GU00982569

# SAILING BARGES

By the same author:

THE YACHT MASTER'S GUIDE
AND COASTER'S COMPANION

Fourth Edition (Sixth Printing)

Eighth Annual Barge Match, 1870.　　Rounding the Mark-Boat at the Nore

[*A lithograph by Josiah Taylor*

# SAILING BARGES

*by*

# FRANK G. G. CARR

CONWAY MARITIME PRESS

1971

Published by Conway Maritime Press,
7 Nelson Road Greenwich London S.E.10,

by kind permission of
Peter Davies Ltd.


*First Edition 1931*
*Revised 1951*
*New Impression 1971*


ISBN 0 85177 024x

Printed in Great Britain by
Latimer Trend & Co. Ltd.,
Whitstable, Kent

TO
MY MOTHER

# Preface to the First Edition

IN compiling this record it has been my earnest endeavour to include within its scope some account of every type of sailing barge to be found in England. While this has involved personal search and inquiry in many districts, the work would have been most difficult, if not impossible, but for the most kind help which I have received wherever I have sought information. For the faults and omissions of this book I am alone responsible; but for any merits it may have as a record, I am chiefly indebted to those friends and admirers of the barges who have supplied me with its material. To some I have made my acknowledgments in the text; to them, and to the following additionally, I have the pleasure of offering my sincerest thanks.

In the first place, I owe a debt of gratitude to Lieut.-Colonel R. C. Bingham, who made the drawings with which the book is illustrated, and who drew and re-drew until the minutest details were correct; then to Mr H. C. Willis, who, having embarked upon a similar work, generously handed over to me all the material and photographs which he had himself collected, and has since been of the greatest help in adding to that supply; to Mr G. S. Laird Clowes for much advice and assistance; to the Science Museum for many photographs of prints and models; to Mr G. A. Foate, of the Parker Gallery; to Mr E. Manning Lewis for information on the surviving Severn trows; to Colonel J. A. Saner, of the Weaver Navigation, and Mr George Cruttenden, of the Newhaven Harbour and Ouse Lower Navigation, for notes on the local barges in their respective districts; to Mr Aubyn Carrick of the Watermen's Company; to Mr A. G. Linney, editor of *The P.L.A. Monthly*; and for much invaluable help in connection with the Thames and Medway barges, to the barge-owners generally, and particularly to Mr George Andrews; Captain Will Everard; Mr Leslie Farnfield; Mr E. A. and Mr Maurice Gill; Mr E. J. Goldsmith; Messrs Albert Hutson; Mr Charles T. Perfect; and Mr Alfred Sully.

Among the bargemen themselves I have had the good fortune to find many friends; they have shown the greatest interest in my work, and have been most anxious to assist me in all possible ways. Although I cannot mention all my helpers individually by name, I would assure them that they have not been forgotten. To bargemen all I tender my thanks, and particularly to Captain Alfred Horlock of the *Phœnician*, with whom I first went "bargeing", to Captain Thomas Strange of the *Davenport*, and to Captain Frank Beadle, of Erith. Finally, I have to thank my old friend, Mr Harry Ward, of Pin Mill, for many a yarn of barges and bargemen and to his son, Mr Harry Ward, Jun., the yacht skipper, who has been with me throughout the year and whose industry and enthusiasm have discovered fresh information wherever we have sailed.

Yacht *Cariad*, R.C.Y.C.                     FRANK G. G. CARR
   *August 17th,* 1931

## Preface to the Second Edition

SINCE the first edition of this book appeared twenty years ago, devastating changes have taken place in the fleets of sailing barges, and of all the many types then to be found around our shores, the Thames barge is the last to survive as a trader under sail alone. Although, happily, she is still with us, her numbers, already greatly diminished, are decreasing so rapidly that much of what this book contains will be out of date before it can be printed, and a few years at most will see the last pure sailorman carry her last freight.

In June, 1949, when I had completed the list of barges that appears as Appendix II, there were in all 150 barges still trading, of which 112 were pure sailormen, the remaining 38 being auxiliary. Fully-powered motor craft were deliberately excluded; they should have no place in a sailing-barge register. By March, 1951, when the list was brought up to date to the time of going to press, the number had been reduced to a total of 113 barges, of which 43 were auxiliary, leaving no more than 70 sailormen "all-told". In less than two years, therefore, there had been a reduction of 37 barges; the pure sailing craft were down by 42, but an increase of 5 in the toll of auxiliaries made up the numbers. These figures speak for themselves.

Of the 113 barges still at work, 65 were fifty or more years old and only 12 had been built since the end of the First World War. The oldest barge still trading to-day is Francis and Gilders' *George Smeed*, built originally in 1882, but re-built in 1922, and now owned by the London and Rochester Trading Company. The oldest in her original state is Wood's *Gipping*, built at Ipswich in 1889; and the last barge built is the *Cabby*, built at Frindsbury in 1928, another of the London and Rochester Fleet.

It is also of interest to record that one of the most celebrated of them all, Everard's beautiful little *Sara* (of London), built at Conyer Quay in 1902, has been moored off the South Bank for the 1951 Festival of Britain Exhibition. Painted and fitted out as in her racing days, she is a delight to the eye of every sailorman, and to all who love London River and its history.

In the preparation of the original version of this book I was greatly helped by those to whom I have recorded my thanks in the first Preface; but I am now indebted in addition to many others who have come generously to my aid in the preparation of this new edition. To some I have already expressed my gratitude in the text; but I want to thank most cordially all who have supplied me with information, illustrations, references, or advice, or who have allowed me to make use of their notes or other resources. In particular I would thank the Trustees of the National Maritime Museum, together with Mr Michael Robinson, of the Department of Prints and Drawings, and Mr Arthur Waite, of the Department of Models; Mr E. W. White, of the Science Museum; Captain F. C. Poyser, of the Nautical Photo Agency; the Editors of the *Mariner's Mirror, Yachting Monthly, Yachting World, Yachts and Yachting, The Trident, Sea Breezes, The P.L.A. Monthly*, and *Spritsail*; Engineer Commander H. Oliver Hill, R.N. (ret.), of the Photographic Records Sub-Committee of The Society for Nautical Research; Mr G. R. Clark, of the Norfolk Wherry Trust; Mr Edgar J. March, author of *Spritsail Barges of Thames and Medway*, and Mr Hervey Benham, author of *Last Stronghold of Sail* and *Down Tops'l*; the Honble R. A. Balfour, of Sheffield; Major W. D. Gosling, of Gay Bowers, Danbury; Mr Frank Hussey, Mr Francis H. Smith, and Mr H. C. Lewcock, of Ipswich; Mr A. C. Boast, of Blyth; Mr A. L. Cross, of Erith, Mr W. H. Kemp and Mrs A. Rolt; Mr W. J. Everard, Mr E. A. Gill and Mr H. E. Andrews; Captain George Blake, Captain A. H. ("Chubb") Horlock, and Captain J. A. Uglow; Lieut.-Commander L. M. Bates, R.N.V.R., of the P.L.A., and Mr Charles Vince, of the Royal National Lifeboat Institution.

To the late Captain "Alf" Horlock's son, Alan E. Horlock, of Mistley, I am particularly indebted; and I am also especially grateful to my three friends, Arthur Bennett, author of *June of Rochester* and other books, Roger Finch, and Philip Kershaw, all well-known experts on sailing barges, who have devoted much time and trouble to answering my questions, improving my manuscript, and reading the whole of the proofs. To Roger Finch I have also to acknowledge several of the drawings; while I have to thank another friend,

Colonel Howard I. Chapelle, U.S.A.R., for some of the most important plans.

In conclusion, I would like to express a very sincere word of grateful thanks to my publishers, Messrs Peter Davies, Ltd., and particularly to Mr F. G. Howe, for their courteous and unfailing help, encouragement and patience; and also to Mrs M. Stuart, who so kindly undertook the preparation of the manuscript during her very limited spare time at home. To all these, to my bargemen friends, and to the many who have helped in other ways, I am proud to acknowledge my deep indebtedness, for it is they who have made possible this record of the Sailing Barges in the last years of their history.

*National Maritime Museum,*              Frank G. G. Carr
   *Greenwich*
     *May 1st,* 1951

# CONTENTS

# PLATES

# FIGURES, PLANS, ETC

The tailpieces are from drawings by W. L. Wyllie, reproduced by permission of the National Maritime Museum and Colonel Harold Wyllie.

# CHAPTER I

# On Barges Generally

It has ever been the character of man to appreciate least those things which are most familiar to him, and perhaps that is why for so many years the humble Thames barge, one of the commonest sights on the London River, plied her trade unhonoured and unsung. Indeed, to the average Londoner the word "barge" probably conjures up little more than a picture of an enlarged and somewhat ugly floating box found in docks and inland waterways; nor was the word "bargee" often used in terms of admiration. Yet actually the sailing barge is one of the most interesting, as well as wonderful, craft the skill of man has ever produced, and now that the age of sail is passing before the advance of the age of power, the Thames barge, alone almost among sailing craft engaged in commerce, continues to hold something of her own. If honour is to be given where honour is due, the Thames barge should have her share.

For just so long as men living on the banks of the River Thames have known the meaning of trade, so long has the barge carried cargoes up and down the stream. As conditions changed, so the barge was adapted to suit the altered requirements. Gradually from the elongated box of the Middle Ages grew the splendid sea-going vessel of to-day. The result is seen in the development of a type of craft, purely English in origin, that will do what no other craft in the world can. Where else can be found a vessel that will carry as much as 180 tons of cargo with a crew of as few as two hands all told? Yet the Thames barge can do this, and do it, moreover, anywhere within the limits of the home trade, from Ushant to the Elbe. River, estuary, sea—it is all one to her. Has she to cross the open sea? She can batten down her hatches and cheerfully set off on a hundred-mile passage, with her decks six inches from the water, letting the swell roll harmlessly over her rail. The sandbanks of the estuary are her friends; she anchors behind them, and in their shelter makes her own harbour miles from the nearest port. Does a bridge bar her way in the river? She can sail boldly up to it, and at the last moment drop all her gear on deck, and shoot through, to heave it up again on the other side. Arrived at her destination, she scorns the services of a tug and handles in the dock under her own sail.

The race of men who man her are among the finest real seamen left in the world, and in handling small craft the bargeman knows no superior. The better type of barge skipper is often a man of considerable education and taste, with a genuine love for his profession. The magnificent handling of the barges in the annual sailing matches, when speeds of over twelve knots were sometimes reached, was a thing to admire and to wonder at.

Yet among all the literature that is now appearing to make known the old sailing ships whose glory is of the past, until a few years ago practically nothing had been written about the barge that is still here, though in her way she is as deserving as any of them. In the following pages some attempt has been made to tell the story of the sailing barge from her humblest beginnings, and to present a picture of her at her work in fair weather and foul, at peace and at war. Long may she continue to uphold the glorious traditions of sail!

In setting out to explore the early history of the barge, however, one is faced at once with a serious difficulty. For the word "barge" is one of the most overworked of nautical terms, and may mean any one of a considerable variety of craft, from a fairly large sea-going vessel of the fourteenth century, down to a comparatively small rowing-boat. So to the sailor, to the historian and to that convenient fellow "the man-in-the-street", the word may well have very different meanings.

Landsmen indeed are sometimes surprised to learn that barges are capable of sailing at all; or that, winter and summer alike, our English barges even to-day make long coastwise voyages. Ideas of barges may range between wide limits, from canal-boats to Caligula's galleys. But one would scarcely connect, unless one knew, the beautiful brown-sailed vessels that are so much admired sweeping past Walton in Essex or battling round the Foreland in Kent, with the dingy, flat craft with lowered gear and water-level decks seen dropping down through London's bridges on the tide. It seems almost impossible that these can be the same ships.

Nor is much more known of the true character of the bargemen, in spite of the popularity of Mr W. W. Jacobs's amusing stories. For "bargees" seem often to be thought of chiefly as somewhat rude gentlemen with expressive if not extensive vocabularies. Hughes, in "Tom Brown at Oxford", sums up the public attitude very aptly when he speaks of "a man who gets up to be a country gentleman with the tongue of a Thames bargee". Indeed, "swearing like a bargee" has become a byword for the high-water mark of proficiency in that art.

Very unjustly so, for though it cannot be denied that a bargeman is probably able to hold his own with any man should the need arise, he is not nearly as prone to use bad language as men in many other walks of life. Considering the annoyances and provocations of adverse winds and tides, and the rank stupidity of dockers in handling "the sailor-men", I have been surprised at the moderation of their language. But sometimes, as a barge skipper's wife said to me, when we had just failed to reach our berth at the end of one of the most trying days I can ever remember, "Can God wonder that we swear?" It was really amazing that they had sworn so little!

As a certain amount of preliminary explanation and classification is necessary, in this chapter barges will be considered generally in all their great variety.

The etymology of the word is interesting. It may be traced from the old French *barge*, which, according to one view, was derived from the medieval Latin *barga* or *barica*. This, in turn, had its origin in the Latin *baris*, from the Greek βᾶρις—a kind of boat used on the Nile. The Coptic root is *bari*, a little pleasure boat. Perhaps the modern usage of the word in the sense of an elaborately decorated boat used for state occasions, with all the pomp and ceremony entailed, is derived from this source. On the other hand, there seems to be no evidence that this use of the word was ever directly transmitted to the West, and it is more probable that the modern word is derived from the Latin *barca*, meaning a ship's boat, used as a lighter for unloading and general ferrying purposes. In this sense, "barge" ultimately came to denote the chief boat of a man-of-war. In any event, the word "barge" from *barca*, was extended to include a boat or small ship with sails, and this is stated to be its first use in English. But after the introduction, by Caxton, of the fifteenth-century French word *barque*, that word came to replace *barge* in the sense of a sea-going ship, and in the form *bark* exists to the present day. After about 1600, "barge" in the sense of a "ship" is no longer found.

Regarding, therefore, the first class of barges as sea-going ships, in the Middle Ages these were medium-sized vessels, rigged originally with a single mast and square sail, like the ships of the Bayeux Tapestry or the Humber keels of a few years ago. Oars were employed to aid the power of wind, and the barges were favourite ships for fighting. Such may have been the vessel sailed by Chaucer's Shipman, for it will be remembered that "his barge ycleped was the Maudelayne". She evidently made long voyages in all weathers, for

> *Hardy he was, and wys to undertake*
> *With many a tempest hadde his berd been shake,*

> *He knew wel alle the havenes, as they were,*
> *From Gootland to the cape of Finisterre,*
> *And every cryke in Britayne and in Spain.*

Turning next to the state barge type, one is irresistibly drawn to Shakespeare's beautiful description of Cleopatra's vessel:

> *The barge she sat in, like a burnish'd throne,*
> *Burned on the water: the poop was beaten gold:*
> *Purple the sails, and so perfuméd that*
> *The winds were love-sick with them.*

Carving, gilding, pomp and ceremony are inseparable from the state barge throughout the ages. She was just a large rowing-boat, expensively furnished and elaborately decorated, used by great persons on state occasions. At one time the Lord Mayor's procession went in state barges upon the Thames, and how this came about is described by Maitland in his "History of London" in the following words:

"John Norman being chosen Mayor of London for the year ensuing (1454), he changed the custom of riding to Westminster (to qualify himself for that Office) to that of going by water: To which End he caused to be built a stately Barge at his own Expense, and on the usual Anniversary, was rowed thither, attended by the several Companies of the City, who, in imitation of their chief magistrate, had likewise built their own Barges; which being all magnificently adorned, formed a most beautiful aqueous Triumph."

This was written in 1760, and although the custom of going by water has long since died out, it was still practised in those days, and for a century after that, the King, the Admiralty, and all the great City Companies had state barges which they used in processions and for all formal occasions. The barges were all built on very much the same lines, and some idea of these ornate and graceful craft may be gained from a well-known etching, by E. W. Cooke, of the Stationers' Barge in 1832.

The Royal Family still have a state barge, called the Queen's Shallop. In 1931 she was presented by H.M. Queen Mary to the National Maritime Museum, and she is to be preserved at Greenwich. King George V used this barge when he visited Henley Royal Regatta in the year 1912. He was then rowed down the course by the King's Watermen in their gorgeous uniforms. There are twelve of them, and they wear long scarlet coats, cut very full below the waist, scarlet breeches and stockings, buckled shoes and peaked jockey's caps of black velvet. The barge is steered by the King's Bargemaster, whose uniform consists of a scarlet Eton jacket and knee-breeches, buckled shoes, white silk stockings and a cocked hat. The barge herself was built by William III for Queen Mary in the year 1689. She is a heavy vessel, forty feet long, and beamy, following the typical Dutch lines of that period; and is brilliantly painted in red and gold, even the oars being painted red.

There is also a state barge preserved in the Victoria and Albert Museum. She is a craft of rather different design, being long and narrow, with a sharp hollow bow, and the lines rather of a Thames wherry or skiff. She was built for Frederick, Prince of Wales, in 1732, and was designed by William Kent. The elaborate carving was executed by James Richards and the painting and gilding by Paul Pettit. She pulled eighteen oars, and was steered with a finely carved tiller from a helmsman's cockpit abaft the cabin. She was emphatically an up-river craft, and would not have been safe battling with the short, choppy seas of the lower reaches of the Thames. This barge also is destined for the National Maritime Museum.

A further type of barge, which may be dismissed in a few words, is the service barge of the Navy. This was a long, light boat, used by high naval officers for journeys to and from the shore and for all ceremonial visits. She was one size larger than the modern Navy pinnace. A barge properly must pull at least ten oars, while a pinnace pulled but eight. The service barge was well equipped with cushions and carpets, and often had a decorated canopy or awning over the stern supported on hoops called bales.

The ordinary canal-boat is another form of barge. She is a development of the simple, long, flat-bottomed box used for inland water transport on the rivers from the earliest days of civilisation in this country. Such were probably the craft Tennyson had in mind when he tells how

> By the margin, willow-veil'd,
> Slide the heavy barges trail'd
> By slow horses.

When the canal systems developed in the latter part of the eighteenth century, these craft tended to become standardised. Their width was fixed by the locks on the canals over which they worked, and fell into two main classes, of wide and narrow gauge, just as did the railways some fifty years later. To get the carrying capacity the length was increased, and a long, narrow and very shallow vessel resulted, known as a "monkey-barge". She had a small raised cabin in the stern, with inward-sloping sides, in which lived the bargee and his family, who worked her. Usually she was gaily painted, and had a sort of flat ridge-pole running down the middle to support tarpaulins for covering the cargo.

Probably the earliest form of motive-power was hauling or "haling" by men upon the bank or "haling-way". This was called "bow-stringing" by reason of the bow-shaped yoke to which the tow-rope was made fast. But very early, horses were used, and bow-stringing, although used occasionally in the Fen districts until recent times, has practically disappeared.

The competition of the railways and their policy of buying up and closing the canals to prevent rate-cutting reduced the barge traffic to a very small amount. For this reason the canals were never enlarged or developed, and the monkey-barge has remained almost unchanged for the last hundred and thirty years. But now, with the improvement of the marine motor and its adaptation to canal craft, a possible new field for development is opened up. In view of the increasing congestion on the railways and roads, it is to be hoped that better use will be made of our admirable system of inland waterways, which has been allowed to lapse into so sorry a state of decay.

These canal barges are often found in the Thames, having arrived by way of the various connecting canals. Among the Thames bargemen their crews are never called "bargees", but are known as "wherrymen". One of the standing jokes on the London river is about the wherryman in trouble on a blowy day in the short, choppy lop of the lower Thames. "That's all right, up above Bridge, mate," he said afterwards, "but when you gits dahn orf Blackwall Point you don't 'arf cop it summat rough!"

This is high comedy to the sailing bargeman, who has seen winter gales in the North Sea.

Yet another general class of barges are the dumb barges or lighters used for unloading ships: "lighting them", as it was once called. They may be seen in great numbers upon the Thames at any time, are built either of wood or steel, to-day always of steel, and have no motive-power but tide or tug. When drifting with the tide they are navigated by one man who keeps them in the run of the stream by means of a pair of huge oars, called sweeps, which he works as needed over one side or the other alternately. These lightermen are a numerous class, and have no connection with any other bargemen. They are very tough customers, quick to anger and merciless in a fight.

In a quarrel between any two of them, when words must give way to blows, it is usual to repair to the hold of an empty lighter in order to settle the matter. This makes an ideal ring, from which there is no escape; and from the decks above their fellow lightermen look down to see the fun. Usually it is a fight to the finish, and quarter is rarely asked or given. Some twenty years ago I joined a barge the day after such a fight had taken place in a lighter near-by. It had lasted twenty-five minutes, and by the end, the hold of the lighter was all bespattered with blood. One of the combatants was removed senseless to the hospital, where he lay for over three weeks. The other was taken to his own home, and remained out of action for ten days! Thus, was I given to understand, did the aggrieved vindicate his parents' honour.

Yet in spite of their rough ways, the lightermen were very elegant in their attire. Double-breasted jackets of the most varied shades, "natty" footwear and bowler-hats were the rule. The sailing-bargemen call them "pokers", from the manner in which they push their way about the docks and drift down-river, thrusting their craft into the oddest corners with nothing but tide and oar to aid them. They are a rough type, but their skill at their work is unquestioned, and they make the fullest use of every eddy in a way that is truly marvellous. Yet theirs is a dying art. In a post-war world, where time is money, lighters are picked up, towed and dropped by tugs, quickly and certainly. Lightermen's wages are too high to leave them driving about the river. It is rare to-day to see a drifting lighter in the Thames.

Finally, there are the sailing barges themselves. Of these, by far the largest class are those found upon the Thames, which are of a type unique and purely English. Other sailing barges there were all over the country, on different rivers and lake systems. They were named variously according to their localities. Thus there were the keels of the Tyne and the Humber; the keels of the Norfolk Broads, now extinct; and the wherries, which will soon be only a memory. The flats of the Mersey, the trows of the Severn and the cutter-rigged stone-barges of Devon and Cornwall were all distinct types brought about by local conditions. These will be dealt with in passing. But it is with the ordinary Thames barge, born and bred in the London River, that this book is mainly concerned.

There was no finer sight upon the coast a few years ago than a fleet of these brown-sailed vessels beating round the Foreland against a stiff breeze and working their way into the Thames by the Horse and Gore Channels off Margate. Or again, standing in towards the land at Clacton in the calm of a summer's evening, sliding through the Spitway into the Wallet; the setting sun tingeing their limp sails with the most glorious shades of golden browns and reds. They may still be seen, even in 1951, though in much smaller numbers; but it is doubt-ful whether the children of the next generation will know them.

Small craft they are, carrying anything from 80 to 180 or 200 tons. A few larger steel barges may carry as much as 300 tons. The crews are ridiculously small, and vary from two to three or, in the largest barges, four hands all told. Their rig, with slight differences, is in general much the same. They have a large mast, stepped well forward in a mast-case on deck, on which is set a heavy tanned fore-and-aft mainsail, of which the peak, or upper, outer end, is supported by a long spar called a spreet, crossing the sail diagonally and anchored to the mast at the lower end. This sail is fitted with small ropes called brails, leading from the leach or after-edge, through blocks on both sides of the upper and forward edges, in such a way that the sail may be drawn up and stowed like a theatre curtain. A sail so rigged may be set and taken in with a minimum of effort by a small crew. Above this mainsail is set a topsail, also fitted with an easy-stowing device. For-ward of the mast is a foresail, and in barges carrying a bowsprit, a jib.

In the stern is stepped a very much smaller mast, on which a little sail called a mizzen is set. This is used chiefly for help in steering, as will be explained later. The sails are dressed with a mixture of oil and ochre, which never gets completely dry, and gives them their beauti-ful reddish-brown colouring, so much admired by artists.

The Thames barges are completely flat-bottomed, so that they can take the ground without listing over. This ability to sit upright when the tide leaves them is one of their greatest assets. It also allows them to carry a maximum load on a minimum draught of water. And this large flat area enables them to sail without ballast when empty—a great advantage over most sailing craft. They used to be found far removed from the London River, which is their home, up and down the East Coast and Channel seaboards, from Hull to Weymouth. Occasionally they would go farther, and I have seen an Ipswich barge in the Spencer Basin at Belfast, and met a bargeman who had been to Ballyshannon in County Donegal. They also used to make long Con-tinental voyages, anywhere within the home-trade limits of Ushant to the Elbe. There was a small barge still afloat in 1931 that used to trade regularly, some seventy years ago, between Newcastle and the Channel Islands, with a crew of man and boy all told. Four barges have sailed out to South America on their own bottoms for service in the River Plate, for which their shoal-draught would render them specially suitable.

Not only will they go to sea—and come safely through surprisingly bad weather—but they will also go up the shoalest creeks, right inland to places like East Mills above Colchester, or Bradwell Quay in the Blackwater River, where one would think it almost impossible for so comparatively large a vessel to penetrate. Their small draught of water is a great advantage to them, enabling them to get where the steamboats cannot follow. As the bargemen put it, "they will go anywhere after a heavy dew", which is illustrated by the following yarn of a barge skipper working on a muddy river, deciding when it was time to "go about" on the other tack.

"Jimmy, me boy," says he, "is that gull a-swimming or a-walking?"

"That's a-swimming, master."

"Then we'll hold on a bit, Jimmy."

A little later: "He's walking now, master."

"All right, Jimmy—ready about."

In clear water they will sometimes stand on until they can see the bottom, and then tack.

The gear on these barges is made to lower, so that they can go through bridges far up the rivers. The gear on the Medway barges, which twenty years ago were constantly "shooting" Rochester Bridge, worked so easily that they would sail right up to the bridge, lower the gear smartly, "shoot" through and heave up again on the other side without so much as stopping to anchor.

Perhaps the most remarkable were the hay-barges, which went to sea with twelve feet of hay on their decks. And they might then be met off the Essex coast or beating up the London River, with the skipper at the wheel, and the mate perched on top of the stack to keep a lookout and tell the helmsman how to steer. The way they went to windward in spite of the deck load was astounding, and inexpicable by all the accepted laws of sailing. The bargemen themselves said that the eddy draught from the mainsail got behind the stack and pushed them up to wind'ard.

At another time the same craft might be seen lying in some farm creek in the Orwell or Stour, whither she had been sailed and pushed until she was right among the chickens in the farmyard; and when the hull was not to be seen from the staith, she looked like some crazy haystack fitted out for the sea.

The cargoes carried by the barges vary enormously, and must comprise practically every form of merchandise—corn, hay, sheep-dip, laundry-blue, cement, bricks, paper, rotten apples and coal, to mention but a few of them at random. There used to be a great machinery trade * for the barges from Ipswich to London, and the gates of the

* Revived in 1950, though by auxiliary barges only.

Assuan Dam on the Nile were carried this first stage of their journey by barge. Writing in 1873, G. Christopher Davies in "Mountain and Mere" speaks of "the bargees, who navigate barges laden with fragrant hay or corn up the stream". But their cargoes were not always so salubrious, as the following Essex story of about the same date will show. A certain old skipper, being also owner of his own barge, secured a contract for the carriage of fish manure to Brightlingsea; which cargo stank unto high heaven. So that, when the wind was in the right direction, his arrival was heralded to the natives, who, with noses sniffing the south-west wind, would say, "That'll be ole Jem come in to-night, bor'!"

The sailing bargemen are a fine race of seamen. Some of the old families, like the Horlocks of Mistley and the Wests of Rochester, have given generations of splendid coasting sailors to the nation. Men better able to handle small craft among the treacherous sands and strong tides of estuary sailing are not to be found the world over. Winter and summer alike, thick or clear, the bargemen ply their trade, and it is a rare thing indeed for a barge to be in serious trouble.

Their love of their craft and the pride they take in them is not sufficiently appreciated. Barges named after their womenfolk are a natural demonstration of their affections for both. But there is a remarkable case actually on record of a girl named after a barge, when a certain skipper had his daughter solemnly christened in full *Francis* [*sic*] *of London W——*.

In the pages that follow, the story of these sailing barges will be told and an attempt made to picture them as they were at different stages in their development, showing the work they did first upon the river, later upon the sea; and the part they so played in building up the Port of London.

# CHAPTER II

## The Old London River

UNTIL the close of the eighteenth century the barge was probably quite unable to go to sea. Her traffic was limited to the Thames itself, and she went no farther seawards than the mouth of the Medway, though she carried cargoes up the latter river well into the heart of Kent. The coasting trade farther afield was carried in a variety of craft known variously as Smacks, Hoys, Sloops, Cutters and so on— which were all of much the same round, tubby shape, extremely slow, but very seaworthy. Time was then of little importance, sailors, when obtainable, were comparatively cheap, and the large crews needed to handle these clumsy coasters were more easily found and paid for than they are to-day.

A point that must be borne in mind is that the greatest development of the sailing barge has taken place only within the last hundred and twenty years, and, curiously enough, is largely due to the very introduction and growth of steam in the merchant service, which sounded the knell of most other forms of sail. The Golden Age of the barge did not really begin until the year 1863, when in the fertile brain of a Mr Henry Dodd was born the idea that has done more than anything else to improve the build of the barges and to raise the status of the bargemen. For in that year the Annual Barge Sailing Match was founded by him and his friends on the Corn Exchange. The innovation was an immediate success, and as early as 1874 barges were being built specially for the race. It came at a most opportune moment, and supplied just that impetus which was required to lift the barge from the clumsy type of lighter with sails into the class of small sea-going vessels; and it has enabled the developed craft to hold her own even to-day against the otherwise all-conquering power.

Thus it came about that the Thames barge grew up as a craft peculiar to the London River. She is unique. She owes both her origin and her subsequent development to a set of circumstances and natural conditions not found elsewhere, and is in consequence quite different from the other barge types found in other parts of this country, or anywhere else in the world. It will be convenient to have in mind a preliminary survey of the scene of her birth.

The Thames has been navigated continuously from Roman times, and has always provided the great route for merchandise to London, both from the West Country and from seawards. But in early times the navigation in both directions was extremely difficult. Before the lower reaches were embanked the river was flanked by wide, flat marshes and sailtings on either side, and the shoals by which the entrance was encumbered were not properly known or charted. The existing channels constantly shifted, and it can have been by no means plain sailing to make the port of London even in days when ships were still very small. Until two or three hundred years after the Conquest the ships trading to London must have been small enough to lie alongside river wharves, taking the ground and drying out as the tide fell. Their cargoes could thus be landed direct, and the need of smaller craft to unload them was not felt. But from about the fourteenth century the practice was for the larger sea-going ships to lie afloat in midstream, and to discharge their cargoes into barges or lighters, in which the goods were carried and distributed to their destinations at wharves in London or up or down the river. It was never good for large ships to have to berth aground in a strong tideway. Docks deep enough to take them were costly to build; and would, moreover, speedily fill up and require constant dredging. Further, as trade increased, there was not room for all the ships to lie alongside, even if there had been sufficient depth of water at the wharves for them to get there. Therefore the need for lighters was felt, and was supplied by simple, flat, box-like craft, which would sit upright on the mud when lying alongside wharves, carry the maximum of cargo for their size and be very easy to load and discharge. The distance the goods were to be carried was generally so short that the ebb and flow of the tide alone would take such a boat to her destination, aided by an oar to keep her in the desired part of the stream. For longer journeys a square sail might be used when the wind was fair. For the navigation westwards, the motive power was supplied by men or horses.

This navigation westwards was always a matter of great difficulty, by reason of the shallows and rapids which infested the course of the river and the bad condition of such locks, weirs, towing-paths and other aids to navigation as were made from time to time. Nevertheless, the early barges, being quite small craft, managed to overcome these difficulties without very great trouble, and a fairly extensive trade developed.

Originally there can have been little difference between the lighters which unloaded ships in the port and the barges which carried cargoes up and down the river westwards; indeed, it may well be supposed that the same craft were used for all purposes. But as the barge gradually tended to increase in size, and the trade of London developed, a distinction arose between the tideway lighters and the barges navigating the upper river. Probably this may be dated from the middle of the sixteenth to the beginning of the seventeenth century. In 1665 one finds Pepys referring to the "Western Bargees" as a separate class, and they are specially distinguished from the "Lightermen" of the lower river in the various acts by which their great organisation, the Watermen's Company, was ultimately founded.

The development of river traffic during the seventeenth and eighteenth centuries was very great, as may be shown by contrasting the "2,000 wherries and other small craft", given by Stow in his famous "Survey of London" of 1603, with the figures given by Brayley in 1796, when the number of small craft (exclusive of wherries and ship's boats) was 3,419, with an aggregate tonnage of 110,156. The "wherries" referred to here were the small rowing-boats used for the transport of passengers up and down or across the river, which were hired in much the same way as hackney carriages, and were one of the most convenient forms of passenger transport in London.

The limits of the Port of London were wide, and reached from London Bridge to the North Foreland in Kent and the Naze in Essex. The western limit, formed by London Bridge, has had a great effect in influencing the barge traffic of the river from the earliest times. Exactly how long there has been a bridge across the Thames at London is not known; but certainly there was such a bridge in the time of the Romans, and after one or two early wooden structures, old London Bridge was begun in the year 1176. The span of the arches ranged from ten to thirty-three feet, but the effective span was greatly reduced by the enormous stirlings of piles filled with rubble by which the foundations of the piers were protected, so that the total waterway was only 236 feet. As that of the present bridge is 690 feet, it may well be imagined what an enormous impediment the old structure caused to the ebb and flow of the tide, acting as a dam across the stream, through the arches of which the river poured with a difference in levels above and below of *over five feet* on the ebb-tide. The noise of the rushing waters was terrific, and the roar of the bridge could be heard afar off. Yet it stood for six hundred years, and throughout that period the daily work of the river barges involved the perils of shooting its narrow arches. The hazards attendant on this operation were very grave, and bargemen and watermen were constantly losing their lives in the attempt.

At one time London Bridge did not form so complete a barrier to the sea-borne trade. When it was first built, one of the spans was in the form of a wooden drawbridge, which would be raised to allow ships with fixed masts to proceed as far as Queen Hithe, there to unload in a small dock "against the midst and hart of the Citie". But long before Stow's time the timber bridge was no longer drawn up, and sea-going ships lay below in the Pool, discharging their cargoes into smaller craft for conveyance to the shore. The dock at Queen Hithe referred to above had thus become nothing more than a "water gate, or harboro, for boats, lighters and barges".

In order to understand the early history of the barge it is essential to have a clear picture of this system of unloading ships, which has lasted from the thirteenth or fourteenth centuries right down to the present time. In the early nineteenth century, the congestion in the Pool and farther down the river became so great with the increase of trade that the great dock-building schemes were begun on a large scale to provide additional accommodation. In these wet docks ships were of course able to lay alongside quays. Nevertheless, the old system of unloading, which grew up when the big ships lay at anchor in the river, was found to be so convenient that it was continued in the docks. For the barges provided not only an economical means of transport up and down the river, but also cheap warehousing for the goods themselves until these were required. Thus the barge and lighter are to-day doing the same kind of work as they have done for the last seven hundred years.

At the end of the eighteenth century the system of unloading in midstream was in its prime, and about 800 ships could lie afloat at low water in that stretch of river between London Bridge and Limehouse called "The Pool". The coasters occupied the shallow part, near the bridge, and the larger ships lay in the deeper berths below. The big East India ships, however, came no higher than Blackwall and Deptford.

Stockdale, writing in 1796 of the state of the river at that time, thus graphically describes it. "A stranger," he says, "would naturally look for the quays and wharves made for the accommodation of this great quantity of shipping; but he would learn, that except the *legal* quays about a quarter of a mile in length between London Bridge and the Tower, the rest of the business is done at the sufferance wharves, irregularly interspersed on the banks, and so inadequate to the purpose, that lighters are obliged to be employed for the loading and unloading of a great proportion of the goods, to the heavy expense and detriment of the merchant. He would also lament the contraction and embarrassment of the stream from the tiers of ships moored in the midst of it, and reaching from each side, so as at some times scarcely to afford a passage, and liable to various injuries."

The "legal quays" were certain wharves (in other seaports as well as in London) at which, by an old Statute of the time of Queen Elizabeth, most goods were required to be landed and shipped. "Sufferance wharves" were places where certain goods might be landed or shipped, such as hemp, flax, coal and other bulky goods, by special "sufferance" granted by the Crown for that purpose. To and from these wharves the barges and lighters plied, going down to the ships with the ebb-tide, loading or unloading alongside, and returning on the flood some hours later. In this way practically the whole of the sea-borne trade of London was carried for some part at least of its journey in barges.

In addition to this lightering trade, the early barges made voyages down the Thames to Gravesend, up the Medway to Gillingham and Maidstone; small barges as far as Tonbridge; and up the River Lea into the heart of Essex. It was for these longer voyages in particular, as well as for those up the Thames as far as Putney and Windsor, that sails came to be used. For the short lightering job, the distance that the goods were to be carried was so small that the ebb and flow of the tide were motive power enough. But on these longer passages the value of sails was so obvious that they came to be used at an early stage in the development of the barge.

The first barges could not lay any claim to being objects of beauty. They were merely long, wooden floating boxes; flat-bottomed, square-ended, but with the ends sloping upwards from the bottom at an angle of about thirty degrees, in a manner very similar to the Thames fishing punt of the present day; or even more like the steel dumb-barges that may be seen in their hundreds upon the Thames.

Actually, the Thames pleasure punt of to-day, which crowds through Boulter's Lock with its gay cargo on Ascot Sunday, is a development, in a different direction, of the old seventeenth-century barge. The pleasure punt is a comparatively recent advance on the lines of the rougher fishing punt from which she sprang, and which was only a small, shallow copy of a barge. The overhanging ends, or "swims", have been drawn out and the lines made more graceful. But for all that, she is only a refined descendant of the same rough old craft, and is therefore a distant cousin of the sailing barge of to-day, although possibly she might not be pleased to acknowledge her ancestry.

The sides of these barges were comparatively straight, and it was not, apparently, until the latter half of the eighteenth century that an attempt was made to introduce a somewhat more shapely form of hull, the sides of which curved round to a rather narrower bow; and although the flat, sloping overhang was retained, the vessel had a form at once more shapely and easier to handle. This form of bow was known as the "swim head", and the overhang was termed the "swim". Although it has now been displaced by the straight stem, a few of the old swim-headers or "swimmies", as they were called, were still afloat into the early 1930's, and this type of bow has become a standard for the modern lighters, or dumb barges, which have no motive-power but tide or tug.

Under the stern of these early barges, which was, like the bow, merely the sloping end to the box, was a vertical fin or "dead-wood", called by the bargemen the "budget", which helped to keep the barge straight. On the after end of this, in sailing barges, the rudder was hung. The barge was not decked at all, except for a short length forward, on which was a simple windlass, worked by hand-spikes, for hoisting the mast and getting up the anchor. Aft was a small cabin, called the cuddy, in which slept the crew of a man and his wife, or a man and a boy; close quarters, usually shared with a dog.

The mast in these craft was generally stepped only a little forward of the midship line, and was fitted in a mast-case, such as in other craft is called a "tabernacle", the after side of the case being open, and the mast secured by a bolt through the lower end and a bar across the top of the mast-case, which could be removed to allow the mast to lower. As far as can be judged from contemporary prints, a single forestay comprised the whole of the standing or fixed rigging of the barge in the seventeenth century. But it is clear that by the middle of the eighteenth century a pair of shrouds each side were fitted in addition, and it is more than probable that their omission in the earlier drawings is due to the lack of a sufficiently discerning eye in the artist who drew them.

A single square sail was set upon this mast, the yard being hoisted by a halyard in the middle and lifts to each yard-arm. The sail was trimmed by sheets and by braces leading aft from the yard-arms to the gunn'l of the barge. Steering was by a long wooden tiller fitted to a large square-shaped rudder.

A more simple rig could hardly be imagined. It was the original square sail of the Vikings, found in England surviving in its simplest form all over the East Coast; in the keels of the Tyne, the Humber and the Norfolk Broads; and in the barges of the Thames and Medway. In its development from the sixteenth century the sail was differently treated in each of these various districts. But in its most primitive form it was found in the Thames barges until the end of the eighteenth century.

The barge shown in Fig. 1 is taken from a picture of Lambeth Palace, drawn by Hollar in 1647. She is bound downstream with a cargo of logs, stowed athwartships and piled high. The square ends and raking swim already referred to will be noticed, and it will be seen that she carries no lee-boards on her sides.* Forward is a small deck, but in this barge there is apparently no cuddy aft. The mast is stepped rather farther forward than was usual, being about one-fifth of the length aft from the bows. The sail is of the simplest possible form. There are no ropes to support the yard-arms—"lifts", as they are called—and the yard is hoisted by a single halyard in the middle.

FIG. 1 Thames Barge of 1647

The mast appears to be unsupported by shrouds of any sort, and has merely a forestay which, owing to the pressure of the wind on the sail, hangs quite loosely "in a bight". The forestay was, of course, necessary for heaving up the mast after shooting a bridge.

Such a barge could not possibly go to windward; that is, sail against the wind. Only when the wind was fair would the sail be hoisted, and at other times the barge, helped by an occasional oar, would depend upon the tide alone to carry her to her destination, like her more humble sister, the dumb-barge. The lowering mast was necessary to cope with the difficulty of "shooting" London Bridge and the low bridge at Putney higher up the river. Such was the first, the most primitive sailing barge or lighter upon the Thames.

At this point it will be convenient to deal rather more fully with the navigation westwards from London Bridge and the "western barges" by which it was carried on.

The water communication between London and Oxford is certainly known to be more ancient that the Conquest. But the river was

* See Chap. III, p. 34.

in many places choked with shallows, so that in summer, when the water was low, it was often impassable. In order to remedy this, staunches or weirs were placed across the stream, by which the water was held up. This system of holding up the water, and letting it down in "flashes", as they were called, was antiquated and unsatisfactory, for the upper reaches were emptied with each "flash" and sometimes barges would lay aground for days or weeks, even for so long as a month, before enough water had accumulated to let down another "flash". During the whole of this time barge traffic up and down was virtually suspended. It was even possible at times to cross the river dry-shod at Marlow after a "flash" had been drawn.

In some reaches a barge would get over the worst places by one "flash", and then have to wait several days for a second to get over some inferior obstacle, as it could not go fast enough to keep up with the water sent down at first. Some shoals were very bad indeed, and even as small a barge as the little *Tamesis*, which drew only 16 inches of water, was often aground; so it may be understood how impossible at times was the navigation for larger barges.

The difficulties of lack of water were so serious that for parts of the voyage from Oxford to London one full load had to be shared amongst three barges in order to lighten the draught sufficiently. And not only was water lacking, but also in many places there was no adequate towing-path. The result was to make water transport from the west both slow and expensive, and owing to the strong current and weed-encumbered channel, the number of horses required to move a loaded barge of 70 tons was at one time almost ludicrous, amounting to as many as twelve horses in some reaches. The weeds and rushes grew so thickly in summer as almost to choke the river, but were never cut, as they "hung up the water over the Shoals to greater Depth than otherwise there would be".

On the Thames and Severn Canal a barge of 70 tons required only one horse, so the state of the Thames can well be imagined. Enormously strong and heavy tow-ropes were required, which in those days cost £11–£12 and lasted, even with careful usage, no more than three voyages. The old Thames barges used at that time to make eight or nine round voyages yearly. In the days when they were smaller, and not so liable to delays for want of water, they had made as many as fourteen or fifteen trips. The normal size was about 70 tons, but some working on the lower reaches were as big as 146 tons. Such a barge, with a 66-ton barge in tow, required no less than seventeen horses to haul it against the winter streams from Weybridge to Windsor. In 1767 there were said to be about ninety barges navigating

the river westwards. Of these, about half were over 100 tons and the
rest were smaller.

The barges were marked for a draught of 3 feet 9 inches, loaded,
and load marks had to be painted on their sides. They were allowed to
load to one inch more. But it did not follow that there would be
enough water for their permitted draught.

The western bargees seem to have been a pretty rough crowd. In
the days when towing by men on the banks was much in use, a gang
of fifty to eighty men was necessary to drag a loaded barge upstream.
These fellows were of the worst possible character, and a terror to the
whole neighbourhood. But the bargemen themselves were of a better
class. The western bargees were great favourites with Samuel Pepys,
and he spent many a merry evening on the water in their company,
singing and jesting, sometimes taking his wife along with him; as on
14th May 1669, when he wrote: "So home, sullen; but then my wife
and I by water, with my brother, as high as Fulham, talking and singing, and playing the rogue with the western bargemen, about the
women of Woolwich, which mads them, and so back home to supper
and to bed."

What was this story of the women of Woolwich can only be conjectured, but it was apparently a favourite joke with Pepys among the
bargemen, for it occurs again on 2nd June 1668, when he returned
from Deptford (whither he had been dallying with the wife of one of
them) at about midnight, "taking into my boat, for company, a man
that desired passage—a certain western bargeman, with whom I had
good sport, talking of the old woman of Woolwich, and telling him the
whole story". Incidentally, this passage is of interest in showing that
the western barges in all probability went as far downstream as Deptford, which involved the dangers of shooting London Bridge on the
way. It is probable that there was a good deal of direct import and
export trade between the West Country and the ships lying in the
Port of London, which would be carried straight through by the
western barges.

To understand the history of the barges with a fair perspective, it is
necessary to have some knowledge of the conditions of their work,
and the places where they plied.

If one could be an inquisitive passenger upon a barge bound downstream some time in the late seventeenth or in the eighteenth century,
London's waterside would present a very different picture from what
is seen to-day. Consider such a passenger upon just such a primitive
barge as has already been described, who, stepping aboard the vessel
one day at a wharf below the old wooden bridge at Putney, has

begged a passage down to Greenwich from her genial and bearded skipper.

It is early morning, and the faint white mist is gradually dispersing before a gentle westerly breeze as the barge casts off from the quay. The wind being fair, the old square sail is hoisted and the sheets are trimmed aft. Slowly she gathers way and glides gently down the river. It is just after high water, and the ebb is beginning to run.

The country about here is all open, although Chelsea Hospital is shortly seen upon the port hand. And below Chelsea, the Tyburn— that stream of dread name, which was long years afterwards to suffer the indignity of being carried in an iron sewer across Sloane Square station—is open and navigable to small craft such as this barge. Indeed, there is a small dock just within its entrance to which she has often carried cargoes. All along Millbank are open fields, and a fine view is obtained of the Abbey and the Houses of Parliament, while Lambeth Palace stands in comparative isolation on the south bank. The Houses of Parliament themselves present but a sorry spectacle. For on the river side there is seen only an untidy pile of ramshackle buildings, overtopped, it is true, by the fine old roof of Westminster Hall. But in front, where in a later century brightly dressed ladies were to take tea with black-coated members upon the stately terrace, there is now only a collection of old and ugly houses, precariously perched upon a muddy bank, with nothing even of antiquity to commend them. Truly, the fire of 1834 was a blessing in disguise, for all that was bad was burnt and little that was fine was lost.

Before the Houses are reached, however, there is a chance to pass the time of day with the horse ferry, which puts off from Horseferry Road on its journey to Lambeth just as the barge arrives. There is plenty of room to pass, and the barge slips under her stern. Below the Houses, where Westminster Bridge was later to be built, are Westminster Stairs, with a constant stream of wherries in attendance, carrying Lords and Commons to and from their duties. Beside the stairs is a small dock, where barges bring necessaries for the City's use. Along the north bank no embankment yet runs in a clean sweep of chiselled stone. But the plain mud bank is broken up by innumerable wharves and river stairs, with occasional docks cut into the bank itself, where flat-bottomed barges can lie upright on the soft mud while their cargoes are craned out into carts or warehouses ashore. On the rising ground above, all along almost to Blackfriars, is a row of tall and stately buildings: Somerset House, the Savoy, the Adelphi and so on, and of course the Temple and its spacious gardens. These stand up well, for they are not obscured and half hidden by a harsh embankment, with a constant stream of tramcars and traffic to divert the eye. Before the Adelphi is a fine terrace "commanding a charming view to the river, when not obscured by the damps and poisonous fogs, which too often infest the air of the lower part of our capital". Fogs are no new product of the growth of the city, but at least there are no groping steamers or prowling tugs to run down the blinded drifting barge of the eighteenth century.

The Surrey side about here is, as yet, but thinly built upon, although, as Southwark is approached, the houses are thicker and the wharves along the bank become more frequent.

From Blackfriars to the Tower the quays and wharves are almost continuous. The ebb runs stronger here, for London Bridge, as yet the only bridge, is being quickly approached. Several other barges put off from the bank, but, apart from a few wherries creeping up close along the shore where the tide is slacker, all the traffic is bound the one way. There is no giant steam to stem the current, and the powers of nature alone can be used. Immediately below Blackfriars Stairs is Puddle Dock, a little basin for lighters and other small craft, named after one Puddle, who owned it in days long past. Then follow Powle's Wharf, Broken Wharf and Queen's Hithe. Next, Downegate, Ebgate (better known as the Old Swan) and several others. With the exception of Queen's Hithe, "Ripa Regina" as it used to be, all these are privately owned. At Queen's Hithe is a dock, crowded with barges. It is quite a large dock, compared with the rest, and at one time, when the wooden drawbridge of London Bridge was opened, it was used as a landing-place where sea-going ships could discharge their cargoes.

As the barge drifts on and the crew prepare to lower mast and sail for the shooting of London Bridge, we have a brief glimpse into the mouth of the Fleet Ditch, which runs into the Thames just below Bridewell. This was at one time open and tidal as far northwards as Holborn Bridge, at the foot of Holborn Hill. It was fed by three tributary streams: the Fleet River, Turnmill Brook and the Old-bourn. Although crossed by four stone bridges, it was navigable by large barges as far as Holborn Bridge; and up to about the fourteenth century, small sea-going ships most probably made use of it, perhaps even the barges of the early sea-going type described in Chapter I. On either side were extensive wharves and warehouses. But a good deal of trouble seems to have been caused by people casting filth into the stream and using it as a convenient receptacle for any rubbish they had to dispose of, so that, in spite of regulations to prevent this, considerable sums of money had to be spent from time to time on scouring it out and keeping it open for barges. This subsidiary

harbour for the City was wholly arched over below Holborn Bridge
between the years 1737 and 1765.

The small stream known as the Wall Brook, which drained the
Moor Fields, was also open at one time, and barges used to be rowed
or towed up this as far as Bucklersbury, and there unloaded. There
was in the Manor of Bucklersbury a large stone house, called "The
Old Barge House" by reason of the painted sign which hung outside
its door. "The Barge Yard" was to exist right into the twentieth
century, though few would know the reason for the name.

There is little time for more than a cursory glance around, however, for the roar of London Bridge grows rapidly louder. This
operation of shooting the bridge is an awe-inspiring business, needing
both skill and nerve on the part of the bargees. The barge must
approach the chosen arch end-on and as near as possible in the
middle. It is no easy matter to keep her straight, for with the swirl of
the tide and the eddies caused by the piers, there is some danger of
getting twisted across the stream. If then she should be caught athwart one of the arches, disaster is certain. Lying like a stick across a
sluice, the barge will most assuredly be capsized and broken up. One
has only to imagine a five-foot fall through the bridge—and then to
fill in the picture.

On this trip, however, no untoward incidents happen. The mast
and sail are lowered as the bridge is approached, but steerage way is
maintained. With a dip and a lurch she sweeps into one of the wider
arches; the piers flash past, and she is spewed forth into the river
below, not without having shipped a quantity of water in her passage.
It is indeed a hazardous matter to shoot the bridge and scarcely a day
passes without a life being lost. It was said that "London Bridge was
made for wise men to go over and fools to go under".

From London Bridge to the Tower, in that part of the river known
as the Upper Pool, the wharves are practically continuous, and from
them steep and narrow lanes ascend into Tower Street. Up these toil
struggling teams of horses, hauling heavy, lumbering carts laden with
merchandise craned from the barges lying at the wharves below.
These in order, from London Bridge to the Tower, are the following:
Fresh wharf, Cox's key, Botolph's key, Lyons key, Billingsgate,
Smart's key, Dice key, Ralph's key, Wiggin's key, Young's key, Bear
key, Porter's key, Custom-house key, Galley key, Chester key,
Brewer's key and Gun wharf.

Galley key was at one time the place where the Genoese and other
Mediterranean galleys were wont to discharge, and the Custom-house
was always a busy place for trade. But of these below-bridge landing-

places, Billingsgate is by far the most important, and is not only the great landing-place and market for fish, but is also the spot to and from which the boats on the "Long Ferry" to Gravesend ply. A bell is rung here on the quay for a quarter of an hour to mark the time of high water and of low water at London Bridge, and this is the signal for the Gravesend boats to depart on their journey, that they may lose nothing of their tide. Here also at noon each day is a market or exchange held on the wharf by woodmongers, and by masters of colliers and dealers in coal, at which the business of the Newcastle coal trade is transacted. Billingsgate is the largest of the docks or water-gates for barges and small ships on the Thames, and besides fish, is the usual landing-place for oranges, lemons, Spanish onions, and other such commodities from abroad.

Near-by, in Water Lane, the Corporation of Trinity House has its offices. Originally at Deptford, the headquarters were moved to London in the early eighteenth century, and remained in the house in Water Lane until in 1795 they were removed to the new Trinity House on Tower Hill. At the time of this barge journey, the Trinity House has still the monopoly of supplying ballast for all ships using the Port of London. The ballast is supplied in the form of sand dredged from the bottom of the river by special ballast barges, of which the Corporation possesses quite a fleet. Sixty barges, carrying two hands apiece, are constantly employed, and the ballast is delivered to the ships for one shilling per ton. In this way—and in this way only—the shoals that grow up and choke the channel are removed, and by this system of "ballasting" the river is supposed to be kept open for traffic. As the barge continues her voyage down the lower river, many of these craft are seen anchored over the shoals, dredging up their cargoes of sand from the river bed. But, as the barge skipper might explain, this method of removing the shoals is most unsatisfactory in practice. For the lighters will only dredge up sand, which can be sold as ballast; while any banks of mud, which may be greater obstacles to navigation but have no commercial value, are left to accumulate untouched. Many are the complaints of the ineffective and uneven dredging by the Trinity House lightermen, but no improvement seems to result.

These Trinity House lightermen are a class apart, and responsible to Trinity House alone. They are privileged by being freed of the jurisdiction of the Watermen's Company, which has authority over all the other lightermen and watermen on the river, subject to certain minor reservations to other authorities in special cases.

The ballast lighters are, the passenger notices, of a different shape from the ordinary Thames barges. They are quite open, but instead of having the square-shaped sloping ends already described, they are double-ended craft, with bluff rounded bows and sterns, moulded to massive stem and stern posts. In fact, they are much like the fenland barges of Cambridgeshire and Lincolnshire, whose form was to remain completely unchanged right into the twentieth century. They seem to carry no sails, and to depend on tide and sweep alone for motive-power.

The ballast lighters are not the only craft of this form on the Thames, and quite a number built on this model are to be seen in other employments. It is altogether a more shapely form of hull than is that of the ordinary box-like barges, and belongs to the same general type as the keels of the Humber. Is it a development of the original Viking ship? There are some grounds for supporting this view, which will be discussed in further detail later. But at the moment the passenger will notice such craft in considerable numbers, and may wonder why there are not more of them; or, indeed, why they have not displaced the less shapely box-like lighter. They seem so much more sea- or, rather, river-worthy.

Perhaps the answer may lie in the consideration of expense, for those bluff, rounded ends will be more difficult to build than the simple square ones. Or perhaps it is that the straight-sided, completely flat-bottomed box-like craft was easier to load and discharge, and would take the ground better alongside wharves. But whatever may have been the reason, the double-ended type was practically to disappear on the London River by the beginning of the nineteenth century.

The Custom-house Wharf, between Billingsgate and London Bridge, is always a busy spot, and a host of barges, lighters and other small craft are seen before it, jostling one another in their efforts to edge in and find a berth to lay alongside and discharge under the customs officers' eyes. The officials seem to be rather slack in attending to their business of checking the dutiable goods; and the resultant delays in unloading are a great grievance to the bargemen, who may thereby lose a tide down to the ship they are discharging with their unladen craft, and have to wait for the next ebb. Then a tide lost means a freight lost, and there are plenty of rivals to do the work.

The breeze is freshening slightly as the Tower is passed, and a much-longed-for ripple of foam begins fitfully to curl away from the barge's flat bow. Below the Tower come successively Wapping, Shadwell, Ratcliffe—a corruption of *Red*cliffe, from the low reddish-coloured cliffs which flanked the Thames at that spot—and Limehouse, so named after the lime-works there. At one time straggling hamlets inhabited mostly by watermen and sailors, these have gradually grown more densely built upon as trade has increased and commerce has shifted farther eastwards. With bigger ships and more traffic, this process was going on through the centuries, and the chief landing-place for the Port of London was to move from Queen's Hithe in the fourteenth century to Tilbury in the twentieth. Where the big ships have gone, the barges have followed.

Already the big ships are beginning to congregate at Blackwall. Below Limehouse is the Isle of Dogs, where bluff King Hal kept his hounds when Greenwich was a royal dwelling; and across the neck of the Isle—which is really a peninsula—stretches the hamlet of Poplar, joining up with Blackwall near where the River Lea runs into the Thames. At Blackwall are the building yards for the big East India-men, and Blackwall is coming to set its own standards of sailorising. In a few more years, to say a vessel was "all shipshape and Blackwall fashion" would be the height of praise. Between the houses and the waterside, along all this stretch of river, are frequent docks and small building and repairing yards, so that the bows of ships can sometimes be seen in places rising up over the street. Wapping and Shadwell had been famous in Stow's time for such filth and stench as called forth his caustic comments, but towards the end of the eighteenth century the chief highway, a long, narrow street, is "well paved and hand-somely flagged on both sides", as far, at least, as Limehouse.

Execution Dock is still to be seen at Wapping, and came into view as the barge swept round the bend of the river there. Here is the famous gallows for the execution of pirates, which remained in use until so late as 1790, "as often as a melancholy occasion required". Possibly the barge's passenger has to view the body of some poor wretch hanging there in chains, where he could be seen all up and down the river as an awful example of the fate of pirates. At one time a simple hanging was not considered sufficient; the older practice had been to hang the culprits at low-water mark, and leave them there to be overflowed by three tides before slinging them aloft in chains.

At Limehouse the New Cut, or Bow Creek, which was begun about 1770, enters the Thames, and if the barge journey be made late enough in the century, the mouth of this canal will be seen. It is only a short cut, about a mile and a quarter long, which, running by Brom-ley, enters the Lea by Bow Lock, thus saving the barges the longer journey down and round the Isle of Dogs.

The Surrey side of the Thames is thinly built upon, although a belt of houses stretches along to the eastwards of the Bridge, where Tooley

Street runs. In front of this are many wharves and small docks, just as
on the northern bank, which are almost continuous as far as St
Saviour's, or Savory Dock. The latter is the chief haven for barges
and lighters on the Surrey side, and is frequented by barges which
discharge "coals, copperas from 'Writtlesea' (i.e. Brightlingsea) in
Essex, pipe-clay, corn, and various other articles of Commerce". The
dock is four hundred yards long, but only thirty feet wide, and very
shallow. Thus no craft larger than a barge can enter it, and even hoys,
cutters and other small coasters have to unload into barges, which
land the goods at this dock. This involves great expense and results in
raising the price of the commodities. But it is all for the benefit of
the bargemen, who would be sorry to see the dock made deeper.

The shipping lies thick in the Pool, and down the river almost as
far as Greenwich the barge has carefully to thread her way among the
great numbers of small craft which attend upon the wants of the
bigger vessels. At last Greenwich is reached, and there the passenger
is to be disembarked. The barge is bound for Barking Creek, some
distance lower down. So a wherry is hailed and the passenger put
ashore. He lands, maybe, upon the north bank, by an attractive
tavern overlooking the river, called the "Folly", from which he can
enjoy the view across the water, as Pennant did in the course of one of
his tours.

"We finished our walk," he says, "and dined at a small house
called the *Folly*, on the water's edge, almost opposite to the splendid
hospitall at Greenwich, where we sat for some hours enjoying the
delicious view of the river, and the moving picture of a succession of
shipping perpetually passing and repassing."

The river below Greenwich ran through fairly open country, with
occasional small villages here and there upon its banks. Greenwich
itself lay just below Deptford Creek, which was at one time called the
Ravensbourne, and was navigable by barges to the place where it was
crossed by the London road to Greenwich. From Greenwich the
river flows northwards down Blackwall Reach to the mouth of the
River Lea, and thence south-eastwards down Bugsby's Reach into
Woolwich Reach. It is interesting to note that the Thames water was
fresh as far seawards as this, and only became brackish at high spring
tides. This Thames water was in great favour for watering ships, as it
had the peculiar property of going rotten at first and smelling
abominably for about a week, after which it sweetened, and would
then remain perfectly good for an indefinitely long time.

Gravesend was of great importance in the history of the barges, for
it was the first port at the entrance of the river for vessels bound up

for London. Here ships were first boarded by the customs officers, and from it they took their departure when bound away. Homeward-bound ships often landed their passengers at Gravesend, and it was also the point to which the "Long Ferry" from Billingsgate plied. Many vessels were continually at anchor before it, and kept busy a small fleet of bumboats, barges and the like, supplying them with fresh meat and vegetables and other necessaries from the shore. There was a considerable barge traffic up and down the river from Graves-end which, for most practical purposes, was the seaward limit of the Port of London. Indeed, the name itself of "Gravesend" indicates this. The officer originally in charge of the town was called the "Portreve", being a shortened form of "Portgereve". Gravesend, in the Saxon was "Gerevesend", and therefore signified the limit of the Portgereve's authority.

Such, then, was the London River of the seventeenth and eighteenth centuries, on which the barges plied. It may be objected that here is too much of the river, and too little of the craft themselves. But owing to the barges being so much part and parcel of the Port of London itself, it is almost impossible to think of them separately, and the early history of the barges is almost the early history of the Port of London itself. In support of this view, I conclude the chapter with a quotation from the speech of the late Mr Erskine Pollock, K.C., to the Joint Select Committee of Lords and Commons on the Port of London Bill of 1903. Having referred to the fact that from 75 to 80 per cent. of the whole traffic of London was carried by barges, he went on to say : "I do not think it is putting it too high to say that the barges have created the Port of London, because all the work is done by the barges, and if it was limited entirely to the docks, there would be a limited area for the work to be done in, whereas we know from the evidence which has been given before the Royal Commission that the barges have transformed the whole of London into one big dock : that they do an enormous business between the limits of Gravesend and Brentford, and instead of the business of London being conducted in a limited number of docks covering a limited acreage of water, the result to London, which is now a barge port, is that the work is done from Erith right away up to Teddington."

# CHAPTER III

# The Barge in Evolution : First Stage

THE Thames sailing barge was left in Chapter II as a simple, box-like craft, with no pretensions to graceful shape in her hull and rigged with nothing more than a single square sail. As such she remained until well on into the later years of the eighteenth century. It was not until the spritsail had been introduced into England for many years, and had become familiar on the Thames in the latter part of the seventeenth century, that any attempt was made to apply this sail to the barges. The generally prevalent idea that the Thames barge, her lee-boards and her rig came in one stage from Holland is completely erroneous. The hull was never Dutch; and the spritsail was not adopted on the barge until long after it had become common in the hoys, wherries and small fore-and-aft coasters of this country.

The points which distinguish the spritsail from other sails are, briefly, these. In the first place, it is a "fore-and-aft" sail. A fore-and-aft sail is best distinguished from a square or cross sail in that with the square sail, which is spread across the ship, whenever she has to alter course and tack, the yard by which the sail is stretched has to be swung round by hand so that the wind always presses on the same side of it, i.e. the *after* side (except in the actual moment of tacking); whereas the wind presses on either side of the fore-and-aft sail with equal effect, and alternately, according to the tack the ship is sailing on. In tacking, this sail does not have to be swung round by force, but adjusts itself automatically to the new point of sailing. In the spritsail, the whole of the sail is abaft and the forward edge or "luff" is attached to the mast, so that if the after part of the sail were left uncontrolled it would fly out like a flag. In Figs. 2, 3, 5 and 6, primitive spritsails are shown. The distinguishing feature of the sail, which gives it its name, is the spar running diagonally from the mast across one side to the upper corner, or "peak", by which the "head" of the sail is extended. The lower after corner of the sail, called the "clew", is controlled by a rope known as the "sheet"; and the upper end of the sprit is steadied by two ropes, called "vangs", leading down to the deck. The heel of the sprit rests in a rope collar surrounding it and the mast, which is termed a "snotter", and is prevented from dropping down by a rope from near the mast-head to its heel, called a "standing lift", which has been corrupted into "stanliff". The sail can be stowed by means of "brails"—lines from the after edge or "leach" rove through blocks on the head and luff of the sail and so down to the deck, by which the sail can be brailed up to the head-rope and into the mast in the same way as a theatre curtain is sometimes drawn up. As an alternative, the heel of the sprit can be freed from the snotter and allowed to come forward, the weight being taken on a tackle from the mast-head to the middle of the sprit, and the sail furled into the mast. This can often be seen in seventeenth-century Dutch paintings, and is still occasionally used for reducing the height of the mizzen in river barge when shooting bridges. This is in its simplest form the sail of the Thames barge to-day.

The spritsail is, as far as is known, a comparatively late-comer to the rigging of ships. It is almost certainly of Dutch origin. The earliest known examples occur in a miniature believed to be by the brothers Van Eyck illustrating The Voyage of the Saints, in the Low Country manuscript "Heures de Turin", of about the year 1420 (Plate 1). The boat in which the saints are travelling would be about 20 feet long, and she is running before the wind with a spritsail set on one mast. The sprit appears, as the boat is seen from aft. It seems to rest in a snotter at the foot of the mast, with a sheet and a vang to the sprit end, all clearly shown. It is worth noting that the sprit was then, as now, carried on the starboard side of the mast and sail. The same thing is shown in another early drawing of a spritsail, which occurs in a pictorial map of Calais Harbour, by Thomas Pettyt, in 1545, which is reproduced in Fig. 2. It will be noticed also that this craft steps a small mizzen-mast, and is not unlike the Thames barge of to-day in the broad features of rig. Finding her there suggests that such craft were probably not uncommon on the North Sea and Channel seaboards at that time.

In 1594 an engraving by the celebrated Theodore de Bry shows Jeromy Benzon arriving at San Lucar de Barrameda, and in this appears a small fishing boat with a spritsail and foresail set on a single mast and shown in some detail. She is of a characteristically Dutch type, with a rounded stern, and is steered with rudder and tiller. She has a pole mast, supported by a forestay and a single shroud each side. The heel of the sprit rests in a snotter near the foot of the sail, and a single vang leads from its upper end to the helmsman's hand. A tackle leads from the mast-head to the middle of the sprit, and this, known as the "yard-tackle", is found in all the larger spritsails after this date. The luff of the sail is laced to the mast with small line. At the mast-head is a little square flag. The boat is manned by a crew of three.

The spritsail became the usual sail for the small river and coasting craft of Holland, but the exact date of its introduction into England is not known. It should be noted that, according to Sir Alan Moore\* the Elizabethan hoys had spritsails as their mainsails, even in craft up to the burden of 200 tons. But there is very little evidence to show

FIG. 2 Spritsail Coaster in Calais Harbour, 1545

that the spritsail was widely adopted in England until the time of Charles II. At this period, a wave of Dutch influence swept over the small shipping of this country. The "yacht" was unknown in England until one of these craft was presented to Charles II by the Dutch; and many similar craft were subsequently built and added to the navy. These yachts were often rigged with either the spritsail, or

\* "Last Days of Mast and Sail," Oxford U.P., 1925.

a variant known as the half-sprit or standing gaff. This latter sail was developed from the lateen sail of the Mediterranean which was used as a mizzen when ships first adopted three masts, and was afterwards altered by cutting off the part of the sail and yard extending before the mast. In this form the sail was shaped like the spritsail, but the head was extended by a gaff, called a "half-sprit", along the head of the sail, the gaff being kept more or less permanently aloft. The sail was stowed by drawing it up with brails, just as the spritsail was, and was largely used in smacks and hoys as an alternative to the spritsail. Unlike the latter, however, the half-sprit has not survived in any great numbers into the present century.

It appears that the spritsail was actually applied to the Thames barges as early as the time of Charles II's Restoration in 1660. For in a Plan of Arundel and Essex Houses, in Ogilby's and Morgan's twenty-sheet plan of London, etched by Hollar, there is a spritsail craft rigged like a modern "stumpy" barge, but without the mizzen, running up the river (Fig. 3). She has a large spritsail and foresail. Vangs are fitted to the sprit, and she carries a square flag at the masthead. Note here too that the sprit is on the starboard side of the sail, as in modern practice. This rig was not, however, common in the barges at that time. It is also interesting to note that this craft is

FIG. 3 "Stumpy", c. 1660

provided with lee-boards, as it is the earliest example of a river craft so fitted that I have been able to discover in this country. As Hollar flourished from 1636 to 1677 and it is practically certain that this plan was etched after the Restoration, this tends to indicate that the lee-board was a Dutch importation, among the many others from Holland at that time.

At about this period, valuable evidence on the spritsail is provided by a manuscript entitled "Of Navarchi", which is in the Pepysian Library at Magdalene College, Cambridge. This was written by a man named Fortree, who was anxious to introduce among other matters to Samuel Pepys, at that time Secretary to the Navy Board, a new kind of sail in which he was interested. In the course of this paper he therefore describes all the sails then in common use, for purposes of comparison with the "New Sail", and among them he treats of the "Smack Sail", the "Hoye Sail" and the "Wherry Sail", of which the two last were sprit sails. The wherry sail was a small sail used to aid the oars in the watermen's passenger wherries on the

Thames. It was certainly introduced for this purpose as early as 1630, as a drawing of that date of Durham House, Salisbury House and Worcester House, now in the Pepysian Library, shows a wherry setting a very small sail of this type. The three sails are shown in little sketches (Figs. 4, 5 and 6) and his description of them runs as follows:

"Of the Smack saile.

"The Smack Saile (Fig. 4) is good by a wind and handy to tack, always hanging behind the mast. But extending only from the midle of the ship and over hanging only one side, it cannot stand so faire before a wind as a square saile; and also by a wind it hath this inconveniency, that being Boom^d or spritted aloft and raised very high it is subject to cause a vessel to lean or heel so much as to put it so out of Trim that it will gripe and straine so hard upon the rudder or healm as to be a great hindrance to the way of the ship: besides to support this kind of spritt the mast must be more lofty whereby it

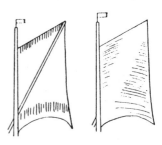

FIG. 4 The Smack Sail          FIG. 5 The Hoy Sail

must be the more wind Tant, and so a proportionable hindrance to the way of the vessel.

"Of the Hoye Saile.

"The hoy sail (Fig. 5) is much the same with the smack saile only this difference that it is raised something more apeake and is supported by the yard or whole spritt, and therefore needs not so tant a mast, but it also hath some inconveniency. For the yard being very long and standing slant is the more wind tant, and when the yard or spritt is to leeward of the saile the saile will bagg and cling so hard to the sail yard or spritt that often times it is very difficult in stress of wind to haul up & furle the saile.

"It may be also a query if there be any difference in the saileing of a vessel whether the spritt is to windward or to leeward of the said saile; For when to windward the saile makes but one great bunt or rounding saile, and when to leeward the spritt divides it, and so makes

PLATE 1  Earliest known representation of a Spritsail

[From a Manuscript of *circa* A.D. 1420
[*By courtesy of The Society for Nautical Research*

PLATE 2  Westminster Bridge from Lambeth, 1744

[*By courtesy of the Parker Gallery, London*

PLATE 3  Westminster Bridge, 1792

[*By courtesy of the Parker Gallery, London*

two less, but the difference doth not seeme to be great for that the driveing part and back saile will be near alike in both.

"Of the Werry saile.

"The wherry saile (Fig. 6) is much the same with the hoye saile only it is squarer at top and not so much raised apeeke, but in all things else the same."

It is clear from the above that the fore-and-aft sail was firmly established in English small craft at this time, and the explanation of the fact that it was not apparently adapted to the Thames barges until the second half of the next century is probably due to these craft being of such primitive and clumsy shape that even when fitted with the fore-and-aft sail they would not be able to sail except with a fair wind. That the form of hull was not improved was probably because of the comparatively small volume of traffic; and because the much smaller ships of those early days were able to proceed almost up to London itself. For the short distance, therefore, that goods would have to be lightered in the barges, the power of the tides was almost sufficient, and the square sail was merely an auxiliary. Up the river westwards the barges could be towed, and the traffic down the river towards the sea was, in the main, carried in smacks and hoys. But, whatever the reason, it was not until the shape of the barge's hull was improved in the latter part of the eighteenth century that the spritsail displaced the older square sail. For purposes of comparison, the pictures facing page 33, Plates 2 and 3, should be regarded together.

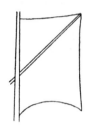

FIG. 6
The Wherry Sail

In the first of them, Plate 2, which is a view of Westminster Bridge in 1744, one of the old square-sail barges is seen navigating down the stream. In the foreground are a number of watermen's wherries which were so popular for passenger transport. The barge represents but a small advance on that of 1647, shown in Fig. 1. But in the next picture (Plate 3), which shows Westminster Bridge as seen from downstream, the transition stage is clearly visible. Out in the river is one of the old square-sail barges bound upwards; while under the crane in the foreground is moored a spritsail barge, of the more modern rig, with sails furled.

That barges of a superior form of hull were in use at that time is clearly shown by the lines of an English chalk barge, Figs. 7a and 7b, published in Chapman's "Architectura Navalis" in 1768. She is 56 feet over all, 15 feet beam and the side 5 feet deep amidships. The very pronounced swim-head and box-like build of hull is most noticeable, and the resemblance to the ordinary Thames pleasure punt can easily be traced. Notice the lee-board, so distinctive a feature of the Thames

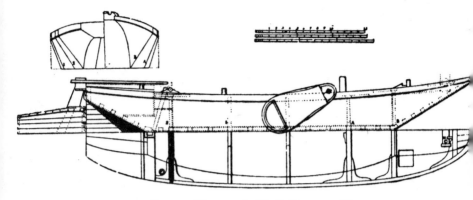

FIG. 7a  Chapman's Chalk Barge, 1768

barge from that date onwards, which can be lowered down the side to prevent the barge making "leeway"; that is, blowing sideways through the water. She is quite open, save for a short deck over the

FIG. 7b  Chalk Barge Sail Plan, 1768

swim forward and a little cabin aft; on the fore deck is a simple barrel windlass, worked by handspikes. She steps one mast, in a mast-case supported by a heavy sailing beam. The sides, which slope outwards from the bottom, so that the barge is wider at the level of the gunwale, are joined together at the top by beams. The main horse, on which the main sheet traverses, is a stout wooden bar across the after end of the hold. She has no external keel, the bottom being perfectly flat, and is steered by a long rudder and wooden tiller.

She is described as a "chalk-barge", and was probably employed carrying chalk from the Kentish pits near Gravesend and in the Medway, up to London. Whether she was also one of the craft used for the regular trade mentioned by Defoe, of carrying chalk into the Essex creeks to put upon the heavy Essex soil, whereby to lighten it, one can only conjecture. But there is no reason why she should not make such a voyage in settled weather, *via* Havengore or New England Creeks, into the River Roach, without going eastward round Foulness Island at all. Certainly by the beginning of the nineteenth century barges went beyond the Nore in summer, so why should not this vessel, of much the same improved and more modern type, also proceed on the slightly longer voyage? The chief point against this view is that, having apparently no hatches (which the barge of 1800 certainly had), she would admittedly be liable to swamping in any lumpy sea. But the distance sailed in only semi-open water from Sea Reach at the lower part of the Thames to Havengore Creek is so short that this danger could be almost avoided by watching the weather carefully.

An interesting comparison is obtained when this barge of Chapman's is compared with two barges of rather later date, whose lines and construction are shown in contemporary plans which have recently reached the National Maritime Museum in the latest batch of original Admiralty draughts, transferred by the Director of Naval Construction. These were discovered in August 1950 by Colonel Howard I. Chapelle, who was then researching among the many thousand plans in the Museum's collection. They are undoubtedly the most important early barge plans that have ever come to light, and they are reproduced here by courtesy of the Trustees of the Museum, as Figures 8 and 9.

The first (Fig. 8) is entitled "A Draught of a Flatt Bottomed Sailing Barge, Rigged with One Mast & Spreet Main Sail and a Fore Sail, with a Jib occasionally and an Outrigger abaft, to be built at Port Jackson, New South Wales, for the Service of that Port". Evidently somebody had thought that a typical Thames sailing barge would be a suitable craft for harbour service at Port Jackson; and a note on the Draught states that "A Copy was sent to Chatham to be forwarded in the *Calcutta* to Port Jackson for the above purpose 22nd. January 1803".

The following dimensions are given on the plan:

|  | ft. | ins. |
|---|---|---|
| Length between Perpendiculars . . . | 56 | 9 |
| „ of the Bottom for Tonnage . . . | 36 | 0 |
| Breadth Extreme . . . . . . | 17 | 6 |
| „ Moulded . . . . . . | 17 | 2 |
| Depth in hold from Ceiling to Deck . . . | 5 | 6 |
| Burthen in tons $54\frac{19}{94}$ |  |  |

She carried two anchors, of $2\frac{1}{2}$ cwt. and 3 cwt. respectively.

Important points to notice in the plans are, among others, the arrangement of the floors and frames, which are similar to those in a modern barge; the four pump wells, one in each corner of the bottom; the two hatches; the budget stern; the hollow construction of the rudder, boxed up in thin planking over a framework; the barrel windlass, for handspike working; the bow chock and sheave for the cable; the bowsprit, pivoted at the heel so that it could be steeved up, as it is in barges to-day; and the small mizzen mast stepped on the rudder head. This last feature is particularly interesting, as it is the earliest example that I have been able to discover of the rudder-post mizzen in a Thames barge.

It is not beyond the bounds of possibility that the well-known New Zealand scow, the sea-going sailing barge used in the New Zealand timber, coal and cattle coastal trade, and also in the inter-colonial trade between New Zealand and Australia, had her origin in this Thames sailing barge plan that was sent out to Port Jackson at the beginning of the nineteenth century. Up to the early nineties, as the Baron de Kerchove has recorded in his "International Maritime Dictionary", most of these scows were built square across the bow, much in the manner of the old Thames barge's swim head. They were flat-bottomed and chine-built, and had a square stern. Later scows were built with a clipper bow. The craft employed in the log-carrying trade had no bulwarks, except at the ends, in order to enable the logs to be lifted on board by means of parbuckling chains; and, of course, the swim-headed barge had no bulwarks. Here is interesting scope for speculation!

The second plan, Fig. 9, shows a barge of a few years later, for it is entitled "Draught of the *Ant* Barge built in His Majesty's Dock Yard DEPTFORD", and is dated "Deptford Yard, 1st. Novem. 1819". She was a rather larger craft, with a length of 72 feet overall, breadth of 20 feet 6 inches and depth of 7 feet 4 inches.

Added to the plan, nearly five years later, is the following note :

Dimensions of Mast, Bowsprit &c for the Barge ordered to be built in His Majesty's Dock Yard at Chatham 15th Jan^y. 1824.

|  | Length ft. ins. | Diam. ins. |
|---|---|---|
| Mast to the Hounds . . . . | 46  0 | 14 |
| ,,   Head . . . . . | 14  0 | — |
| Topmast to the Hounds . . | 34  0 | 7 |
| ,,   Pole . . . . . | 5  0 | — |
| Bowsprit . . . . . . | 29  4 | 10¼ |
| Boom . . . . . . | 51  0 | 12 |
| Gaff . . . . . . . | 33  0 | 8 |
| Squaresail Yard . . . . . | 33  0 | 6 |

From this it is clear that this barge was cutter rigged ; and it interesting to note that she carried a squaresail yard.

Also noted on the plan is the following :

15th Jan^y. 1824. The Dimensions of Mast, Bowsprit &c with the iron knees and alterations as ticked in red was got in on this drawing and a Copy was sent to Chatham Officers for building a Barge named ———.

N.B. To stow 25 Tons of Iron ballast at the sides of the keelson under the temporary flat.

By studying these plans of 1803 and 1819 respectively, together with the etching reproduced at Plate 4, which shows a Thames barge of 1809, a very fair idea can be obtained of what these early nineteenth-century craft were like. It will be seen that the form of hull is very like that of Chapman's chalk barge of 1768 ; but the barge of 1809 is rather bigger. She is, moreover, completely decked, and has a large main hatchway, with coamings and hatch-covers, each side of which is a narrow waterway. The cabin is aft. The heavy rudder and long tiller should be noticed, the latter with a belaying-pin through the head for temporarily making fast the tiller-ropes when steering. Chapman's chalk barge of 1768 was rigged in much the same way as the barge shown in this picture. The arrangement of brails, with a main brail, two uppers leading to the head of the sail, and a single pair of lowers, can be seen clearly. The mast is stepped in a mast-case or tabernacle, and made to lower. It is supported by a forestay with powerful forestay tackle, a pair of shrouds each side and running backstays. The main sheet travels on a wooden horse just the foreside

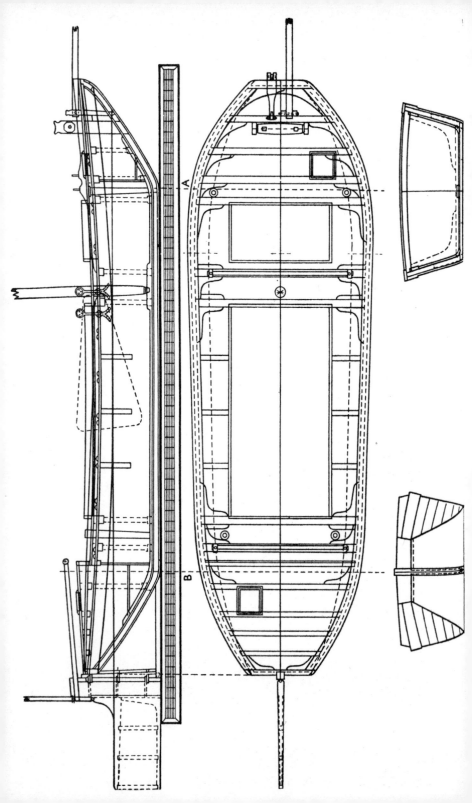

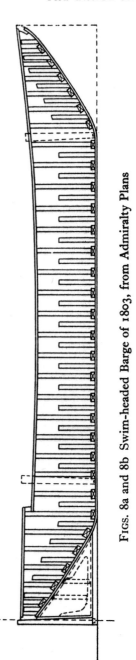

FIGS. 8a and 8b Swim-headed Barge of 1803, from Admiralty Plans

of the cabin top, and the sheet is rove in much the same way as in the modern barge. This ingenious arrangement enables the sail to be "sheeted", or hauled out very flat, and was certainly in use on the Thames barges as early as 1794; for a very full account of the rigging of the ordinary Thames sailing barge is given in the rare "Rigging and Seamanship" by Steel, published in that year. For the benefit of readers who may be interested in the technical details of the rigging of barges, I have quoted this somewhat fully below, as it is the earliest detailed account of the Thames barge that I have been able to discover.

In the first place, it is fairly obvious that there were as many sailing barges rigged as cutters or sloops with gaff sails as with spritsails. "*Sailing Barges*," says Steel, "are vessels with one mast, and sometimes a bowsprit. Those that have boom-sails are rigged similar to sloops; but having few hands on-board, the boom and gaff is more easily hoisted or topped, the power being increased by the addition of blocks." On the other hand, "*Sailing Lighters or Barges*, with a sprit-mainsail, rig with a sprit-yard at the head of the sail, hanging diagonally to the mast ".

In both, the mast was supported by shrouds and "Runner-Pendants" (i.e. backstays), which went over the mast-head singly, with eyes spliced in the ends, or in pairs, with the bights seized close to the mast, resting on a "trudding" or grommet, driven down to the stops on the mast-head. The forestay went over all, with a running

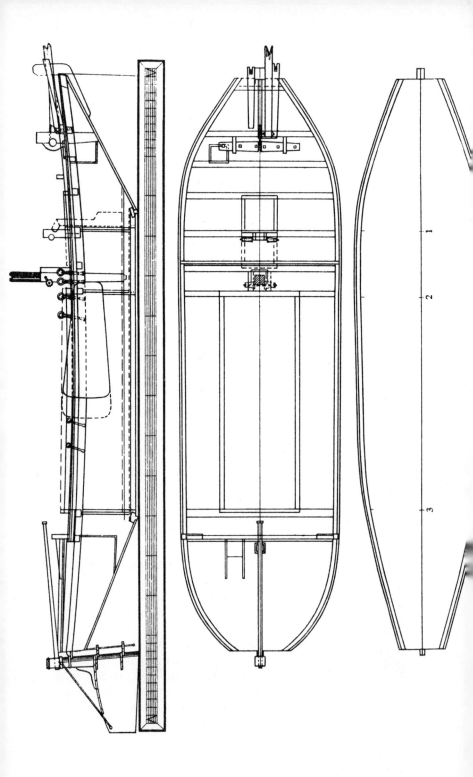

1

2

3

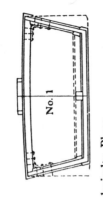

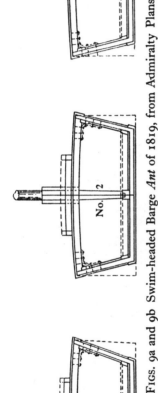

Figs. 9a and 9b  Swim-headed Barge *Ant* of 1819, from Admiralty Plans

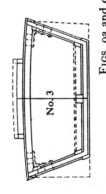

eye, and the lower end was set up with a powerful three- or four-fold tackle hooked into a large iron strap over the stem. The mast was generally made to lower, for "*Sloops, Smacks, Barges* and *Lighters*, that go through bridges, have the mast confined in a trunk or wooden cap, above the deck and fastened in by an iron strap on the aft-side: some have a strong iron hinge at the heel of the mast, or a bolt through the heel; so that it can be lowered at pleasure, by the stay-tackle easing away the fall by degrees. To raise the mast, the fall is brought to the windlass and hove upon, until the mast is up in its place: The fall is then stopped to the windlass bitts." In Fig. 10 this is being done, the barge having just shot London Bridge on the ebb-tide. This drawing is made from a picture of about the year 1796.

The sling from near the mast-head to the middle of the sprit, now called the "yard-tackle", was then called the "Sprit-yard Pendant". One end was spliced into a rope collar or "grommet" round the yard, the other led through a block near the mast-head and down, with an eye spliced in the end into which a tackle was hooked, the lower block of which was attached to a ring-bolt in the deck. The standing lift (now "stanliff"), used to "top up" the sprit, was spliced round its lower end, led up through a block at the mast-head and down, with a similar tackle. The snotter by which the sprit was kept in to the mast was made of two or more turns of rope spliced and marled together, encircling the sprit and the mast, with a seizing between making, as it were, two loops. It was then bound with leather and greased, and a collar or shoulder on the lower end of the sprit rested in it. Nowadays this is replaced by an iron "muzzle". The upper end of the sprit, which rested in a rope grommet worked into the sail, was controlled with vangs, and could be pulled down by means of a line called a peak down-hauler when the yard was being "topped up" with the standing lift. The sail could then be easily stowed on deck or unbent from the spars, for the luff of the sail, above the point where the sprit rested in the snotter, was confined by sliding mast-hoops. Below the snotter it was attached to hanks travelling on a "horse" consisting of a rope going with an eye over the mast-head and having the lower end set up

FIG. 10 Barge of 1796 heaving up her Gear

with dead-eyes and lanyards to an eye-bolt near the heel of the mast. The throat of the sail, referred to throughout, as to barges' sails in Steel's work, as the "nock", could be lowered by a single halyard rove through a block at the mast-head and down to the deck.

The rigging of the main sheet is important, as it is universal in the barges, and almost unique. In 1794 "one end bends to the clue of the sail, the other reeves through a block that traverses on an iron or wood horse (fixed athwart the vessel near the stern), and again reeves through a block, hooked to a thimble in the after leech of the sail, four feet above the clue; then leads aft, and belays round the pin of the block on the horse". The barge of the present day has precisely the same arrangement, only a second block on the after-leech is added above the first, and the block travelling on the horse is double instead of single.

The brails "are made fast to cringles on the after-leech of the sail, then lead up on each side of the sail, and reeve through small blocks, seized into the head-rope, and then through blocks lashed to the upper part of the shrouds on each side; and lead down through trucks* seized to the shrouds below the middle, and belay round pins in the shroud-rack".† This arrangement remains much the same in the modern barge. But the brails referred to above are those known as the "uppers". The main brails "go with two short legs; one spliced in the head-rope near the nock, the other about four feet up the head; the leading-part comes down one side of the sail, and reeves through a cringle, on the after-leech, five or six feet above the clew, and comes up on the other side, and reeves through a block, seized to the nock of the sail, and leads down by the mast". In the barge of to-day, this is generally hauled up by a winch; otherwise the rigging is very similar.

The barges' sails were generally tanned, and to preserve them the bargemen used a composition of horse-grease and tar, mixed to a proper consistence and coloured with red or yellow ochre. This was heated up and painted on to the sails. Another favourite method was to spread the sail on the grass, and after thoroughly wetting it with sea-water, to pay it over on both sides with brown or red ochre mixed to a cream with sea-water, after which both sides of the sail were well rubbed over with linseed oil. The sail could be used within twenty-four hours of the oiling.

A few further comments on the rigging of barges call for notice. According to Steel, both the squaresail (set on what was called a crossjack-yard or "crojick"-yard), topsail and jib set on a bowsprit were carried additionally by "large barges" at that time. It is probable that this refers in the main to cutter-rigged barges of the type shown by Cooke in the etching reproduced in Plate 5. But it is also likely that the larger spritsail barges carried jibs, topsails and square-sails. Another point to notice is that none of the barges described by Steel has more than one mast. The little mizzen had certainly appeared, however, in some barges, by 1803, when it is mentioned in the Admiralty draught of that year, described on page 35, and illustrated in Figs. 8a and 8b.

To conclude this survey of the barges of the late eighteenth and early nineteenth centuries, there is an excellent description of life aboard these vessels given by the immortal Captain Marryat in "Jacob Faithful". The boy Jacob was born in a dumb barge or

---

* Wooden blocks shaped like beads with a hole in the centre, through which a rope is led.
† Wooden battens lashed horizontally to the shrouds at a convenient height with belaying-pins through them.

lighter, navigated on the River Thames by his father and mother as only crew, and until he was ten years old he had never set foot ashore. At that early age he had the misfortune to lose both his parents in one fell swoop, the one by fire and the other by water. As Marryat describes her, his mother, though her virtue was unimpeachable, was often found in bed with that foul seducer of women—gin! On the fateful day when Jacob became an orphan, she had retired to her couch, which is a wise precaution when one can no longer stand. But by an evil whim of fortune, she was so filled with fiery spirit that she perished by fire. In a word, she ignited, and, dying from spontaneous combustion, left nothing but a few smoking ashes in her bed as legacy to her only surviving child. His father, her lawful spouse, was so frightened by this sudden change, into something strange at least, if not rich, that he leapt up the hatchway and fell overboard. In the morning, remembering his father's last words, that the lighter must be at the wharf above Putney Bridge first thing on the following day, little Jacob took her there unaided.

Jacob was then sent to school, but his yearning for the water being stronger than his love of letters, he was apprenticed under the rules of the Watermen's Company, and sailed as boy on a sailing barge. With his many adventures this book is not concerned, but some of his descriptions are well worthy of study for the light they throw on the barges of the period. Take this account of his introduction to the barge, for example; just such a spritsail barge as has been described, and as is illustrated in Plate 8.

"I followed him down to the barge, which was one of those fitted with a mast which lowered down and hauled up again, as required." This suggests that there were then barges with fixed masts; and this view supports some of Steel's descriptions in the work already referred to. Probably the fixed-masted barges were cutter, not sprit-sail rigged. "She plied up and down the river as far as the Nore, *sometimes extending her voyage still farther*; but that was in the summer months." The italics are mine, and this phrase bears out the suggestion made earlier, that already the barges were penetrating beyond the confines of the river. But I doubt very much whether she would go round the North Foreland. Margate was probably her farthest port. "She had a large cabin abaft, and a cuddy forward. . . . 'This will be your berth,' said Marables, pointing to the cuddy-hatch; 'you'll have it all to yourself. The other man and I sleep abaft'."

The cabin he later describes thus: "I caught up the light, and held it in my hand, as I hung over the table. On each side were the two bed-places of Marables and Fleming, which I had before then had many a partial glimpse of. In front of the bed-places were two lockers, to sit down upon. I tried them—they were not fast—they contained their clothes. At the after part of the cabin were three cupboards; I opened the centre one, it contained crockery, glass, and knives and forks. I tried the cupboard on the starboard side; it was locked, but the key was in it. I turned it gently . . . the cupboard had three shelves. . . ."

Finally, there is this delightful description of the river on which he was to work, as it appeared to him between Putney and Westminster in the early morning on the day he joined the barge.

"The heavy dew which had fallen during the night studded the sides of the barge, and glittered like necklaces of diamonds; the mist and fog had ascended, except here and there, where it partially concealed the landscape; boats laden with the produce of the market-gardens in the vicinity were hastening down with the tide to supply the metropolis; the watermen were in their wherries, cleaning and mopping them out ready for their fares; the smoke of the chimneys ascended in a straight line to heaven; and the distant chirping of the birds in the trees added to the hilarity and lightness of heart with which I now commenced my career as an apprentice."

# CHAPTER IV

# Early Days on Thames and Medway

SEA fights in the river among small craft were by no means unusual, and even as late as 1528 such an incident as the following occurred. A French crayer of 30 tons, with a crew of thirty-eight, fell out, off Margate, with a Flemish crayer of 27 tons and a crew of twenty-four. A running fight started, and the Fleming chased the Frenchman right up to the Tower Wharf, London. There, because of the bridge, the chase could proceed no farther. Sir Edward Walsingham, Lieutenant of the Tower, promptly arrested both ships and cast captains and crews into prison; where they were left to cool their heels and repent their rashness in so insulting the king's peace on the Thames.

The humble bargeman was always in danger of losing his craft by forfeit to the Crown as a "deodand" if any man should fall out of it and be drowned; for by common law any instrument or thing causing a death was forfeited to the king. Sometimes the bargeman might thereby lose his livelihood. But the rule was not always enforced. For example, in 1414 a barge called a "schoute", belonging to William atte Broke and John Dawe, had been seized for the king's service and laden with stone to take through London Bridge to Westminster "for the work of the church there". She was swept by the tide against the piles of the bridge and sunk, her crew of three being lost. But although forfeited to the king, she was granted back to her owners. And in an earlier case, in 1401, the king took compassion on an unfortunate boatman. "Whereas one William de Woxebrugg on Wednesday last on the Thames when casting an anchor out of a boat . . . was unfortunately wrecked in the Thames and drowned, and so the boat was forfeited to the king; the king, because the said John (the owner) has not wherewithal to live besides the said boat, of the value of 20s., grants it to him." Deodands were not actually abolished until so late as 1st September 1846.

Great storms caused much havoc on the river in the old days of small, unseaworthy barges, moored or anchored with unsound hempen cables. One of the earliest in which damage to small craft particularly is recorded was in the reign of Edward VI, when, in 1548, "in the latter end of Januarii was soche vehement windes that damaged sore the western barges, and the lade barges from London to Gravesend to London : a grocer of this citie, his wyfe, his seruant all were drownyd in a whery, sauing the seruant and one of the whery men". In 1703, one of the most fearful storms ever known arose at ten o'clock on the evening of 26th November and continued to blow hard all night. Over a thousand chimney-stacks were blown down in London, and the lead on the roofs of several churches was rolled up like skins of parchment by the wind. All the ships in the Thames between London Bridge and Limehouse, excepting only four, were broken adrift and driven ashore. Over four hundred wherries were lost ; more than sixty barges were driven foul of London Bridge in the greatest confusion, and as many more between the Bridge and Hammersmith were either stove in or completely sunk. Many lives were lost, both on the river and ashore, and, in days when damage to barges was not covered by insurance, grievous loss resulted to the bargemen and wherrymen of the river.

Again, in 1768, on 1st September, there was a similar gale, with an exceptionally high tide. Over forty small craft below the Bridge were sunk, driven on shore or stove in, and a collier in Long Reach drove from her anchors and beat her keel off. With barges adrift, ships driving foul of one another and the crews sweating and swearing in their efforts to clear one another, the scene in the Pool was one of a confusion that almost baffles description. The year had begun with a very severe frost, which, following on a shortage of food forcing up prices to exorbitant levels, caused great distress among the humbler river-folk. The old London Bridge of those days, acting as a dam, checked the force of the tide, so that the river was more easily frozen over. Below the Bridge in this year the river had the appearance of a general wreck; ships, barges and other small craft lay about all jammed and confused with ice ; and many barges and lighters were overset or sunk and frozen in. So severe was the frost that in Deptford Creek a fishing boat was discovered choked with ice and her crew all frozen to death in the cabin. The youngest of them, a lad of about seventeen, was frozen just as he had been sitting—as upright as if alive.

During the Great Fire of London, 1666, the barges were pressed into service for salvage work, and most of the wealthy inhabitants of houses along the Strand loaded their furniture and valuables into barges and lighters, in which they were carried to other houses some miles out of town. Others were used as grandstands for sightseers. One can only guess that sometimes improper uses were made of barges from a note among Pepys's "Naval Minutes" for the year

1681, when he writes: "Reflect on the scandalous barges made of lighters upon my Lord Mayor's Day." Samuel Pepys was always very interested in barges and other small craft, in spite of being mainly concerned officially with the larger navy vessels. He realised that the barge-builder's art was a craft of its own, and that a distinct skill was needed to build a river barge: "he that can build a Ship Royal being possibly not able without further information to build a western barge or wherry so well as an ordinary boat-builder".

Accidents to the barges in the old days were very frequent, and many were due to the dangers involved in shooting the arches of London Bridge. An early example of this, in which a schoute was lost, has already been referred to. A typical later case occurred on 11th May 1798, when a spritsail barge, laden with hay, was coming up the river, and left the lowering of her gear too late. In endeavouring to make the centre arch of the bridge, the set of the tide swung her round and she drove through stern first, so that the end of the sprit struck the balustrades, carrying them away for about ten feet. Two men and a boy, who were standing looked through, were flung into the roadway and severely injured by the stones falling on top of them. They were immediately taken to St Thomas's Hospital, where the boy, whose thigh was broken and skull fractured, died soon after-wards.

Accidents due to the negligent mooring of barges and lighters alongside one another were very common, and gave rise to many actions in the Admiralty Court. An interesting case involving the question of demurrage occurred as early as 1557. This was the case of Thurlstone v. Moore. The contract was for the carriage of forty loads of hay from "the wharf called the Waterside of Ham Marshes to the wharf or harbour called Haye Wharf, or the Three Cranes, in the Vinetree of the City of London". The consignee failed to receive the forty loads at the proper times, and the owner of the lighter had to expend 9s. 6d. in discharging the hay. Also, as the hay was left in the lighter, it got wet, heated, swelled and thus made the lighter leaky. The damages awarded were 53s. 4d. for the freight of forty loads, 10s. for expenses and loss of profit and 20s. for damage. Charges for lighterage were very low in those days; in an earlier case, in 1551, only 2s. a week was allowed for the hire of a lighter. So, also, were the charges for ordinary carriage of goods. In the case of Rich v. Knee-land, in 1614, the defendant, a common bargeman carrying for hire from London to Milton and other places in Kent, received only two-pence for the carriage of a portmanteau containing 30 lb.

A case in 1726, in which the East India Company was concerned,

PLATE 4 Thames Barge of 1809, by Varley

PLATE 5 Cutter-rigged Barges in 1828

*[From an Etching by E. W. Cooke, R.A.*

PLATE 6 Hay Barges in the Thames in 1828

*[From an Etching by E. W. Cooke, R.A.*

throws some light on the system of hiring lighters for the unloading of its ships. Although the company owned a number of hoys for that purpose, the greater part of the work was done by hired barges and lighters. Most of these were what were called "close lighters", that is to say, barges with hatches and hatch-covers, and when the loading was completed, a representative of the company, called a "guardian", was put aboard the lighter; who placed the company's lock on the hatches and went with the goods to see them safely delivered at the warehouse. In the particular case referred to this had been done as usual, and when the goods were lost or stolen, the lighterman was held not to be liable, as the company's representative was in charge.

An interesting collision case in which a barge was concerned was that of the *Baron Holberg*, in 1835. Here a barge, heavily laden with chalk, was beating up Woolwich Reach with a flood-tide under her, when she was run down by the *Baron Holberg*, a foreign sailing ship of 500 tons, coming down the river with a westerly wind. The ship was in charge of a master of thirty years' and a pilot of eight years' experience, and it was argued that, as the barge was in the hands of two watermen only, the ship should be exonerated. This view was not upheld, however, as it could not be shown that the barge was de-signedly mishandled, and the ship, running before the wind, should have kept clear of her. A further point arose over the value of the barge, which was over-estimated at £165, as in 1832 she had cost only £125.

Another collision case occurred in 1837, in which the point turned on the well-established Rule of the Road at Sea that a ship close-hauled on the port tack gives way to one close-hauled on the star-board tack. Here the barge *Susan*, laden with chalk, was run down by the *Carolus*, a foreign vessel of 67 tons in charge of a pilot. The barge was on the larboard (now *port*), the *Carolus* on the starboard tack. But the barge was hailed to "keep her luff", i.e. to "stand-on" on her course. This was held to exonerate her when a collision occurred through her doing so, for the other vessel should have kept clear.

Doubts have occasionally arisen as to whether an ordinary river sailing barge was a "ship" within the meaning of the law, but this was finally settled in the affirmative in 1904, in the case of Corbett *v.* Pearce, concerning the spritsail barge *Alexandra* of 38½ tons burden, registered as a British ship and employed to navigate the estuary and tidal reaches of the River Thames from Sea Reach to Vauxhall.

By the end of the eighteenth century, and before the great dock-building schemes had come into operation, the river became exceed-ingly crowded below the Bridge, and not only was the fairway almost

4

blocked with the larger shipping, but great numbers of small craft were needed to cope with the unloading of ships lying out in the stream. The following table gives the aggregate number of small craft employed on the Thames in the year 1796:

| NO. OF VESSELS | DESCRIPTION | AMOUNT OF TONNAGE | TONS EACH |
|---|---|---|---|
| 2,596 | Barges* | 85,103 | 33 |
| 402 | Lighters | 15,454 | 39 |
| 338 | Punts | 6,810 | 20 |
| 57 | Boats | 1,332 | 24 |
| 6 | Sloops | 161 | 27 |
| 10 | Cutters | 711 | 71 |
| 10 | Hoys | 585 | 53 |
| 3,419 | | 110,156 | |

\* About 400 of these craft were employed in the deal and the remainder in the coal trade.

The lack of proper wharfage and other facilities for handling the merchandise passing through the port, which by 1798 had reached an annual total value of over sixty millions sterling, led to an appalling system of river plunderage, in which about eleven thousand persons were engaged, the extent of the losses amounting to over five hundred thousand pounds annually. To cope with this trouble, the River Police were founded on lines suggested by Mr Colquhoun, an able London Magistrate, with their headquarters at Wapping New Stairs. As the system came into operation, and was modified by experience, it proved "astonishingly efficient in checking that daring system of rapine which before existed, and in breaking up the formidable conspiracy by which it was supported and had been carried on".

It must be admitted that the bargemen were sometimes responsible for a good deal of the plunderage. But, then, their wages were small; opportunities to plunder were frequent; and the temptations great. Samuel Pepys had many troubles with bargemen purloining gear from naval yards. His method of dealing with them, however, gave them short shrift; as an entry in his diary on 5th August 1665 shows, when he tells how he left Woolwich by water, "having ordered in the yard six or eight bargemen to be whipped, who had last night stolen some of the king's cordage from out of the yard".

Various slang terms came into use to describe river thieves employing different well-recognised methods in their depredations. The

"Light Horsemen", for example, used to cut lighters adrift, boarding them later, when the stream had carried them away, and robbing them at their leisure, or sometimes even claiming a reward for salvage. The "Heavy Horsemen" did their work in the daytime, when they went aboard as "lumpers" to clear the ships of their cargoes.

Mr Justice Hawkins, in a note to his "Life of Johnson" published in 1787, refers to an interesting case involving a practice common among bargemen and lightermen then, and until recently. It appears that, with a strong tide under her, a barge was driving up the river, and fell athwart the hawser of a vessel lying at anchor in the Thames. The barge was in danger of capsizing, and a young fellow who was at the helm leapt overboard the vessel and let slip the end of her cable. The crew opposed him in his attempt and a scuffle took place, in which the lad knocked down one of the crew with a handspike. The noise of the fight brought the master, an elderly man, on deck, who indignantly asked the lad what he meant by knocking his man down. "I did it," was the reply, "in my own defence; and if you had been in his place, and your old grey locks had not put me in mind of my own father, I would have knocked you down too!" As Hawkins remarks, here was the very sentiment that restrained Lady Macbeth from murdering Duncan:

> . . . Had he not resembled
> My father as he slept, I had done't.

In the early nineteenth century the barges were sometimes used for smuggling. Hay-barges in particular were peculiarly suited for this purpose, as the stack of hay, loaded high on deck, provided ideal hiding-places for smuggled goods. These would be loaded at night in the lower reaches of the river, out of ships arriving in the Thames from foreign parts. The ship would then proceed up the river, to be boarded by customs officers next day, while the barge, with the smuggled goods carefully hidden among her cargo, would sail up unsuspected, as it was well known that she was quite incapable of making a Continental voyage, and it was easy to prove she had never loaded nor been outside English waters. Nevertheless, barges were sometimes caught in the act, and two fine coloured lithographs illustrate such captures. Of these, the first shows "H.M. Revenue Cutter *Vigilant* towing the barge *Alfred* of London, a valuable prize, captured 17th December 1828, having on board 1,010 half-ankers of contraband spirits concealed in a coasting cargo". The other, of rather later date, shows the same revenue cutter, which was obviously alive to the possibility of smuggling in barges, towing the stumpy barge

*Charlotte*, "captured on the 13th December 1849 having on board nearly seven tons of contraband tobacco concealed under straw".

In the latter part of the century, when barges were making Continental voyages, many of them were built with hollow beams, false bulkheads and the like, where smuggled goods might be concealed. Clever devices were adopted by some of the bargemen for evading the vigilance of the customs. One skipper bored holes through the keel of his barge's boat, through which loops of wire were threaded. In these, bottles of spirits or cans of tobacco were slung, and before the customs officer boarded the barge the boat was placed in the water and towed astern. At the first convenient moment after the search, the boat was hauled up and the smuggled goods were retrieved.

To conclude this section, here follows a brief history of the Watermen's and Lightermen's Company, by which the affairs of bargemen and wherrymen were ordered until its chief activities were transferred to the Port of London Authority in 1909.

The activities of the watermen and bargemen on the Thames are first officially referred to in an Act of Henry VIII's in 1514–15. This Act compelled wherrymen and bargemen to work normally for 6*d*. a day, and to charge only the authorised fares: and, moreover, it compelled them to make the passage for this fare, so that a regular service might be maintained. But this provision was apparently insufficient to regulate the conduct of the watermen, and in 1555, in the time of Philip and Mary, was passed "An Act touching Watermen and Bargemen upon the river of Thames".

The recital to the Act relates that "whereas heretofore for Lack of good Government and due Order amongst Wherrimen and Watermen exercising, using and occupying Rowing upon the River of Thames, there have Divers and many Misfortunes and Mischances hapned and chanced of late Years past, to a great Number of the King and Queen's Subjects, by Reason of the rude, ignorant and unskilful Number of Watermen, which for the most part been masterless Men, and single Men of all Kinds of Occupations and Faculties, which do work at their own Hands, and many Boys being of small Age, and of little Skill, and being Persons out of the Rule and Obedience of any honest Master and Governor, and do for the most Part of their Time use Dycing and Carding, and other unlawful Games, to the great and evil Example of other such like, and against the Commonwealth of this Realm . . . whereby divers Persons have been robbed, and spoiled of their goods, and also drowned".

To remedy this the statute enacted that out of all the watermen between Gravesend and Windsor the Court of Aldermen of the City of London should choose eight "Overseers", as they were called, who were to keep order over the whole body.

There was a further provision under James I in the year 1604, to regulate the training of apprentices. In the preamble of this Act there is again a long dissertation on the unskilfulness of the men handling wherries, tilt-boats and barges, for carrying goods and persons, resulting in great hazards and considerable loss of life.

These early Acts all failed to achieve their objects, however, chiefly because of the lack of adequate powers given to the overseers to enforce their authority, and as, by 1700, "the Numbers of Wherrymen, Watermen and Lightermen" had become "more numerous and disorderly than before", a new Act, 11 and 12 Will. III, cap. XXI, was passed, which was the real foundation of the Watermen's Company. For the first time also the position of the lightermen was regularised, and they were brought within the scope of statute law. By this Act the lightermen were associated with the watermen and the Watermen's, Wherrymen's and Lightermen's Company was formed. All persons owning or working "any Lighter or Flat Boats, commonly used for the lading and unlading Goods and Merchandise, to or from any Ship or Ships" might register as lightermen at the formation of the Company. No other persons might work lighters, save certain employees of Trinity House, under pain of paying a penalty of five pounds for every week they should so work on a lighter.

By the constitution laid down for the company, the Lord Mayor and Court of Aldermen were to elect yearly eight of the best watermen and three of the best lightermen to be overseers and rulers. The watermen were to choose assistants, not less than forty nor more than sixty; and the lightermen similarly were to choose nine assistants from their number, who were to be stationed at the various stairs to preserve good order and government. Some of the earlier orders of the rulers strike a curious note to modern ears; for example, the rule that "watermen using any lewd expression on the river Thames, are to forfeit two shillings and six pence for every offence". The Watermen's and Lightermen's Company retained the rights over the registration and licensing of vessels, and the regulation of lightermen and watermen, until these powers were transferred to the newly constituted Port of London Authority by the Act of 1908 which brought that body into being.

In the early days of the river barges, their longest voyages were probably made carrying cargoes between London and the various towns and villages on the Medway, frequently sailing as high up the latter river as the town of Maidstone, well into the heart of Kent.

Small barges even went as far as Tonbridge. In the time of Elizabeth Maidstone was quite a small town, with only 294 houses and four landing-places. Five ships and hoys belonged there, of burdens from 30 to 50 tons. But by about 1780 the town had increased considerably, and a large number of barges were regularly trading from there to London. It was a great distributing centre for wheat and flour, some being sent for the use of the Navy at Chatham, and much more to Rochester and to London. Fulling and paper mills in the vicinity also sent their produce by barge to London. Vast quantities of timber from the Weald of Kent were brought to Maidstone by land carriage and there loaded on barges and conveyed by water to different parts. Besides the barges engaged in these trades, there were several large hoys sailing weekly to and from London with general cargoes.

Stockdale, writing in 1796, describes the barge trade on the Medway in these words. "Large hoys," he says, "of 50 tons burden, are constantly going to, and returning from, London, exchanging for other goods, at that great mart, the various articles of produce already mentioned. Warehouses and stowage-rooms are provided for hops, and large wharfs for English and foreign timber, giving this place and its environs a very busy appearance. The number of barges and all kind of craft upon the Medway, in and near the town, is extremely great; and if the projected union between that river and the Thames should take effect, it probably will be much augmented." The "projected union" was the canal from Gravesend to Strood, built shortly afterwards, by which the barges were to be saved the hazards of a short sea passage round the Grain Spit into the Medway; and, incidentally, a considerable amount in distance.

Later he writes: "If the traveller looks to the water, other pleasures await him; the leaping fish leaving behind the many, circling waves; diverging from its centre, the dashing water falling over its tumbling bays; barges sailing or hauled along, loaded with timber, hops, stone, chalk, lime, coal, coke, bricks, fine white sand, fuller's earth or bales of party-coloured rags; and frequently the painted boat richly bedecked without, but graced within with the richest treasures of Britain, our fair Country-women, often such that beggar all description." Such was the Medway nearly a century and a half ago.

Faversham, built on a creek running out of the East Swale, part of that channel which divides the Isle of Sheppey from the mainland, was also a great Kentish shipping port for small craft. In the time of Henry VIII vessels of only 20 tons could come up to the town, but later it was improved, so that vessels of 80 tons burden and upwards, "of which size," says Hasted, "are the common corn hoys," could come up to the town quays. In 1774 there were twenty-nine coasting vessels, of burdens between 40 and 150 tons, belonging to the port. At that time, the principal shipping trade was carried on by six hoys, which went alternately every week to London with corn; the amount carried annually being sometimes as much as 40,000 quarters.

Some indication as to the shape and rig of these hoys is given in a map showing the whole Isle of Sheppey, with the River Medway and the Swale. In this, no less than four small cutters are seen navigating these waters. They are probably, indeed almost certainly, the hoys referred to above; therefore their rig and form of hull are of the greatest importance, and although the drawing is crude and on a small scale, certain broad features are very obvious. They are all cutter-rigged craft, pole-masted, with a boomless gaff-mainsail, foresail and jib set on a bowsprit steeved well up. The head of the jib is carried high enough up the mast to balance the strain of the peak halyards. But the most important point is that all these craft have the square, sloping swims of the barges of that period. Indeed, they are exactly a primitive form of the cutter-rigged barges illustrated in Cooke's etching of 1828 (Plate 6), and correspond very closely to the rig of the hoy shown and described in Steel's *Rigging and Seamanship* of 1794. They all carry the usual long flag or streamer at the mast-head; the "bob" as the bargemen call it. There is other evidence to show that the ordinary sailing barges of the Medway were sometimes called "hoys", which, if it increases the difficulty of defining a "hoy" as a particular build and rig of ship, yet supports the general indication that the hoy was merely a generic term for a small short-distance trading coaster of the humblest class.

Mr Edgar J. March, in his "Spritsail Barges of Thames and Medway" (1948), gives a full and detailed account of the old Kentish "Hoy-barges", which were run by what were called "Hoy-Companies", such as the Margate Hoy Company, who had the well-known hoy barge *John Bayly* of 56 tons, "spreetie" rigged and built at Sandwich in 1895, named after their chairman; and the Ramsgate Shipping Company. These and others ran regular weekly services between London and the Kentish coast ports, Margate, Ramsgate, Sandwich and Dover, with fast sailing barges carrying general cargo. For long they were able to compete successfully against the railway; but the increasing competition of road motor transport as the century advanced at length drove them to other trades.

One well-known hoy barge was the *Dorcas*, which forty years ago ran to Sandwich and Dover with general cargoes. The red, white and green of her painted hull earned her the name of *Hokey Pokey*. Built in 1898 at Rochester, she was burnt out soon after the First World War, and was rebuilt by Pipers at East Greenwich in 1922, when she was re-named *Squeak*. Her hull was "rose-on" (i.e. built up and made deeper) and she was re-rigged as a river staysail barge, shorn somewhat of her former bowsprit glory. In her later days she traded mostly in the sand and ballast trade. She was dismantled in 1948, after nearly sinking in Sea Reach; and her hulk now lies at Greenwich.

At one time there was in Maidstone an old tavern known as "The Bargemen's Arms". It bore a painted sign on which were the words:

> *Oh all ye bargemen that pass through this town*
> *Pray lend me a hand, for my barge is aground.*

The origin of this couplet I have never been able to discover. An old Rochester barge skipper I know, remembered it quite well, but the tavern has long gone and the sign is no more.

Before leaving the old days on the Medway, it is perhaps worth pointing out that the immortal Francis Drake first learnt his seamanship on this river; for he was apprenticed to a Gillingham hoyman trading with France and Flanders.

The corn hoys of Kent and Essex were a numerous class of vessel, and were employed carrying corn to London from as far afield as the ports of Sandwich in the south and Ipswich in the north. When Queen Anne came to the throne, there was some agitation because of the action of the Customs authorities in imposing heavy duties and requiring corn shipped in these vessels to be "coquetted", that is, broadly, to have had certain duties paid. By an Act of the first year of her reign, hoymen trading within these limits with corn were relieved from these duties, a total payment of a maximum of 3s. 5d. per voyage for a "transire" being all that was required of them.

Among these corn hoys were great numbers trading from Margate to London. Margate in the eighteenth century was a great corn shipping port, and towards its close the town blossomed forth as a fashionable resort for sea bathing. This developed a regular service of passage boats, not only for passengers, but for luggage and general goods, and an average number of no less than 18,000 persons were carried annually. The "Margate Hoy" is famous in song and fable. The hoys sailed from Wool Quay, near the Custom House, London, on Wednesdays and Thursdays, and with a favourable wind the passage to Margate was made in twelve hours. In adverse circumstances, as much as three days might be spent over it. The hoys bound the other way sailed from Margate on Fridays and Saturdays. The fare in 1772 was the very modest sum of half-a-crown, and, as evidence of the safety of the passage, Fisher, writing in that year, was able to state that there had not been a hoy lost for over one hundred and fifty years; a great contrast to the "Long Ferry" to Gravesend, on which the tilt-boats were constantly getting into serious troubles.

The history of the Gravesend "Long Ferry" can be traced far back into the past. As early as the time of Edward I, in 1293, "a complaint was made, that the Bridge and Chalk Causeway leading to the water here, was much out of repair, and that the Watermen took extra-ordinary money of the people, to the great injury of passengers . . . *viz.*, where they used to take of a man on foot going to London a *half-penny* for his passage they now exact a *penny*".

In 1797 the charge had increased to one shilling for the single journey. The "Long Ferry", as the Gravesend passage was called, was much used by passengers for Calais *via* Dover, as well as for the ordinary traffic into Kent, owing to the cheapness and comfort of the voyage and its comparative rapidity, one tide only being more than sufficient for the journey. The arms of the Portreveship of Gravesend and Milton are interesting, for they throw light upon the "tilt-boats" used for this passage. The boat is a typical heraldic boat, but certain points may be noted : The single mast is stepped almost amid-ships. There are a forestay and a pair of shrouds each side to support it. The sail is a simple square sail, such as the ordinary sailing lighters carried. It is supported by a halyard, and lifts from the yard-arms.

The five oarsmen are all on the foreside of the mast. Further details are available from contemporary accounts. Aft of the mast, although it is not shown, was the "tilt" or awning from which these boats took their name. This was supported on semi-circular bales, and the sides were open, though sometimes fitted with let-down curtains. Under the tilt sat the passengers, who were provided with clean straw every tide strewn on the bottom of the boat, and over it a large rug or blanket with which they might cover themselves in cold or bad weather. The tilt extended aft as far as the steersman.

The number of tilt-boats lost from time to time was surprisingly large, and compares very unfavourably with the excellent records of the Margate Hoys. The last disaster of the kind happened in November 1750. A man named Cooleby was master, and twelve or fourteen persons were drowned, six only being saved.

About this time boats covered with wooden decks were first used, the boats were enlarged, and after their improvement no more acci-dents happened, certainly until the end of the century. At Graves-end the boats were met by coaches to carry the passengers to Rochester.

The arrangement for sailing the tilt-boats, which departed at tide-time at any hour of the day or night, was as follows: A bell was hung at Billingsgate, whence the boats started, and another on the causeway at Gravesend. An officer was appointed at each of these places and it was his duty to ring the bell at the time when the first of the ebb and the first of the flood began to run. He continued to ring it heartily for fifteen minutes, in order to give due warning to intending passengers and to the tilt-boats and wherries that the time for sailing had arrived. Any tilt-boat master or wherryman bound for Gravesend remaining after the bell had ceased ringing, or delaying on the passage so that the tide was done before the destination was reached, was liable to heavy penalties, unless he could manage to set his passengers on shore within two miles of their journey's end, when it was

FIG. 11 Gravesend Tilt-boat, 1753

considered that they would have no reasonable grounds for complaint if they should have to walk the rest of the distance!

The tilt-boats had to be of a least burthen of 15 tons, and might not carry more than thirty-seven passengers to start the journey, or pick up more than three additional passengers by the way. The drawing reproduced in Fig. 11 is copied from a sketch by Pierre Canot showing a Gravesend Tilt-boat of the year 1753. She is clinker-built, and fairly fine forward with a clean run aft to a narrow stern, not unlike a Norfolk wherry. She is rigged with a single pole mast, supported by two shrouds aside and a forestay and fore-topmast-stay, but no backstays. She carries a bowsprit supported below by a bob-stay; a gaff mainsail; and foresail and jib are both set with hanks on stays. At the mast-head is the usual vane. Forward is a short deck. The tilt or awning, which gave the boat its name, was like a raised hatch-

cover over the middle of the boat, supported on pillars and open at
the sides, with a canvas awning over. It seems as though curtains or
weather-cloths were furled under the tilt at the sides, which could be
let down in bad weather. She looks an able enough craft, and should
be fairly fast. Having shoal draught, embarking and disembarking
were made comparatively easy.

The tilt-boats continued running until they were displaced by the
Gravesend steamboats, early in the nineteenth century.

In addition to the hoys, smacks, barges and tilt-boats frequenting
the London River in the old days, were great numbers of other small
craft bearing different names and used for different purposes, but all
more or less connected with the early barges. The hatch-boat, for
example, of which Cooke made a fine etching in 1828, was a small
vessel, with a double-ended hull not unlike a Norfolk wherry in
shape, rigged with a gaff mainsail, foresail and jib. Aft she had a small
cuddy for the crew's accommodation, and her deck was almost entirely
composed of hatches, from which she derived her name. A smaller
vessel with the same double-ended form of hull was the Peter-boat,
used for fishing; but she was rigged with a sprit mainsail, and foresail.

The hatch-boat does not seem to have survived to within living
memory. But a craft not unlike her at the bow end, though with the
transom stern of the barge instead of the sharp stern; round-bilged;
and rigged with a sprit mainsail, stay foresail and no mizzen, was
known in the middle of the nineteenth century as a "luff-barge".
There is a drawing, reproduced here as Fig. 12, in "The Book of the
Thames", by Mr and Mrs S. C. Hall, published by Virtue & Co. in
1859. On page 365 we read of luff-barges as "a smaller class of barge
than the square barge of the Thames, being sharp forward, and
altogether more like an ordinary vessel. Perhaps this accounts for the
name of clipper-barge, which it sometimes receives. Luff-barges are
rigged with a sprit and foresail, without a mizzen, and generally carry
goods where larger vessels are unable to go; their trade is mostly confined to London and the upper part of the river ".

The accompanying picture, Fig. 12, shows a craft not unlike in
some respects the 1840 model of the Medway barge *Ann*, p. 73 and
Plate 10. It was suggested there that the bow of the *Ann* represented a
transition stage between the old swim-head and the later round bow.
I believe myself that the luff-barge was the successor to the hatch-
boat; combining the round bow of the hatch-boat, and probably a
rounded bilge, with the other features of the smaller Thames spritsail barge. I also think that the term "luff-barge" was given to these
craft *because they had a rounded bow*, as distinct from a swim-head.

The word "luff" or "loofe" was not only used as an order to the helmsman, meaning to bring the ship's head up more to windward; it also meant the fullest or roundest part of a ship's bows. That is one of the meanings given to it in Smyth's " Sailors' Word Book" of 1867; and it seems to me to offer the most likely explanation for the term "luff-barges" as opposed to barges with a swim-head, known later as "swimmies".

Mr Edgar J. March, who refers to luff-barges in his "Spritsail Barges of Thames and Medway", informs me that an old barge-man told him they were also called "Paddy-boats". This would fit in

FIG. 12 Luff-barge, 1859

very well with what is known about "Paddy-boats", which twenty years ago were described to me as round-bottomed and sloop-rigged barges, carrying about 60 tons. They were so called because they were manned almost entirely by Irishmen. A Paddy-boat skipper was the man originally concerned in the oft-told yarn of the barge and the liner, which has now become almost traditional. A Paddy-boat was holding on her course when a P. & O. liner approached. Having very little room, she blew her siren to indicate that the Paddy-boat should keep out of her way. The latter took not the slightest notice until, as the liner was practically on top of her, and going astern on both engines to avoid a collision, the Irish skipper looked up from the helm, and "What would ye be hootin' for?" said he.

"Get out of the way, you ——!" yelled the infuriated Chief Officer.

"Sure, an' who are you?"

"I'm Chief Officer of this ship."

"Then spake to yer aquals," replied Paddy, "for I'm *master* of this!"

The Paddy-boats have all gone now, though twenty years ago one or two of the Irish bargemen were still left sailing in the English barges, or picking up a precarious living as watermen upon the Thames.

FIG. 13 Hay Barges

Hay barges (Fig. 13 and Plates 6 and 12) are no longer seen on the Thames to-day. But at one time, when London's streets were full of horse-drawn traffic, most of the hay required to feed the horses came by barge, and a fleet of hay barges working up the river was a common enough sight. It was almost uncanny to watch such a vessel turning to windward in all the traffic of the London River, with 12 feet of hay on her decks, the mast apparently stuck into the middle of it, a pocket-handkerchief of mainsail and a tiny triangle of foresail only left above the stack, and the mate perched on top of the hay letting the master know what lay ahead of him. Plate 6 shows a number of hay barges in the Thames in 1828, and a drawing by T. S. Robins of slightly later date shows "Hay barges off the Reculvers", just above Margate. They have probably recently left the latter port and are bound into the Thames. The heavy, old-fashioned swim-heads are clearly shown. The picture is interesting because it proves that the hay barges along the Kentish shore sailed from ports well below the Nore. On the Essex side, the hay barges regularly sailed out of Harwich for London ; and a few barges still carried on this trade, almost up to the Second World War. They were specially built for it, being rather shallower than the ordinary barge, to enable them to enter the farm creeks. They also had special gear for holding the stack firmly in place when at sea. The photograph, Plate 12, gives a very good idea of the appearance of these amazing craft when under sail.

By a strange turn of the wheel of fortune, "stackies" have returned to the Thames Estuary since the Second World War, though they no longer trade into the London River. Mr Hervey Benham, in his delightful book, "Last Stronghold of Sail", published in 1948, tells how the last few years have seen a sudden and unexpected revival, with a big demand for straw for paper-making mills near Queenborough in the Swale. Thus once again one may be lucky enough to see a barge under sail, with a stack of straw from an Essex creek high on her deck, standing across the Estuary bound for the Kentish mills. Mr Benham gives a vivid description of such a passage : "We went bucking and bowling across in the teeth of a strong sou' westerly, which just allowed us to fetch the East Swale. Aft at the wheel, under the lee of the stack, one hardly realised it was blowing, for with so bulky a cargo the barge was in ideal trim and as lively as a life-boat."

Another class of barges common at one time were the "Sandies". These were small barges employed for dredging silver sand from the bed of the river. The sand was afterwards carried to London and sold for scouring and scrubbing, for sanding the floors of taverns and dwelling-houses, and other domestic uses. The trade is very ancient. Forty or fifty years ago, a "sandy" might be seen anchored under the lee of almost every point. At low tide, if the berth was suitable, the barges could lie aground while the sand was shovelled aboard. But generally it had to be dredged for, which meant hard work for very little profit. The "sandies" were supposed to supplement their income by stealing sheep grazing on the marshes behind the river walls. The standing joke when sailing past a "sandy" was to shout "Baa" repeatedly in loud and life-like tones. A volley of earth, bricks, mud and every other available missile was the instant retort. One or two "sandies" were left working right up to the First World War. Barges needed licences to allow them to dredge sand, and these are no longer granted.

An interesting account was given to me by Mr F. C. Prideaux

Naish, who lived at Gravesend as a boy about the turn of the century. He said that two or three "sandies" could generally be seen over on the Essex side of the river, just above Coalhouse Point, at the bottom of Gravesend Reach. The sand there was much sought after by iron founders for making castings. It was particularly good for moulding, as it was sharp, and bound together well, having a little clay with it. It was dredged up with poles which had big leather scoops on the end. The tide washed the sand into the scoop, which was then hauled up with a tackle, and capsized into the hold of the barge.

The last two "sandies" were the *Band of Hope* and the *Blue Ribbon*.

At one time a number of barges were rigged with a lugsail in place of the ordinary spritsail. These were sometimes called simply "lug-boats". A solitary survivor was still working on the Medway in 1931. She was a small swim-headed barge, and carried her cargo only a few hundred yards; but she was fitted with lee-boards, a microscopic mizzen, lowering mast, etc., and was in all other respects an ordinary barge.

Among lug-rigged barges in the last years of the nineteenth century were those on the following list; the names being given with place and date of building: *Chiltern*, *Cheviot*, and *Dartford*, all Blackwall, 1888; *Brothers*, Blackwall, 1889; and *Blackthorn*, Grays, 1901. The *Success*, in which George Chapman started as mate, was a swim-headed lighter, rigged with a stay-foresail, standing-lug mainsail, fitted with brails as in a "spreetie"; and a diminutive sprit mizzen stepped on the rudder-head. She was steered with a tiller, and my friend the late George Doughty, of Martlesham, sent me a sketch of her drawn from George Chapman's recollections, in which all these features appear.

A variant of the lugsail in barges was the split-lug, which was cut as shown in Fig. 14, and was really a mainsail and foresail set on the same yard. It had the advantage of some of the driving power of the big dipping-lug sail, without the disadvantage of having to dip the fore end of the yard and sail round abaft the mast every time the vessel was tacked; or, if this were not done, of having the sail set badly when it was on the weather side of the mast. It is, however, forty to fifty years since this sail was seen in the river barges. In the days when the old sailing collier ships lay in the Lower Pool and were unloaded into lighters, a number of small lug-boats made a living dredging up the coals which inadvertently fell into the water in the process of trans-shipping.

I close this chapter with the following account of the use of barges for salvage work in the old days, sent to me by the late Mr George Andrews of Sittingbourne. I have included it verbatim, affording as it does yet another example of the sailing barges' remarkable versatility.

"Away back in the 'seventies and 'eighties, when many sailing ships used the East Bay of Dungeness for anchorage and shelter, wrecks were frequent at this place. The salvage of their cargoes was done by sailing barges owned by the late Mr George Smeed, and Smeed, Dean & Co., Ltd., of Sittingbourne; for which services the sum of four or five pounds per day per barge was paid, the craft being towed to and from Dover. Sailing barges named the *Jessie, Isabella, Wave, Harry, Favorite, Georgina, Elizabeth, Mary Ann* and *Sarah Ann* did much of the work. Several of these were swim-headed. Their average size was 110 tons D.W.

" It of course frequently happened that they were caught at this

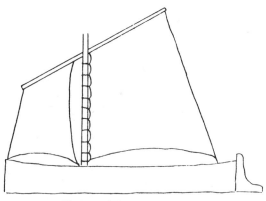

FIG. 14 The Split-lug Rig

dangerous work by bad weather, and before the tide floated them, the tug was compelled to leave for shelter. Many a time the crews (master and mate only) rode out the gales, and not infrequently have slipped cables on the high water and run into what was then Romney Hoy, now reclaimed to the foreshore. It was a deadly risk, but they did it again and again. I have known these craft to be in tow away from the wreck with a rising south or south-easterly wind, by day or night, in the direction of Dover, when the crews, refusing further to risk their craft sinking one another in tow, have slipped hawsers and run back under the steep beach of the West Bay, and left the tug to her own course.

"They were brave and capable bargemen of the dare-devil order, and I do not remember that any of the crews were drowned. In shoal water and on a lee shore, sailing barges well handled act marvellously."

# CHAPTER V

# The Barge in Evolution : Second Stage

In Chapter III the development of the barge was traced down to the early eighteen hundreds. In this, it is carried a stage further to the later years of the nineteenth century. The improvements in the barges during this period can conveniently be considered under the two headings of developments of hull and developments of rigging. A considerable advance in both took place between 1800 and 1830. Among them the most important was the addition of the mizzen and the unique use made of it for assistance in steering the barge.

The reason for its introduction was that at this time the barges were increasing considerably in size; and this increase in size was being gained chiefly by adding to the length. The longer and, by comparison, narrower vessel which resulted, was difficult to turn about when tacking, for it is a well-known and obvious fact that a short, tubby vessel is more easily turned round than a long, narrow one. The more modern barge was consequently apt to fail to come about, "missing stays" as it is called, and something had to be devised to enable her to handle as easily as before. The device adopted was the addition of that small after or mizzen-mast and sail, which is so characteristic of the barge of to-day; and very ingeniously stepping that mast on the rudder-head itself, and sheeting the sail to the outboard end of the rudder-blade, as shown in the sketch by the late Edward Wigfull (Fig. 15). The result was that the sail turned with the rudder, and as soon as the helm was put down, the mizzen sheet was automatically pulled up to wind'ard, and the sail itself, acting as a backsail, pushed the stern of the barge round. In effect, the sail acted as an additional rudder in the air, and had an advantage over the ordinary rudder, in that it was effective as long as there was any wind, whereas the rudder could act only if the barge had "way on" or movement through the water. For many years the mizzen mast continued to be stepped on the rudder-head, and as long as barges were steered with big wooden tillers no other arrangement was possible, as an after mast would have prevented the tiller swinging across the deck. When wheels were introduced, Harry Munns of Erith, the famous racing skipper, is reputed to have been the first man to step the mizzen on deck, although according to others, his brother Johnny actually did so before him.

It is interesting to note that the mizzen working with the rudder appeared also on the German barges, known as *Evers*, on the lower

FIG. 15  Mizzen stepped on Rudder-head
*[By courtesy of the " Yachting World"*

Elbe, at about the same period. The *Ever's* mizzen, like that of some early barges, was a lug-sail "rudder in the air". Such a craft, of about 1840, called a "Kniep-Ever", is illustrated opposite page 16 in Szymanski's "Der Ever der Niederelbe" (Lubeck, 1932).

The small lug-mizzen is stepped on the rudder-head. She is lug-rigged, transom-sterned, fitted with lee-boards and carrying a stack of timber on deck. The German *Ever* was in many ways the counter-

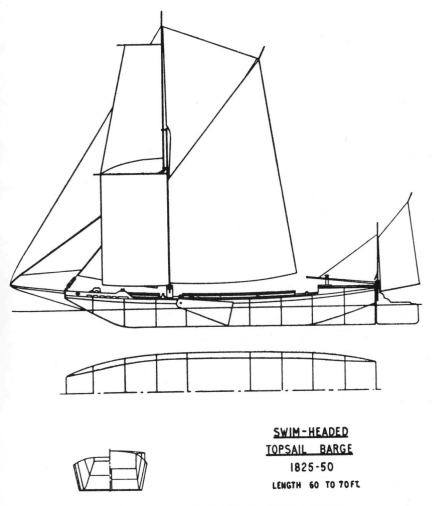

SWIM-HEADED
TOPSAIL BARGE
1825-50
LENGTH 60 TO 70 FT.

REDRAWN FOR REDUCTION FROM AN ORIGINAL PLAN BY HOWARD I. CHAPELLE

FIG. 16

part of the Thames barge, working in similar waters of river and shoal-infested estuary.

Barges with topsails had become quite common by the 1830 period, and square sails, square topsails and sometimes even square to'gans'ls were carried in the larger barges. The illustration (Plate 7) from an 1829 etching of E. W. Cooke's, shows such a barge in a fresh breeze, running up Northfleet Hope, from Tilbury to Grays, in the lower reaches of the London River. She makes a splendid picture. The high-peaked mainsail and short topmast will be noticed. By the kindness of my friend, Lieut.-Colonel Howard I. Chapelle, U.S.A.R., of Cambridge, Maryland, U.S.A., to whose painstaking and learned researches into the history of sailing craft, large and small, on both sides of the Atlantic, we owe so much, I am privileged to make use of his beautifully drawn plans of a swim-headed spritsail barge, carrying square canvas, of a type well known in the period 1840–1870 (Fig. 16). She is a craft very like that seen in Cooke's etching (Plate 7) already mentioned, and will well repay careful study.

One of the last old-time barges to carry square tops'l and to'gans'l was the *Septimus*, in which my old friend Harry Ward of Pin Mill sailed many years ago. She had a big gaff mainsail with a long main boom reaching right aft, and a little lug mizzen set on a mast stepped on the rudder-head. She was steered with a tiller, and the mizzen sheet pulled right out on a long boom. Another like her was the *Francis*, Captain Cowey. There were at that time (nearly sixty years ago) several barges named with Latin numerals, of which the *Septimus* was one. They are treated more fully in the chapter on "Boomies".

The famous *Record Reign*, of much later date, was originally fitted with square tops'ls and to'gans'ls, as shown in Plate 33.

In barges carrying a squaresail yard this was carried permanently aloft, and fitted with lifts to the yard-arms and braces led aft for trimming it. The squaresail was generally set flying, the foresail halyards being used to hoist the sail, with head earrings from the yard-arms to pull out the head of the sail. My ex-pilot cutter *Cariad* carries a squaresail rigged in exactly the same way at the present time.

Sometimes, however, the yard was carried on deck, and the sail bent on to it when required with separate stops or with a lacing. The yard and sail were then hoisted together on the foresail halyards. This had the advantage of simplicity, and was useful when a small square-sail only was carried. But, as against this, the spar was too heavy to handle comfortably on deck, and had to be laid across the rails forward of the mast before being hoisted. It was also more difficult to lower and unbend the sail in a breeze of wind than when, as where the yard was kept aloft, the sail only was hoisted and "set flying". The permanent yard could be "cock-billed", that is, tilted on end, when not in use, by hauling up one yard lift and slacking away the other,

PLATE 7 Thames Barge off Northfleet, 1829

*[From an Etching by E. W. Cooke, R.A.*

PLATE 8 Spritsail Barges, 1828

*[From an Etching by E. W. Cooke, R.A.*

PLATE 9 Swim-headed Barge, 1840 Period

[*From a Model in the Science Museum*

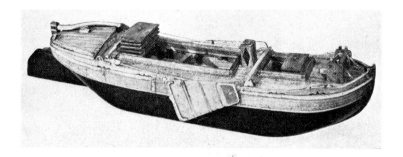

PLATE 10 Round-bowed Medway Barge *Ann*, 1840 Period

[*Model made by Mr E. W. Gill, and now in Rochester Museum*

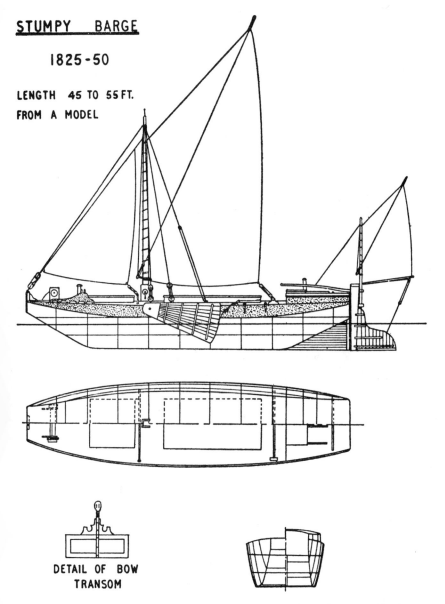

## STUMPY    BARGE

### 1825-50

LENGTH   45 TO 55 FT.
FROM  A  MODEL

DETAIL  OF  BOW
TRANSOM

REDRAWN  FOR  REDUCTION  FROM  AN  ORIGINAL PLAN  BY  HOWARD I.CHAPELLE

FIG. 17

until the lower yard-arm could be secured by a lashing round the forward shroud on one side, so preventing chafe.

With the addition of topsails, barges became divided into the two classes of topsail and "stumpy" barges. The latter were the barges

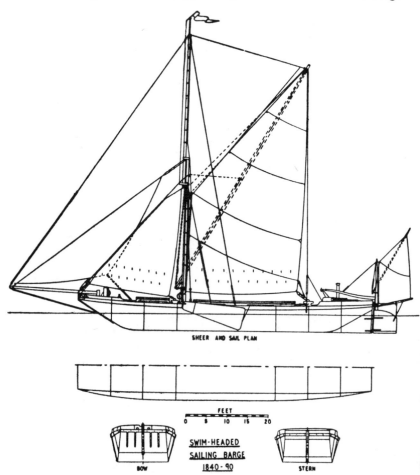

SHEER AND SAIL PLAN

FEET

0   5   10   15   20

SWIM-HEADED
SAILING BARGE
1840-90

BOW        STERN

REDRAWN FOR REDUCTION FROM AN ORIGINAL PLAN BY HOWARD I. CHAPELLE

FIG. 18

carrying no topsails, like those shown in Plate 8. I am again indebted to Colonel Chapelle for the plans of an early small "stumpy" barge of the period 1825 to 1850 (Fig. 17); and of a typical big topsail barge of about the same time (Fig. 18), which may thus be compared. In those days the "stumpies" were, in fact, often as fast, or even faster, than the topsails, and as the old spritsails were cut with a much higher peak, raised by a spreet far longer than is customary nowadays, the difference in sail area was not so considerable as might be supposed. It was common for a barge of less than 80 feet in over-all length to carry a spreet as much as 64 feet long. The topsails, when carried, were consequently smaller than those of to-day, and were cut much squarer in the head, so that the leach was not far out from the horizontal. This was the more pronounced because both masts and topmasts were shorter in comparison with modern practice.

Some time within the next thirty years after 1830, the cutter-rigged barges disappeared and were succeeded by barges with a cutter's mainsail and a gaff mizzen set on a mast stepped well inboard, being thus rigged as ketches. As the foot of the gaff mainsail was spread by a boom, they were known as boomsail barges, or, more shortly, "boomies". There were then three types of barges: "topsails", "stumpies" and "boomies". The story of the "Boomies" forms the subject of Chapter VII. Up to about 1840, however, all the barges appear to have been built with the old-fashioned swim-head.

A fine example of a swim-headed topsail barge of the 1840 period is seen in the photograph (Plate 9) of a model in the Science Museum, and in the plans by Colonel Chapelle of the same craft (Fig. 19). She is fitted with a high-peaked mainsail, stowed with main brails, two pairs of uppers and two pairs of lowers. The foresheet and mainsheet traverse the deck on heavy wooden bars called horses. Forward is the old-fashioned barrel windlass, worked with handspikes. The main-mast is stepped on deck in a heavy mast-case. She has only one hatch-way, on which is coiled a long warp. On the fore deck another warp is coiled down. Forward of the mast are chocks and tholepins for work-ing the long oars or "sweeps", by which she can be manœuvred in a calm or when the gear is lowered on deck. The sweeps can be seen lying alongside the hatch. The cabin is under a raised deck aft, with well-rounded beams. Notice that the lee-boards are raised and lowered with tackles led aft to near the main horse. Crab-winches for the lee-boards were a comparatively late innovation. Notice also the mizzen-mast stepped on the rudder-head, as shown in detail in Fig. 15, which shows how the mizzen stay sets up to the tiller itself. In the early barges the deadwood or "budget" was strengthened and held in place by iron straps. The budgets and rudders too, of these early swim-headed barges were built hollow and boxed up with thin wood. This can be seen in the etching in Plate 4 and in Figs. 8a and 8b. The barge of 1840 carries a bowsprit which can be "steeved up" into a vertical position when desired.

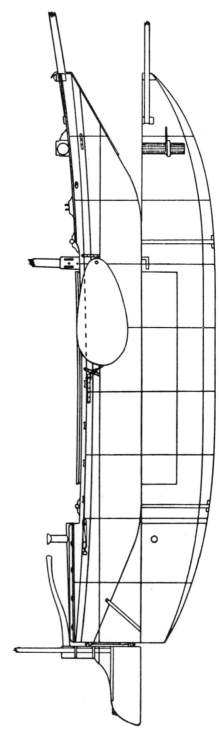

TOPSAIL BARGE

1840

FROM A MODEL

REDRAWN FOR REDUCTION FROM AN ORIGINAL PLAN BY HOWARD I. CHAPELLE

There is then nothing projecting forward over the bow which can get in the way when handling the barge in confined waters. It is supported by a bobstay beneath, leading down under the swim; a topmast stay above; and bowsprit shrouds on either side. On it is set a jib, the tack of which is hooked or shackled to a sliding iron traveller on the bowsprit, on which it can be hauled in and out. The luff of the topsail is seized to wooden hoops sliding on the topmast, and the sail then, as now, is stowed aloft by means of the clew-line. This light rope leads from the after corner or clew of the sail, up to a block at the head and down to the deck through a block at the lower mast-head. By hauling on this, when the topsail halyard and sheet are let go, the clew and head of the sail are drawn together and bunched up snugly at the lower mast-head. For greater security, if it is blowing hard, short ropes called gaskets hanging from the mast-head can be passed two or three times round the sail, and all made secure.

In about 1840 a great improvement was made in the shape of the barges, when the swim-head began to give place to the round bow. Canal barges and ballast barges on the Thames had for a long time been built with the round bow, but until this period the sailing barges of the Thames and Medway had retained the old swim-head. In the Museum at Rochester is a most interesting model of one of the first of these round-bowed barges, built by Mr E. W. Gill of Rochester, the father of Mr E. A. Gill, M.I.N.A., of the London and Rochester Trading Company, whose genius has been responsible for so many fine barges and whose enthusiasm was so largely responsible for the success of the Medway Barge Races in the years between the wars. This model, which is seen in the photograph (Plate 10), is of the hull alone, but it will be noticed at once that this barge is built on very pretty lines. She represents, as it were, the transition stage from the swim to the round bow. She slopes up from the forward end of her bottom as if she were going to have a swim-head; but this is not carried out, for the sides are brought in to a short rounded stem, and the result is a really attractive round bow not unlike in shape the short spoon bow that is often seen on the modern cruising yacht.

Various other points in the construction of this barge are worthy of comment. Although completely flat-bottomed and chine-built* in the typical barge fashion, she has a wide flat outside keel, which is unusual, as well as a pair of small bilge pieces. The lee-boards are attached at the forward ends by eye-bolts and toggles of the pattern in use to-day. Observe the raised cabin-top and sliding hatch over the

---

* Chine-built: having a square corner, not a rounded bilge, where the sides join the bottom.

companion ladder. The forward end of the cabin-top is decorated with carved and painted panels, on which the name of the barge, *Ann*, is inscribed. She has a short fore hatch as well as a main hatchway. The decks are wider and the hatches narrower than in the modern barge. Forward of the fore hatch is a short fore-peak. Across the middle of the main hatch is a removable tye-beam. The curved wooden tiller ships into the rudder-head, and is kept in place by iron straps. A wooden bracket should be noticed between the upper edge of the rudder blade and the after side of the rudder post. The mast is stepped in a heavy wooden mast-case on deck, supported by the substantial sailing beam below.

This form of round bow did not live long, however, for whether or not many barges were built on those lines, it was soon displaced by the more modern straight stem as found in nearly all sailing barges at the present time. In this the stem is nearly vertical, and rises straight up from the forward end of the keel of the barge, in the manner shown in Colonel Howard I. Chapelle's plan of a Thames Barge of 1865 (Fig. 20) and in the model of the *Thelma* (Plate 13). This comparatively modern barge, *Thelma*, was built in the year 1901, and is referred to in greater detail later in the book; but, leaving aside for the moment the question of rigging, she does not represent a great advance, so far as the broad features of hull are concerned, from the round-bowed, straight-stemmed barge of the eighteen-sixties (Fig. 20), when the general lines on which the barges of to-day are still built became established.

The advance in the shape of the bow during the nineteenth century has been described; and during the same period the stern was also very much improved. The stern common at the beginning of the century is well illustrated in Plate 4 and Figs. 8 and 9. That of the middle of the century is seen in the model of the Rochester barge *Ann* shown in Plate 10. A considerable improvement is immediately noticeable. The barges of that period had narrow, comparatively deep transoms, and the lines up from the bottom to the stern, called the "run", were not so fine as in the later craft. This point is clearly seen in the fine model of a barge of the 1870 period named the *Verona*, now in the National Maritime Museum at Greenwich. The narrow, deep transom is still, generally speaking, the mark of the "old-timer". For the clean run, the barge races were largely responsible, with their great influence in improving the build of the barges in all directions. The barges of the later years of the century had broader, shallower and flatter transoms, like that of the barge *Torment* in the fine photograph, Plate 47. This pattern stern has remained for most barges, except the

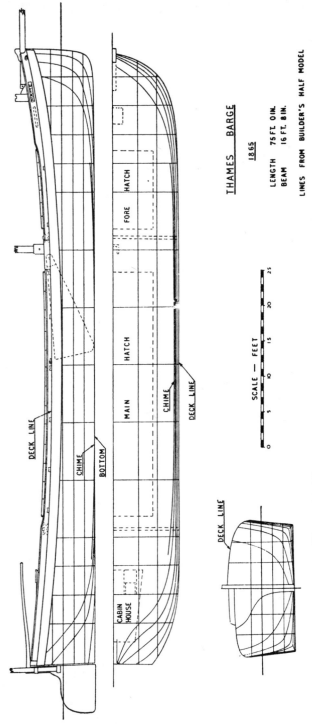

THAMES BARGE

1865

LENGTH 75 FT. 0 IN.
BEAM 16 FT. 8 IN.

LINES FROM BUILDER'S HALF MODEL

SCALE — FEET

0 5 10 15 20 25

REDRAWN FOR REDUCTION FROM AN ORIGINAL PLAN BY HOWARD I. CHAPELLE

FIG. 20

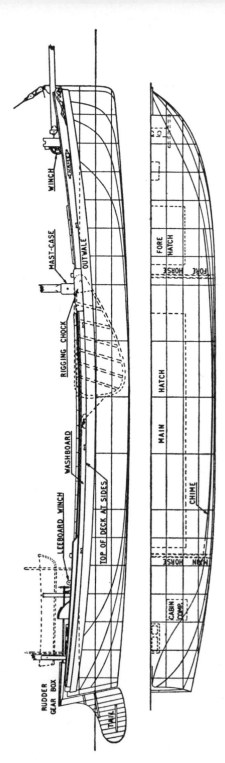

WINCH

MAST-CASE

OUTWALE

RIGGING CHOCK

WASHBOARD

LEEBOARD WINCH

TOP OF DECK AT SIDES

RUDDER
GEAR BOX

TAIL

FORE
HORSE

FORE
HATCH

MAIN HATCH

CHIME

MAIN HORSE

CABIN
COMP.

SCALE - FEET

0    5    10    15    20    25

DECK LINE

TRANSOM

TOPSAIL BARGE

CHAMPION CLASS

1895

LENGTH   85 FT. 0 IN.
BEAM     18 FT. 8 IN.

REDRAWN FOR REDUCTION FROM AN ORIGINAL PLAN BY HOWARD I. CHAPELLE

FIG. 21

PLATE 11  A "Swimmie" off Cubit Town in 1884

[*By courtesy of the National Maritime Museum*

PLATE 12  A "Stackie" at Sea

[*By courtesy of the Nautical Photo Agency*

PLATE 13 Champion Barge *Thelma*, 1901

[*From a Model in the Science Museum*

large iron barges, until the present day; although in later years the transom has become somewhat deeper, while the fine lines of the run remain. An idea of the beautiful hull form, encouraged by the competition of barge racing in the closing years of the nineteenth century, may be formed from the Plans shown in Fig. 21, where Colonel Howard I. Chapelle has drawn out the lines of a Topsail Barge in the Champion Class of 1895.

A number of the "boomie" barges were built with clipper bows and counter-sterns, like the *Lord Tennyson* (Plate 34), the *Pearl* of Harwich (Fig. 25) and the *Lily* of Whitstable, and very pretty ships they were. But at least one famous "spreetie", the *Haughty Belle*, built by Piper of Greenwich in 1898, had a counter-stern. This handsome barge had the lines more of a yacht than a barge, and being painted instead of tarred when she first came out, she looked a very lovely vessel. The photograph (Plate 45) shows all the grace and beauty of her hull; and I doubt if a more handsome barge ever sailed. Her keelson, instead of being straight, had a spring to it fore and aft, so that it followed the line of her sheer. And when heeled in a breeze, the fore foot, which was considerably rounded up, came almost out of the water. Another, even more famous barge, built with a spring to her floor, was the celebrated *Giralda* (Plate 46), also built by Piper, and many times Champion both of the Thames and of the Medway. In her the spring of her keelson was so marked that she was actually deeper amidships than forward. Half-models of both these fine ships are still in the possession of the builders. From that of the *Giralda*, Mr Edgar J. March, of The Society for Nautical Research, took off the lines and drew them out. They appear in his "Spritsail Barges of Thames and Medway", published in 1948. A beautiful craft she was. The counter-stern of the *Haughty Belle* did not, however, prove a success. Projecting so much, it was found to be in the way and was liable to serious knocking about and damage from which it could not be adequately protected. It was therefore removed about the year 1904. These considerations have prevented the counter-stern being adopted generally by the barges, and the flat transom stern became standardised, except for the "boomies".

After the swim-head had been superseded, a number of experiments were made in the design of the round bow; and the amount of round-up to the forefoot where it joins the stem varied between such wide limits as the Rochester barge model of 1840 (Plate 10) and the *Thelma* of 1901 (Plate 13) with her perfectly straight stem; with *Haughty Belle* (Plate 45) as an intermediate design. One barge, the *Alexandra*, built by Piper, had a Dutch-pattern bow, rather like a boeier's, which was round as an apple and "tumbled-home" about the water line; together with an almost V-shaped deep transom stern. But she was not a success, and the design was never copied.

Another important improvement in the barges made in the latter part of the century was the change-over to wheel steering. The first barge to be fitted with a wheel was the *Anglo-Norman*, one of Stone's best barges. She was fitted with a wheel taken from the old broken-backed schooner *Azalia* at Erith in about the year 1882. An interesting old photograph taken at the time shows Mr Stone, his sons, some of his friends and some of his bargemen, gathered round this famous wheel on board the *Anglo-Norman* on the day of the Barge Race, 1882. The original wheel was still in existence in 1930, when it was in the possession of Mr Douglas Stone of Brightlingsea.

The improvement in the design of the barges fitted them for more extensive voyages, and in the latter part of the century, fine sea-going spritsail barges were sailing far beyond the limits of the river where they had their origin. The lines and sailplan of a "Channel Barge" of this period are shown in another drawing by Colonel Chapelle, from which Fig. 22 has been taken. Such craft were able to compete in the coasting trade which was then carried in hoys, smacks, schooners, billyboys and the like. The effect of the combined competition of the barges, with the small coasting steamboats which were introduced and increased rapidly in numbers during the century, was almost to drive the older vessels off the seas. The reasons for this were the following. The hoy and smack type of coaster was a round, tubby ship, of comparatively deep draught of water. She was slow and, her gear being very heavy, she required a big crew to handle her. The former consideration meant that she had no great advantage over the small steamboat. For, where there was water to float a hoy, a steamboat could follow; and that more certainly and quickly. The large crew needed and her heavy gear made her more expensive to run than the barge; while the latter, with her light draught, could get where the steamboats could not follow. So, for small cargoes, the barge provided a more economical means of transport than any other that could be devised. Her motive power, the wind, cost her nothing, and she could carry her cargo into the smallest navigable creek. When her hull and rig were improved, she could also make long coastal voyages.

Thus it was that in the latter part of the century, Thames barges were trading down-channel to Falmouth; across to the Channel Islands and Brest; down the East Coast to the Humber and the Tyne, and over to the Belgian, Dutch and German seaboards. Nor did they stop at that. The *Edith Mary* was the first barge round Land's End;

MULE-RIGGED COASTING BARGE — 1895

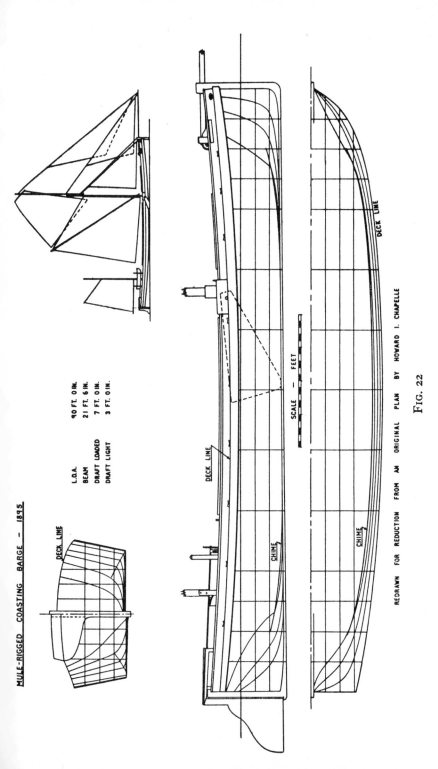

| L.O.A. | 90 FT. 0 IN. |
| BEAM | 21 FT. 6 IN. |
| DRAFT LOADED | 7 FT. 0 IN. |
| DRAFT LIGHT | 3 FT. 0 IN. |

DECK LINE

DECK LINE

DECK LINE

CHIME

CHIME

SCALE — FEET

REDRAWN FOR REDUCTION FROM AN ORIGINAL PLAN BY HOWARD I. CHAPELLE

FIG. 22

and after her voyage, the west of England and the Irish ports frequently saw the Thames barges. Harry Ward of Pin Mill went to Ballyshannon, County Donegal, in a "boomie" barge; the first to visit the north-west coast of Ireland. About sixty years ago, Captain Tom Strange, whom I knew as master of the *Davenport*, was the first man to take a barge to the Shetland Islands. Nearly sixty-five years ago, Captain Walter Ward of Pin Mill took the barge *Arundel Castle* to Christiania from Antwerp, and brought her back across the North Sea with a six-foot stack of timber on her decks. The voyage is described in greater detail in Chapter XII. Captain David Garnham, of Pin Mill, sailed the *Eastern Belle* (a barge known as a "hard-hearted old devil") out to Lisbon and home at about the same time or a little later. One could continue almost indefinitely. North, south, east and west, the barges of the London River sailed far beyond the limits of the stream where they had been bred and born, to wrest their living from the sea, carrying safely across it the merchandise of all Western Europe. River lighter no longer, the sailing barge had become a sea-going ship.

PLATE 14  Barges in Ipswich Dock Entrance, 1903

[By courtesy of Messrs Smiths, Suitall, Ltd, Ipswich

PLATE 15 "Stumpie" Barge, 1888

[*By courtesy of the Nautical Photo Agency*

PLATE 16 Model of Barge *Hero*, showing frames

[*By courtesy of the Science Museum*

PLATE 17 Model of Barge *Hero*, showing keelson and floors

[*By courtesy of the Science Museum*

CHAPTER VI

# The Modern Barge and how she is Handled

THE most noticeable advance in the modern sailing barge lies in the great increase in size, and in the employment of iron and steel in place of wood. The rigging has changed but little since the latter part of the nineteenth century. Mast and topmast are taller, the topsail longer in the hoist, and the upper end of the spreet no longer appears to fall backwards directly over the main horse. But otherwise the barges are much the same in rig as they were some sixty years ago.

In the hulls, apart from the fact that the later barges were built very much larger, the chief change was the increase in the size of opening of the hatches, with narrow cambered decks, made necessary by the need for accommodating modern cargo machinery, such as "sucker"-type grain elevators, and large mechanical grabs, together with the avoidance of unnecessary labour in trimming cargo.

The construction of a wooden barge had the advantage of combining simplicity and strength with cheapness. The number of sharp bends, necessitating the use of natural-grown wooden crooks for the framing, was far less than in a round-bottomed ship, and there were few awkward twists in the planking. An idea of the construction of a barge can be gathered from the photographs (Plates 16 and 17) of a model in the Science Museum of the barge *Hero*. From the specification for the building of a typical modern wooden barge, the following dimensions have been extracted:

She was to have an over-all length of 82 feet, beam of 18 feet 6 inches and to be 6 feet 6 inches deep. Her keel, no part of which was to project below her perfectly flat bottom, was of English elm, 12 inches wide and 4 inches deep. Stem and sternposts to be English oak, 9 inches by 12 inches; stem and stern knees to be of the same, through-bolted with $\frac{7}{8}$-inch bolts. The floors were to be $5\frac{1}{2}$ inches by 8 inches, and well tree-nailed.* The keelson, which runs down the centre of the barge on top of the floors and keel, and gives longitudinal strength proportionate to that afforded by the keel in a normally built vessel, was to be 14 inches by 14 inches of Oregon pine. The corresponding longitudinal strength of frame at the sides was

---

* I.e. fastened with hard *wooden* bolts called "treenails".

6

given by side keelsons of 7-inch by 16-inch pitch-pine in one length. The planking of the bottom was to be of 3-inch Oregon pine, with 1-inch pine sheathing diagonally laid over it set with tar and hair, while the ends were to be worked out with 2½-inch English elm for three strakes out from the keel, and afterwards in oak. The decks were to be laid of well-seasoned pine, in 6-inch planks 3 inches thick, painted both sides and properly caulked. The hold inside had to be "ceiled"; that is, lined throughout with planking. The rudder to be of pitch-pine on an oak post, and the lee-boards to be of 3-inch oak.

Her mast was to be 33 feet in the hoist, and of pitch-pine; her sprit 56 feet long, and of Oregon or red pine. The topmast was to be a Swedish spar, 36 feet with a 5-foot pole. Mizzen-mast 16 feet, and mizzen sprit and boom in proportion. She was to have a 27-foot bowsprit. Her mainsail, topsail and foresail were to be of best No. 1 canvas; her balloon foresail of duck; and mizzen, mizzen staysail (an unusual sail in a barge), spinnaker and two jibs to be of 18-inch and 16-inch cloths. Five months from the acceptance of the tender were to be allowed for building her, with a £5 Penalty Clause. A proportion of the price was to be paid as soon as she was in frame, a further and equal sum when "skinned" (i.e. planked) and the decks laid; and the balance on completion, with the exception of a small sum which was to be withheld until the barge had been in service for two months.

A very fine example of all that is best in wooden barge-building after the First World War is seen in the *Phoenician* (Plate 18), which was skippered and partly owned by the renowned Alfred Horlock of Mistley, and sailed under A. H. Sully's flag. To her skipper and to Mr Alfred Sully I am indebted for the following account of her building and of her principal dimensions. Her building Contract and Specification appear as Appendix III. She was built in 1922 at Sittingbourne, by Messrs Wills & Packham, and started work in 1923. Her estimated cost was £2,500, and the builders lost £1,000 in building her. A condition of the building was that she had to be of the maximum possible size to go through Mutford Lock, into Oulton Broad from Lowestoft, to enable her to take part in the trade up the Waveney to Beccles. This was effected by rounding her quarters in sharply to a transom stern somewhat narrower than is usual, to enable the lock-gates to close clear of her. She was also to be fast. I had good proof of her powers turning to wind'ard when we sailed from Harwich after breakfast one morning in early January, and after having had to turn every inch of the way against a strong sou'-westerly wind which backed and veered and headed us in every reach, we brought up in the Lower Hope below Tilbury before it was dark

enough for us to need our sidelights. Few yachts would have done it;
we were sailing light—that is, without cargo—and there was just as
much wind as we could stand with all plain sail; but too much for the
other barges lying in Harwich, for we were the only barge to get to
London that week, and it blew half a gale for the next few days.

The late Captain Russell Dent, who was recognised as one of the
finest barge skippers of all time, and who was killed when his barge,
the *Bankside*, was mined in December 1942, had raced many times
aboard the *Phoenician* as a member of Captain Alf Horlock's racing
crew; and in his opinion she would outsail all others in a really strong
wind with a sea running. She won in the Thames Races of 1932, 1933,
1935 and 1936; and was second in 1931. In the Medway matches her
wins were in 1931, 1932, 1933, 1935 and 1936. A truly wonderful
record.

The *Phoenician* is 84·1 feet in over-all length, with a beam of 20·8
feet and a depth of side of 7·3 feet. The round-up of the beams is
13 inches, giving considerable camber to her decks. As a sailing barge
the lengths of her spars were as follows: Mast, deck to hounds, 35
feet; sprit, 59 feet; bowsprit, 32 feet outside of stem; topmast, 40 feet
under hounds, and 4 feet 6 inches topmast head; mizzen mast, 16
feet; boom, 17 feet; and sprit, 28 feet. She set 6,000 square feet of
canvas in all. Her registered tonnage as a sailing barge was 79 net and
97 gross, and she carried 150 tons to sea or 175 tons in the river.

On 6th June 1940, during the "Blitz", she was lying by Marriage's Mill at Felixstowe Dock when an English bomber crashed on
her, and in the resulting fire her gear and part of her decks were
burnt. After that, she was used as an ammunition hulk for the rest of
the war; and when she was released, was taken to Sittingbourne for
repair. She lay in the builder's shed there for over two years, being
extensively rebuilt, and converted to a purely motor barge. It was sad
to see her great racing lee-boards lying beside her in the yard, never
to be used again. It was decided to install two Deutz Diesels, from a
Fairmile D-type M.L. which had been captured by the Germans
during the war. After a refit lasting some two years, she was completed early in 1949 and is now trading again as a fully powered
motor barge, under Captain Fox.

The first iron barge was built away back in the 'fifties, or there-
about, and was named *Frederic*. She was a Kentish vessel, belonging
originally to Huggins of Sittingbourne, and was known to all bargemen as the "Old Iron Pot". Captain Frank Beadle of Erith had her
in the days when she was owned by Stone Bros, and told me that a
handier barge never turned up the river, in spite of the fact that she

had only one lee-board at that time, her owners never troubling to replace the other, which she had lost. For some reason she was sheathed inside and out with wood, so that she had the appearance of a wooden vessel. When she was eventually broken up, in about 1905, the plates in her bottom were found to be in as good condition as the day they were put into her. The "Old Iron Pot" was, however, a lone pioneer far ahead of her time, and it was not until the eighties that more barges built of iron appeared. The first was the *City of London*, 55 tons, built at East Greenwich in 1880 for Messrs A. H. Keep Ltd. Shortly afterwards, in 1881 and 1882 respectively, Messrs E. J. & W. Goldsmith had the *Bras de Fer*, of 54 tons, and the *Electric*, of 58 tons, both built at Blackwall. *Bras de Fer* survived to sail in the Southend Barge Race in 1904. In 1884 two more iron barges, *Atlantic*, 69 tons, and *Pacific*, 60 tons, were built for A. H. Keep. Mr March records that all these vessels survived into the second decade of the twentieth century, their iron plates still in good condition. *Pacific* is still trading, at the time of writing, as a motor barge belonging to the London & Rochester Trading Co.

Iron, however, in its turn was to give way to steel, and the largest modern barges are steel-built. Of these, some built between the wars reached very large dimensions for craft carrying the ordinary Thames barge's spritsail rig. Two large ones were the *Barbara Jean* and *Aidie*, belonging to Messrs R. & W. Paul of Ipswich. They were both built at Brightlingsea in 1924, and were fine big craft carrying about 260 tons, and of 119 tons net. Unfortunately both these barges were lost at Dunkirk, as recorded in Chapter XVI.*

But the largest spritsail barges ever built were the splendid steel ships, costing some £5,000 each, which were built by Fellowes, at Great Yarmouth, in 1925 and 1926, for Messrs F. T. Everard & Sons Ltd., the well-known barge-owners of Fenchurch Buildings, E.C.3, whose yard is at Greenhithe. There were four of these craft originally, *Alf Everard* (Plate 19), *Ethel Everard*, *Fred Everard* and *Will Everard*, all named after members of the family. They were 97·6 feet long, 23·1 feet in beam and 9·6 feet deep; and were very fine ships loaded, though in the opinion of some competent bargemen they were rather narrow for light sailing. Perhaps that is why they really never achieved success in the Barge Matches, although the *Alf Everard* came second in the Medway Race in 1928. They loaded about 300 tons. From truck to keel they measured no less than 112 feet, and had sprits 65 feet in length. They set 5,600 square feet of canvas, exclusive of balloon canvas; and it must be remembered that even with this

* *Aidie* is now a coal hulk for tugs at Dunkirk.

PLATE 19 *Alf Everard* leaving Newlyn, 1928

[*By courtesy of Eng.-Cdr H. Oliver Hill, R.N.*

PLATE 18 *Phoenician* in the Medway

[*Photograph by J. N. Willis, High Street, Chatham*

comparatively large sail area, they were specially kept snugly rigged for Channel passage-making in the depths of winter. When first launched, they carried a crew of four hands, with skipper, mate and two boys; but afterwards worked as three-handed ships, it being found that one strong and efficient man was more useful than two inexperienced lads.

A few examples of passage-making in these craft will show what they could do loaded. In 1928, for example, the *Alf Everard*, under Captain E. Mole, a smart Essex bargeman who was only twenty-three when he first had charge of this ship, made a very smart run from Weymouth to Hull, and the following details were kindly supplied to me by Mr Philip Kershaw, from Captain Mole's rough log. The barge got under way at 10.30 a.m. on 25th October; passed St Catherine's Point at 5.0 p.m. that afternoon; and was off Dungeness at 6.0 a.m. next morning. The North Foreland was passed at 10.30 a.m., the wind then being S.E.'ly; by 6.0.p.m. Yarmouth was abeam, Cromer at midnight; and at 7.0 a.m. she was passing the Bull Light on entering the Humber. The wind was then E.N.E., and fresh. At 11.30 a.m. the barge was anchored in Hull Roads, 49 hours out from Weymouth, and eventually arrived at Keadby to load at 5.20 p.m. that afternoon.

On another occasion she left Poole in very light winds; but after passing the Owers, she got a slashing S.W. breeze, and made Cromer Light in 27 hours. As the wind had then veered to N.N.W., she had to beat from there to the Humber.

On the other hand, being a comparatively deep-draught vessel for a barge, she sometimes had to wait for spring tides to trade to such lesser ports as Wells, in Norfolk. At least once, when bound there with 285 tons of oil cake, she just missed her tide, and had to anchor for a week off Wells bar before she could cross and reach the quay.

Her last passage under sail was made in 1938, and shortly before the war the *Alf Everard* was converted to a fully powered motor barge, all her sailing gear being taken out of her. When built originally, these barges all had special stern-frames fitted, so that they could easily be converted. On conversion, they were fitted with a raised bridge and superstructure, so that they looked much like an ordinary motor coaster. The last entry in Captain Mole's rough log reads:

"Jan. 11, 1939—Berthed yard (Greenhithe) 4.0 p.m. to be dismantled for motor."

*Alf Everard* is still trading as a motor barge, under the same owners.

The *Ethel Everard* was lost at Dunkirk, as recorded in Chapter XVI. She was one of the barges entered in the first post-war Thames

Race of 1927, but she did not win anything. She had, however, many
fast passages to her credit when trading. Mr A. J. Dover, who once
served in this ship, recalls an occasion when they were towed out of
Newlyn, Cornwall, by one of Everard's motor coasters; who gave
them a good offing and then cast them off. Both were bound for
Margate. With a strong fair wind, *Ethel Everard* made a fast passage;
the motor coaster getting in on the high water, and the sailorman
arriving at half-ebb only about three hours later.

*Fred Everard* has also been converted to a fully powered motor
vessel, and extensively rebuilt, with raised bridge and superstructure.
She was converted to power in about 1940. When war came in 1939,
she was one of Everard's craft employed as Ammunition Store
Issuing Ships, and was attached to the Home Fleet at Scapa Flow.
She is still trading to-day as a motor coaster.

Thus *Will Everard* remained alone of the four to continue under
sail only, and was, until recently, the largest surviving spreetie at
work. At the time of writing, she is said to have been the last purely
sailing vessel to trade north of Boston. Her wartime adventures
under Captain J. A. Uglow are recorded in Chapter XVI. She was
lately trading fairly regularly with coal and coke from Keadby in
summer, and sugar from Ipswich in winter. One of her fast passages
laden was from Keadby to Margate, with coal, in 30 hours. It is
with regret that I have to record that she also has now become an
auxiliary.

Smaller steel barges, with fine lines and almost yacht-like hulls,
were being built regularly, up to the early 1930's, by Messrs F. W.
Horlock at Mistley in Essex. The latest of these craft, like the *Blue
Mermaid*, built in 1931, and the *Resourceful*, replaced the old-
fashioned dead-eyes and rope lanyards by which the standing rigging is set up, with the more modern turn-buckle-type rigging-screw.
But in the opinion of many experienced bargemen this was by no
means an improvement, as the rigging-screw has not the give and
elasticity of lanyards, is liable to strip its thread and will not adjust
itself to an even strain if one shroud is set up harder than another.
But apart from this, the new Mistley steel barges were splendid
vessels, and could "sail like the wind". Unhappily, *Blue Mermaid*
was sunk by a mine during the Second World War on 9th July 1941,
about 8 miles from Clacton, near the West Hook middle buoy; both
master and mate losing their lives. *Resourceful* has had the gear taken
out of her and has been trading as a fully powered motor barge since
1933. She was under requisition from February 1940 to July 1946,
employed in the Clyde.

A number of staysail river barges were built of steel by Piper of Greenwich between the wars. Two were named *Pip* and *Wilfred*, and they represent the last word in modern steel staysail barges. *Squeak* (Plates 58 and 59) ,which completed the once-famous trio of children's favourites, was the old hoy-barge *Dorcas*, rebuilt after having been burnt out, as recorded on page 56. *Pip*, 88 tons, built at Greenwich in 1921, was run down off Purfleet some years ago by a steamboat, her crew being drowned. She was dismantled later to be made a pure motor barge, but the engines, ordered in Holland, could not be delivered because of the war. She now lies, a hulk, at Greenwich, owned by T. Scholey. Her sister-ship, *M. Piper*, is still going. *Wilfred*, of 98 tons, built in 1926, is a motor barge, now in ballast work; also in sand from Brightlingsea.

In 1931 there were still quite a large number of "stumpie" barges in service, several of them being fairly modern ships. Messrs Eastwoods, the brickmakers, had a little fleet of them, used for carrying bricks from their Kentish brickfields to their various wharves in and near London. The Associated Portland Cement Manufacturers Ltd. had eight, the *Clyde*, *Edwin*, *Emma*, *First Attempt*, *Overcomer*, *Regent*, *Scarborough* and *Wednesday*. Of these, the oldest was the *Scarborough*, built in 1882, and the smallest was the *Regent*, built, in 1896, specially to be able to go through all the locks from end to end of the Regent's Canal. *Clyde* was sold to Messrs J. Mowlem & Co. in 1933, and *Edwin* was bought by Messrs C. H. Musselwhite & Son in 1931. She now lies on the mud at Erith. *Emma* was sold to Mr W. H. Theobald in April 1933; in which month also *First Attempt* was bought by Flt.-Lieutenant Semphill and *Overcomer* by Mr W. D. Inglis. *Emma* was to have the distinction of being the very last stumpie trading, and was certainly working until 1944, but by 1951 she was being converted at Leigh.   I have no further news of *Overcomer*, but *First Attempt* was converted, and belonged for some time before the war to the Misses Joyce and Peggy Evers.   The last report I had was that she was lying by King's Ferry Bridge, and not likely to fit out again. *Regent* was sold to Mr H. J. Thomas in June 1932 and *Scarborough* to Messrs Braithwaite & Co. in March 1933. The "stumpy" *Wouldham Hall*, whose photograph appeared in the first edition, was sold to Mr Moore in May 1928, and I have no subsequent news of her.

The *Wednesday* was one of a fleet of barges named after the days of the week. Messrs Albert Hutson of Maidstone still owned four "stumpies" in 1931. The *D.E.F.* and *U.V.W.* were originally built by a cement manufacturing firm who named their craft with groups of three letters taken successively from the alphabet. *D.E.F.*, 42 tons, built Rochester, 1889, is now at Maidstone, used for lightering coal. *Jim Wigley* was originally a 100-tonner, but later carried about 90 tons, and used to be employed carrying coals to Tonbridge Gasworks from Rochester. She was found to be beyond repair and has been used as a store barge.

Their fourth "stumpy", *Wouldham Court*, of about 90 tons burden, was generally employed in taking stone from quarries to sea-walls. She was requisitioned by the Ministry of War Transport for mine watching in the Thames. She was very seriously damaged when a German F.W. 190 bomber, brought down in the Medway, crashed on her when she was lying on the Lower Moorings off Strood Dock, with *Herbert* and *Kingfisher*, also destroyed. She was too badly damaged to repair for trading again, and is now a motor yacht barge at Chelsea.

A number of other firms also owned "stumpies", and many of these were quite fast and able to hold their own against some of the slower topsail barges turning to windward in the London River.

Strangely enough, the last sailing barge built on the Thames was a little wooden "stumpy", built by Hyam and Oliver at Rotherhithe in 1931 to the order of the War Department, specially for carrying arms and ammunition between Waltham Abbey on the River Lea and Woolwich Arsenal. She has gone right back to olden times in her rig, with tiller steering, and mizzen mast stepped on the rudder-head itself. She is still very much "alive", and Arthur Bennett told her story in "The Trident" for March 1949.

Although all the "swimmies" have now gone, a few of these were still left in 1931. Messrs Goldsmiths had two, the *Atom* and *Juliet*, both large barges then only about thirty years old. They might often be seen lying off Grays. The Associated Portland Cement firm had one, the *Ant*, but she was even then dismantled and has been broken up. There were perhaps half a dozen altogether left at that time. It is a mistake to imagine that the "swimmy" was necessarily slow, for off the wind a fast "swimmy" would often beat a round-bowed barge. *Atom*, 78 tons, was built at Grays as a wooden lighter in 1903, and afterwards rigged as a spritsail barge. She was eventually run down off Grays and afterwards broken up. *Juliet* was a big "swimmy", of 105 tons, built at Sittingbourne in 1896. Both these "swimmies" were employed in the river trade.

Another class of barges, of which I believe there were only a few, were pointed-sterned craft. These were known as "nipcat" barges. They were originally built as lighters for ferrying off the stone to the Eddystone Rock for the building of the new lighthouse there. When this service was finished, they were eventually bought by White of Crabtree Dock, Fulham. Lee-boards' and ordinary spritsail barges' gear were put into them, and they started working as ordinary sailing barges. Being chine-built, the only difference lay in the pointed stern. Two of them bore the names of *Bee* and *Spider*. *Spider* eventually became a lighter on Woolwich buoys, where she was destroyed by a bomb during the Second World War.

A small "nipcat" barge of about 40 tons, the *Chance*, built at Lewes in Sussex, used at one time to belong to an Erith bargeman named Robert Austen. "Robert the Devil", as he was universally called, was a well-known riverside character at Erith twenty years ago. He had been a man of wild ways in his youth, and his various escapades had earned for him the nickname he bore with a not inconsiderable amount of pride. He would lie on his back and have a granite kerb-stone broken across his chest with a sledge-hammer for a gallon of beer, and many a time swum the river from Erith to Coldharbour Point and back for a pint.

For the benefit of those who may be interested in the details of the rigging of a modern barge, as shown in the plans of the "spreetie" *Nautilus* in Fig. 23, the following brief description may be of some value. The mainmast, a heavy pitch-pine spar, has the heel squared for about the first six feet up from the deck, and is stepped in a strong iron mast-case, as shown in Plates 22 and 23, bolted firmly through the deck to the heavy sailing beam below. The mast-case is like a three-sided iron box, open at the top and at the after side, in which the heel of the mast fits snugly, and is secured by a bolt through its lower end and a removable iron bar across the after part of the case.

On either side of the mast-case, mounted on it, are small hand winches, known as "mast-winches". They generally have two drums each side, one operated direct by the handle, and the other low-geared. They are used for warping, particularly from ahead; and for any other purpose when extra power for heaving on a rope is needed. Very useful they are, too! If it should ever be necessary to work the cargo in and out by hand, without cargo machinery, a big-wheeled gin-block can be slung on the end of the sprit and the mast-winch used as a cargo winch.

No part of the mast extends below the deck, but it is supported by a stout strut or stanchion rising up from the keelson below. At the mast-head (Plate 21), two forged iron straps, called mast-caps, one below the other, encircle the mast, and provide two rings on the fore-side through which the topmast can slide up and down. The topmast is hoisted by a wire heel-rope shackled to the mast midway between

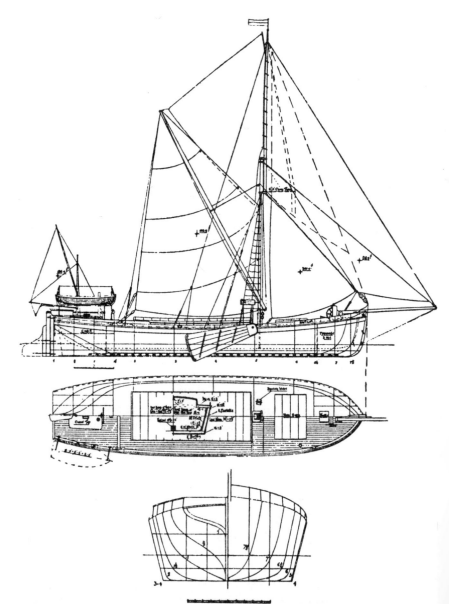

**THE THAMES "SPRITTY" BARGE NAUTILUS**

FIG. 23

*Plans by W. M. Blake*

[*By courtesy of the Editor of the "Yachting Monthly"*]

the caps, leading down through a sheave in the heel of the topmast, and back up to a sheave on the mast between the caps on the opposite side, the fall having a tackle on it by which it can be hauled down to the deck and the topmast hoisted. An iron bar called a fid can be shipped through a hole, called a fid-hole, in the heel of the topmast, which, resting across the lower cap, prevents the topmast slipping down when the heel-rope is slacked up.

The mast is supported by three wire shrouds each side, set up with dead-eyes and rope or wire lanyards, and by the forestay, set up by a three- or four-fold purchase to the stem-head, called the stay-fall tackle (Plate 20), by which the mast can be raised and lowered by leading the stay-fall to the windlass, whereby sufficient power to heave up the mast may be obtained. When not in use, the stay-fall tackle is generally kept coated with a painted canvas cover. Additional to the shrouds are backstays which can be set up to a point along the side about half-way aft from the after-shroud to the main horse. When under way, the weather backstay is always set up, and when working cargo in or out, both backstays can be unhooked and taken in to the main shrouds out of the way.

The topmast is supported by one shroud each side, set up with a light tackle or a length of small chain; a pair of backstays; and a topmast stay leading forward to the stem-head, or, in barges carrying a bowsprit, to the bowsprit end. The topmast shrouds are spread by iron cross-trees which can be "topped up" or raised, so that the shrouds fall in close to the mast when going alongside cranes or other dockside machinery. In barges carrying a bowsprit, this spar is held in place by a bolt through the heel so that it can be "steeved-up", or raised into a vertical position, when working in the river or in docks, so that no part of the gear projects beyond the stem. It is kept down when in position by a chain bobstay leading from well down the stem to its outer end, and set up inboard, and is supported sideways by bowsprit shrouds. The mizzen-mast is stepped in a small iron mast-case on deck, and supported by a pair of shrouds each side and a mizzen-stay set up to the deck forward with a tackle, by which it can be lowered like the mainmast.

The lower end of the main sprit (Plate 23) is confined to the mast by an iron collar called the muzzle, the weight downwards being taken by a chain "stanliff" from the mast-head near the hounds. The upper end ships into the peak of the mainsail, and the weight is taken by the head-rope of the sail. The strain is so great that a very large head-rope has to be employed, and in cutting and making up a large new sail, as much as three feet may have to be allowed for stretch. The arrangement of the brails by which the mainsail is stowed remains the same to-day as it was in the barge of 1794 described on page 42, but the main brails, leading down from the throat, are usually hauled up by a small crab-winch placed on deck on the port side of the mast, and in large barges an additional drum on this winch is employed for hoisting the topsail. The main sheet is rigged as in 1794, with the addition of an extra block about eight feet up the leach (Plates 29 and 58). The luff of the foresail is attached by sliding hanks on to the fore-stay, and the sheet is of chain, and travels freely across the deck on a wooden or iron horse. In addition to the sheet, the clew may be made fast to the forward shroud on either side by means of a short length of rope called a "bowline" which is passed through a metal ring called a cringle near the clew of the sail and back to a cleet seized to the shroud.

The jib on a large barge is usually set with hanks to a stay leading from the lower mast-head to the bowsprit end, and is stowed on top of the bowsprit by gaskets passed round the sail and spar. The topsail has a short yard at the head, and is set on mast hoops sliding on the topmast. The sheet by which the clew of the sail is hauled out to the spreet end is a short length of chain with a rope spliced into it, and a rope whip on the fall to haul it out. In setting the sail, the sheet is first hauled right out, the head of the sail then hoisted and finally the lower corner or "tack" is hauled down with a tackle. In stowing, if bringing up for a tide only, in fair weather, the head of the sail alone is dropped and the sheet left hauled out. But in blowy weather the sheet also is let go, and the sail snugged into the mast with the clew-line, and stowed with gaskets as described on page 73.

The mizzen of a barge calls for little comment, beyond the fact that in all except some of the largest, and in the mule-rigged barges, the sail is sheeted to the outer end of the rudder.

New sails in a barge are allowed to stretch and take their shape before they are dressed. But when ready, they are dressed, and kept dressed, with a composition in which the chief ingredients are oil and red ochre. This never dries, and although it makes the sails very heavy, keeps them always supple, and gives to them that rich, reddish-brown colouring which artists find so attractive. But it has the dis-advantage that it rubs off and soils anything that touches it, and one cannot stow a foresail or pass the gaskets round a tops'l on a barge without getting hands and clothes coloured with the same warm tints as the sail.

The older type of steering gear consisted of chains (in some early barges, ropes) leading from a short iron tiller, through blocks out by

PLATE 20  Stay-fall Tackle

[*By courtesy of W. H. Kemp, Esq*

PLATE 21  Lower-mast Head

[*By courtesy of Arthur Bennett, Esq*

PLATE 22  Mast-case and Winches

PLATE 23  Heel of Spreet

[*By courtesy of W. H. Kemp, Esq*

the rails and round a drum on a spindle running fore-and-aft down the centre of the top of the cabin, with the wheel at its fore end. A dog-toothed cog wheel just by the steering wheel enabled a hinged iron bar to be dropped in place between two cogs to lock the wheel in any position; or in some cases there was a screw-down band brake. Such was the gear in the old *Davenport*, in which I served as mate.

More modern barges are fitted with the gear shown in Plate 24, where the steering gear of the *General Jackson* is seen with the cover removed. Two steel links, of unequal length, are bolted to the ends of a thwartship yoke or cross-head on the rudder-head. The inboard ends of these links are secured to nuts, one with a right-hand, the other with a left-hand thread, which are threaded on the spindle of the wheel, while the spindle itself is threaded right- and left-handed away from the middle. A moment's consideration will show that turning the wheel one way screws the nuts towards each other; turning it the opposite way separates them. This movement is transmitted to the rudder-head by the links and cross-head, and the rudder is turned.

The old-fashioned type of wheel with curved spokes used in the smaller barges, and familiarly known as a "chaff-cutter" wheel, is shown in Plate 25. Bigger and more modern barges have wooden wheels of the usual turned-spoke pattern.

A chain, called a "kicking-strap", is secured to the end of the rudder blade, and leads through a fairlead, generally on the port quarter, where it is loosely belayed to a cleat. When under way, the chain is left slack. But when at anchor, the chain can be hauled in tight and belayed; and the wheel is then put over against it, and locked with the brake. This keeps the rudder steady and quiet, and prevents most of the banging and knocking which otherwise can make sleep in the cabin almost impossible in unruly weather conditions.

In smaller barges the lee-boards are raised and lowered with a chain pennant and a rope tackle; but in larger barges, where the boards are heavier, small lee-board winches are fitted like that shown in Plate 27. Notice the cranked handle and the chain from the lee-board. Notice also that there is an independent drum, worked by separate gears, which can be used for warping, etc. This gives extra power aft when required, similar to that given forward by the mast winches.

The windlass on a barge is simple and slow, but immensely powerful. It has to be, otherwise two men could never heave a barge up to her anchor and then break it out and weigh it. The photograph, Plate 26, shows its construction so clearly that little explanation is necessary; but notice the cotton line wound on the small drum across the upper fore part of the upright "bitts". That is a long line, light but very strong, which it is easy to run out in the boat, secure to anything handy and then heave on for warping out to a buoy or across a dock.

When heaving up the gear, after the mast has been lowered, the chain cable is "lighted-up" with spunyarn stops to the small drum mentioned above, so that it hangs in loops round the barrel, which can then turn freely within them without pulling in the cable. Several turns of the stay-fall (see page 91) are then taken round the barrel, and the gear is hove up with the windlass.

As a barge is flat-bottomed, there is very little room for any bilge-water to accumulate, especially when heeled; nor is there any lowest part of the hull where it will always collect, in a sort of centre well from which it can be pumped out. For that reason, a barge is fitted with several pump wells, so that whether she is trimmed by the head or the stern, or is sailing on the port or starboard tack, the pump can be rigged in one of them and the water can be sucked out. Usual positions are: one each side aft, a little abaft the end of the main horse; and one right out by the side forward, right out by the rail, and about level with the middle of the four-hatch coaming. A barge resembles a flat wooden box and it is obvious that if you have a pump in each corner of the box, however you tilt it any water in it *must* run to one or other of the four corners, and a pump rigged in that corner will suck it out. That is exactly how it is with a barge.

The ease with which a barge can be handled by so small a crew is due to several causes, and in this short account of the handling of a barge these will quickly become apparent. When a barge lying at anchor gets under way, the procedure will vary according to the conditions of wind and tide. But, taking the simplest conditions by way of example, with the barge lying to both wind and tide ahead, the first stage in getting under way is that the skipper and mate go forward, ship the handles on the windlass and heave in the chain until it is short and only enough is out just to hold the barge. The very powerful gearing on the windlass enables two men to do this without additional help, and unless the wind and tide are very strong, the chain comes in quickly, the pauls clanking merrily, with an occasional rest for "fleeting" the chain; that is, throwing it across the barrel of the windlass, as it tends to work over from the starboard to the port side, and has to be thrown back again. This is a task needing some degree of care and skill.

The topsail is then set, and the master helps the mate to break the anchor out of the ground. The barge has been given a sheer with the helm to make her "cast"—that is, start off—in the required direction, on starboard or port tack. As soon as the anchor is broken out, the master goes aft to the wheel, and the mate, after heaving the anchor clear of the ground, sets the foresail, generally with the bowline made fast to wind'ard to help pay her head off on the right tack; this done, the bowline is let go, and the sail blows across and trims itself on the loo'ard side. The mate then heaves the anchor (which may weigh over 5 cwt.) up to the chain snatch on the stem single-handed, while the master carries the main-sheet block aft and hooks it into the iron traveller ring on the main horse. The brails being let go, the sail is soon hauled out with the main sheet and properly trimmed. The mizzen is set in a few moments; and if in a coaster bound seawards the bowsprit is steeved-up, it is rigged by master and mate together in the lower reaches of the river, and the jib is then set.

Should it breeze-up during the passage, sail may be reduced either by lowering or "rucking" the head of the tops'l, or by brailing in the mainsail wholly or in part. In either course, the task is done by one hand in an almost incredibly short space of time. When the squall has passed, sail is made again with equivalent speed and simplicity. The mizzen may be stowed altogether, and in many barges this is necessary in a strong breeze, as otherwise they carry too much "weather-helm": that is, they tend to fly round into the wind's eye owing to the pressure on their after canvas. The foresail of a barge is sometimes reefed, the mainsail rarely (except by brailing) unless when carrying a stack it is necessary to enable the foot of the mainsail to clear the top of the stack. But two or three reef-points in the mainsail are often tied to enable the man at the helm to see under the foot of the sail and keep a look-out on the lee bow. Small river barges often had a short iron rail at each side just abaft the main horse, for the helmsman to lean against when taking his periodical walk to loo'ard for the purpose of looking round the mainsail.

When bringing up in a barge, the process of getting under way is simply reversed. The barge will handle so well, with perfect control, under foresail, tops'l and mizzen alone, turning about in her own length, and never "missing stays" or failing to come round, that she can be sailed right up to her berth in a dock and laid alongside so gently that she would scarcely crack an egg. Even running into a place like Ipswich dock-gates with a following wind down the cut, she can run in under the tops'l, or under bare poles alone. The mate takes a check-rope to a buoy off the entrance in the boat, and the skipper gently checks her with it until her way is stopped, by which time she is near enough to the dump-head to get a heaving-line from the shore, and in a couple of minutes she is moored up.

When a barge is negotiating a narrow creek, driving up with the tide through the London bridges, or "shooting" Rochester Bridge under sail, an extra hand called a "huffler" may be shipped. The "huffler" has been confused with the Deal boatman called a "hoveller", and even the "Oxford English Dictionary" has fallen into this error. In fact, the "huffler" derives his name from the "huff" which was the square part of the overhanging swim of an old swim-headed barge. The "huffler", when shipped, let his boat trail astern and immediately went into the bows and *stood over the huff*, whence he directed operations, helped to lower and raise the gear and to work the sweeps or setting-booms. This work is termed "huffling". An inn at Dartford is called "The Hufflers' Arms", spelt in that way. The "hoveller" is a totally different person, who is the English equivalent of the South Sea beachcomber. He is a long-shoreman who makes his living partly as a sort of unlicensed pilot, partly by helping vessels in distress and to some extent, in the old days especially, by recovering lost anchors left behind by ships which had been forced to cut and run. The Deal boatman is the prince of hovellers. A profitable salvage job is spoken of as "a rare good 'hovel' ". In Devon the words used are "hobblers" and "hobbles". I believe that this has nothing to do with their living in hovels on the shore, as is generally supposed, but with the fact that in the old days a partly disabled ship, labouring in a heavy seaway, was assisted by the "hobblers" to "hobble" into port; and in Kent "hobbler" became "hoveller" by mere change in pronunciation. The "hoveller" is the shark of the sea, to be avoided at all costs if possible, as a salvage job may involve charges out of all proportion to the services rendered. Bargemen certainly have no love for the Deal hovellers. But due credit must be given them for extreme bravery and skill in saving life when life is at stake, and for their almost reckless courage on such occasions.

"Huffling" on the other hand is a highly respected riverside profession, and the huffler generally does no other work. It was indeed marvellous to watch the skill shown by barges "shooting" Rochester Bridge in the old days with the flood tide under them. A barge would approach the bridge with all sail set. When her topmast was within a few feet of the top, the stay-fall (of the forestay) was eased away and everything dropped down on deck as the barge, carrying her way, shot through. She was then allowed to soak away up on the Strood side, and the gear was hove up as it was with all sail set, as in Plate 28, and only very rarely was the anchor let go. The Rochester Bridge hufflers were skilled men, and theirs was a very ancient craft. Up to the early 1930's barges were still shooting Rochester Bridge under

Screw
Steering
Gear

PLATE 25
"Chaff-
cutter"
Wheel

PLATE 26
The
Windlass

PLATE 27
A Lee-
board
Winch

24

Nos. 24,
25 and 27
by courtesy
of W. H.
Kemp, Esq

No. 26 by
courtesy
of Mrs A.
Rolt

25

PLATE 28 Heaving up after shooting Rochester Bridge

*[Photograph by the Author*

PLATE 29 Main Sheet and Mizzen Rigging

*[By courtesy of the National Maritime Museum*

sail. But the practice to-day is to lower all gear at anchor, or at a buoy, before being towed through the Bridge by a tug. Barges proceeding above Rochester usually tow or use their engines now.

The term "huffler" was also extended to cover extra hands employed for "tracking", that is, towing barges up the Medway above Maidstone, in Dartford Creek and in other places. The Salmon family were landlords of the Long Reach tavern and hereditary Dartford Creek hufflers for three generations. The Clarks had long been the hufflers for Barking Creek. Hufflers were employed at Colchester to help barges up to Hythe, or on spring tides, when they lower their gear and go up as high as East Mills, above the main-road bridge. Deep-laden barges lying there are seen from the Bridge in Plate 30. In later years the huffler might be a man of some substance, and often owned a motor-boat, so that he was sometimes tugmaster as well. This was so at Ipswich, for example, where a small motor-launch still finds work towing barges in and out of the dock, so killing the old trade of the Ipswich huffler. Likewise at Colchester, a motor-boat is available, though the hufflers would sometimes work without, and the price charged depended on whether the boat were used or not. Hufflers were also employed, two to each barge, when turning out of Brightlingsea Creek, to push the head of the barge round from bank to bank with poles called "setting-booms", as the navigable fairway is barely wider than the length of the barge, and was often crowded with yachts into the bargain.

When there is no wind, a barge will often drive for miles up or down the river, by the process known as "dredging", always pronounced "drudging" by the bargemen. The anchor cable is hove short, until the anchor starts to drag on the bottom. This allows the barge to drop down stern first with the tide, but the drag means that she is moving more slowly over the ground than the tide is doing, and she is therefore actually in effect moving *ahead* through the water. This enables her to be steered across the tide either way by means of the rudder. Should she be dragging too fast to one side, the mate, who stands forward by the windlass, pays out enough chain to hold the barge and prevent her dragging. She is then "sheered", that is, canted across the stream the other way with the helm, and the cable is shortened in until she starts to drag again. In this way not so long ago barges could be seen any day "drudging" up and down through the bridges of London. It was well worth while to stand for a few moments on Westminster or any other bridge, and watch the consummate skill shown by the bargemen in negotiating the narrow arches. "Drudging" is, of course, only possible where the river bed

7

is not obstructed by moorings. It is often most useful for getting a barge out of an awkward berth inshore to the open river, where she can set sail in safety.

Sometimes, when the wind was fair, barges used to carry special "bridge sails" for going through the bridges (Plate 32). A small, square-headed lug-sail, hoisted on a light pole mast, sometimes a little fore staysail and the ordinary sea-going mizzen were used. The mast had a pair of shrouds, and a forestay with a gun-tackle purchase by which it might easily be lowered and set up again. The sail was either kept at the mast-head and mast and sail lowered together, or the sail would be lowered first and then the mast, when going through a bridge. The sails, though of small area, gave the barge steerage way, and enabled her to keep in the best of the tide. Small barges negotiating bridges may also be rowed with a pair of huge oars, called sweeps, worked over the bow. Barges were sometimes rowed for long distances in this way, and I have known of barges some years ago often being rowed from Butterman's Bay in the Orwell right up to Ipswich, a distance of over eight miles.

Yet another method of driving up a river with no wind, or, in a clear river, in fog, is to allow the anchor to hang a fathom or so below the bottom of the barge. This is called "jilling". The vessel then drives up with the tide, and should she get too near the mud one side the anchor touches and, holding her head, brings her up and casts her off shore again. Should it be necessary to bring up suddenly, a few fathoms more chain let go will hold the barge instantly. I have in this way driven up the River Orwell from Harwich nearly to Pin Mill, in a dense fog, with no wind; and only brought up below Pin Mill to avoid the risk of fouling yachts lying there.

It is by reason of the handiness of her gear, her ability to handle perfectly under very little sail, which can be taken off her in a moment, and by the use of the methods of working outlined above, that the barge can be managed with so small a crew. Some of the bargemen are almost wizards at their work. They know their ships and know exactly what they can do with them. They know, moreover, every shoal and every eddy in the London River and the estuary of the Thames. Under the lee of most points from Sea Reach up the river, there runs an eddy tide, flowing against the direction of the main stream. By skilful use of these eddies, the bargeman will work his ship for miles against the tide, with wind too light even to hold his own against the main current. The modern barges are wonderful ships and their crews are wonderful men.

For the use of the bargemen, lightermen and tugmen, the late Mr

Charles T. Perfect, of the Associated Portland Cement Manufacturers Ltd., wrote a Handbook dealing with the London River and
the handling of barges. This book was prepared originally only for the
men employed by this firm, but proved so successful that it went into
a fourth edition. The value of the Handbook was immediately
realised, and at the request of the Sailing Barge Owners Association
Mr Perfect prepared another edition of the same work for general use
among the bargemen.

The book contains concise sailing and navigating directions; Rule
of the Road, simply explained; chartlets of the Thames, Medway and
Swale; a list, in order, of all the wharves on all the rivers and creeks;
life-saving information; first-aid instructions; all the information, in
fact, that a barge-skipper is most likely to need in the everyday working of his craft. Short "aids to memory" verses embellish the book.
Having learnt that pumping is very necessary when under navigation
in a strong wind, one reads, for example:

> *Don't get the "wind-up" in a breeze,*
> *But try your pumps, and be at ease.*

The Handbook opens with a verse which appeals to me particularly.
It is addressed "To Captains All".

> *If your job you'd carry through*
> *In a way that's straight and true,*
> *Steer your barge, and all things do*
> *As though the craft belonged to you.*

Before leaving the subject of the modern barge and the handling of
her, mention should be made of some of the long voyages made
between the wars by various barges which had been sold for service in
far-distant parts of the globe. Two of Messrs Goldsmith's barges, the
*Norvic* and *Cymric*, of about 260 tons burden each, sailed out to
South American for work on the River Amazon, for which their flat
bottoms and shallow draught peculiarly suited them. The spreets
were taken out of them and they were boom-sail ketch-rigged for the
passage, carrying a half cargo of coal by way of ballast. Certificated
merchant service officers had to be taken for the passage out, as the
barges were proceeding beyond home-trade limits; and these were
responsible for the navigation, while the barges' ordinary crews
sailed and handled the vessels.

Three barges also made the voyage out to British Guiana, and particulars of these vessels were kindly sent to me by Messrs S. C.

Chambers & Co., the Liverpool shipbrokers, who were responsible for commissioning these ships and sending them out there. They were the *Kindly Light*, which sailed out in 1926, followed by the *Clymping* in 1929 and the *Goldfinch* in 1930. These little vessels were afterwards employed running out of Georgetown, Demerara, mostly up and down the river acting as "feeders" to the Liner trade. In their new owners' hands they did much useful work, and as far as I know two may still be working. Before sending them out to Demerara, Messrs Chambers spent a considerable amount of money on the vessels, sheathing them with zinc (yellow metal could not be used on account of their galvanised fastenings) to preserve them from the attacks of marine worms, providing new rigging, new sails and generally fitting out to Board of Trade requirements. The *Kindly Light*, a 200-ton ketch, made the passage out from Plymouth in forty days; *Clymping*, also a ketch, was thirty-eight days; and *Goldfinch*, a 250-ton schooner-rigged barge, took fifty-five days for the voyage. Particulars of these interesting little ships are given in Appendix IV. It says much for the build and capabilities of the modern barge that she was able to make such voyages in perfect safety, and proved, if proof be needed, that the barge in her later days had become an ocean-going ship.

The latest news of one of these craft, the *Goldfinch*, was published in the " Faversham News " of 13th May 1949. Her former owner, Captain J. M. Waters—who had commanded her from 1902 until he sold her for service in British Guiana in 1930—had then recently heard from the Harbour Master at Georgetown that his old ship had at last had to be condemned. During the eighteen years she was in the colony, she had done a prodigious amount of work, carrying to various places on the coast and up the rivers, general cargoes imported from England, and taking back to Georgetown sugar, rum, rubber, mahogany and teak for trans-shipment to this country.

In British Guiana, of course, she had been worked by a native crew, and Captain Waters feared she might not have had the care and maintenance which he had always lavished on the ship he loved so well. However that may be, now at last has come the end of her voyagings after a working life of fifty-five years. She was the last big wooden barge to be built in Faversham, and her record is one of which Faversham barge builders may well be proud.

PLATE 30 Barges at an Essex Mill
Where they may still be seen, at East Mills, Colchester

7‡

PLATE 31  The First Real "Boomie": the *Stour*, 1857

[*From an old photograph in the possession of the Author*

PLATE 32  Barge with Bridge Sails off Cannon Street, 1884

[*By courtesy of the National Maritime Museum*

# CHAPTER VII

# The Boomies

FOR the information contained in this chapter I am indebted principally to the notes compiled by my friend, the late Mr George Doughty, as a result of years of practical experience and painstaking research. Had he lived, it would have appeared here entirely under his name. As it is, I have had to arrange and edit the material that he left, and combine with it certain more recent information from other sources. I mention this, that he may not be held responsible for any errors or faults which may be found. The shortcomings are mine alone, but I would like this chapter to be associated with his name, and in paying my tribute to his work, I hope he may feel that I have tried to prepare it for publication in a form which he would himself approve.

In addition to his notes, I am also indebted to the researches of Mr Basil Greenhill on the same subject, and of Mr Roger Finch, who have both most generously placed their material at my disposal. I would refer particularly to the information collected by Mr Greenhill for his forthcoming book, "The Merchant Schooners", shortly to be published; a monumental work, as I can testify from having read the manuscript, worthy to rank with Basil Lubbock's classics on the clipper ships; and also to Mr Finch's valuable contributions to "Spritsail", the quarterly journal of the Thames Barge Sailing Club.

The origin of the ketch-rigged boomsail barges, known as "boomies", although comparatively recent, is unfortunately complex and obscure. The true boomy did not appear until the late eighteen-fifties, and it then came upon the scene quite suddenly. It is perhaps nearest to the truth to say that she was born of a marriage of two different types of craft, rather as the Scottish "Zulu" fishing boat appeared as a combination of the straight stem of the "fifie" with the raking sternpost of the older "scaffie". How this came about I will endeavour to trace; but the reader should appreciate that the conclusions I have reached are only one interpretation of the known facts, for which I make no higher claim than that they seem to me to offer the most likely explanation.

We know that boomies, that is ketch-rigged barges, are of fairly recent origin. There were none afloat in 1828, when Cook published his "Shipping and Craft". At that time the Thames barge did not venture far outside the Estuary. There were plenty of cutter and sloop-rigged barges, like those in Plate 5. These, however, like the "spreeties", were swim-headed and not suitable for a long sea voyage. In course of time, just as the mizzen, stepped on the rudder-head, was added to the spritsail barge, as described on page 65, so a similar mizzen was added to the sloop-rigged barges, making them what were then called "dandies". That was a very important step, which will be referred to later.

It was some years, however, before this rig developed; and meanwhile the sloop-rigged barge disappeared almost entirely. The late Mr C. Woodruff, born in 1842, and who had been at sea from the age of 12 until he was 72, was asked about this by George Doughty.

"There were no boomies when I was a boy," he said. "Billyboys, smacks, brigs and schooners came to Woodbridge in those days. Later on, little barges started to creep round. We called them ditch-crawlers. Boomies came later, and took the place of schooners."

Although a gaff sail is more suitable for sea-going craft, the sprit-sail is much handier for river work, and far more economical; and it proved quite good enough for the short trips to Ramsgate and Ipswich, which barges were making about 1840 to 1850. Barges were, of course, increasing in size all the time, and thereby becoming more suitable for coastwise voyaging. This is shown by a study of the early registers and Mercantile Navy Lists, etc. Roughly speaking, barges built in the eighteen-twenties, thirties and forties were of less than 40 tons net; those built in the fifties were under 50 tons; and those in the sixties, of under 60 tons net. There were, of course, exceptions to this general rule, and George Doughty compiled a list of some forty larger barges which exceeded the usual tonnage of their time. These do not, however, affect the general line of argument that barges were increasing in tonnage, and therefore in suitability for coastwise trading. Smaller barges, of course, of about 30 tons, were common throughout the period.

As the century progressed, moreover, spritsail barges were coming to be built and owned farther afield than in the rivers Thames and Medway. Maldon, for example, was building "spreeties" in the eighteen-thirties, when the *Rogue in Grain* (did ever a barge have a more charming name?) was built there; a swim-headed "spreety" of 45 tons net. And Mr Philip Kershaw has discovered in the archives at the National Maritime Museum a Certificate of British Registry of a barge called the *Betsey*, built at Chelsea in 1788, registered at Colchester in 1817 and re-registered there on 22nd December 1825, the date of the Certificate in the Museum Library. Adam Glendining Junr. was Master and Part Owner; the barge was of $48\frac{20}{94}$ tons burthen, and was certified in the following terms:

"That the said Ship or Vessel has One Deck and One Mast, that her length from the fore part of the Main Stem to the after part of the Stern Post is Fifty seven feet six inches her breadth at the broadest part taken above the Main Wales is Seventeen feet five inches her Depth in the Hold is Five feet three inches that she is Barge rigged, with a Standing Bowsprit, and Lee Boards; is Square sterned Carvel built; has neither Galleries, nor figurehead."

This description would fit, almost exactly, the early spritsail barge shown in Figs. 8a and 8b. When such barges were found to be suitable for short coastal trips, the sloop rig fell temporarily out of favour; and an old bargeman assured George Doughty that when he first went to sea in 1866 there were no sloops and no boomies on the London River; nor were there any dandy-rigged vessels of the half-way stage, such as one might expect. We know from other unimpeachable evidence that this was not strictly true; but this, and the evidence of Captain Skinner, which follows, proves that there cannot have been many.

The late Captain Skinner was born in 1853, and went to sea when he was 13. "There were no sloop barges then," he said, "nor boomies, nor dandies; but spreeties were already going further afield. Spreeties in the London River became so big as to be unhandy, so boom and gaff sails were fitted about 1870 to 1880." Captain Skinner at that time was in the London and down-Channel trading, and no doubt, therefore, did not know of the boomy barges *Septimus*, *Stour* and *Flower of Essex*, owned down Harwich way. The "Illustrated London News" in 1859 also refers to what it calls "the Clipper Barge *Thames*".

During the period 1840–1860, as we have seen, great improvements were made in the hull design of barges, and the stem head began to take the place of the swim. The run was hollowed out and the lines of the vessel improved all round. They were also built larger, and started to make longer passages. With this desire for seaworthy barges, we see in one or two cases a reversion to the old sloop or dandy rig, discarded a few years back. These, however, were few and far between, and the builders on the London River preferred to build larger and better sprities, as they have continued to do until quite recent times.

It is not possible to say with certainty when the small mizzen was first added, to convert what would otherwise have been a sloop-rigged barge into a "dandy", but the earliest dandy-rigged barge that George Doughty was able to trace was the *Flower of Essex*, built by Messrs Hartnall & Surridge at Limehouse in 1857. Fig. 24 is drawn by Mr Roger Finch from an original contemporary photograph, owned by Miss Meashem of Harwich; this had unfortunately been painted over, and was unsuitable for reproduction in its original state.

The *Flower of Essex*, of 67 tons net, was built obviously for a man who wanted a particularly big barge, and one that was designed and rigged suitably for sea work. She was probably constructed to the

FIG. 24  First Dandy-rigged Barge, *Flower of Essex*

order of John Watts of Harwich, as he was her owner a year or two later. She had a straight stem, slightly raked, and a counter-stern. She was dandy-rigged, with a running bowsprit, and a lug mizzen sheeted to an out-ligger. She was still classed as a "dandy" in the Mercantile Navy List of 1930, though then a ketch, owned by Mrs Emma Rayfield of Gravesend. She represented the first stage in the development of the old sloop-rigged barge towards the later ketch-rigged craft. Perhaps, given time, the boomy might have developed completely by evolution through the dandy; but, in fact, something else, something altogether more dramatic happened. A new type of vessel was suddenly born.

It was in the smaller East Coast ports that the genuine boomy originated. Spritsail barges had crept round to ports like Brightlingsea, Harwich and Ipswich; and by 1841 spritsail barges were being built at Ipswich. *Primus* of Harwich, a swimmy of 36 tons net, was built there in that year; and was the first barge Doughty came across built at that port. The first barge to visit Woodbridge in the fifties is believed to have been the *Lady of the Wave*, built in 1856. These coasting barges took the place of the old-fashioned trading smacks, being far less trouble, with their shallow draught, and twice as economical. Owners in these ports then wanted to find a similar substitute for schooners, to bring coal from Newcastle, make the long voyages and carry all the cargoes hitherto carried by schooners.

For these purposes deep-draught vessels were not at all suitable in the shallow waters of the East Coast. They often wasted several days kedging up narrow rivers, and were frequently beneaped. In many places part of the cargo had to be discharged into lighters before they could come alongside. They needed ballast, which often had to be bought, and no one wanted it at the other end. Altogether they involved much waste of time and expense.

A schooner would require about 40 tons of ballast, which might be difficult to find. At Woodbridge schooners would sometimes buy sand at 3s. a tumbril load, and try to sell it in the North. A schooner of 200 tons D.W. would draw 10–11 feet of water. *Ariel*, a fore-and-aft schooner of 84 tons net, loaded 160. *Lothair*, a ketch barge of 108 tons net, was said, by the son of the man who built her, to carry 300 tons, though 250 tons seems a more likely figure. Both had a crew of five hands.

The silting-up of the smaller East Anglian ports was also increasing the difficulties of the deep-draught coasters. Hence, the handiness of the spreety barge, with her flat bottom and shallow draught, requiring no ballast, inspired the local builders and owners to combine the advantages of the two types. The result was the prototype of what became the boomy in her most perfect form.

John Watts, Middleton and John Vaux, all of Harwich, were the pioneer boomy owners. John Watts's first boomy was the *Flower of Essex*, already described. In the same year, 1857, Vaux built the first *real* boomy, the *Stour*, at Harwich. He had a coal business, and, owning several brigs and schooners, was quick to realise that a flat-bottomed vessel would do away with much unnecessary expense.

The *Stour*, Plate 31, was of 99 net tons and carried 200. She was practically a flat-bottomed schooner, having a clipper bow and counter-stern, and high bulwarks. She had a fixed bowsprit, carrying a jibboom; and a mizzen stepped well inboard, with a fidded mizzen topmast. She also carried a squaresail and square topsail, was provided with channels, cat-heads and whiskers, and was indeed a real sea-going vessel, with very little resemblance to the old sloop-rigged barge. She was, in fact, a cross between a schooner and a barge; and was in those early days described as a "schooner barge".

A shipbuilder described the older boomies as being not really barges, but "schooners with the bottom cut off". It was an apt description. It was found, however, that a barge had not the quarters, or the draught aft and necessary grip of the water to carry a schooner's mainsail; so the after-mast was shortened to a mizzen. These vessels were also, of course, cheaper to build than were the schooners. They had mostly the straight planking of a barge, with a schooner's bow added. Round-bottomed vessels required a lot of moulding; their curved frames were more costly in time, timber and skill.

Of the fleets of these pioneer boomy owners, the largest was that of John Watts. In addition to the *Flower of Essex*, the dandy already described, he owned the spreety *John Watts* and the boomies *Dovercourt, Harwich, Brightlingsea, May Queen, Lothair, Alice Watts, Emerald* and *Enterprise*. John Watts was also interested in the ancient trade of dredging for stone* from the West Rocks, off Harwich. Yachtsmen to-day are familiar with the Stone Banks Buoy. The stonemen dredged up this stone at low water, and it was loaded into vessels for Holland and Germany. There it was broken up by women, burnt in kilns and sold as "Roman cement". When Mr Watts bought the *Who'd a Thought It?* they said, "Who'd a thought it, the Stone Man bought it!" In 1881 he found himself short of money, and most of his vessels were sold.

Middleton, also of Harwich, owned the little boomy *Era*, and the larger *Laura, Gloriana* and *Mary Lyne*, as well as two spreeties. John Vaux, in addition to his schooners, square-rigged vessels and smacks, owned the pioneer boomy *Stour* and the schooner barges *Lymington* and *Jubilee*. Although he owned few boomies, he built a great many.

Between the years 1860 and 1870, several boomies were built on the East Coast, at such ports as Brightlingsea, Harwich, Ipswich and Yarmouth. Between 1870 and 1875 many more were built, and from 1875 onwards they became too numerous to keep count of them. Thus at Brightlingsea were built the *Era* and *Jabez*, both in 1863; the *Dovercourt*, 75 tons, in 1865; *Harwich*, 77 tons, in 1867; *Startled Fawn* (enchanting name!), 100 tons, 1868; *Brightlingsea*; and *Antelope*, 98 tons, in 1869.

* Septaria.

At Yarmouth, the boomies built included the *Garson* (now a hulk used as a store barge for the Erith Yacht Club) in 1864, of 69 tons; and the *May Queen*, 94 tons, in 1870. No doubt there were very many more. Strangely enough, very few were built at Ipswich and Harwich between 1860 and 1870; but from 1870 to 1880 there were far too many to enumerate. Thus it came about that while the London builders were turning out "extra big and seaworthy river barges", the other ports of Essex and Suffolk and Kent were turning out "schooners with the bottom cut off".

The reason for this is not difficult to find. Coal from the North was the main cargo for which they were intended. Coal came to London in brigs and steamers, and there was no need for small, seaworthy vessels to fetch it, as there was in these smaller ports.

The first real boomy that Doughty could find to be built in the London River was the *Lily*, built at Millwall in 1873; but after that date quite a number were built. Nevertheless, the majority of the boomies were built at other ports.

The early boomies were all rather in the nature of experiments: some owners and builders preferred clipper-bowed, counter-sterned, schooner-like vessels; others preferred vessels built more on the lines of a barge. Some reckoned that a good sea-going vessel must needs have square topsails; others who were less conservative considered such things were nothing more than a nuisance.

It is impossible, and unnecessary, to give an account of all the various early boomies. It is enough to make a few general remarks and to give detailed descriptions of one or two vessels of different types.

The term "clipper-bow" has been used here not in its strict technical sense of a much hollowed entrance, such as the tea clippers had, but as it was generally used when speaking of the bows of a typical West Country schooner of the period. With the exception of the famous boomies *Record Reign*, *Cock of the Walk* and perhaps *Laura*, *Gloriana*, *Alice Watts*, *Lothair* and *Malvoisin*, which might truly be called "clipper-bowed", the others can more appropriately be called "fiddle-bowed", to be on the safe side.

Some boomies had raking stems with a gammon knee (forming a fiddle head) which were very graceful. Others had a knee, but the stem was nearly upright. Those which had running bowsprits, of course, had no knee. Some of the old boomies had figureheads, but most were adorned only with scroll-work. They had either a round counter-stern—some more graceful than others—or a square transom stern like a spreety. The sheer and general proportions of the vessels varied according to the owner's requirements and the builder's fancy. The boomies built at Littlehampton all had their bowsprits in line with their sheer, for example; and Rye-built vessels could be recognised by the tapering head of their mizzen masts.

The earliest boomies had tillers, and these were of necessity very long, so that the mizzen mast had to be stepped well inboard. Captain Smith said that the tiller on a big boomy would be 15 feet and sometimes as much as 20 feet in length. Wheels were put into boomies before spreeties had them. The long tiller of 15 feet or more was a great nuisance when carrying round timber (tree-trunks) on deck. In later years the mizzen became smaller and was stepped farther aft.

In the older boomies, the larger ones had jibbooms, with proper cat-heads and whiskers for the jibboom guys. Even the little *Era* had a jibboom, though she only carried 140 tons. The smaller vessels mostly had running bowsprits. All these were soon altered to the fixed single-spar bowsprit. George Doughty thought that there were one or two with steeving bowsprits like a spreety's, but could not give their names. The gear on the bowsprit was eventually simplified, and the old-fashioned cat-heads and channels disappeared.

In the old-fashioned rig, the mainsail and gaff topsail were shorter in the head, and not peaked up so much as were the later sails. The old sails were baggier, and the jibs cut lower in the clew, as was then the fashion. There were three rows of reef points in the mainsail, two in the mizzen and one in the foresail. In one or two there was a row of reef eyelets in the standing (or inner) jib. All of them set a square-sail. The yard was slung aloft with truss and sling. It was fitted with lifts to the lower-mast head, and with braces. When not in use it was cock-billed, and the lower yard-arm was lashed to the rigging. The squaresail was set flying, as in a schooner. Latterly many of them kept the yard on deck. When the sail was to be set, it was taken from the locker and bent on to the yard with stops. A strop was then put round the yard, and yard and sail together were hoisted up on the foresail halyards. The foot was boomed out to windward with a boom used for that purpose, and the sheet was led aft. Many of the early boomies set a square topsail; but this was usually nothing but a fair-weather sail, and set only when the wind was free. It was not set on a wind. It hoisted about halfway up the topmast on an iron jackstay, which ran up the foreside, so that it did not interfere with the hoops of the gaff topsail.

Some of them had topsail and topgallant as well, the topsail either hoisting up the doublings of the topmast, as in the old-fashioned billyboy, or being slung at the lower-mast cap, as with double top-

PLATE 33  The *Record Reign*, with Square Tops'l and T'gans'l set

[*From a painting in the possession of Messrs John Sadd & Sons, Maldon*

sails. The topgallant usually hoisted up a jackstay, as in the account of the *Alice Watts*, described on page 111.

These square topsails were latterly dispensed with when economy became the order of the day, though the *Goldfinch* and *Record Reign*, built some years later in 1894 and 1897 respectively, both had double topsails. It is interesting to note that in the earliest boomies the square topsail was very common, although not very effective. A few had the small topsail and topgallant, which were more efficient; and apparently only two barges had really powerful double topsails, which were the most efficient of all.

Vessels with single square topsails were the *Garson, May Queen, Dovercourt, Harwich, Brightlingsea, Stour* and the shallow little *Ida*.* An old bargeman said, "Dozens of the old boomies had a square topsail when they first came out, so I was told. But that was before my time. I only remember one or two—I don't mean them like *Lothair*."

Boomies with topsail and topgallant were *Lothair, Alice Watts, Lucy Richmond, Stour, Lord Lansdowne* and *Kingfisher*. Proper *double* topsails were carried only by *Goldfinch* and *Record Reign* (Plate 33).

The lead of the flying jib halyards is also interesting. In many of the older vessels they had a tailing block, that is, a block spliced into a rope, the end of which led through a fixed block on the lower-mast cap and down on deck. The halyards passed through this tailing block and through the block on the topmast head, and down on deck. In a breeze the tailing line was hauled upon and the halyards eased, so that the strain was taken off the topmast. Latterly it was more usual for the halyards to lead direct to the lower-mast cap, having hanks on increasing lengths of line, as shown in the picture of the *Lord Tennyson*, Plate 34. Many swore by this method. Others maintained that the flying jib was a fine-weather sail and, above all, should set well; and that when it was blowing hard enough to endanger the topmast, the proper place for a flying jib was stowed neatly at the end of the bowsprit. They therefore led the halyards direct to the topmast head.

The boat was stowed on the main hatch, and the runners and tackles from the lower-mast, used also for supporting the mast, were employed for hoisting it aboard, with a burton from the mizzen. Latterly the boat was hoisted on davits on the quarter.

The later boomies were on the whole smaller than the early ones, though there were some notable exceptions. As it is quite impossible to define a typical "old timer", four particular vessels will be described which show roughly the different earlier types. Of these, the *Stour* represents the earliest big boomy, with single square top-

* She later carried double tops'ls.

sail. The *Gloriana* was an early boomy with *no* square topsails. *Alice Watts* had a small topsail and topgallant ; and *Gem of the Ocean* was a small barge with a square stern.

The *Stour* in her early days had a square topsail, and was fitted with a jibboom and a mizzen topmast. She had a tailing block on her flying jib halyards. Her standing rigging consisted of three shrouds aside—four were usual—with the old-fashioned channels ; runner and tackle ; running backstay from the topmast ; and three mizzen shrouds. She was a particularly interesting vessel, as she had various alterations to her rig which were in many ways typical of the times.

The first alteration was to do away with the mizzen topmast—mizzen topsails are pretty useless sails at the best of times, and no doubt hers was quite unnecessary, and only a nuisance. Her jibboom was also troublesome to rig in and out, and was altered to a single-spar bowsprit. She was given a wheel instead of a tiller. Captain Smith knew the *Stour* in 1875 ; she had a wheel then, and he never heard of her ever having a tiller. Mr Middleton, on the other hand, said that they *all* had tillers at first.

After this her rather useless square topsail was altered to a topsail, with the yard slung on the cap, and a topgallant with the yard slung round the topmast ; the gaff topsail was dispensed with altogether and the square topsails were set on every point of sailing. The final change came when she was again altered to the ordinary fore-and-aft rig of the later-day boomy.

*Gloriana* was an early boomy, built by Vaux of Harwich in 1871. She never had square topsails—as a builder remarked, "a barge is a lee-wardly vessel without square canvas to make her more so". She had a lovely bow which might fairly be described as "clipper", with a pine-apple for figurehead. She was built with great sheer, and was later raised 12 to 15 inches amidships, which enabled her to carry 50 tons more.

Another ship very similar to her, and built by Vaux in 1873, was the *Laura*. She had a figurehead, and was named after Laura, the daughter of Samuel Stocks, who had a share in her. Not many could afford to own a whole barge in those days. The figurehead, however, was supposed to represent Emily, sister of Mr T. Middleton, who later owned the barge outright.

These barges had their jibbooms taken out about 1880. The *Laura* was afterwards bought by a man called Saunders, who put a boiler in her for pile driving. She was later bought by the London and Rochester Barge Company, and had a motor installed. In the First World War on her first trip across the Channel under her new owners she struck a mine and blew up.

*Alice Watts* was built in 1875 by Robertson of Ipswich. She carried, as already stated, a small topsail and topgallant. Named after the daughter of John Watts, the first owner, she originally had a figurehead representing Miss Watts, which was a very good likeness, with long black hair. It was later removed (the figurehead, not the hair). She (the barge) was 100·2 feet in length, 24·2 feet beam, 8·0 feet deep; and her tonnage was 119 net and 130 gross. *Lothair*, built by Robertson of Ipswich in 1872, and similar in every way, was 101·8 feet long, 23·2 feet in beam, with a depth of 7·5 feet. She was 108 tons net and 129 gross.

*Gem of the Ocean* was typical of a small boomy, with a square stern, smack-like bow and running bowsprit. These vessels were more like little smacks. Some of them had counter-sterns. The jib was not on a stay, but set with halyards and purchase, and hauled out on a traveller like a smack's. In bad weather a small jib was set. The bowsprit had a bobstay and shrouds, and was never reefed in when jibs were shifted. It was run in when in port.

After these early vessels, the build and rig of the boomies tended towards a more or less standard type; but before dealing with these, mention must be made of two famous barges, referred to elsewhere in this book. Instead of doing away with square topsails like the others, these were given proper double topsails, set like those in modern topsail schooners. and being really good powerful sails. The braces led aft to the mizzen rigging. As can be seen in the picture of the *Record Reign*, Plate 33, they had standing backstays set up with dead-eyes like a schooner. The gaff topsails were jib-headed, and kept in to the mast by a jackstay or "switching line". Both had tall mizzens stepped well inboard and set mizzen topsails. They were called "jackass schooners".

The *Record Reign* was a fine vessel with a lovely sheer, graceful counter and a real clipper bow with a figurehead of Queen Victoria. A full description of her is given on p. 246. The *Goldfinch* was zinc sheathed in 1930, and sold to the West Indies. She made the passage from Plymouth to Demerara in 45 days.

As an example of a really smart boomy of later date, George Doughty would have liked to describe the *Sussex Belle*. She was of 80 tons net, and built at Rye of good Sussex oak in 1892; a real tough, handy, seaworthy little ship. Unfortunately she was wrecked at Yarmouth some fifteen or twenty years ago; and he chose therefore the *Pearl* of Ipswich, a ship he knew well, having worked in her. Her lines also were taken off by the late Mr W. M. Blake, and his detailed plans were published in the "Yachting Monthly" for April 1934; by

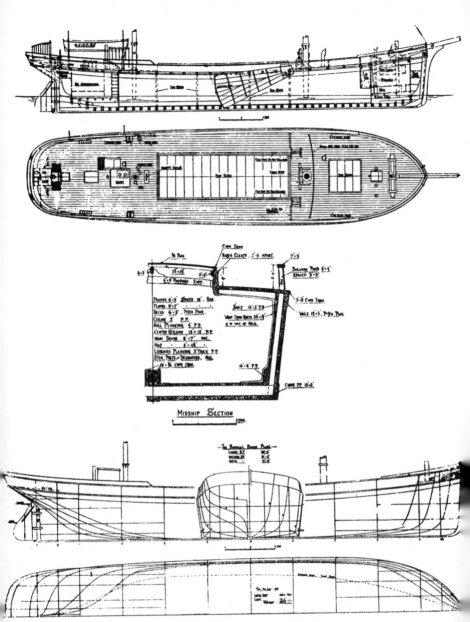

**THE " BOOMY " BARGE PEARL**

*Lines and construction plans, showing scantlings and deck arrangements.*
*Note the large pitch pine keelson, 15 in. by 15 in.*
*Her register tonnage is 75 $\frac{80}{100}$ tons; displacement 102 tons (light).*

FIG. 25a

[By courtesy of the Editor of the " Yachting Month

the courtesy of the Editor I am able to reproduce them here, as Figs.
25a and 25b.

The *Pearl* was not quite so graceful as the *Sussex Belle*. Her lower-
mast was much taller, and the topmast shorter than those of the
average boomy. Her mainmast was a lovely spar. When George
Doughty knew her, she had been brought well up to date, having
roller reefing on the mainsail; and her throat, peak, topsail, foresail,

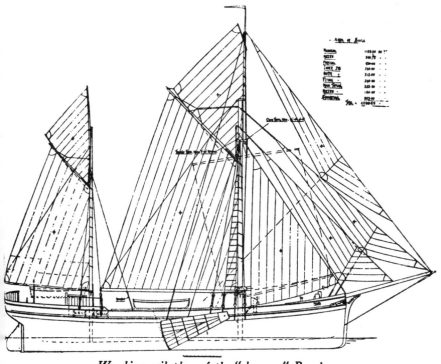

*Working sail plan of the " boomy " Pearl.*

FIG. 25b

[*By courtesy of the Editor of the " Yachting Monthly"*

standing jib and boom jib halyards, all hoisted on the various barrels
of two large winches, one on either side of the mast. She had davits
on the port quarter, and her flying jib halyards then led direct to the
topmast head. Halyards on winches are, however, by no means an
unmixed blessing.

*Pearl* represented the typical modern boomy, i.e. a barge which had
a fiddle bow, standing bowsprit and a counter or transom stern. She

8

was built with the flat bottom and square chine of a barge, and fitted
with lee-boards. The standing rigging consisted of four shrouds aside,
set up with lanyards and dead-eyes, and rattled down with rope or
with wood ratlines. The topmast shrouds, sometimes called standing
backstays, were spread by crosstrees usually of wood. Older vessels
had a runner and tackle from the lower-mast, which was used also for
hoisting in the boat. The modern ones did not. Running backstays
were fitted from the topmast head, set taut by a luff tackle, with no
runner, to an eye-bolt on the rail. The lee one was let go when running. They had *two* shrouds aside on the mizzen mast. The had a
flying jib-stay, boom jib-stay, standing jib-stay and forestay. The bobstay was rigged with a bridle, set tight aboard. Sometimes there was a
short chain bobstay from the cranze iron of the standing jib-stay;
though most of the later ones did not have one, as the standing jib did
not come far outboard. The mast was stepped on the keelson, and not,
as in a spreety, in a mast-case. The jibs hanked on to the stays, with
the usual sheets, halyards and downhauls, and were stowed on the
bowsprit. The square yard was either carried aloft, on truss and sling,
with lifts, braces and yard ropes, otherwise known as head outhauls;
or else it was kept on deck.

All the boomies latterly had roller-reefing mainsails. The boom
was turned by a tackle hooked into a chain, and a weighted pawl kept
the boom from turning back. Some barges had roller reefing on the
mizzen as well. The mainsheet was a two-fold purchase, with a lug
on the upper block, the hauling part being led down through a bulls-
eye, and made fast round a big cleat on deck. The mainsheet was
sometimes a bass rope, about 6 inches in circumference, and having
more "give" than manila. When gybing, the sheet was hauled in as
much as possible, one hand keeping a good turn and taking in the
slack on the cleat; and was eased out after the gybe. Running at night
with the wind aft, a stout bass rope was often made fast to the boom
and the end made fast to the lee rail. This prevented an accidental
gybe, by bringing the boom up amidships.

The gaff topsail had a head stick, and hoisted up the mast on hoops.
The halyards, when not on a winch, were rigged with a purchase.
There were the usual sheet, tack and clewline. The latter was made
fast at the clew, passed through a block on the end of the head stick,
down to another block on the after-shroud and thence through a bulls-
eye or truck on the shroud to a cleat. The sail was stowed aloft, like a
spreety's. The foresail sheet travelled on an iron horse, and had the
usual bowline. The mizzen was an ordinary gaff sail.

Most boomies had mizzen topsails, but they were very seldom set.

They had a yard, and were set flying. They were silly little sails, just enough to upset the steering, and not enough to do any good. As is often the case in small fore-and-afters, they were looked upon rather as a joke, and a poor joke at that. A captain who carried them a lot would be called "mizzen topsail So-and-So".

One man in particular was famous for his mizzen topsail. On one trip, when it was blowing hard, another boomy got to port before her; and when she arrived the owner asked, "Well, what's happened to the old *Britannia*?" The mate answered at once, "She won't go when they can't set her mizzen topsail." "Why can't they set it?" said the owner. The mate, thinking that a silly question, gave a silly answer, and said, "Her skipper left it at home." "Left it at home?" he was asked. "What do you mean? How? Why?" "Well," said the mate, "he thinks the world of that sail, and when he's in port he takes it home and sets it in his back-yard. This trip he came away in a hurry and forgot it!"

Another fancy sail which was sometimes set was a raffee, a three-cornered sail set above the squaresail when running. It was hoisted on the flying jib halyards, and the weather sheet (or rather the tack, as it should be called) was led through a thimble on the weather yard-arm, and set tight aft, like a brace, the sheet being belayed in the lee rigging. The trouble with this sail was that any old piece of junk would have to do for the sheets; and it always seemed a pity to pull a sail down just when it was really beginning to do some good. What happened next in many cases was that one sheet would part, followed of course by the other. The raffee then waved gallantly aloft like a medieval banner, and caused much strain on the topmast. It would eventually wrap itself round the flying jib stay. With reliable gear, however, it was a good sail. I carry one in my pilot cutter *Cariad* to this day.

A handier sail was the mizzen staysail, which was sometimes set. This was usually an old foresail with the bolt-rope taken off the leech and foot. It hoisted to the mizzen mast-head, and was tacked down to a ring bolt on the weather side of the main hatch. It was sheeted home aft, abaft the mizzen rigging. This was only of use with the wind any-where between just abaft the beam and on the quarter. It could not be set close-hauled and was no good with the wind aft, but when it did draw it was a good help.

One boomy at least set a huge spinnaker jib. She was the *Harold*, a very fast barge, and the sail was always called "Bill White". It was tacked down to the bowsprit end and hoisted right up to the topmast head, on the topmast stay. The clew came well abaft the forestay, and it was sheeted home abaft the rigging. The sail was light, and could be rolled up and put into an ordinary-sized sack. It was a splendid sail in light winds. The late Captain Chapman had a similar sail made for the mulie barge *Emma*. For the five minutes it was set, the old barge forged ahead and nearly doubled her speed, but the bolt-rope was not man enough. There was a loud crack and the whole sail blew to ribbons. "Chuck it away," said the skipper, "and never mention the word 'spinnaker' again." When Doughty sailed with him six years later, he still felt sore about that lovely jib he'd had made!

Most boomies had the old-fashioned pump-handle windlass, though some were turned with a handle like a spreety's. The *Harold* had a patent windlass with three gears, gypsies and a brake. The pump-handle windlasses were not the diabolical, dangerous, awkward things people make out. It was hard work heaving up, but so it is on any windlass worked by "Armstrong's patent". Provided that the windlass was in good working order, however, and that those working it were not half-wits, they were no trouble, though dragging the cable up is never much fun anyway. Nor were the old handspike wind-lasses as bad as they were made out to be; there was a knack in work-ing them, and there was nothing like them for breaking the anchor out when it had a tight hold.

Abaft the windlass was the foc's'le scuttle, and then came the fore hatch. The chain lockers were at the after end of the foc's'le, one on either side of the ladder. Just forward of the mast was the iron fore-horse; and on many boomies there were winches on either side for the throat and peak halyards, often with additional drums for other hal-yards as well. Winches for halyards are not altogether an unmixed blessing, however, and Doughty didn't like them. The *Sussex Belle* had a winch for her peak halyards only, he said, and, once started, the throat could be pulled up by one man faster than the peaks on the winch.

Abaft the mast was a dolly winch, and then the main hatch, on which the boat was stowed; though latterly it was customary to have davits on the quarter. Abaft the mizzen there was often a galley, just a little wooden box lashed to the deck; and abaft this came the com-panion, skylight and wheel. Sometimes there was a wheel-house. The wheel worked either with chain and barrel or with screw gear.

The crew berthed in the foc's'le, at the fore end of which was usually a sail locker, and space for tackles, cargo gin and other gear. The skipper and mate berthed aft in the cabin. These cabins were often roomy and smart, with the usual polished panelling and brass fittings; and the mate very often had a separate little state room on the port side, as well as the skipper, who always had his to starboard. The hold was continuous, there being no bulkhead between fore and main hatch. The main pumps were usually of the patent kind, with a long lever one could really put some weight on. Unlike the miserable little things fitted in some craft, these would fetch up about a gallon a stroke.

They were all painted in much the same way. The tarred hull was surmounted by black bulwarks with a white or yellow streak and scroll-work. The rail was painted or varnished. Bowboards and quarterboards were white, or the topgallant rail if she had one. Inside of the bulwarks was white, and deck fittings were varnished or mast-coloured. Most boomies were black-leaded up to the wale, which made them look smart. This made them slip through the water, though the effect soon wore off. Weed seems to grow on it just the same as on tar, but it scrubs off more easily. Doughty said they used to mix their black-lead with salt water, but another friend said they used fresh, with a bit of lime in to make it a lighter colour. It was put on with a broom.

Most boomies had white sails, though latterly many had them dressed. The mixture was cod oil, brine and red ochre, put on with a broom. The brine and ochre had to be mixed first. The big early boomies carried a crew of five hands. In later years four was the usual crew, or rather three men and a boy, though often they sailed three-handed. The big barges belonging to Mr Smith, in the coal trade to Dover, etc., used to carry five strong men. These were required to "jump" the coal out, as was done in the old collier brigs.

Boomies were good seaworthy vessels, though of course a barge has not the same grip of the water as a vessel with a keel, and in a nasty sea they will not go to windward so well. When coming about, the weather lee-board has to come up smartly or you may lose it. When loaded or with the wind free, it was not necessary to have the lee-board down, and one or two barges boasted about keeping their lee-boards down in the hold. Nevertheless, a boomie could not do much without them when light, and a great many felt the benefit of a lee-board down when loaded. The lee-boards hoisted up by little winches aft, though no doubt the earliest had merely a tackle.

Boomies were definitely good sea-boats and could stand any weather when properly handled. They were far more efficient and comfortable in bad weather than a big spreety or "mulie", where the weight remains aloft after sail has been reduced. Well reefed down, a boomy would stand up to anything, and would lie-to comfortably under a close-reefed mainsail.

A smart boomy with a skilful master or pilot could also tack and turn about in narrow waters quite easily, though they were of course not so handy as spreeties. It is told, however, that when old Peter Broom, Pilot, brought the *Harold* up to Woodbridge with wind north-west, and put her about quickly in the Ham, she did spin round and run up the mud half-way to Cross Farm, before he had time to ease the helm.

Of the early boomies, few were as smart as *Lothair* and *Alice Watts*. The latter, with her yards removed, was sound and working until 1930 or later. Some of the fastest boomies were built by White of Sittingbourne. The *Harold* was considered the fastest; others were *Teresa* and *Medina*. These were all rather lightly built. It was said that when they lay aground, water would run to either end. They had square transom sterns, and huge rudders, and good steering made all the difference to them. It was an old gag to shout, "Whose old lee-board are you towing?" in reference to this.

These boomies used to be trimmed slightly by the head; and then they would go to windward like witches—submarine witches, as they only came up to surface every sixth time! It must be remembered that those boomies which sailed best trimmed by the head were of course regular submarines.

The main trade was coal from Newcastle, and other coal ports, sometimes Cardiff. They also carried round timber, often with a big deck load. They carried all sorts of cargoes and traded to the Continent, and down Channel to Portland for stone, and to the Channel Islands, and much farther afield. See elsewhere in this book the voyages of *Arundel Castle* to Christiania; *Eastern Belle* to Lisbon; and others. See too *Kindly Light* and *Clymping*, and also *Goldfinch* and *Leading Light*, sold foreign and sailing to Demerara.

It was a common failing for boomies to be built too light, and one or two "busted out" when loaded with coal. This started a craze for sheathing them—and many good sound barges were sheathed which did not need it. After this, many of them leaked like baskets, and would have been much better left alone.

The *Sussex Belle* was best trimmed by the stern. The skipper maintained that you could *not* wet her forward of the mast. She was quite fast, and taken all round one of the best boomies there was. She was Rye-built, and good work and good Sussex oak were put into them there. Another smart vessel was the *Cock of the Walk*, built at Millwall in 1876, of 90 tons net, and belonging to Mr Cox, of Weymouth. She had a lovely clipper bow, and on her counter was a gilded cockerel, wings outspread, standing on a globe, with the text, "While

I live I'll crow." She was a beautiful vessel; everything in her was of the very best quality, from truck to keelson. Even her cabin was described as being "like a palace"!

But when she first came out they said, "She would not go for toffee." After Captain Harry Strange took over, however, and made many alterations and shifted the mast forward, nothing could touch her, except perhaps the *Harold* when close-hauled. She was sunk by the Germans during the First World War. They put a bomb in her, since that was considered the best way of sinking shallow-draught vessels. Several boomies were very fast off the wind, like *Mazeppa* and even the old *Stour*. The *Genesta* was another smart vessel, though she did not have much sheer. She carried a great spread of canvas.

It is impossible to give a complete list of all smart boomies. Most firms and private owners took a great pride in their vessels, and to most people the vessel they are in is the smartest afloat.

Mention must be made of the fine fleet of boomies owned by the English and Continental Shipping Co. These started off with *Western Belle*, a mulie, *Eastern Belle*, boomy, *Southern Belle*, mulie, and *Northern Belle*, boomy. After these, they were all called "Lords". In the 1891 register there are fifteen of these "Lords", most of them built at Littlehampton, but four built at Ipswich. They were roughly of two sizes: the larger carrying 250–260 tons and the smaller about 150. The largest was *Lord Alcester*, built by J. & W. B. Harvey of Little-hampton in 1891. She was of 144 tons gross, 133 net, and was 101·0 feet in length, 24·0 feet in beam and 8·8 feet in draught. Her mean depth was 9 feet 6 inches, and her freeboard amidships was 1 foot 3½ inches. A smaller vessel was the *Lord Tennyson*, built by Messrs Orvis & Fuller of Ipswich in 1891. Her tonnage worked out at 78 gross, 74 under deck, and 61 net. Her dimensions were 82·0 feet by 19·8 feet by 6·9 feet, and she is shown in Plate 34.

The English and Continental Shipping Company must have been a flourishing concern at the turn of the century; but by 1905 all their ships except eight had been sold to other owners. The period from 1880 to 1900 may be taken as the hey-day of the boomy.

This brings me to the remarkable record in ketch barge building of that famous yard of J. & W. B. Harvey of Littlehampton, which, as Mr Basil Greenhill puts it, "carried the good name of Littlehampton to seas far away from the coast of Sussex". Renowned as builders of barques, brigs, brigantines and schooners, in 1878 they started to build ketch barges, and continued to build them until, when *Moul-tonian*, the last boomy to be launched, left their ways in 1919, no fewer than twenty-nine had been constructed at their yard.

These ships had been built in three distinct series, of which the first consisted of six barges. These were the *Susie*, launched in 1878; *Sallie*, 1879; *Maggie*, 1880; *Nellie*, 1882; *Rosie*, 1886; and one other.

In the following year began the second, and biggest series; the well-known "Lord" barges. Ten of them were built in the four years between 1887 and 1891; all were named after Victorian earls. *Lord Salisbury* came first, in 1887, followed by *Lord Churchill* in 1888. *Lord Wolseley*, *Lord Nelson*, *Lord Beresford* and *Lord Hamilton* were all four launched in 1889. 1890 saw two more, *Lord Lansdowne* and *Lord Dufferin*; and the last two, *Lord Alcester* and *Lord Napier*, came out in 1891.

The present foreman of Harvey's Yard told Mr Greenhill—to whom I am indebted for all this information about the Littlehampton and Rye ketch barges—that from 1899 to 1916 they had built eight ketches of about 200 tons D.W. capacity, besides a small steam passenger boat during their slack time. The ketches cost about £1,750 each and were usually taken by the men on very easy terms of instalment purchase. These eight, with the *Moultonian*, completed the third series, consisting of *Nell Jess*, 1902; *Kindly Light*, 1904; *Leading Light*, 1906; *Boaz*, 1908; *Clymping*, 1909; *Worrynot*, 1910; *Gippeswic*, 1912; *Wellholm*, 1916; and *Moultonian*, 1919. In addition to these, five boomies were built, which must be classed as "miscellaneous", as they do not fit into any of the three main series. These were *Dolgwandle*, in 1891; *Athole* and *Eric*, in 1892; *Princess May*, in 1893; and *Bona*, in 1898.

Rye was another Sussex port at which ketch barges were built; and among the early ones were *Enterprise*, *Surprise*, *Sunrise*, *Mountsfield* and *Diana*. These vessels traded with coal. They went to Scotland with shingle, also oak bark, and came back with coal from the Forth. Boomies were also built at Rye in later years, and the last of them, launched in 1913, was still afloat in 1947, as a sprit-rigged vessel. Another survivor, still trading as a motor barge, is the *Sarah Colebrooke* (see page 248). Her owners, Messrs Colebrooke, also had the *Katherina*, a steel ketch barge, one of the last sailing vessels to be owned in Rye.

The biggest boomy that George Doughty was able to find was the *Llama*, built at Harwich in 1875. She was 149 tons net. Bigger barges than this were rigged as three-masted schooners, and these are described later. Another big barge was the *Unity*, a Rye-built boomy of 120 tons net. She was not a great success, however, as she was rather crank, dipping her main boom when light. She was the only boomy known to have required ballast. Smith of Burnham had some big barges: *Thistle*, *Vanguard*, *Magnet* and *Emily Lloyd*, as well as the three-masted schooner *Friendship*. The *S.D.* (Smeed Dean), usually called "Sudden Death", had a big ugly square stern, and looked bigger than she really was.

Such were the boomies which took the place of the schooners on the East Coast. After this type of vessel was firmly established, no more schooners were built in these parts; and a great many of the old ones were sold away to the West Country, where conditions were different and round-bottomed vessels were essential.

They ousted the schooners because they were more handy and economical. For exactly the same reason, they were in turn ousted by large spreeties and mulies. It is true that at first some of the early coasting spreeties were considered too big for the sprit rig, and were altered to ketch rig; but it was not many years before the opposite procedure was taking place.

While boomies were being built in large numbers in all sorts of ports from Yarmouth to Littlehampton, other builders, especially those on the London River and Estuary, were developing the spritsail and mulie barges, and building fine big vessels. Steel spritsail barges were even being built in foreign yards; as at Papendrecht, for example. These carried just as much as the boomies; some carried more. They were handier in narrow waters, simpler to load and discharge and cheaper in every way; particularly in requiring one less hand, needing only two men and a boy instead of three men and a boy.

Small steamers and also Dutch motor vessels all had a share in driving the boomies off the sea; but the two main reasons for their extinction were the railway and the improved mulies. In the first place, when the railway came, small ports became far less self-supporting, and so many small local businesses, which had always been fed by water, were closed down. The main reason was that Newcastle coal was carried by rail, and the spritsail rig was considered quite good enough for all the other work left to barges. As a consequence, the spritsail or mulie rig have taken the place of the ketch for coasting barges.

The modern coasting barge is indeed a fine vessel—I do not suppose there ever was or ever will be such an amazing combination of sea-going qualities combined with handiness in shallow waters, shallow draught and large carrying capacity, speed and economy.

Nevertheless, by no stretch of imagination can anyone believe that the sprit rig is suitable for heavy weather in a nasty sea. A boomy's mainsail could be reefed down snug and she would take no harm; but a mulie's mainsail, half brailed up and scandalised out of all shape, is a miserable sail to windward; and the weight of a great heavy sprit heaving about aloft does not make for safety and an easy motion. Between the staggering mulie and the snugly reefed boomy there is no comparison.

It is true that a mulie with good gear and the right man in charge can come through pretty well anything in the shape of dirty weather, and they have done so times without number. Only those who have tried it, however, will know what it is like for those on board. Still, barges are not built for comfort or run for pleasure. As long as they are brought safely to port, that is all that matters. The old mulie gets there, and the sodden, sleepless, aching bargemen rig the gear, and suffer the harbour officials, customs, sanitary inspectors, enthusiastic bystanders and all the collection of tiresome people, which are the real trials of a bargeman's life.

There are now no boomies left, rigged as such. Most of the old timers have been lost in the last twenty years. Of those which were left in the late nineteen-thirties, the *Pearl*, of 76 tons, built by Orvis in 1889, and still under Captain Mynheer as her owner-skipper, was used only for lightering. Her bowsprit was unshipped and her gaff kept permanently aloft, as a half-sprit, her mainsail being stowed by brailing up, though she retained her boom and had a foot outhaul. When her skipper's advancing years made him retire, she lay for a long time in Ipswich Dock, until she was towed round to Erith by a *sailing* barge and used as a houseboat by the keeper of the Erith dump. She then lay at Gravesend, and was eventually converted to a powder hulk in 1947–48.

The *Davenport* in her later years also had a gaff aloft and no boom. *Justice* became a motor dredger, and looked like nothing on earth. The old *Garson*, built at Yarmouth in 1863, is a hulk belonging to the Erith Yacht Club; and the *Azariah*, *Alice May*, *Major*, *Dannebrog* and a few others were altered to spreeties or mulies. The *Dannebrog* and *Major*, once part of the Groom family's fleet, are still in commission; so are the *Ena* and *Thallata*, now mulie-rigged and owned by R. and W. Paul Ltd. *Alice May* is now a mule-rigged yacht owned by Mr Tony Lapthorne.

Mr Roger Finch has recorded in the 1948 Summer Number of "Spritsail" that the very last survivor trading with full ketch rig was the *Martinet*, of Goole, of 99 tons, owned by Everards, and built by G. and T. Smith at Rye in 1912. She was a fine example of the type, with a counter-stern, fiddle bow and "pump-handle" windlass. Before the Second World War she traded between the Humber and Margate with coal. She was sunk during the war, foundering at anchor in Hollesley Bay from stress of weather in February 1941.

Fortunately Mr E. J. March was able to take off her lines when she came into Margate with coal in September 1938; and he published the plans he prepared, from the measurements then made, in his " Spritsail Barges of Thames and Medway". She loaded 204 tons on a draught of 7 feet 6 inches; and was 95·2 feet in overall length, 22·8 feet beam, with a depth of hold of 8 feet.

Mr Greenhill states that the *Moultonian* was the last ketch barge to be built. By 1928 she had been fitted with an oil engine, and was trading as an auxiliary. She, and one like her, the *Wessex*, were rigged with pole mainmasts and sliding bowsprits.

The days of the boomy are now over. She came to the fore, flourished and faded out, following the old law of the "survival of the fittest"; or, perhaps more correctly, in the shipping world, the "survival of the cheapest".

To conclude on a lighter note, there is a story worth repeating of an old lady and her daughter watching the crew hoist a boomy's mainsail at Southwold. "No wonder them sailor chaps do swear so," said she sympathetically, "the more them poor fellows pull *down*, the fudder that there thing keep a going *up!*"

# CHAPTER VIII

# The Big Barges

CLOSELY connected with the ketch barges are those which were rigged as three-masted schooners, barquentines and brigantines. Those have been referred to briefly by the first Lord Runciman in a chapter entitled "The Smeed Barges" in his book, "Collier Brigs and Their Sailors". The reasons which he assigns for their introduction were the shallow and impractical nature of the north-east coast ports, which emphasised the advantage of a shallow-draught craft which would pass out on neap tides fully laden; and the fact that the Thames barge had a form of hull which could sail without ballast, and therefore save the cost of an unremunerative return cargo which had to be bought and carried on the voyage north to load coal.

According to Lord Runciman, the first big barges of this type built by the Kentish firm of Smeed Dean were two barquentines and a brig-rigged barge. One was the *Emily*; another, the *Eliza Smeed*. They carried about five or six hundred tons each; and were followed by a big barge rigged as a barque, which could load no less than 800 tons, and was said to be a very fast ship with the wind anywhere abaft the beam. But in spite of their lee-boards, said Lord Runciman, "beating to windward in a jumpy sea, they sagged badly to leeward".

Mr Edgar J. March has told the story of some of them in his "Sprit-sail Barges of Thames and Medway", including the well-known *Friendship* (Plate 35) and the *Zebrina*, most famous of them all. But there were in fact many more of them than have so far been described in print, and it is unfortunately very difficult to get any detailed information about them, except for some few that lived until more recent years. Most of them do not seem to have lasted very long.

Biggest of all the barges was the *Esther Smeed*. She was the craft which Lord Runciman said could carry 800 tons, and she was rigged as a barque. She was built at Sittingbourne in 1868, and was owned by Mr George Smeed of Gore Court, the originator, so far as can be discovered, of those very big barges; and certainly he was their biggest employer. In 1875, Mr Smeed decided to change his brickmaking concern into a limited liability company, under the title of Smeed, Dean & Co. Ltd., with his son-in-law, Mr George Hambrook Dean, as Managing Director; and this great firm achieved a high reputation as one of the principal barge-owning firms. The *Esther Smeed* must have been the biggest barge ever built. She had the tremendous net registered tonnage of 494 tons—which gives a very fair idea of her size. She last appears in the Merchant Navy List in 1878; but I have been unable to discover what happened to her.

Another enormous barge, built two years earlier, also at Sittingbourne, was the *George Smeed* of Rochester, a barquentine of 477 tons net. She was named after her owner and he kept her until she was sold foreign to Norway on the 29th December 1879.

The *Emily Smeed*, one of the barges mentioned by Lord Runciman, was built at Sittingbourne, Kent, in 1872, and owned at first by Mr George Smeed, and afterwards by Messrs Smeed, Dean & Co., who kept her until 1881. She was of 272 net and 299 gross tons; 133·3 feet in length, 25·8 feet beam, and of the extraordinary big depth, for a barge, of 13·3 feet. When launched, she was rigged as a barquentine. Her great depth of hull would make one doubt whether she could be correctly described as a "barge" but for the fact that another big craft, the *Nellie S.*, of almost the same size (295 tons gross), built three years later at Whitstable in 1875 and listed in Lloyd's Register as a "Wooden *Barge* Barquentine", has a depth of 12·8 feet and a moulded depth of 13 feet 7 inches.

*Emily Smeed* was one of the few of these big barges to have a long life. In 1896, having changed hands some time before, she was owned by J. H. Bull and registered at Newhaven. Captain J. Bennett had then been in command since 1882. Her rig had by then been changed to a three-masted schooner, no doubt to enable her to reduce the size of her crew. In 1919 she was owned by Craske, registered in Aberdeen, and under Captain A. Garner, who had been her master for eleven years. She was still rigged as a three-masted schooner; but by 1930, when she was registered in Peterhead and owned by Frederick O. Mulliner, of Lowestoft, she was described as "jury-rigged", and had no doubt degenerated to some sort of towing lighter.

*Emily Smeed* was followed two years later by another big barge, named after another member of the family. She was the *Sarah Smeed*, a three-masted schooner, of 241 tons net, registered at Rochester and built at Murston, Sittingbourne. She was built partly of second-hand materials, which one might reasonably surmise came from warships broken up in Chatham Dockyard. She was 125·7 feet in length, with a beam of 25·7 feet and a depth of 11·0 feet. She appears for the last time in the register in 1882, at which time Captain J. Hadlow was her master.

No doubt when the big coal merchants saw that the boomies were not crank and awkward to handle, they decided to copy these on a larger scale; for, as far as the hulls of these big barquentine and schooner barges were concerned, they were like very large boomies. They could not be called at all graceful, but the large cargoes they carried on a small draught more than made up for that. They were flat-bottomed, with a square chine, and lee-boards just abaft the fore-mast. Lord Runciman says they could not be constructed with the same strength as an ordinary vessel; and there must obviously be a weakness in a long, flat craft not present in a deeper round-bottomed hull of normal construction. Perhaps that is one reason why the big ones were sometimes not very long lived.

An exception to this, however, was the celebrated *Zebrina*, a most interesting vessel, built by H. H. Gann & Son at Whitstable in 1873. She was an oak-built and copper-fastened three-masted schooner barge, but unlike most she never carried lee-boards. Her tonnage was 185 gross and 169 net, she was registered at Faversham and her dimensions were 109·1 feet in length, 23·9 feet beam and 9·9 feet draught. She was built for the River Plate, and certified for nine years. On the voyage out to South America she carried a cargo of cement, and then worked in those waters for eight years. After that for some reason she ceased to pay out there, and was sailed home to Whitstable, arriving with a Negro crew, which caused a stir in the town that was remembered for long afterwards.

On her return to England she was owned by the Whitstable Shipping Co., and employed in the coasting trade, where she certainly did pay. The late Captain R. Skinner, who was master of the *Zebrina* and later of the same company's schooner barge *Belmont*, described the trade to my old friend George Doughty. "The Whit-stable Shipping Company's ships were registered at Faversham," he said, "as Whitstable was not a port for registration. They had brigantines which they turned into barquentines, the sails being smaller and easier to handle; but the ship did not sail so fast. An extra mast, a small mizzen-mast, was added aft.

"We went all round the coast, looking for cargo. This was called 'seeking'. We would take chalk from Gravesend or Northfleet to the Tyne—Newcastle. For some years the company did not insure their ships, and with the money thus saved they had a barge built, the *Belmont*, and asked me to choose the rig. She was rigged as a topsail schooner, with two masts, setting a squaresail, topsail and topgallant on the foremast. She had no mizzen topmast, but carried a jibboom, and was steered with a wheel.

"The first voyage of the *Belmont* we went to Milford Haven (that was in 1895), where there is a naval base. We loaded with coal at a little place called Hope. The coal was brought in farm tumbrils and put aboard down wooden shoots—square troughs. We carried this cargo to Ipswich, where we discharged 317 tons."

The *Belmont*, referred to above, was built in 1895 at Whitstable by the Whitstable Shipping Company, her owners, and registered at Faversham. Of 169 tons gross and 145 net, she measured 104·0 feet in length with a beam of 24·1 feet and depth of 9·6 feet. Her moulded depth was 10 feet 8 inches, and her freeboard amidships 1 foot 5½ inches. In 1919 she was still in the Register, being owned by H. A. Payne and commanded by Captain T. J. Jones. She disappears from the Register after 1920.

To continue with the *Zebrina*. She was originally barquentine-rigged, having a proper fore course with all its gear, though she had no fidded topgallant mast—topgallant mast and topmast were all in one. She was a lucky ship, and used almost always to get a freight both ways. I believe that if she had to make a long passage light she needed a little ballast. She had a fiddle bow, which could be recognised miles off. It raked inwards above and stuck out below like a battleship's ram—it may have been specially strengthened for meeting tree-trunks and other floating débris in the South American rivers. She had a counter-stern and a raised cabin top, like that of a small sprit-sail barge. As has already been stated, she never carried lee-boards.

She was so successful that the Whitstable Shipping Co. had the *Belmont* built in the same style, but rigged as a two-masted schooner. She also was chine-built, but carried no lee-boards. She had a normal bow, however, and a counter-stern.

When Captain Skinner took the *Belmont*, in 1895, Captain H. Bedwell took the *Zebrina*, and she continued trading and doing well until, in the 1914–18 war, she had an extraordinary adventure, which gave rise to a mystery of the sea that has remained unsolved and is strikingly like that of the famous *Marie Louise*. Edgar J. March tells the story. She left Falmouth in October 1917, bound with coal from Swansea for St Brieuc. Two days later she was found ashore on Rozel Point, south of Cherbourg, her hull undamaged, rigging in some slight disorder, but without a soul on board. It was assumed that the crew were taken off by a U-boat, which was about to sink the *Zebrina*, when she got scared and cleared off, being later sunk herself with the *Zebrina*'s crew aboard. That is only a guess, but David Master has investigated the mystery, in his book "When Ships Go Down", in a delightful piece of maritime investigation.

The ship was salvaged practically undamaged, and re-fitted. In 1919 she was owned by Hopkins, Saunders & Co. of Cardiff. She then had a one-cylinder paraffin engine of 14 h.p., made and fitted in 1917 by the Invincible Engine Co. of Keighley. She was then rigged as a three-masted schooner. Captain Martin had her at that time. By 1930 she had had a bigger engine, of 55 h.p., installed, and was then owned by the Ajax Shipping Co. of 16, Water Lane, E.C.3. In 1928 and 1929 she lay as a coal hulk in Ramsgate Harbour; and after this, resumed trading as a pole-masted motor schooner. While on a passage from Blyth to Truro with coal, her cargo caught fire, and she put into the Solent. The hull was so damaged that she never left those waters again; and her hulk lies to this day in the Vedder Creek of Langstone Harbour. To Mr Greenhill my thanks are due for much of this information.

Another big barge launched at Whitstable was the *Nellie S.*; a barquentine of 262 tons net, built there in 1876 by H. H. Gann & Co., and registered at Faversham. She was salted, copper-fastened, felted and yellow-metalled; and Mr March says considerable quantities of English and African oak from Chatham Dockyard went into her construction. With length 131·2 feet, beam 26·0 feet and depth 12·8 feet, she loaded about 500 tons, and was classed A1 at Lloyd's. Her moulded depth was 13 feet 7 inches, and her freeboard amidships 2 feet 7 inches; undoubtedly she was a fine hefty vessel for a barge. She traded very little in home waters and was eventually sold to a firm in Brazil. Her name was removed from the list of British vessels after 1898.

Most of the big schooner barges were rigged as ordinary three-masted schooners, with double topsails on the foremast. The *Friendship*, however (Plate 35), had staysails between fore and main, instead of the more usual gaff sail. She had a fat, old-fashioned head and slab sides. She was one of several three-masted schooners built by Taylor of Sittingbourne, at a cost of about £1,000 each. They were said to have been somewhat lightly built. Edgar J. March says prospective owners fitted them out to their own requirements as to rig. The *Friendship* was built in 1890, was 117·0 feet in length, 25·5 feet beam and 10·6 feet in depth. She was registered at Colchester and owned by T. Smith of Burnham, and with a net tonnage of 200 and gross 223 she would carry about 420 tons. Her last voyage was from Dover to the Humber, light, in about 1912, when she was run down and sunk by a steamer in that river.

Another of the big schooners was the *Enterprise* of Yarmouth. She was built at South Town in 1891, and classed A1 for nine years. Of

PLATE 34 *Lord Tennyson*

[*By courtesy of the St Clement's Shipyard, Ipswich*

PLATE 35 The Three-masted Schooner-barge *Friendship*
Towing out of Dover Harbour

[*By courtesy of the Nautical Photo Agency*

PLATE 36 Humber Keel

[*From a Model in the Science Museum*

PLATE 37 Norfolk Keel

[*From a Model in the Science Museum*

190 gross and 168 net tons, she was 109·5 feet in length, 24·8 feet beam and 10·3 feet depth, with a moulded depth of 11 feet 0 inches and freeboard amidships of 1 foot 6½ inches. She was rigged as a three-masted schooner and set a topgallant sail over her double topsails, but was not *really* a great success according to her owners, Messrs Bessey & Palmer, for whom she was built. Mr Dawson, in their office in Yarmouth, told George Doughty that she was apparently a bit clumsy. She later had her yards taken out of her, leeboards removed and an engine installed. She was lost some thirty-two years ago.

Lack of space forbids more than a brief mention of other big barges; such as the *Ellen Smeed* of Rochester, a three-masted schooner of 147 gross and 134 net tons, built at Sittingbourne in 1872; 107·8 feet in length, 22·6 feet beam and 8·8 feet depth. Captain R. Eve had her twenty years later, in 1892, and she lasted until 1912. *Seven Sisters*, of Faversham, one of the very early ones, was built for George Smeed at Sittingbourne in 1862. She registered 174 tons net, and when she first came out was rigged as a schooner. She retained that rig until, in about 1881, she was sold to Charles E. Doughty, of Margate, when she was rigged as a brigantine. In 1882 her port of registry was changed to Rochester, but by 1883 she had disappeared from the Register.

Sittingbourne, however, was not the only port to build these big barges. Greenhithe saw the launch, in 1874, of a three-masted schooner barge, built by Keep, and named after her birthplace. *Greenhithe* had a net tonnage of 162 tons, was registered at London, and in 1882 was owned by J. P. Bryant and commanded by Captain E. Lothian. Mr March says she loaded about 400 tons, and was eventually sold to the French, which would be about 1883.

Ipswich also saw the birth of a big three-masted schooner barge named *Parkend*, built there by Bayley in 1873. When she came out she was of 145 tons gross and 132 net, 101·7 feet long, 24·0 feet beam and 8·0 feet deep. She was afterwards "rose-on" and altered to a ketch; her dimensions then being 103·1 feet long, 24·0 feet beam and 10·5 feet deep, increasing her tonnage to 192 and 175 gross and net respectively. She was a ketch in 1896, when she was registered at Bridgwater and owned by Sully & Co. Ltd., of that port, Captain T. Owens being her master. In 1919 she was registered in North Shields, commanded by Captain G. W. Eastwick and owned by the Theodore Shipping Co. Ltd. She disappears from the registers after 1922.

Harwich too entered the lists. *Lymington* was a wood three-masted

9

schooner of 163 tons gross, built and owned by J. H. Vaux, builder of
the celebrated *Stour*, at Harwich, in 1880. She survived until 1888.
*Jubilee* was another three-masted schooner barge of 189 tons gross,
also built by Vaux at Harwich in 1887 and owned by him; she last
appears in 1910, when she was owned by Walter T. Howard of
London.

Returning to Kent, we find J. M. Goldfinch, of Faversham, turning out the *Nancy*, built there in 1890. This little schooner barge, of
117 tons net, was registered at Ramsgate. She belonged first to J. J.
Greenstreet, but was later owned by her skipper, Captain G. Smith of
Sandwich. It was while he had her that she was run down and sunk
on 10th December 1909, when anchored near Clayhole, on a voyage
from Boston to Sandwich. Her crew was saved.

It was not only in south-eastern England, however, that big
schooner barges and their sisters were built; for Foster of Emsworth
built at his yard there in 1870 the wooden barquentine *Thorney
Island*, of Portsmouth, registering 185 tons gross. This ship, with an
overall length of 102·0 feet, beam of 24·7 feet and depth of 11·4 feet,
was particularly interesting in having a raised quarter-deck, a most
unusual feature for a barge. Captain R. May had her in 1892, and for
some years after, when she was owned by S. Ash. She finished her
days as a hulk at Emsworth, where she lay from about 1898 to the end
of the First World War.

The same builder, in 1878, launched a little brigantine-rigged
barge, of 124 tons net, with the attractive name of *Annie Florence*,
registered at Portsmouth and owned by Crampton. She was only
96·5 feet in length, 23·1 feet beam and 8·7 feet depth. Captain T.
Dyer had her for a time, but in 1884–5 her port of registry was
changed to Faversham, and alterations were made which reduced her
net tonnage to 115 tons. She had been re-rigged as a schooner, following her sale at that time to Stapleton Payn, of Faversham. She
disappears from the lists after 1894.

The most interesting barge built by Foster at Emsworth, however,
was the beautiful little *Fortuna*, launched there in 1892. She was
unique in having a centreboard in place of lee-boards. Of 133 tons
gross and 121 tons net, her dimensions were 100·0 feet in length,
24·3 feet beam and 7·8 feet depth. Although she appears in the
registers as a schooner, her rig might perhaps be more accurately
described as that of a brigantine. From information supplied to Basil
Greenhill at Harvey's Yard, Littlehampton, by men who remembered
her, her rig when they knew her was not like that of an ordinary
brigantine, as her mainmast was shorter than her foremast, and in

lieu of staysails between the masts she had a gaff and boom foresail like a schooner's donkey. Her square foresail was not bent to the fore-yard, but set flying like a schooner's. Unfortunately, as might be sup-posed, it was almost impossible to prevent leakage in her big centre keel trunk. He was told that they used to pour chaff into this in order to stop the leaks—a very good, though temporary, remedy. According to the Littlehampton men the *Fortuna* gave endless trouble, and her reputation prevented more experiments with centreboards. No doubt the structural weakness of a big centreboard case to resist thwart-ships wringing strains, together with the undoubted obstruction to cargo carrying of such an object in the hold, contributed to this result, in spite of the fact that centreboards in large barge-like craft have proved successful in various parts of the world, and particularly in the well-known New Zealand scows.

On the other hand, in marked contrast to this reputation, is the account of her given by one of her masters, my old friend Captain William Bate, for many years Deputy Harbour Master at Fowey. Captain Bate was a grand old master mariner of the old school, a sea-man if ever there was one, who had served his time in sailing ships large and small, in both coasting and blue-water voyaging. Those who have read Rex Clements' inspiring book "A Gipsy of the Horn" will recall the account there of his captain, a splendid portrait of a mag-nificent old seaman. Although it is not disclosed in that book, Rex Clements was one of Captain Bate's apprentices, and the portrait that he gives is of him.

Captain Bate was so enthusiastic about the *Fortuna* that he wrote to "Sea Breezes" about her; and his account, with a photograph of the ship, appeared in that journal for January 1929. By the courtesy of the Editor I reproduce it here.

"One of the few coasters I have ever known which combined the light draught of the Thames barge along with the sea-going attributes of the ordinary schooner," he writes, "was the *Fortuna*—of which vessel I was master for a time before the (1914–18) war. Built of oak at Emsworth in 1892, she carried a deadweight cargo of 230 tons. She was rigged as a square foresail brigantine, and was peculiar in con-struction in that she was fitted with a big wooden centre keel which worked in a trunk and was raised by means of a hand-winch on deck. When this keel was dropped, on starting out on a passage, the *For-tuna* drew 17 feet loaded, which naturally gave her a good grip of the water. On entering a shallow-draught port, the keel was raised, and she then drew only eight feet—a great advantage when entering or leaving such ports as Truro, Par, Charlestown, etc., on neaps. Not only did this centre keel help her tremendously in making a passage, but it also enabled her to sail without ballast. Thus it was an all-round time and money saver.

"The *Fortuna* made many smart passages; the best that I can remember whilst I was in her was when she left the Isle of Wight one Tuesday in ballast for Dean Quarries, near the Manacles, loaded a full cargo of stone and arrived back in Southampton on the following Saturday, thus covering 320 miles, besides loading a full cargo, within five days—a record which a steam coaster of equal tonnage might find it hard to beat.

"The *Fortuna* was an early war casualty, being sunk by a submarine off Portland in 1914."

The photograph illustrating Captain Bate's account shows that her rig, when he had her, differed from that described to Mr Greenhill. As she appears at the time the photograph was taken, her mainmast and main topmast are much taller than her foremast and fore topmast. Fore topmast and topgallantmast are one spar. Her fore course is furled on the yard. She sets fore course, single fore topsail, fore topgallant and fore royal. Her (main) gaff topsail appears to be stowed aloft, as it is in a spreety barge. In the picture she is seen from ahead, in tow of a small tug, and is deep laden. There is no doubt that she was a handsome vessel.

An unusual experiment with a schooner barge was made by Bayley of Ipswich. This was the *Problem*, a schooner of 128 tons net, which he launched from the St Clements' Shipyard there in 1861. An iron-fastened vessel, of 92·1 feet in length, beam 22·6 feet and depth 9·7 feet, she was destined for Mediterranean voyages, for which she was zinc-sheathed in 1867 and again in 1877, after undergoing considerable repairs in 1874.

*Problem* was unique in that, although she was built with a flat bottom like a barge, she had neither lee-boards nor centreboard, but had three fixed keels instead. These consisted of one fairly shallow keel amidships, and two big bilge keels which it was thought should, in theory, hold her up when heeling, without making her draw a lot of water when upright. The theory does not seem to have worked, however, for she was not a success. She used to sag to loo'ard badly, and was lost about 1886. Among her masters were Captain W. Biggs, who had her in 1868; and Captain T. Hart, commanding in 1882.

The changing conditions of the coasting trade in the twentieth century, which gradually drove the boomies off the seas, affected the big schooner barges in the same way, but with greater and earlier force; yet, while they lasted, they must have been fine ships and done their work well. Though, to my regret, I never saw one, I have tried here to set down something of their history.

To conclude in lighter vein, here is a story told of the schooners in days when the galley was no more than a wooden box lashed down to a couple of ring bolts on deck, an arrangement common in both the schooner barges and some boomies.

"It was a dirty night," runs the yarn, "and we were taking them over green. Me and my mate got into the galley to have a warm. Suddenly after a heavy sea we saw a schooner go tearing past to windward of us—only missing us by a few feet.

" 'Heavens!' says I, 'that was a near one!'

" 'Hell!' says he, 'she's *ours*!' "

CHAPTER IX

# The Keels

In addition to the Thames barge, which is unique, there have been in England in the past many varieties of local barge and coaster types which are more or less confined to a particular district or found more especially upon a particular stretch of coast. Yet although these craft exhibit very varied rigs and developments of hull and equipment, it is a fact both interesting and striking to observe how, in so many types, the double-ended form of hull, derived from the Viking model, has persisted.

In describing these local craft, a somewhat arbitrary division will be adopted, and this chapter is devoted to the barges known as *Keels*, which are nearest of all to the Viking model. These vessels can be grouped in three distinct classes: namely, the keels of the Tyne, the Humber and the Norfolk Broads. The name *keel* itself is very ancient, and is derived from that given to the old Viking longships. It was in three *Ceolas* that Hengist and Horsa were supposed to have landed when they founded the Kingdom of Kent in A.D. 449; and the word *keel* was always pronounced "kee-ul" on Tyneside.

It is hardly surprising, therefore, that this common name and common ancestry should be found more strongly marked in those very districts which propably suffered most from the visits of the Viking raiders. The *keels* bore the following common features. They were small, comparatively shallow-draught craft. They were almost alike in bow and stern, being pointed at each end; although the Humber keel was very bluff, and the Norfolk keel actually had a narrow transom instead of a sharp stern, sharing with her namesake on the Tyne a rather flat, dish-shaped form of hull. Both were originally clinker-built, although the later Tyne keels were carvel, which the Norfolk keels never were. The Humber keel, however, was far more straight-sided and flat-bottomed, and had not the suggestion of flare about her bows noticeable in the other vessels. Possibly this was because the estuary of the Humber approached far more to open sea conditions than did either the Tyne or the Broads of Norfolk and Suffolk, so that a more weatherly ship was necessary.

The connection between the Humber keel and the medieval

coaster is in many ways remarkable, and makes an interesting study which will be considered later; and it is almost certain that at one time the Humber keel went sea-going coastwise voyages beyond the limits of the river. A further point in favour of this view is that the now obsolete small coaster known as the Yorkshire Billyboy, of which the *Brilliant* of Goole, referred to in Chapter XII, is an example, had the same form of hull and was really nothing more than a larger, sea-going keel, rigged fore-and-aft instead of with the older squaresail alone.

Of these three classes, perhaps the Tyne keel has the oldest documentary records. She was built for a particular purpose, and her employment was in the Newcastle coal trade. Of other work she had practically none. Her work was simply to load coals from the pit staiths or "dykes" up the river and bring them down to the sea-going collier ships lying in the port below. Having done this, and discharged, she returned to the staiths for more. This work was carried on, like the lightering on the London River, chiefly by the aid of the tide. Down with the ebb, back with the flood she went, and sail or oar helped her on her way.

The Newcastle coal trade is far more ancient than is generally imagined, and as early certainly as the middle of the fourteenth century coasters were regularly carrying coals by sea to London. These vessels were too large to go right up the shallow river to the pits, and therefore smaller craft were needed to carry the coals for the first stage of their journey. The form of hull most familiar on the coast was that developed from the ancient Norse model, and the little vessels of the Tyne followed the standard lines on a smaller scale. The first keels were probably clinker-built, but later the carvel method of building was adopted, and this lasted until about 1840. From about 1832 the employment of steam tugs for towage on the Tyne called for a larger and cheaper craft than the very strongly built keel, and brought about the development of the clinker-built type known as Tyne wherries. After this, keels were no longer built, at least not in any considerable numbers.

What may well be the earliest local account of keels was discovered by Mr W. Stanley Metcalfe (see below) in the Rolls of the Parish of Norham, contained in Raine's "History of North Durham", page 271. Here there is payment of 20*d*. "for a kele with wool from Newcastle to Wardeley"—a manor belonging to the prior and convent of Durham near Gateshead. Other fourteenth-century documents refer to keels employed in the coal trade on the Tyne at that time; and the keelmen, who are sometimes called "kelers", appear in the

Chartulary of Tynemouth monastery in the fourteenth century as "servants of the prior of Tinmouth who wrought in the barges".

The earliest mention of the Newcastle keel that I have been able to trace in an Act of Parliament occurs in the year 1421, when by statute of Henry V, I, cap. X, it was enacted that all these vessels should be measured and marked by Commissioners, and that their portage should be twenty chaldrons of coal only. The wording of the original petition is found in the old Rolls of Parliament. It sets forth that "in the same Port be certain Vessels called Keels, by which such Coals be carried from the Land to the Ships in the said Port; and every of the said Keels ought to be of the Portage of Twenty Chaldrons". After the passing of the Act, any unmeasured and un-marked keel carrying coals was liable to be forfeited to the king.

This statute continued to govern the licensing of keels until it was amended in the year 1678 by "*An Act* for the Admeasurement of Keels and Boates carrying Coales", and dealing with keels "in the Port of Newcastle upon Tyne Sunderland upon the River Ware Callercoats Seaton Sluce Blythe Nooke and all and every other the Members Havens Creeks and Places whatsoever to the said Port of Newcastle belonging or otherwise appertaining". Markings were to be "either by Nails upon Bulke heads or partitions to be affixed to the fore and after Beame of every such Keele or Boate or by Nails to be driven into the Stemm or Sterne Post of every such Keele or Boate . . ." or by such other method as might be approved of by the Commissioners. The keels, moreover, were only to be measured be-tween 25th March and 29th September, which bears out Defoe's statement that the collier trade in ships was carried on only during the summer months. It appears, however, that the working of these Acts was still not effective, and in 1695 another Act, 6 & 7 Will. III, cap. X, had to be passed further to regulate the trade.

During the eighteenth century the "keel" as a measure of coal became fixed at eight chaldrons of 53 cwt. each, and the burden of the "keel" was therefore 21 tons of coal. This term was once used in connection with the loading of collier ships which were chartered "to load a full and complete cargo of (so many) keels of coal". As late as 1901 sailing ships for certain Baltic and Spanish Mediterranean ports were chartered in this way, but otherwise the practice has been gradually dying out since 1863.

The old coal-keel carrying eight chaldrons was a tubby, grim-looking craft, almost oval in shape, rounded fore and aft and about 42 feet long by 19 feet in beam. The plans produced herewith (Fig. 26) were drawn by Mr Hugh R. Viall from a model in the Castle

# TYNE KEEL

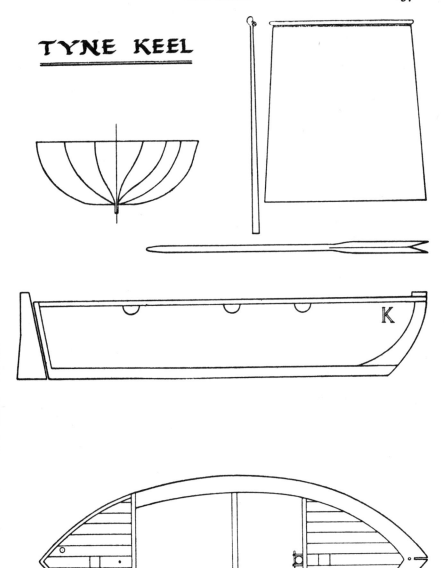

FIG. 26 Tyne Keel, by Hugh R. Viall, Esq

[*By courtesy of the Society for Nautical Research*

Museum at Newcastle, and published, with a valuable account of the keels, in the "Mariner's Mirror", Vol. XXVIII, page 161. I am indebted to Mr Viall and to the Editor for permission to reproduce them. Fully loaded, the keel drew approximately 4 feet 6 inches of water. In her later days she was carvel-built, and was rigged with a single large square sail set on a light mast stepped well into her, in a mast-case just the foreside of her hold, called in these craft a "tabernacle". This mast could be easily lowered for going through the low Tyne Bridge. She was steered with a long oar, called a "swape", used as a rudder over the stern of the vessel. She was undecked, except for a short deck forward and a little cabin or cuddy aft, called a "huddock" or "huddick".

"I huik'd him an haul'd him suin into the keel, an' o' top o' the huddock aw rowl'd him aboot" ran the words of an old song. Admiral Smythe quotes another:

> 'Twas between Ebbron and Yarrow,
> There cam on a varry strong gale;
> The skipper luik'd out o' th' huddock,
> Crying, "Smash, man, lower the sail!"

This huddock was entered by a scuttle in the after-deck, and was so small that when a keelman stood upright in it his head and shoulders appeared above the deck. It is said that in cold weather, in some few keels fitted with rudders, this was a favourite position with the skipper, who could thus keep his nether extremities warm while he handled the tiller above. There was a small hatch into the fore peak and another in the hold, at the after end generally, through which it was possible to get inside the keel to inspect the timbers.

In the absence of wind or if the wind was ahead, the keel was rowed by the united efforts of her crew of four, who were known as "keel-bullies". Although they were a very hardy class of men, they were not by any means so quarrelsome as their name "bully" would suggest, for the word is really derived from an old word "boolie" meaning "beloved", a cheery term of fellowship common among brother workers in the collieries. The rowing was done by three members of the crew, who plied one huge oar over the starboard side of the bow while the skipper kept her on her course with the "swape", worked near the stern, over the port side. In the shallow higher reaches of the river the keel was sometimes punted along with long poles, called "puoys", which the keelmen struck down to the bottom and then, thrusting upon the end set into the shoulder, walked the keel along, just as the Norfolk wherry-men "quant" their craft. The keelmen, however, called this "setting".

The square sail of the keel was sometimes set as a form of standing lug, when on a wind; the tack being brought to the mast and the sheet led aft. About the year 1840 the old squaresail of the keel was displaced by the spritsail and small jib, and the keel then had an

## TYNE WHERRY

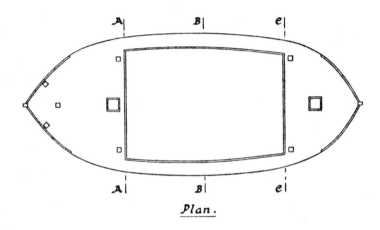

Plan.

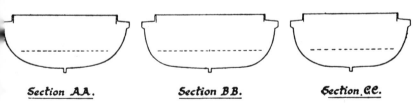

Section AA.          Section BB.          Section CC.

FIG. 27 Tyne Wherry

[*By courtesy of the Society for Nautical Research*

appearance not unlike a "stumpy" barge on the Thames. She carried no bowsprit, the jib being tacked to the stem-head. Vessels larger than the keel, but clinker-built and modelled on much the same lines, were also being introduced at about the same period, as has already been mentioned. These were called "wherries", and the plans of a Tyne wherry, Fig. 27, show how closely she resembled a keel.

The loading of the keels varied to some extent. Large coal was shot in and piled up fairly high. Small or "tender" coal was carried in tubs. Keels carrying these tubs appear to have shown some slight difference in construction or equipment, and were called "pan-keels" or "pan-boats".

Mr Viall states that the floor of the keel's hold was only about 2 feet from the deck line, and on it the coals were piled up in a conical heap, and kept in place by deals stacked on end, called "jells". The collier brig was provided with special coal ports, one forward, one amidships and one aft on each side; and into these the keelmen discharged their cargo by casting it with shovels, literally "coal-heaving". The remuneration of the keelmen ranged from 11s. 8d. to 13s. 4d. a keel, with an allowance for beer known as the "can". As the collier could have a keel—sometimes two—on each side, and other laden keels were waiting to take the place of those discharged, she was loaded in a remarkably short time for those days without machinery.

A development of later date was to make the deck narrower on one side of the keel than on the other. This made the casting of the coal easier, the "throw" into the brig was shorter and the keelmen always had coal running down into their shovels as they worked. The hold ceiling was called the "shute", and there was generally a strengthening beam amidships.

The keels were extremely strongly built, with oak planking generally, though some had elm below the water line, fastened with wooden treenails to sawn timbers of grown oak. The price of a keel depended on the closeness with which these timbers were spaced, and in the most costly they were so close that only the width of a man's fist would go between them.

In addition to the model in the Castle Museum, there are three rough ones in the Municipal Museum at Newcastle, and one very poor one in the Science Museum at South Kensington.

The keel-bullies were a numerous class, well known in song and fable, when they were often termed "keel-laddies".

> *My bonny keel laddie, my canny keel laddie,*
> *The bonny keel laddie for me, O,*
> *He sits in his keel, as black as the de'il,*
> *And brings the white money to me, O.*

is a good example. Best known of all, of course, is that charming old song:

> *Oh, weel may the keel row, the keel row, the keel row,*
> *Oh, weel may the keel row, the keel my laddie's in.*

The keelmen often worked hard to get their loads off in one tide, and Mr Viall tells a well-known yarn of the Tyne, in which one evening down at Shields an empty keel managed to get foul of the moorings of a man-of-war. The officer of the watch, full of dignity and importance, looked down on the keel and said, "Do you know, my man, the consequences of interfering with one of Her Majesty's Ships?" to get the ready answer, "D'ye knaa, mistor, the consequens of wor missin' this b—— tide?"

There is a good account of the keelmen and the way they worked in R. W. Johnson's "The Making of the Tyne: Record of Fifty Years' Progress"; and a most valuable source of information is a paper on "The History of the Keelmen and their Strike in 1822", which was read to the Society of Antiquaries of Newcastle-upon-Tyne by Mr W. Stanley Metcalfe in 1935, and published in "Archaeologia Aeliana", 4th Series, Vol. XIV, to which I am much indebted. The eighteenth-century keelman in holiday attire was a veritable dandy. He wore a short blue jacket, yellow waistcoat and slate-coloured trousers. The trousers were cut tight at the knees and bellied out below. On his head he wore a black hat with a flat brim and a black ribbon tied round it in two bows, with five or six inches of ends left streaming. The outfit was completed by a black neckerchief tied in a reef knot. A very high proportion of the keelmen were Scotsmen from Edinburgh, which is perhaps why "The Keel Row" is generally, though incorrectly, regarded as a Scots song. It is essentially a song of the Tyne.

The keelmen's wives and daughters were known as "keel-deeters" or "keel-dighters", because it was their privilege to sweep up or "dight" the keels, taking away the sweepings of coals for their pains. The keelmen as a class were said to be very superstitious, and many were the uncanny stories current among them. But the keel and the keelmen have now faded away into the almost forgotten past, and no longer does keel go down the Tyne to load the ships with sea-coals. The collieries on the western outcrop of the field were worked out, and newer collieries had all the advantages of railway transport for direct shipment. Thus gradually the number of keels diminished year by year, until in 1915 it was stated that only three of them were left. Yet at one time hundreds sailed on every tide, and less than a hundred years ago Samuel Smiles was able to write: "One of the most curious sights upon the Tyne is the fleet of hundreds of these black-sailed, black-hulled vessels, bringing down at each tide their black cargoes for the ships at anchor in the deep water at Shields and other parts of the river below Newcastle."

One has only to come a few miles farther down the East Coast, however, to find in the River Humber and the inland waterways of Yorkshire a type of keel which existed in considerable numbers until quite recently, and bears to-day the distinction of being almost the only craft in the British Isles in which the primitive squaresail rig of the Vikings has survived until the present time. Even as late as April 1949, a solitary survivor, the *Nar*, was still fully rigged, and her skipper, Captain Albert Barras, still liked to make his passages under sail. The *Nar* belongs to Messrs Furley & Co., of Princes Dock Side, Hull, who were kind enough to supply me with this information. They say that Captain Barras, who has been with them for over forty years, is one of the best men with a sail (square rigged) on the Humber. This firm are the last keel owners on the Humber; and although they still own two or three square-rigged keels, they have only one suit of sails, as it has become uneconomic to sail these keels, and, with the exception of the *Nar*, they are therefore always towed. Messrs Furley are, however, gradually turning over all their craft to motor power, so that in the next twelve to eighteen months there will be no sailing keels left at all.

The form of hull and of rig in these vessels is well illustrated by the photograph (Plate 36) of the splendid model in the Science Museum lent by the Sheffield and South Yorkshire Navigation Company; and by the plans, Fig. 28, drawn by the late Mr George F. Holmes of Hessle, near Hull, which were published in the Humber Yawl Club Year Book for 1901, from which they are reproduced here by the courtesy of the Club. The dimensions of a typical keel are: length, 62·5 feet; breadth, 15·5 feet; depth, about 8 feet; draught, 7 feet with a load of about 100 tons. They are thus much larger than the keels of either the Tyne or the Norfolk Broads, although they vary a little in size, with smaller keels trading to Sheffield, while larger ones, with a length of 68 feet, can carry about 170 tons. They are carvel-built, flat-bottomed and straight-sided, like a Thames barge, with a very bluff bow. They are double-ended, however, the stern being slightly more rounded than the bow. The stem projects above the deck, and alternate timber-heads in bow and stern are brought up to form stanchions, capped by a strong oaken rail. Between these stanchions short timber-heads appear, which can serve as bollards and fairheads. The stern-post is cut off flush with the deck, to allow the tiller to work over it. The keel is decked in at bow and stern, with narrow waterways on either side of the main hatch, which is covered with a tarpaulin over eighteen well cambered hatch covers. Aft is a small cabin, and forward a short fore-peak, bulk-headed off from the hold.

Like the Thames barge, the Humber keel has lee-boards, which are used to enable her to get a grip of the water when sailing to windward, and these are raised and lowered by wires from the after ends led to

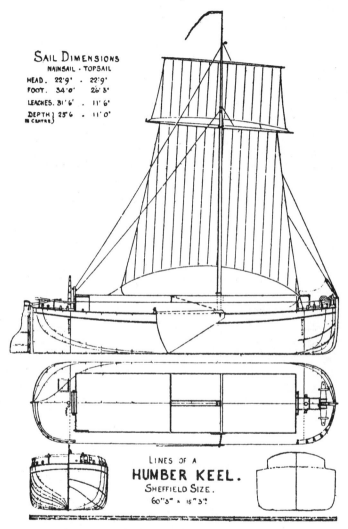

SAIL DIMENSIONS
NAINSAIL · TOPSAIL

| | MAINSAIL | TOPSAIL |
|---|---|---|
| HEAD. | 22'9" | 22'9" |
| FOOT. | 34'0" | 26'3" |
| LEACHES. | 31'6" | 11'6" |
| DEPTH (IN CENTRE) | 25'6" | 11'0" |

LINES OF A
**HUMBER KEEL.**
SHEFFIELD SIZE.
60''3" × 15"3".

FIG. 28 Humber Keel, by the late George F. Holmes
*[By courtesy of the Humber Yawl Club*

geared crab-winches on either quarter. The mast is stepped well into the keel; it is, indeed, very little forward of the midship line, and is fitted in a tabernacle for ease in lowering and raising when passing

bridges. As in the Thames barge, the heel of the mast does not project below the deck. The mast is stayed with a forestay, topmast stay,
a pair of lower shrouds and one topmast shroud each side, with one
shifting backstay and one topmast backstay which can be set up to
either quarter as required. These are all of wire. The shrouds are set
up with lanyards rove through *pear-shaped* dead eyes—an interesting
feature. Although the single squaresail is the oldest rig in the country,
it is noteworthy that every mechanical device known to modern rigging has been employed to make the keel easy to handle by her crew
of two, skipper and boy, and it is really surprising how close to the
wind these craft will sail, and how quickly and easily they can be put
about. Nine geared steel winches are generally fitted, and the running
rigging is of wire. The Humber keelman has nothing to learn from the
Dutchman in this respect, although his anchor is still raised with a
primitive barrel windlass worked with hand-spikes—a survival of
ages long past.

In addition to the windlass, mechanical contrivances include: (1)
The mast rollers, at the fore end of the hatch, which have multi-
plying gear for hoisting and lowering the mast. These are also useful
for warping the vessel. (2) The mainsail and topsail halyard rollers at
the after end of the hatchway. (3) The tack rollers for winding up the
tack chains, at the fore end of the hatch—under the mast rollers, and
placed fore-and-aft at right angles to their work. (4) The sheet rollers
at port and starboard sides of the after end of the hatchway. (5) The
small roller, set perpendicularly under the stern rail, for winding up
the fall of the lee-board purchase.

The running rigging is as follows: the yard is hoisted by halyards
consisting of a single wire tye with a purchase, as used in the seventeenth-century ships, and is kept in to the mast with parrels, having
two rows of trucks.* The braces, with which the yard is trimmed to
the wind and swung around when the keel is tacked, consist of a
single hemp rope, one end being fast to each yard-arm and the bight
led aft near to the helmsman. The head of the sail is stopped to the
yard, and is provided with two deep reefs at the head, being reefed up
to the yard. The sheets and tacks are single wires, rove through sheaves
on the forward and after rails, and led to winches. To make the sail
set flatter on a wind, bowlines are fitted to both leaches of the mainsail, and the weather one leads through a block on the forestay and is
set up from the deck. The sail can be roughly hauled up to the yard
by a buntline led from the foot of the sail up its fore side, though a
cheek-block at the mast-head and down to a position near the helm.

* Wooden balls threaded with thin ropes.

PLATE 38 Vessel discovered under the Bed of the River Rother in 1822

[By courtesy of the Society of Antiquaries

PLATE 39 Norfolk Wherry

[*By courtesy of J. P. Hodge, Esq*

Above the mainsail is set a topsail, a shallow sail set on a yard only slightly shorter than the mainyard. The topsail sheets lead through sheave-holes in the main yard-arms, into cheek-blocks on the after part of the yard near the slings and down to the deck. By releasing the pawls of mainsail and topsail rollers, everything can be lowered instantly if required. Some keels in the 'nineties were said to have carried a third squaresail, a to'gallant-sail, on the same mast. But this was rare, and the sail can only have been a fine-weather one, and possibly rather of the pocket-handkerchief variety, with a short yard at the head. Smaller keels used mainsail only.

With a leading wind the keel rig most decidedly "had its points", as gybing was robbed of its terrors and sudden jars and the sail had quite a lifting tendency, a very desirable point in craft with such terribly hard bow lines. The method of working the sail in tacking was the same as in any square-rigged ship, and wonderfully handy and quick in stays the keels were, as anyone who has watched them will agree.

Amongst the deck furniture, in addition to the quants or "stowers" mentioned below, were two long boat-hooks, any amount of bass warps, a heaving line, a ton or so of chain cable and a water cask with dipper on chocks on the starboard side of the after-deck. In the old days the captain often had his wife and family aboard with him, sailing as his crew; and an order to his wife, who was steering, to "Put your hellum hard ower to watter cask!" was occasionally heard near a dock entrance. In concluding his account in the Humber Yawl Club Year Book, from which these notes were taken, Mr Holmes ended with a tribute to the keelman, whom he knew so well as an amateur yachtsman sailing in those waters.

"Any word about the keel," he wrote, "would be imperfect without some reference to its captain. In a fairly long experience of the class, I have never met with anything but courtesy and ready help from them, and in consequence must own up to a feeling of respect for both the keelman and his keel."

The painting of the keels was very attractive; for although they were tarred below the water-line their topsides and gunwales were varnished bright, and the rails and timber-heads were painted and picked out in gay colours. Failing wind in shallow waters the keel was punted with a quant, as was the Tyne keel or Norfolk craft. But the Humber keelman have a term of their own for the quant used, calling it a "stower" (pronounced "stoer"). It has wide iron jaws on the lower end. Soundings in shallow water are taken with a sounding-pole on which the depths are marked.

10

The dimensions given above must be taken as average figures only, for the size of keels naturally varies to some extent. From evidence given before the Royal Commission on Canals and Waterways in 1906, it is apparent that somewhat smaller keels were in use on some of the lesser waterways; the old wooden keels on the navigation from Hull to Driffield, for example, carried a maximum of 63 tons only; although more modern keels built of iron carried 75 tons. The number of keels was still considerable in 1906, and about 150 keels and similar river craft were then trading up to York alone.

Early records of the Humber keels are conspicuous rather by their absence than by their number. I have been able to trace little mention of them either in the Statutes or in the Rolls of Parliament. But a certain amount of information is contained in various early State papers, and it is clear that they were a distinct class of vessels as early as the fourteenth century. The similarity of the Humber keel to the medieval coaster is remarkable and was first pointed out to me by the late Mr G. S. Laird Clowes, of the Science Museum, South Kensington. In the year 1823 the hull of what was almost certainly a coasting vessel of the Middle Ages was excavated in the old bed of the River Rother in Romney Marsh. Plate 38 shows her as she was laid bare. She was a double-ended craft, flat-bottomed and without any external keel. Bow and stern were round and very full, formed almost alike, the stem and stern-posts nearly vertical and the sides almost straight. She was exceedingly strongly built of oak, still perfectly sound and very hard. The planks were riveted together with iron and caulked with moss—she was clinker-built—and were fastened to the timbers with oak treenails, wedged at both ends. Her topsides were joined above with five principal beams. She had two cabins, under two short decks, one forward, the other aft; and before the after cabin was a space with an arrangement for a tilt or shelter over it, which had been used as a galley for cooking. The middle of the ship was open, but a certain arrangement of stanchions made it obvious that at one time she had had hatches or gratings or some kind of awning over her, though this had since disappeared. She carried a single mast one-third of her length abaft the stem, on which was set a square sail. And she was fitted with a rudder of curious design, apparently worked with ropes.

Her dimensions were the following: length, 63 feet 8 inches; breadth, 15 feet; depth amidships to the top of the beam, 4 feet 2 inches, above which was a bulwark 1 foot 2 inches in height, making a total depth inside of 5 feet 4 inches; allowing for the thickness of hull, about 6 feet. She was ceiled, or lined within, with planks, which would be very necessary in a cargo vessel and is the practice to-day. The finding among her gear of a lead-line for sounding indicates that she was a sea-going vessel, not a mere river craft. One of her boats was found near her, and was 15 feet long, 5 feet in beam, flat-floored, very shallow and caulked with hair.

Now for the sake of comparison turn to page 142, where the dimensions of a modern Humber keel are given, and note how very small are the differences. Compare the shape described above with the vessel in Fig. 28. How very remarkable the similarity! The chief difference lies in the lighter draught of the ancient ship. But then it must be remembered that medieval ships in general had to draw less water than the ships of a later date, owing to the shallowness of many of the havens they frequented, and as late even as the time of the old Muscovite Company their ships drew so little that they were able to cross bars with no more than 5 feet 6 inches of water over them.

The antiquaries of 1823 formed the opinion that this vessel was wrecked in the great storm of 1287, when the town of Winchelsea was overwhelmed and the course of the River Rother changed. One may fairly safely assume that she belonged to the latter part of the thirteenth century. Compare the craft with the Humber keel in the twentieth century. The rigging has been modernised, the topsail has been added; but the square sail and the position of the mast remain the same. Lee-boards were introduced from Holland, probably late in the seventeenth century; but otherwise the Humber keel of the Middle Ages was probably not very different from her modern descendant.

Nor need we stop at the Middle Ages; for if we study the ships, depicted on the Bayeux Tapestry, in which William the Conqueror transported his invading army across the Channel, we find a remarkable resemblance. It must be remembered that most of them were purely transporting vessels, built in a hurry and burnt upon arrival. Most of them were, therefore, cargo ships intended to have maximum carrying capacity for their size. It is noticed at once that the lines are fuller, the ends more rounded, than in the Viking longships. The rig remains the same, with a single mast stepped almost amidships, on which is set a square sail. Some of them have oar-ports along the sides, but most of them have not, and are sailing craft only. This is particularly noticeable in the craft shown with horses aboard. The stem and stern in every ship rise up high, but the gunwales have less sheer than in the longships. They draw very little water, for a man is shown jumping ashore on arrival at the beach, carrying a small anchor. This means that they must have flat or nearly flat bottoms;

and the masts were made to unship, as in at least two of the ships this is being done as soon as the voyage is over.

I have dealt somewhat fully with the construction of these craft to demonstrate how very closely, both in form of hull and in rig, they resemble the Humber keel of yesterday. They are even similar in size, though some of the Norman vessels were larger than others. But rob William's ships of the exaggerated stem and stern-posts, fit them with decks and hatches, hang a rudder over the stern and a pair of lee-boards over the sides and one would have a vessel which might pass tolerably well as a Humber keel. The medieval coaster was undoubtedly developed on lines following closely those of the Conqueror's ships; and it is only one stage further to the Humber keel herself.

Before leaving the Humber keel, one amusing story is worth quoting. Many years ago one of these vessels, the *Mary*, made a voyage to the Thames, and there proved rather a puzzle to the port authorities, to whom the term "keel" meant nothing. The problem was eventually solved by an official who, with more ingenuity than accuracy, entered her in the books as a "one-masted brig"!

Another type of sailing barge which was common on the Humber up to a few years ago was the Humber sloop. She is more conveniently considered here than among other local barges, because she is a direct development of the keel; and, in fact, with minor differences, she is simply a craft with the hull of a keel rigged as a sloop. She has the flat-bottomed round-ended hull, fitted with lee-boards, and with the same form of rudder, big main hatchway, hand-spike windlass, fore-peak in the bows and cabin in the stern. The illustration, Fig. 29, is from the plans prepared by the late Mr George F. Holmes from a typical sloop of the turn of the century, built by Mr W. L. Scarr and owned by Mr John Deheer. It was published in the Humber Yawl Club Year Book for 1903, and is reproduced here by the courtesy of the Club. The information as to rig and other particulars are gratefully acknowledged to the same source.

Generally speaking, the sloops tended to be rather larger than the keels. They traded less up the canals, and were therefore not so limited by the dimensions of the locks through which the keels had to pass. The vessel shown in Fig. 29 has carried as much as 170 tons. The old-time sloops often carried bowsprits, rigged to steeve upwards, as in a Thames barge; and these were in effect practically one-masted, and therefore sloop-rigged, billyboys. In summer, they traded as far south as the Deben. These craft with bowsprits often had high bulwarks all round, instead of the open rails fore and aft of the keel; and sometimes they had two hatchways: a small one forward of the mast and a larger one abaft it. The later sloops were often built of steel.

Like the keel, the sloop was provided with mechanical gear in the form of winches, etc., for doing all the heavier work. The mast rollers, fixed just against the fore headledge, for raising and lowering the

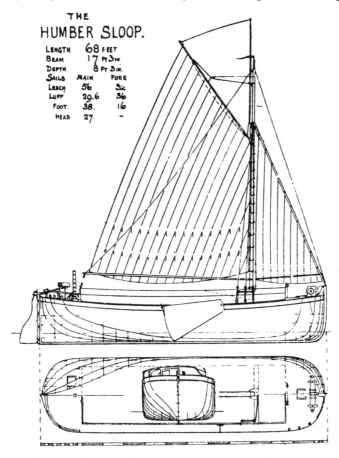

THE
HUMBER SLOOP.

| | MAIN | FORE |
|---|---|---|
| LENGTH | 68 FEET | |
| BEAM | 17 FT 3 IN | |
| DEPTH | 8 FT 3 IN. | |
| SAILS | | |
| LEECH | 56 | 52 |
| LUFF | 29.6 | 36 |
| FOOT | 38. | 16 |
| HEAD | 27 | - |

FIG. 29 Humber Sloop, by the late George F. Holmes
*[By courtesy of the Humber Yawl Club*

mast, were even more powerful than in a keel; for the mast was a much heavier spar. Both throat and peak halyards were taken to rollers fixed abreast of the mast above the coamings; and the topsail halyard was taken to a smaller supplementary roller above the main one. The lee-boards were hoisted with purchases, of which the falls were also taken to rollers fixed vertically on the after-rail.

The crew of a sloop consisted of two men and a boy; although two men or even a man and a boy were sometimes considered sufficient. On the whole, the female element was less frequently met in the sloops than in the keels. Mr Holmes considered this strange, as the accommodation was as good, or better; and those with experience of sailing both seemed to agree that the labour was less in the "flat-rigged" (i.e. the fore-and-aft rigged) craft.

In the early years of this century Mr Holmes had also met some rather interesting examples of miniature sloops at places up river. The smallest was a little craft about 30 feet in length, carrying about 20 tons. She was just like her larger sisters, flush-decked, with a rail aft and a windlass forward. Her owner sailed her single-handed on her "market" trips. Owston Ferry, up the Trent, appeared to be the place with the greatest variety in sloops—scarcely two were alike.

Being perhaps more modern in rig, the sloops trading under sail seem to have survived until recently in slightly larger numbers than the keels. Probably the last firm to own sailing sloops is Messrs James Barraclough & Co. Ltd., of Imperial Chambers, Bowlalley Lane, Hull. Up to the time of writing they had two still trading under sail. These were *The Sprite* and the *Ivie*. But the gear of *The Sprite* was about to be taken out of her to use her as a towing barge; so that, unless any other unknown example is still trading, the *Ivie* must be the last sloop to sail on the Humber.

Captain W. J. King has sent me some further information from Germany; for which I owe him my thanks. He states that the sloops were owned mostly on the Lincolnshire side of the river, being built at one yard at Barton Haven, whose activities go back far into the days of the last century and the Yorkshire Billyboy. In the early years of the twentieth century the sloops had a busy time transporting bricks from the many brickworks on the Lincolnshire side of the river; and as they were also employed for the transport of sand from Paull, and limestone from the Lincolnshire quarries to the cement works at Hull, the building trade was well served by these craft.

As a schoolboy, Captain King served for a month on the sloop *Mafeking* during one holiday. She was then in the limestone trade. They loaded about 80 tons at the quarry jetties on the Lincolnshire side, and with only a few inches of freeboard set sail for the River Hull. On entering that narrow river, sail was stowed, and it was all hands to the dolly winch, to warp her upstream, running away the warping line in the boat, towed astern. He also remembers "drudging" with the anchor on the bottom with a fair tide, as described on page 97. The cargo was worked by captain and mate, using the dolly winch. They averaged the round trip in less than a week. One of the thrills was when, one day, the captain decided to set the spinnaker to make the most of the light fair wind. The long boat-hook or "stower" was used as a spinnaker boom to boom out the foot of the sail, and he and the mate had the honour of setting the sail.

Considering the bluff lines of these craft, he writes, they sailed well; and the captains were very skilful in handling them. Up to the 1914-18 war, a regatta was held every summer, when there was a sloop race over an eight-mile course from off Barton to around Reed's Island, and back. "It was an exciting time awaiting the appearance of the leader round Barton Ness on the way to the finishing point," he writes. "The winner was presented with a silver cup, which was raced for each year."

But the sloops have almost gone; and the waters of the Humber will be the poorer when we can no longer see a fully rigged sloop, as Mr Holmes could describe her, "turning up or down the Humber against a strong breeze, making a fine picture as she crashes through the short seas and flings their crests in spray half-way up her gleaming red sails".

Of the keels of Norfolk and Suffolk, records are very scanty indeed. One can safely assume that the natural waterways of these two counties, spoken of collectively as "the Broads", must have been made use of for the ready transport of passengers and goods from the earliest days of trade in that part of the country. It is quite possible, and indeed probable, that the name and general form of the keel was a survival from the Viking raiders; but what the early keels were like and when the pointed stern gave place to a narrow square or transom stern must be matters for pure conjecture. The earliest mention of the keels as a particular type of vessel that I have been able to trace occurs in 1533, when the order of the various Crafts on the Corpus Christi Day Procession in the city of Norwich was laid down, and eleventh came "the Fishmongers, Fresh-water-Fishers, and Keelmen, with their two Banners; whose Gild is the 9th *Sunday* after *Trinity*". There were in all twenty companies, who wore distinctive liveries, and had their patron saints painted on their banners. At the swearing of a new Mayor, on their Guild Days and at other functions, these paraded through the streets with the Masters of their Crafts before them, bands playing and all a very merry display. These keelmen were the crews of the river barges, then called keels, in which the regular cargo traffic between Norwich and Yarmouth was carried, and in 1543 some of the chief cargoes down to Yarmouth consisted of "divers kinds of Victuals, Leather, Tallow, etc." The other way, the keels carried "Salt, Coals, Corn, etc., and herrings . . . packed in Cades and Barrels".

The name "keel" occurs again in Norfolk in 1561, and in 1669 the keels are mentioned in the Act by which the River Waveney was to be made navigable for barges from Beccles up to Bungay, involving the construction of four locks between Barsham and Bungay. In connection with this navigation, it is worth mentioning that there is reason to believe that at one time there was through-water transit by this route, up a small tributary of the Waveney, passing through the parish of Eye, communicating with the Little Ouse and thence by way of the Great Ouse to the sea at King's Lynn. Anchors and other traces of ancient navigation have been discovered in its bed; and in 1549, during Kett's rebellion, a small pinnace was prepared at Yarmouth to convey twenty men up to Weybread, which is twelve or fourteen miles higher up the river than the limit of the present artificial navigation. It may well have been that this so-called "pinnace" was in fact a Norfolk keel—one of the ordinary cargo-carriers of the district.

Whatever may have been the form of the earliest keels, small vessels used as cargo-carriers, with a transom stern and a square sail set on a mast stepped almost amidships, are seen in prints of Norwich of 1723 and 1741, and of Yarmouth in 1725. What is probably the earliest example of a sharp-sterned or double-ended cargo boat can be seen on a horn cup of 1783 in Norwich Museum. These craft are unmistakably of shallow draught, and quite small. Probably they were also clinker-built and had much the same rather dish-shaped hull as is seen in the wherries of to-day. In 1722, in the reign of George I, an Act for improving the harbour of Great Yarmouth declares that, "The Channel of the River *Yare*, leading from *Great Yarmouth* to *Norwich*, called *Brayden*, and that part lying between the New Mills in *Norwich* and *Hardly Cross* in *Hardly*, and also the Rivers *Waveny* and *Bure*, commonly called the *North River*, are to be depthnd and made more navigable for Boats and Keels. . . ." This is the earliest mention I can find of the traffic on the River Bure. Later, in 1726, in order to raise money for repairs to wharves, gates, roads, etc., the city of Norwich was empowered to erect a boom across the river, with a Customs House, to collect customs from all cargoes carried higher than Thorpe Hall.

During the next hundred years the keel must have had her heyday, for as early as 1830 she was already being spoken of as "very rare". Her place was being taken by the wherry, a craft which differed from her in several particulars, but more especially in being double-ended, with finer lines and setting a fore-and-aft sail instead of the old square sail. This, of course, made her a much handier craft to work up and down the very winding rivers than the keel, which was far more dependent on a fair wind. The last of the keels survived until about 1890, when she was still at work near Norwich. Then, in company with others of her class, long derelict, she was sunk somewhere along the river-bank of the Yare between Whitlingham and Brundall Gardens, to mark and confine the channel. From this position she was partially excavated in 1912 to enable the measurements to be taken from which the model (Plate 39) in the Science Museum was built. Afterwards she was allowed to sink gently back into the rushes and ooze, and so perished the last of the keels.

The dimensions of this particular vessel may be taken as typical of the later keels. Her length over all was 54·5 feet; breadth 14·5 feet; and depth 4·1 feet. She drew, therefore, rather less than 4 feet of water, and would carry from 30 to 32 tons. She was clinker-built and had a short transom stern, but the quarters were rounded off so much that the appearance was very like an ordinary sharp wherry stern (see next chapter) cut off just short of the stern-post. She had a well-rounded section, perhaps rather fuller than the ordinary wherry, and the bow had rather more rake. She was quite open amidships, without hatches, and had a small cabin or cuddy forward. The mast was stepped amidships in a very heavy case called the tabernacle, built into the keelson, but unsupported by any deck-beams. On this was set a single primitive squaresail.

# CHAPTER X

# Other Local Barges

As was shown in the last chapter, the keels of Norfolk are no more; and to-day, of all the many black-sailed cargo wherries which were once so familiar to those who spent their holidays sailing or motor-boating on the Broads, not one remains still trading under sail, if we except the now famous *Albion*, subsidised and run by that excellent organisation The Norfolk Wherry Trust. One can hardly regard as typical the four or five sailing pleasure wherries surviving at the time of writing, even though at least two have no auxiliary motors.

Yet the Broadland wherry was a craft possessing certain unique features both of hull and rig which made her an object of particular interest in the family of sailing barges. With her beautiful, delicate hull, whose lines remind one of some lovely yacht rather than of a humble cargo-carrier, she has a history quite distinct from that of her obsolete sister, the keel. It may at first strike one as surprising that these two craft, so alike in many ways, yet so different in others, should have been found in the same waters engaged in the same work. Yet the explanation, I think, lies in the fact that this was not always so; and I believe that originally the keel, which was the more ancient craft, carried cargoes, while the wherry, of finer and faster lines, carried passengers. In later years, with the improvement of roads, the introduction of steam and the development of railways, this work was taken from her, and she was left to compete with, and ultimately to supplant, the keel as a cargo-carrier.

There is a considerable amount of evidence in support of this view. As far as I can find, the wherry in Norfolk is first mentioned in July 1625. The plague had started in Yarmouth at that time, and the Mayor of Norwich "wrote to the *Bailiffs* of *Yarmouth* desiring them to order the *Wherry-men* to carry no Persons dwelling in any infected Places in their Town, to the City". A later mention, occurring in 1812, records that "nearly twenty persons, in their passage for Norwich from Yarmouth in a wherry were drowned in Braydon". There is no evidence to set against this that I have been able to discover, of any early mention of wherries or wherrymen *in connection with the carrying of cargoes*. This view is, moreover, borne out by the form of the vessels themselves, and is rather suggested by the actual name. For the shape of the wherry is very like that of the old Graves-end tilt-boats, which had much in common, as far as the shape of their hulls was concerned, with the wherries of the Thames water-men, once the most popular form of passenger transport on the river. The Gravesend tilt-boats had, moreover, the fore-and-aft mainsail, which, although differently rigged, is found in the Broad-land wherry. Probably, in the late seventeenth century, this was a spritsail, for Fortree, in the MS. already referred to, describes the wherry sail as being a spritsail with a head cut square and less peaked-up than the ordinary hoy's spritsail. This fore-and-aft sail would be very necessary for the carriage of passengers in the winding rivers, where a fair wind could not always be commanded and where the banks were often too marshy for towage. Goods might wait more easily than persons, and the inborn conservatism of the keelmen may have caused them to retain the squaresail in their craft long after the more efficient wherry sail had appeared. The tilt-boat had, as its name implies, an awning to cover the passengers, which was later almost a raised deck with open sides beneath. What is more likely than that the Norfolk passenger wherry should be similarly equipped and that when adapted to cargo-carrying, this deck should be lowered and divided to form hatch-covers, which the wherry had and still has, but the keel apparently never?

The hull of the wherry has probably changed but little, except for a possible increase in size, from the early passenger-carrier of the eighteenth century; and the modern wherry is well illustrated by the photograph (Plate 39) and by the detailed plans (Figs. 30a and 30b) of the wherry *Gleaner* measured up by the late Mr W. M. Blake and published in the "Yachting Monthly," Vol. LIV. I am indebted to the Editor and to the Director of the Science Museum (from whom copies can be obtained) for permission to publish them here. She is a shallow, almost dish-shaped craft, clinker-built, with well-curved floors, fine lines, sharp at bow and stern and allowing plenty of "flare" to the bow, which is much fuller on deck than below the water. She has a considerable amount of sheer, rising in an even sweep fore and aft. Forward is a short deck, on to which is built the heavy tabernacle for the heel of the mast, extending to the keelson. A long open hatch, without any cross-beams, extends from abaft the mast to the forward end of the little raised cabin in the stern, and a narrow waterway called a "quant-walk" is left either side. Cambered hatches cover the hold, and the capacity of the keel can be increased by the addition of boards called "shifting right-ups", which add to

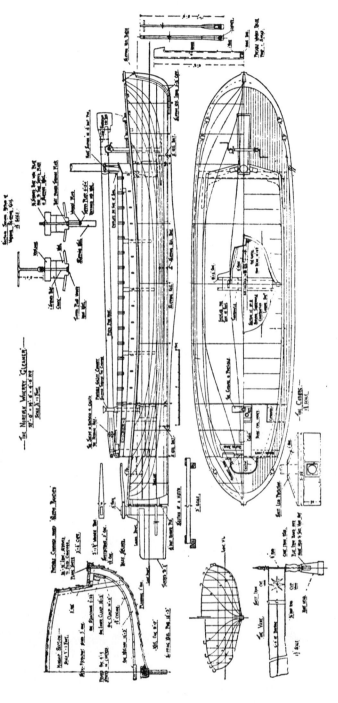

**GENERAL PLANS OF NORFOLK WHERRY GLEANER**

*LOA 57 ft. Beam 14 ft. Moulded depth 4 ft. Details of the "slipping keel" are shown, with method of fixing, as described in the article.*

FIG. 30a

[By courtesy of the Editor of the "Yachting Monthly"]

the height of the coaming, but can be readily unshipped for unloading.

According to Mr Bunn of Messrs Jewson & Sons, former wherry
owners, a typical wherry had a length of 45 to 50 feet, beam of 16
feet and loaded draught of 4 to 5 feet. The mast was 45 feet in length,
the heel being weighted with 2 or 3 cwt. of lead. A 30-foot gaff supported the head of a sail with an area of 500 square feet. The hold was

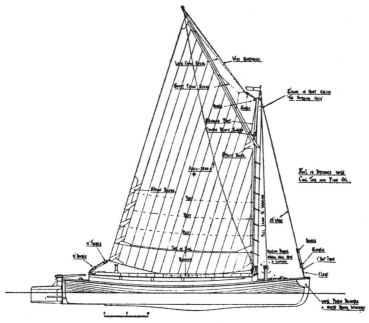

*The sail plan of Norfolk Wherry Gleaner*

FIG. 30b

*[By courtesy of the Editor of the "Yachting Monthly"*

covered by twelve wooden overlapping hatches, extending from mast
to cuddy. The "quant" (a kind of glorified punt-pole, with a spiked
foot like a halbert) was 24 feet long. In the Science Museum at South
Kensington is an excellent fully rigged model of a wherry. The
original, from which the model was constructed, was a large wherry,
55 feet long, 16·5 feet in beam and 3·3 feet deep. Her burden was 32
tons, by wherry-builder's measurement.

In order to improve their sailing qualities, wherries were provided with a false keel, which varied a little in depth in different vessels. In wherries working on the Waveney, this false keel could be unbolted, and was left upon the bank above Beccles by craft going through the locks and higher up the river. Neglecting this false keel, the average draught of a fully-laden wherry was about 4·0 feet.

Mr G. R. Clark, the Hon. Secretary of the newly formed Norfolk Wherry Trust (which proposes to build a new wherry and to preserve one or more of these typical Norfolk sailing vessels in commission as traders, with professional skippers and volunteer amateur crews), tells me that the *Gleaner*, from which Mr Blake prepared his plans, was not quite typical, being rather too "skimpy". She is, however, quite adequate to show the general characteristics of the type. She was built in 1894 at Coltishall by Allen & Hunter—who built the last wherry, the *Ella*, in 1912—for Messrs Woods, Sadd & Moore. Her pitch-pine mast was made by Ellets of Great Yarmouth. When launched, her name was *Orion*, but was changed to *Gleaner* when she was bought by her present owner-captain, Jack Gedge, one of a long line of master wherrymen, under whom she is still trading, but with her mast removed and an engine installed. She had a burden of about 28 tons; that is, she was essentially a North River (Bure) craft. In 1931 she was struck by lightning at Acle. There have been two other wherries named *Gleaner*, which has always been a popular name for these craft.

The rigging of the wherry was peculiar, and was in many respects unique among British vessels. The mast, a very heavy spar, was stepped in the tabernacle well forward and pivoted above the level of the deck. The heel extended right down to the keelson and was weighted with lead, so that the mast almost balanced and could be raised and lowered with very little effort. The heel swung up through a long opening hatch in the fore deck. The only standing rigging consisted of a wire forestay, with a stay-fall tackle rove through two sheaveless blocks and made fast to a cleat lashed to the strop of the lower block. On this mast was set a single fore-and-aft mainsail, cut rather square at the head, and with a very long gaff.

To his sail plan of the *Gleaner* (Fig. 30b), Mr W. M. Blake added many informative notes. The dimensions of the sail, which had an area of 1,200 square feet, were as it was made by Mr Robert Pike of Great Yarmouth, in 1903. The material was Coker half bleached double No. 1 canvas, with 1¼-inch seams. It was dressed with coal tar and fish oil, which tanned it almost black.

The "bonnet" was set in light weather. It was 4 feet deep, and was laced to the foot of the sail with fifty-one latchets through fifty-one holes. It could be removed when carrying a stack or deck cargo. When the main sheet was eased off a little the gaff would "leer off", as the wherrymen would say, lifting the foot of the sail clear of the hatches and so giving an uninterrupted view ahead.

The sail was hoisted by a single rope halyard, which was led in such an ingenious way that the same halyard hoisted simultaneously both the throat and the peak of the sail. It led up the mast from forward, through a sheave in the mast called the "herring hole", down, through a block at the jaws of the gaff, up to a double block at the mast-head, down to a single block on a chain bridle or sling joining two shorter bridles supporting the gaff evenly along its outer length, up to the mast-head double block again and down to the gaff near the jaws, or sometimes to some point between the inner bridle and the jaws, where it was made fast. The fall or hauling part was led to a winch on the fore side of the tabernacle, which could be swung out of the way when the mast was lowered. Hoisting sail was therefore merely a matter of turning a handle. On lowering away, when the halyard was let go, the peak dropped first until the gaff was horizontal, and so it came down. The end of the gaff was controlled when lowering by a gaff-line led to some point near the helmsman. The main sheet was rove through two large blocks, the lower working on a short horse, and to a cleat on this block the end was made fast. The fore-end of the gaff was kept into the mast by parrels, which could be readily cast adrift, so that the gaff might be moved aside out of the way when the mast was to be lowered. The forward edge, or luff of the sail, was attached to the mast with sliding hoops or parrels.

In the absence of wind or when the wind was hopelessly ahead, the wherries were poled along with long poles called "quants". The lower ends of these were provided with wooden prongs to prevent their sinking into the ooze. The upper had large wooden buttons which fitted into the shoulders of the men using them, who would walk slowly along the side decks pushing the wherry forward. But when there was any wind at all, the wherry was able in narrow waters to sail almost into its very eye by reason of the shape of her bow and the flatness with which the sail could be sheeted home. An ordinary sailing craft in a narrow river hugs the weather bank as far as possible. Not so the wherry, for she would skim along as close to the lee bank as she could; and by reason of the almost hollow flare of her bow, a great wedge of water was compressed between her and the bank, which forced her up to windward and checked and prevented her tendency to make leeway. If necessary she could be helped along and kept off with the quant. The normal crew of a wherry was two men. Below the deck-level the hull of a wherry was tarred, except for two quadrants of white on each bow, which are said by some to have been derived from the "eyes" of the ancient Egyptian craft and from the Chinese boats of all time. The fore end of the main hatch and the cabin-top were always gaily painted, as was the slender, tapering mast-head, which was surmounted by a vane and streamer. The metal part of the vane was nearly always cut out in the shape of a girl in the national costume of Wales, including the hat. This somewhat surprising feature is explained by the fact that such a device was worn many years ago by a very fast wherry called the *Jenny Morgan*, which was so successful in beating all her rivals that the other wherries adopted the same design.

At one time wherry races for trading wherries were featured at regattas; but at Barton Broad Regatta, in 1937, there were only three starters; and, so far as I am aware, there has been no racing for commercial craft since that date. This race was won by the *Cornucopia*; the other competitors were *Hilda* and *Despatch*. It is interesting to note that the wherries raced with the bonnet laced on to their mainsails, to increase the area. A photograph showing the winner leaving, flying her winning flag and with the bonnet laced on, was published in Vol. IX of "Ships & Ship Models" in 1939.

Norfolk wherries varied in size from 12 to 83 tons. A few iron wherries were built from time to time. The largest wherry ever built, I believe, was the *Wonder* of Norwich. She was 65 feet long by 19 feet beam, drew 3 feet when empty and nearly 7 feet with a full load of 83 tons.

Between the Humber and the Broads, in the Fenland waterways of Cambridgeshire, Huntingdonshire and Lincolnshire, a type of fenland barge was found, not unlike a Humber keel, but smaller. Although latterly towed only by horses or a primitive steam tug, they used at one time to carry a squaresail when the wind was fair. Flat-bottomed, without lee-boards, they could carry about 20 to 25 tons on an average length of 42 feet. The last to carry a sail was the *Pride of the Lark*, and twenty years ago she still had the original mast, though used then only for towing; she was said to be over 100 years old at that time. Her sail was reputed to be the largest ever carried in these fenland barges.

Turning next to the West of England, one finds on the River Severn a now almost obsolete type of sailing barges of great antiquity, known as "trows". Their long and interesting history would fill a large volume; but an excellent and fully detailed account of them, by

PLATE 40  Severn Trow *Ark* and Ketch *Fanny Jane*

[*By courtesy of the Nautical Photo Agency*

PLATE 41  Mersey Flat

[*By courtesy of the Nautical Photo Agency*

PLATE 42 Square-sail Barge on River Teign

PLATE 43 Spritsail Barge on the Sussex Ouse

Mr Grahame E. Farr, was published in the " Mariner's Mirror " for April 1946 (Vol. XXXII, No. 2), which is outstanding as a model of what such a study should be. To accompany the article, which was profusely illustrated, the lines of the trow *Norah*, built in 1868, were taken off and complete plans drawn out by Mr Edward Bowness, and by his permission and the courtesy of Mr Farr and the Editor of the " Mariner's Mirror ", I am able to reproduce these plans here. I am also much indebted to an earlier article by Mr Basil Greenhill, which appeared in the " Mariner's Mirror " for July 1940 (Vol. XXVI, No. 3); and to an admirable paper on "The River Trade of Montgomeryshire and its Borders" by Mr A. Stanley Davies, reprinted from the "Collections Historical and Archeological relating to Montgomeryshire and its Borders" (Welshpool, 1933), issued by the Powys-land Club. Mr C. P. Hinman, of the Severn and Canal Carrying Co. Ltd., was also kind enough to collect and supply copious notes from trow builders, captains and his own company's records.

Unfortunately, space forbids more than the briefest summary of the history of the trow (Plate 40), one of the oldest and most interesting trading craft of Britain. The word, which in the Severn valley is generally pronounced to rhyme with "crow", seems to have been derived from the Anglo-Saxon word "trog", meaning a drinking trough or other hollow vessel; and occasionally, some form of dugout canoe or small boat. The latest "open-moulded trow", which was straight-sided and open from gunwale to gunwale, has to this day the suggestion of a "trough". The word "trow" is found as early as 1411 in the Rolls of Parliament; and for many years after there are constant references in those early records to a type of barge known by that name, which traded all up and down the Severn. In 1429, in the reign of Henry VI, they were carrying wheat, malt and flour by river and sea to Bristol.

It is impossible to divorce the history of the trow from the history of the river; and it is known that the Severn was navigated for some time before the Anglo-Saxon invasion. It is also important to recall that in A.D. 890 the Viking raiders sailed up the Severn as far as Worcester; and reasonable to suppose that they may have left wrecked craft behind them, which served to some extent as a model for the local inhabitants to study. There is every reason to believe that the early trows followed very much the same double-ended Viking model as the Humber keels; and until the nineteenth century they carried a very similar squaresail rig. Be that as it may, after about the middle of the seventeenth century a very distinctive form of vertical deep transom stern, shaped like a broad letter D, with the flat side

11

above, began to appear; and gradually this supplanted the round stern, and became typical of all the later trows. Trows illustrated in Nash's " History of Worcester " 1781, show this D-shaped stern very distinctly; in one of them, what appear to be two stern windows are seen within the D; and this is by no means impossible, as such windows were seen in the rather similar sterns of the German river barges, the *Evers*, of the lower Elbe in the nineteenth century. Nash's trows carry a single mast, with a fidded topmast, stepped a little forward of amidships, with both lower and topmast shrouds "rattled down". A deep squaresail and shallower square topsail are set, and there is a short bowsprit, but no sign of any headsails. A purchase from the lower-mast head to the stem was fitted for raising and lowering the mast when bridges had to be negotiated.

Later trows, early in the nineteenth century, appear in contemporary pictures with the addition of a mizzen mast. On this is sometimes set a mizzen with a standing gaff, to which the sail is brailed up like the mizzen of a mule-rigged Thames barge; and sometimes the mizzen takes the form of a lateen sail. In 1837 appears the first picture of a trow with headsails—staysail and jib being shown. Two ketch-rigged trows are seen in the picture; one has a short mainmast with a single square sail; the other a mainmast and topmast with two yards. Both have a lateen yard on the mizzen, but with the sail laced to the mast, and the fore-end of the yard left bare.

During the 1840's and 1850's practically all the trows were converted to fore-and-aft rig as ketches, cutters or sloops. All single-masted types were locally classed loosely as "smack-rigged". A few small trows were still trading under the old squaresail rig well into the seventies, however; among them the *Fame*, 27 tons; *Paul Pry*, 26 tons; and *William*, 22 tons, built at Ironbridge in 1843, and not to be confused with the long-lived and famous *William*, built at the Bower Yard, Shrewsbury, in 1809 and still trading up to 1939. There were also small square-sailed barges trading on the Avon to a later date.

Mr Edward Bowness' plans of the *Norah* (Figs. 31 a, b and c), and the photograph (Plate 40) of the appropriately named *Ark*, 55 tons, built at Framilode in 1871, give a very clear idea of what the "open-moulded" trow was like, She was decked only at bow and stern. Under the fore deck was the foc's'le, with its accommodation for the crew, the master occupying the cabin aft. But from the after side of the foc's'le bulkhead to the foreside of the cabin bulkhead the hull was completely open, crossed only by thwartship beams—very strongly reinforced in the way of the mast—with no side decks. The decks in bow and stern were protected by high bulwarks; but these

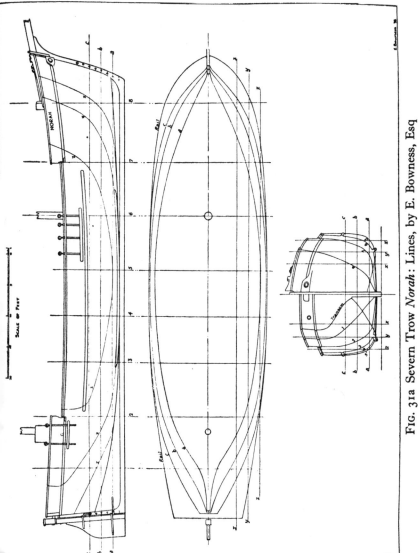

FIG. 31a Severn Trow *Norah*: Lines, by E. Bowness, Esq

were cut short off at the ends, and along the sides of the open hold was an arrangement of stanchions with a rail on top, to support the canvas side-cloths, by which the effective freeboard was increased when at sea.

Notice that, in section, the trow was not like a Thames barge; for although in the true original trow the bottom was flat, with no

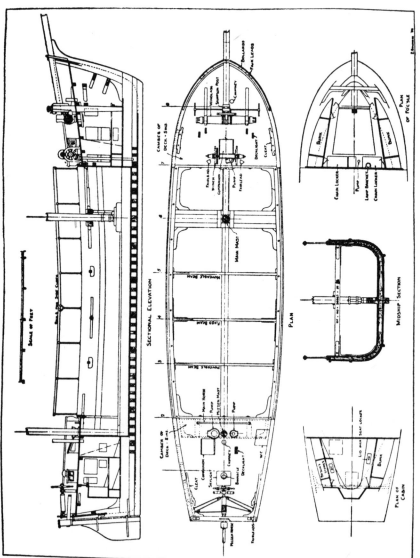

Fig. 31b Severn Trow *Norah*: Construction, by E. Bowness, Esq

external keel, she had a rounded bilge instead of a square chine. Also, she carried no lee-boards; instead, she had a removable false keel, without which it was quite impossible to get her to windward. The arrangement was rather like that sometimes used for the Norfolk wherries, already described. Each vessel was supplied with a keel plank 28 feet long, 2 feet wide and 3 inches thick. This plank was fitted at its upper edge with two pairs of brackets near the ends. To the outer ends of these brackets were fixed chains. The plank was dropped over the side and the chains on that side were made fast on deck at the predetermined correct length. The other chains were passed round the vessel's stern (to avoid the trouble of passing round the bowsprit and bow) and were hauled up on the other side of the vessel until the plank was properly placed under her bottom. Owing to their light draught, the trows nearly always lay wind-rode, and

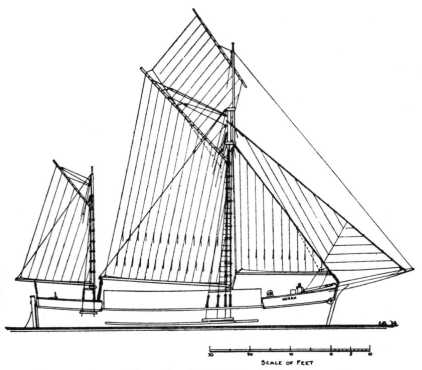

SCALE OF FEET

FIG. 31c Severn Trow *Norah*: Sail Plan, by E. Bowness, Esq

[*By courtesy of the Society for Nautical Research*

therefore it was usually an easy matter to put the plank over on the leeward side, so that the tide helped to push it under to its proper place.

When, for various economic reasons, the trowmen were driven to forsake the upper Severn for the lower, and more estuary trading was done, it became the fashion to add side decks and build high hatch-coamings to the open-moulded trows, to make them more sea-worthy. These altered craft were known by special names. In the

"box trow" the hatch-coamings were built up all round and waterways made at each side of the hatch—some at deck level, others at
rail level. The bulwarks were built up in a continuous line from stem
to stern, sometimes with a removable section to facilitate loading.
Either proper hatch covers or a tarpaulin over a central rail covered
the cargo. A "half box trow" had the bulwarks built up and the hatch-
coamings built up and out at each end of the hold, to join them. There
were no side decks or waterways. As there were no hatch covers, a
form of side-cloth was usually retained, with a tarpaulin on a rail over
the hold.

Ten trows were built of iron between 1843 and 1876 for Messrs
Benjamin Danks & Sons of Stourport, the predecessors of the Severn
& Canal Carrying Co., of which four were open-moulded at first, but
afterwards "boxed", the others being box trows to begin with. These
craft were sufficiently distinctive to be known as "Danks' trows".

The longevity of the trows has already been mentioned in referring
to the *William* of 1809, but she is by no means alone in that respect.
She was typical of the upper Severn trows of the early nineteenth
century, and her dimensions were 74·5 feet in length, 16·7 feet beam,
6 feet depth, her tonnage being 56·7 gross and 50·3 net. Rigged as a
ketch at the end of her career, she must have carried the old square
rig in her youth. When she was wrecked in 1939 she was the oldest
trading vessel in the country.

The last open-moulded trow to trade under sail alone was the
*Alma*, a ketch of 58 gross and 41 net tons, built at Gloucester in 1854,
and rebuilt in 1916. She was in the coal trade in her last years, trading
under sail well into the Second World War. In 1943 she was in Bristol
Docks, with her gear taken out, and used for lightering; where she
now remains, in good condition, used as a barge. In February 1949
she was up for sale by her owners, at that time Messrs Alfred J.
Smith & Co. Ltd., of Bristol; and is now used as a towing barge on
the coal run from Lydney to Bristol.

*Palace*, of Bridgwater, a ketch-rigged trow of 43 tons net, built at
Brimscombe, Gloucester, in 1827, was also trading in stone from the
quarries near Tintern almost up to the war. Another of the last trows
to survive as a rigged vessel, the *Hannah*, is a flush-decked trow,
trading up to 1949 as an auxiliary ketch, and carrying grain from
Avonmouth to Gloucester; but being decked she is not quite typical
of the older form of trows. *Safety*, another flush-decked trow, was
still trading under motor in 1949, with two paraffin engines to drive
her on the coal run from Lydney to Bristol, at the highly respectable
age of 111 years. *Olive Annie* carried her masts and sails until the

Second World War, but was then condemned, and now lies a hulk on the Torridge.

Trows still "going strong" as towed barges include *Spry*, *Victory*, *Higre* and *Wasp*, all, like *Hannah*, carrying grain from Avonmouth to Gloucester; *J. & A.R.*, recently taken off this run, but still afloat in Gloucester Docks; *Ada*, in use up and down the Avon; and *Water Witch*, *Edith* and *Yarra* all, like *Safety*, on the coal run from Lydney to Bristol; *Edith* and *Yarra* now being motor trows.

A fuller history of the trows than is possible here will appear in Mr Basil Greenhill's book "The Merchant Schooners," shortly to be published by Percival Marshall & Co.; to which reference will be made, in addition to the authorities cited above.

The next type of local sailing barges to be described is the Mersey or Weaver Flat. The photograph (Plate 41) shows one of the more recent of these craft under way in the Mersey, and represents a vessel common about sixty or seventy years ago. She is a flat-bottomed craft, although she has a hard, rounded bilge and is not sharp-edged or "chine"-built. She is double-ended, and bow and stern are almost alike, although these craft were somewhat finer aft. Stem and stern-posts both rake slightly, a feature which is noticeable in many early pictures of these barges. The general appearance of a typical flat can be seen from the photograph. The following points should especially be noticed. The mast is stepped rather more than a quarter of the overall length abaft the stem, and is fitted in a tabernacle and made to lower. It is supported by a pair of shrouds and a topmast shroud each side, and a forestay with a powerful tackle for lowering, brought down to the stem-head. The flat is fully decked, and before the mast is a short fore-hatch, with the windlass just the fore side of it. A small square hatch in the deck abaft the stem-head leads to the little forepeak, bulkheaded off from the hold. The main hatch extends from the after side of the mast to within a few feet of the stern. Under the after-deck is a small cabin. Both in the bows and round the stern the timber-heads have been brought up above the deck level, as in the Humber keel, but in the flat they are not surmounted by any rail, and are left as mere uprights to serve as bollards for securing warps, etc. A large rudder, with the outer end of the blade curved up in rather a pretty line, is fitted, and steering is by means of a long wooden tiller. It should be noticed that she carries no lee-boards, and must have made much leeway when light. She is rigged fore-and-aft, her sails rather prettily cut and well balanced. The foresail is set on hanks running on the forestay, and the sheet is arranged like a Thames barge's, being made fast to an iron traveller traversing on an

iron horse crossing the deck forward of the mast. The mainsail is cut
with a generously high peak; the head is laced to a gaff and hoisted
with peak and throat halyards in the normal way. The foot of the sail
is extended by a long boom, the end coming just over the stern, but is
not laced. The main sheet reeves through double-blocks, the lower
being attached to the after end of the main hatch. A topping-lift to
take the weight of the boom and a gaff-line to control the peak when
the sail is lowered complete the running rigging. The mainsail is provided with three rows of reef points. On the hatch-cover lie a pair of
long oars or sweeps by which some forward motion may be induced in
calms. The normal crew of such a vessel was two hands.

The flats were very well-built craft, all the timbers and the bow
planking being of English oak. The four bilge planks, 4 inches thick,
were of rock elm; the bottom planking of softwood; and the mid-
ships planking of oak or of pitch-pine. Decks were of pitch-pine. An
admirable account of them was prepared for the Liverpool Museums
Catalogue, before the Second World War, by Dr Douglas A. Allan,
then in charge of the Museums, and now Director of the Royal Scottish Museum at Edinburgh; and I am greatly indebted to him for
much of the following information.

The history of the Mersey flats is comparatively short, for until the
year 1720 the Rivers Mersey, Irwell and Weaver, on which these
craft used to ply, were not navigable except in the lower reaches. But
in that year schemes were set on foot to make the Mersey and Irwell
navigable as far as Manchester, for the benefit of the cotton manufacturers of Lancashire, and the Weaver as far as Winsford Bridge, a
distance of twenty miles, for the benefit of the salt mines of Cheshire.
The improvement was effected by the usual methods of locks and
weirs, etc., and from that date a considerable barge traffic arose and
grew within the rivers draining into the Mersey estuary. The craft
used at first were small, flat-bottomed, squaresail barges, but the
lines of the hull differed but little, if at all, from the flat in the photograph. The same rounded bows and sterns, flat build and extended
timber-heads are most noticeable in pictures of the middle of the
eighteenth century. In the higher reaches, when the wind did not
serve or was too light, the flats were towed by gangs of men upon the
bank, and horses were not used for this work until the opening of the
first of the Duke of Bridgwater's Canals in 1761, when the river
bargemen copied the canal practice.

That the barges were then quite small is indicated by the often-
quoted fact that when the new, and at that time "engineering
wonder", aqueduct bridge of Barton was built in 1760–61, although

the centre arch was only 68 feet wide and 39½ feet high, the largest barges navigating the River Irwell below were able to sail through it with masts and sails standing. The flats at that time carried a single square sail of the most primitive type, on a short mast stepped not far forward of the midship section. But early in the nineteenth century the squaresail was displaced by the spritsail, and a picture of the entrance to the old dock at Liverpool in 1836 shows this very clearly. A number of typical sharp-sterned Mersey flats are entering the dock with sail set. They are rigged exactly like the early Thames spritsail barge shown in Plate 4. When the gaff mainsail was adopted can only be conjectured; but I am inclined to believe that it was contemporary with the introduction of the spritsail, as probably happened on the London River. In any event, the squaresail survived for some years after the spritsail was introduced, for another published view of Liverpool of the same date (1836) shows both squaresail and spritsail flats in the same picture. These early flats probably carried from 70 to 80 tons. The later ones were much larger, and carried 200 tons and even more.

With the development of the carrying trade the flats were built to carry the maximum possible cargo within the limits of the dimensions enforced by the locks through which they had to pass. In the Museum at Liverpool was a fine model of a flat with a square stern, the *Elizabeth*, built at Dobson's Yard, Wharton, in 1827; 62 feet in length, with a beam of 17 feet and a depth of 6 feet, she had a tonnage of 62. She was rigged almost exactly like the flat shown under way in Plate 41. In hull, she had a snub, rounded bow, the stem slightly curved towards her 8-inch central keel. Her bottom was flat, with a hard round bilge. The early Weaver flats had square sterns, partly to secure the maximum hold space permitted by the length of the locks, and partly to obtain a longer bilge and so to make them stiffer under sail. Apart from the shape of the stern, however, the *Elizabeth* and other flats of her type were fitted and rigged almost exactly like the later sharp-sterned flats. After changing hands in 1861 and again in 1877, she disappeared from the records in 1886, probably becoming a coal hulk.

Another model in the same Museum is the *Avon*, a sharp-sterned Weaver flat 57 feet in length, 15 feet in breadth, with a registered tonnage of 76 tons net, built at Winsford in 1868. She had the sharp stern which became the general practice from about 1860 onwards, when better lines were permitted by the increased length of the reconstructed locks. The *Avon* model was made by a Liverpool dock-gateman in 1880, and is shown flying the pennant of Messrs Worsley,

Battersby, Liverpool. In 1897 she was sold to W. F. Price of Liverpool, and in 1897 to the Rea Transport Co. Ltd., Liverpool and London. Finally, their successors, Messrs Rea Ltd., Liverpool, took over the business and the *Avon* was used to carry coal from various points in the Liverpool Dock System alongside Cunard, White Star and other liners. A common employment of the flats was for coaling liners in days before oil fuel. She was broken up on Tranmere Beach in September 1931 and sold for firewood.

Yet another model in the Liverpool Museum was of the "jigger-flat" *Pilot*. She was built by Isaac Pimblott at Northwich in 1894 for the "Pilot Flat Co. Ltd.", Liverpool. With a length of 78·9 feet, beam of 21·1 feet and depth of 8·6 feet, and a gross tonnage of 103 tons, she was the largest flat ever built at Northwich. She was typical of the larger flats, which were "jigger-rigged", having the mainmast stepped about one-third of her length abaft the stem and her small jigger-mast about one-sixth of that distance from the stern-post. On her jigger-mast she set a gaff mizzen which was a miniature edition of her mainsail. The jigger-flats carried topsails, but had no bowsprits. They also set a little jib-topsail, which was a very pretty sail.

Some of the jigger-flats were employed in the local coasting trade. Before the 1914–18 war, *Pilot* was trading between Fleetwood, the Menai Straits and Anglesey ports. During the war she was unrigged and employed as a lighter. In 1925 she was fitted with an auxiliary engine and was trading between Point of Ayr and Bramborough; and was afterwards carrying coal and fertilisers along the Welsh coast as far as Bardsey Island, Port Dinlleyn, etc., returning with macadam and slates from the Rivals Quarries and Port Dinorwic. Captain W. Beswick, now Master of a motor barge in the sand trade, served his time in the flats; and he has kindly sent me information of the trading work of the jigger-flats in the old days. They were mostly used for the coasting trade from Liverpool to all the North Wales ports, such as Mostyn, Penmanmawr, Bangor, Menai, Beaumaris and through the Menai Straits to Caernarvon, and round the Isle of Anglesey. This trade was brought to an end by the 1914–18 war, when all the flats were ordered to Liverpool, and it has never been resumed. The majority of these flats were owned by the Liverpool Lighterage Co., and one feature of these craft was that many of their names ended in the word "Star", such as *Guiding Star*, *Bright Star*, *Polar Star*, etc. A few of them are still going strong as dumb barges, which have to be towed; but they only work in the Mersey, to Birkenhead, Bramborough, Warrington and Manchester.

The Union Alkali Company at one time had a fleet of twenty-two sailing flats, of which four were jigger flats, trading to the Fleetwood works of that company. These were the *Winifred, E. K. Muspratt, Santa Rosa* and *Eustace Carey*. When the I.C.I. Company was formed, they broke up all but six of the flats they took over, and these they unrigged and made into towing lighters for carrying chemicals from Western Point. One of these, *E. K. Muspratt*, had an engine installed, and is unique in that respect. She is still trading. The jigger-flat *Herbert*, built at Winsford, was sunk at Ellesmere Port with a cargo of cement, but raised, and purchased by Messrs Abels & Sons, who took out her mizzen and employed her in the sand trade. Latterly, she has had her mast taken out and, turned into a barge to carry general cargo, has been renamed *Keskadale*. She has the distinction of being the last flat to work under sail alone.

The river traffic up to Manchester was badly affected by the opening of the Duke of Bridgwater's Canal to Runcorn, which provided a quicker and cheaper route; and in later years first the railways and then the Manchester Ship Canal almost destroyed the traffic on the river. At the present time none of the flats is left still trading under sail. The number in 1931 was said to be about twenty, which was perhaps two per cent. only of those in existence a comparatively short time before. Most of them had even then had the masts taken out on account of the difficulty of getting under the mooring ropes of vessels lying in dock. It was found that much time was lost in unrigging and re-rigging the gear, and the hulls of the flats are now towed by steam tugs instead of using their sails. No less than 189 flats were still in existence in 1931, but of these nearly all were mere dumb lighters. The longevity of the Mersey and Weaver flat is amazing; for of those 189 vessels, 41 were built before 1860, 11 before 1850, 2 before 1840 and the oldest, the *Fletcher*, was built at Northwich, Cheshire, in 1826. The few sailing flats left then were working mostly in the Mersey estuary, and two or three were trading from Widnes to Liverpool. They carried chemicals, salt, coal and sand. To-day only about 27 flats remain, working as dumb barges; of which 21 are owned by the Liverpool Lighterage Co. Ltd. Mr W. Hallwood, the company's Traffic Manager, who was brought up in the flats and has been with this firm since 1896, supplied me with much helpful information. He built a most attractive model of one of the jigger-flats for the company.

In addition to the various main distinctive types of sailing barges found in this country, there were also a number of small local barge types which were not without interest, although comparatively few barges of each kind existed. Among these were the sailing barges working on the River Teign, in Devon, and the Stover and Hackney Canals which connect it. A photograph of one of these picturesque craft appears in Plate 42. This was taken some years ago by Mr J. Knowles of Teignmouth, who also kindly sent me particulars of the barges. They all carried the single primitive square sail as seen in the photograph, and thus shared with the Humber keel the distinction of retaining the old Viking sail right into the twentieth century. The barges were about 50 feet long, 14 feet beam and 5 feet deep. They had flat bottoms, round bows, flat transom sterns and were built of wood. There were sixteen of them in service in 1931; but the sails were not often used, motor tugs being more usually employed to tow them. Their work consisted in bringing down from the head of the river potter's or china clay, of which a considerable quantity was exported, and in taking up coal and other goods to Newton Abbot. It is perhaps worth mentioning that when London Bridge was rebuilt with granite from Haytor, Dartmoor, in order to facilitate the shipping of the granite, in 1821, a quay was built at Teignmouth; and it was from this quay that the granite was shipped to London, after having been brought down to the Stover Canal and the River Teign by a special granite tramway from Haytor, whence it was almost certainly carried down to Teignmouth in these river barges.

The rivers of Cornwall also had small barges of a somewhat similar type, and an early picture of Wadebridge in 1758 shows such craft under way on the River Camel. They have a single square sail, with a double row of reef-points along the foot. The mast is obviously made to lower readily, as barges are seen sailing both above and below the bridge. These barges appear to be double-ended, however, like the Fenland lighters referred to on page 160. It may, in fact, be safely assumed that this type of double-ended barge was once found generally all over the country; and certainly a few of them were found upon the Thames in the eighteenth century, as they appear frequently in contemporary pictures. Many, if not all, of the Trinity House ballast barges on the Thames were of this model.

On the Sussex Ouse small sailing barges were still in service in 1930 between Lewes and the port of Newhaven. A picture of one of these appears in Plate 43, where it may be seen that she has a double-ended hull, with a single mast setting a spritsail and carrying a high stack of sacks. The sizes of these barges varied. Some were quite small craft of about 45 feet in length, 12 feet in beam and shallow draught, carrying from 18 to 20 tons, often poled or drawn along with manual labour, working with the tide. These were chiefly used for carrying chalk for the repair of the river banks, etc. Others were from about 50 to 100 tons' capacity, and these were either sailed or towed up by power boats. The rig in some was the primitive squaresail, in others the spritsail, as in the photograph, or sometimes as carried in the Thames "stumpy" barges. One of the sailing barges, belonging to Mr Glover, carried a lugsail. The medium-size barges carried clay, etc., for making cement, and the largest barges brought iron girders and other iron goods for the Phoenix Iron Works; also fire-bricks and other material for cement works; and some of them were used to carry cement on short coastal voyages. Similar craft were in use on the River Arun, between Arundel and Littlehampton; and on the River Rother, working up and down between Rye and Rye Harbour. An illustrated article on these Rye barges, with complete plans, appeared in 1935 in the " Mariner's Mirror ", Vol. XXI. They carried lugsails. Very similar double-ended barges, lugsail rigged, traded on the River Slaney at Wexford, in Ireland.

On the South Coast of England there were also two more types of barges worthy of mention. Of these, the first were the cutter-rigged stone barges of Devon and Cornwall. These were employed in the coastwise stone trade, and might often be seen in Plymouth, Falmouth, the Helford River and other West Country ports. They were handsome, heavily built vessels, with round bows and flat transom sterns, the top of the transom being sometimes roughly carved. They were rigged with rather an old-fashioned cutter rig, and certainly looked very attractive vessels at sea. They carried about 120 tons when fully loaded, and had a crew of only two hands. None of them are now trading, though a few, without sails, are fitted with engines and carry stores for the Navy at Plymouth.

A little farther up-Channel, between Poole and Chichester and within the waters of the Isle of Wight, were found a number of small ketch-rigged barges, not unlike the smaller Thames barges in build, but usually rigged either with "boomy" mainsails or with half-sprit mainsails, like the *Davenport*, mentioned in Chapter XIV. They were employed in trading among the smaller ports within these limits, and carried a great part of the trade between the Isle of Wight and the mainland. They loaded about 100 tons. The Cowes ketch *Arrow* and the Portsmouth barge *Rollo* were two of them, once well-known in Solent waters between the wars.

In the waters of Langstone Harbour there were also small barges, known as Langstone barges, flat-bottomed, ketch-rigged, many of them with a sharp or "nip-cat" stern. Others had a transom stern, not unlike a Thames barge. They worked in the confined waters of Langstone, Chichester and Portsmouth Harbours, with an occasional longer voyage to Southampton Water. They had no lee-boards, very

little sheer and were pole-masted, but fitted with running, not steeving, bowsprits. They were employed mostly carrying shingle and coal ;
but none are working now, although a few are still afloat, as derelicts,
in various creeks of the three harbours, according to Commander
P. J. Norton, D.S.C., R.N., to whose kindness I am indebted for
much of the information concerning these and the Plymouth stone
barges.

# CHAPTER XI

# The Barge Races

THE spirit of rivalry and the love of racing have always existed among the bargemen, and whether loaded or light, barges sailing together on a tide will always "have a crack" at one another as long as they are in company. Few bargemen like to be passed under way, and the impromptu races with other craft which are part and parcel of every day's sailing add a zest to life on the waterways.

It was not, however, until the year 1863 that barge racing was put on an organised footing, and it was then due to the enterprise and enthusiasm of Mr Henry Dodd, a prominent contractor, that the Annual Barge Sailing Matches were started. Mr Dodd showed great public spirit and considerable financial generosity in working hard to bring about these fine sporting events, and to him bargemen and owners alike owed a debt of no little gratitude. Mr Dodd's view, in originating the Barge Matches, was not only to produce sport, but also to improve the build and equipment of the barges themselves, by offering some inducement and encouragement to owners and builders to produce craft which would be things of beauty as well as of utility, and speedy without sacrifice of carrying power. A further object, not less important, was the improvement of the status of the bargemen, who were not then regarded with that degree of respect and consideration which their calling as master mariners and mates most certainly entitled them to receive. It was hoped that the Annual Barge Races would provide a spur to smartness, good seamanship and efficiency, and would present, in the championship of each class, a pinnacle of glory to be aimed at. These hopes were fully justified, and it was indeed a great encouragement to the bargemen to realise that services which required dispatch, attention, energy and thought were rewarded by some tribute of appreciation.

To write a full history of the Barge Races would require a bulky volume, and considerations of space allow of only the more outstanding events being recorded here. Of the first two races, of 1863 and 1864, the records are very scanty. In both years the race was held under the auspices and management of the Prince of Wales Yacht Club.

The first race was so successful that it was repeated the following year, and in the second race in 1864 no fewer than forty barges competed. The 1864 race was so successful that at the dinner following the closing trip of the Club, the Commodore referred to it in the following terms, in the course of his speech, as reported in " Hunt's Yachting Magazine " at the time. "One of your races this year," he said, "I may fairly say has not been surpassed upon the Thames for years. We must consider that a great compliment was paid to us in our being entrusted with the great barge race. It was certainly a most beautiful sight, and I hope that next year we shall be again favoured with a repetition of it if possible with increased success."

In 1865 the management of the third annual race was entrusted to a committee of members of the Corn Exchange and of the Thames and Medway General Craftowners' Association. In this year, a second race for the Championship of the Thames was sailed a few weeks after the annual sailing match had been decided, and in promoting this second race Mr Henry Dodd was again the moving spirit. Full accounts of both races appeared in "The Times", from which the following has been extracted. The first race took place on 15th August, and there were two classes of barges entered.

In this race the first class consisted of topsail barges (i.e. spritsail barges, with topmasts and topsails), of a maximum tonnage of 100 tons' burden, which is less than two-thirds the size of the average barge entered in the races between the wars. For these were given: first prize, an £18 cup to the owner and £10 10s. to the crew; second prize, a £12 cup to the owner and £5 5s. to the crew; and third prize, an £8 cup to the owner and £3 3s. to the crew. No time allowance was made for differences of tonnage. For this class twenty-two barges entered.

The second class of vessels were stump-rigged barges; that is to say, spritsail barges without topmasts or topsails, and for this there were sixteen entries. Their maximum tonnage was to be 80 tons' burden, and three prizes were awarded similar to, but of less value than, those given in the topsail class.

It is interesting to note that of the barges entered in this early race, no fewer than six were still in commission in 1931: the *S. Taylor*, *Robert Stone*, *Agnes*, *Henry*, *Emma* and *George*.

The course in both classes was from Erith to the Nore and back. The barges got away at 10.53 a.m., with a good breeze from the south. The first barge round the Nore was the *Agnes*, and she was closely followed by the *Surprise, Francis, Matilda and Amy, Henry* and *Robert Stone*, all within 3 minutes 40 seconds after her. These were

PLATE 44 Fifth Annual Barge Match, 1867. *Renown* leading *Monarch* and *Blackfriars*

[*From a print by Josiah Taylor, by courtesy of the National Maritime Museum*

PLATE 45 *Haughty Belle* racing

all in the tops'l class. The leading stumpies were the *Maria*, with the *Charles*, *Volante* and *Queen Caroline* in close succession. The wind then strengthened considerably, and as the tops'l barges rounded in the squalls, they struck their topsails. The *Agnes* carried away her backstay falls; the *Henry's* topmast came down with a run as she gybed round the Nore with her topsail up; the *Swale* rounded *minus* her bowsprit; and various other casualties occurred. The wind had gone round more into the west, and although they were able to reach to the Mucking Light (above Shellhaven), they had to work up from there. It was a ding-dong race all the way; many changes in position occurred, with much skilful manœuvring, and at the finish the result was declared as follows:

| TOPSAILS | | | | STUMPIES | | | |
|---|---|---|---|---|---|---|---|
| | | H. M. S. | | | | H. M. S. | |
| 1st | *Agnes* . . | 5 14 50 | | 1st | *Maria* . . | 5 47 10 | |
| 2nd | *Surprise* . . | 5 24 45 | | 2nd | *Charles* . . | 5 55 0 | |
| 3rd | *Matilda and Amy* | 5 28 30 | | 3rd | *Elizabeth* . | 6 11 45 | |

A spirited picture of this race appears in the "Illustrated London News" for 26th August 1865. It is particularly interesting as the earliest known picture of a barge race; it shows the racing barges rounding the Nore. The rudder-head mizzens are clearly depicted.

This race was followed on 29th August by the second, and "Champion" Race, for the first three barges home in each class in the first race. On this the Championship of the Thames was to be decided. The start was made at 10.5 a.m., with a light wind from N.N.W. The craft had been stationed in two rows, and lay at anchor, with the main-sails hanging in the brails and the tops'ls lowered, but the sheets hauled out, when the signal to start was given. This has generally been the rule in the Thames Race, the barges starting with their anchors down. Some idea of the smartness of handling may be gathered from the fact that the *Agnes* had her anchor weighed and all sail set within 45 seconds. There was a pleasant little breeze at the start, but it did not hold, and later in the day the race unfortunately developed into a drifting match. By the time the young flood came up they had got no farther than the Lower Hope, and as it was impossible to reach the Nore, the Committee boat was anchored there, and the barges rounded her and returned. This disappointing absence of wind was a sorry contrast to the fresh breeze in which the first race had been sailed. The result at the finish was a win for the *Matilda and Amy*, with *Surprise* 25 minutes later and *Agnes* a further 10 minutes behind. *Maria* won in the stumpie class, with *Charles* a fairly good second.

12

After the race had been decided and the cups awarded, a pleasing incident was the presentation to Mr Henry Dodd by the bargemen of a very handsome silver snuff-box, bearing this inscription: "Presented to H. Dodd, Esq^{re}., by bargemen, as a token of respect and esteem, and in acknowledgment of the interest he has taken in their welfare, Aug. 29. 1865."

In 1866 is the first mention of Mr J. A. Farnfield, the solicitor to the Bargeowners Protection Society, who then undertook the duties of Hon. Secretary to the race; and the Committee Meetings for the Thames Race were held in the same room at his offices, in Lower Thames Street, from that year until 1899, and again after the race was revived in 1927. The late Mr Leslie Farnfield was the Hon. Secretary up to the last race sailed, in 1938, so that the office has been in the same family, with one break only, for over sixty years.

A very full account of the fourth race is printed in "Hunt's Yachting Magazine", Vol. 15; and the race was sailed in a light westerly wind. There were two classes, topsails and stumpies; the former was won by *Bessy Hart* and the latter by *Defiance*.

Referring to the improvements effected by the stimulus of the races, Hunt says: "The improved appearance of the vessels since they have been inaugurated speaks trumpet tongued of the beneficial effects exercised upon the crews; in fact, the Thames bargees, always a peculiar race in themselves, are now positively becoming nautical swells, and most fastidious in the rig, gear, sails and general smartness of their flat-bottomed fleet. No greater evidence of this could be seen than the appearance of the fleet on the 10th (of July); not a patch disfigured the canvas, nor was there that dingy worn look of the hulls that the earlier matches witnessed: the sails were in as good condition as yachts, and shone forth in the sun—a picturesque compound of snow white, dark brown, indian red and brilliant yellow; the vessels painted with the most correct 'bargee' taste, their bottoms scrupulously black-leaded, and the blocks, rudder-heads, tillers, windlasses, tabernacles, and stem heads, displaying that gorgeous profusion of brush that bargemen delight to flourish in vivid greens, lightning chromes, poppy scarlets, virgin whites, and the brightest of varnish, all of which look so cheerful and homely on the water. Nor were the crews themselves behind hand, all looking smart and clean, and many clad in the waterman's traditional coat."

After giving particulars of the prizes to be won and the barges competing, the anonymous scribe continues: "The course was from Erith to the Nore and back, and the vessels were moored in two tiers off Erith; the scene presented at the start was most novel and exciting, for besides the 40 barges about starting, the *Princess Alice* saloon steamer was engaged by the barge owners' society, and had a numerous assemblage on board; the *Oread* steamer was engaged by Mr Henry Dodd, on board which he entertained a large party; the *Ibis* steamer was under the patronage of the Rev. Mr Spurgeon, who was accompanied by an immense number of his congregation, and besides these there were the *Penguin, Widgeon, Earl of Essex*, and *City of Rochester* steamers crowded to excess; if to those we add number-less barges, their decks black with a countless multitude, smacks, rowing boats, and though last not least a pretty average number of yachts, the stirring spectacle may be imagined, but nothing save actual presence could convey a correct idea of the reality.

"At 12h. 15m. the starting gun was fired, and then arose such a babel of sound as fairly beggars description; the clanging of the pawls as hundreds of stalwart arms hove up the anchors, the rattling and cheeping of blocks as the gear flew through them, the flapping of the great mainsails as they were sheeted home, short-sharp-hoarse com-mands jerked out with all the energy of barge captains' lungs, and above all the ringing cheers that arose from the partisans of the  dif-ferent crews, made Erith Bay ring again. . . .

"The spectacle presented in the Lower Hope was really beautiful, the barges forming a long line, with their sails a good full, the white foam rolling out from under their bluff bows, the flashing sun-rays glinting upon their coloured canvas, and sparkling on their brilliant paint work, whilst astern and to leeward were a throng of steamers, barges, smacks and yachts, with their crowds of occupants cheering on and encouraging the merry laughing crews of the bargees, who danced about the decks, smoked their pipes, and returned the fire of *badinage* that was levelled at their frolics, with all the *gusto* that 'sand-boys' are proverbially reputed to enjoy."

Owing to lack of wind, the course had to be shortened; and the Committee boat was anchored near Southend, for the barges to round. "They rounded in excellent style, quite equal to yachts, and though there were some two or three collisions, yet the good temper and kindly feeling that prevailed, might well be imitated in many a yacht match." A fine tribute this, the significance of which in a yachting journal needs no emphasis!

An interesting point in connection with this year's race is that at a Committee meeting beforehand there was some difference of opinion respecting the use of "gripes" (forefoot) placed on barges; but after discussion it was agreed unanimously that the barges should be sailed either with or without the use of gripes. The "gripes" referred to would appear to be some form of false forefoot, presumably designed to place under the swim of a swim-headed barge, to give her a better grip of the water and enable her to turn to windward more like a stem-headed craft.

The next race was the fifth, sailed in 1867. So great an interest was taken in the barge match of that year that no fewer than seven steamboats filled with spectators followed the race. Nineteen topsail barges, not exceeding 50 tons register, and seventeen stumpies, not exceeding 45 tons register, were entered. In reporting the race, "The Times" commented on the fact that there were nearly 8,000 barges on the Thames and Medway, and in praising the fine seamanship displayed by the bargemen, said emphatically, "It has ever been found that from this hardy stock the British Navy has found its best recruits".

A fine picture of this race is shown in Plate 44. The Committee boat chartered for this occasion was again the ill-fated *Princess Alice*, and she appears in the background of the picture. The leading barges are three of Lee's stumpies, the *Renown*, *Monarch* and *Blackfriars*. They all had black sails, except for the white jibs carried on their bowsprits. Nowadays, stumpies never carry bowsprits, but in those days they were common in racing barges. I understand that the artist omitted a detail of some interest—the white "ramping horse", the "Invicta" of Kent, which all Lee's stumpies had painted on their black mainsails.

The race was sailed in a nice tops'l breeze from the E.S.E., with splendid weather. As it was a beat down, the race had to be shortened, for the ebb was spent when the Mucking Light was reached, and the *Princess Alice* was there anchored for the racing craft to round. This they did in the following order: *Maria* (spritsail), *Monarch* and *Blue Bell* (tops'ls), *Blackfriars* (spritsail), *Bertha* (tops'l) and *Renown* (spritsail), all rounding within four minutes, and eight or ten more in the next five, which shows how keen was the racing. When the race finished at Gravesend, the tops'ls crossed the line with *Monarch* leading, followed by *Bertha* and *Blue Bell*; and in the spritsails, *Renown* was first, with *Monarch* and *Blackfriars* following her, as shown in the picture already referred to.

In 1868 an additional class was formed for tops'ls exceeding 50 tons register, a proof of the increasing size of barges. This new class race was won by the *Excelsior*, 56 tons, belonging to Richard Horlock (Plates 50 and 51), grandfather of Alfred Horlock (see page 204), and sailed by his two sons; but only two vessels completed the course and there was no second prize.

The class for topsails of less burden, with fifteen starters, was won

PLATE 46 *Giralda* with her Champion Flags

[*Photograph by the late F. C. Gould, Gravesend*

PLATE 47  *Torment* in a fresh breeze

[*Photograph by the late F. C. Gould, Gravesend*

by *Alexandra*, with *Invicta* second. Fifteen stumpies started, and *Maria* won in that class, with *Severn* second and *Defiance* third. A full account of this year's race appears in the "Illustrated London News", with a whole-page picture.

The 1870 race was divided into three classes, of tops'ls not exceeding 50 tons register, sprstsails not exceeding 54 tons and second-class spritsails carrying only three working sails. In a nice working breeze from the north-east, the race for the tops'ls was won by that celebrated racing barge the *Annie Lloyd*, with *Bessie Hart* a good second. In the first-class spritsails, *Renown* won, followed by *Defiance*, and the second-class spritsails race was won by the *Frederick*, *Edwin* being second.

The picture reproduced as the frontispiece of this book shows the barges rounding the Nore in this race. The long tillers for steering and the mizzens stepped on the rudder-posts can be clearly seen, and also the smart striped jerseys, stockingette caps and white canvas trousers of the racing crews. Another point to be noticed, both in this picture and in that of the fifth race (Plate 44), is that the tops'l barges then carried much shorter masts and topmasts, with far longer spreets, than is the modern practice, and the tops'ls were in consequence much shorter in the luff, so that the leach of the sail was not far out of the horizontal. A comparison with any of the pictures of later barges will make this difference apparent immediately.

In a single chapter it is obviously impossible to give in detail the events of every race, and I have had to pass over without mention many an interesting encounter.

The barge *Anglo-Saxon* appeared for the first time in the race of 1873 ; and was the first barge ever fitted with a wheel. This celebrated wheel is seen in a contemporary photograph, which shows Mr Stone, her owner, his sons and some of his friends and his bargemen aboard her during the barge race of 1882. It was the practice in those days to fit out a number of barges for the accommodation of the various owners' friends. A floor was built up in the hold at a convenient height below the hatchway coamings, on which was rigged a long table running down the centre. Plenty of good cheer, both solid and liquid, supplied the groaning board, and the barge following the race provided an admirable mobile grandstand for such privileged spectators as the owner liked to invite. Merry parties indeed have been carried on race-days by some of the older barges. Doubtless the ancient craft now look back upon those good days with feelings of regret for their Golden Age that never will return !

This practice of following the race in a sailing barge was revived in the nineteen-thirties by a group of members of the old Shiplovers Association, under the leadership of Mr Francis T. Wayne. By the courtesy of the London and Rochester Trading Company, a barge—in some years two—was chartered for the day, and an excellent view of the racing was enjoyed by all the numerous party aboard. *Foxhound*, *Godwit*, *Greta* and *Sir Richard* were four of the barges which carried such parties at various times.

Arising out of the Barge Race of 1873, a private race for £200 was sailed. The *Anglo-Norman*, owned by Stone, and the *Sapho*, owned by Woods, both met with accidents in the annual match, the *Sapho* actually losing all her gear; and, to settle a dispute between the owners as to which would have been the faster barge if both had completed the race a match was arranged, popularly known in London River history as the "Race between Wood and Stone", for a wager of £100 a side.

The race was sailed in a fresh breeze, and resulted in a win for the *Anglo-Norman*, Skipper Sam Beadle, who led from the start, and after rounding the Nore, continued to increase her lead all the way on the beat up to Gravesend, eventually winning by some miles.

By 1874 the Annual Thames Match was so firmly established that the *Anglo-Dane*, *Anglo-Saxon* and three or four more new barges were built specially for the race, and from that year the race continued to be sailed annually with the greatest possible keenness.

The race of 1881 was won by the celebrated *Challenger*, 43 tons. She was a vessel noted not only as a champion barge but also as being the fastest barge loaded of her day. She was built in 1875 by Gill of Rochester, for Sam Burford, who kept the "Gibraltar" Public House, near Chatham Station. He wanted her to beat the *Gundulph*, built by G. W. Curel at Strood for James Boulden, who kept another public house, the "Gundulph", by Rochester Bridge. Boulden and Burford challenged each other, although neither owned a barge at this time. The challenge aroused great interest in the 1875 race. The *Challenger* was converted to a barge-yacht some years ago. She was at Pin Mill recently as a barge-houseboat, her gear having been landed at Maldon.

The winning barge in the 1882 contest was a well-known vessel, the *Whimbrel*, 46 tons, new that year and sailed by her equally well-known skipper, Captain Samuel Beadle of Erith. She won the Championships of both Thames and Medway in that year, and although she was not allowed to race again in 1883, owing to the rule then in force that debarred the winner of the previous year's races from entering, she won both races for a second time in 1884, and was certainly a very fast barge. She was known as the "Lion Tamer", as she beat the *British Lion* in the Thames race. *British Lion* had been built by Gill for Sam Burford to beat his own *Challenger*.

The *Whimbrel* was, incidentally, reputed to be the first barge ever to set a flying jib. Coming over from Dunkirk one night, the wind being light but free, Samuel Beadle decided to send up a small six-cloth jib, setting it "flying" (that is, not hanked to a stay) above their working jib. Later, in the river, with the bowsprit "topped-up", they set it flying over the foresail, from topmast head to stem head. The practice was copied by other barges, although the new sail was generally made of lighter canvas and was set by hanks to the topmast stay. The bargemen call this a "spinnaker", though it is not what the yachtsman understands as such. It is only lately that the practice has crept in of calling it, perhaps more accurately, the "fore-topmast stay-sail".

*Whimbrel* became one of the London & Rochester Trading Company's fleet. She was trading during the Second World War as a purely sailing barge, but was badly damaged by a collision in 1944, after which she was broken up.

A tragic event occurred in a private race sailed on the Sunday following this match as a result of a challenge issued by Mr Austin, junior, to Mr Goldsmith to settle an argument arising out of the race as to the speed of their respective barges. The owners were to sail their own barges, and Mr Austin, the challenger, sailed his *Victoria*, whose speed was the subject of the dispute; Mr Goldsmith sailed *Satanita*. It was a hard, squally day when the race was sailed, and some little distance above the Mouse Mr Austin allowed the *Victoria* to come up into the wind and lose way. This is fatal in a barge in a strong wind—she must be kept *sailing*—and when the *Victoria* fell away and filled again, she was laid right over on her beam-ends and went bottom up. Her owner and one hand were drowned, the other two members of the crew being saved.

The race of 1896 was won by the *Haughty Belle* (Plate 45), a fine new barge, built by J. R. Piper of Greenwich specially for racing. She was a lovely ship to look upon, and was successful in attaining the object for which she was built. She carried special iron racing lee-boards. Her later history is recorded on pages 77 and 274. She was followed in 1897 by the *Giralda*, perhaps the most famous barge ever launched. Plate 46 shows her with her winning flags after the Jubilee Race on the Medway in 1898. She was another of Piper's vessels, and was built to the order of Messrs Goldsmith for the express purpose of winning the Gold Cup for the Championship of the Thames in

Queen Victoria's Diamond Jubilee year. The genius of her building was said to be Mr Jack Currell, then foreman at Piper's Yard. When completed, everybody laughed at her. She was so straight and flat and ugly that by comparison with the lovely *Haughty Belle* of the previous year she looked like an orange-box. Jack Currell's reply was simply this: "She was built to win the Gold Cup, and she'll win it!" She did. Below the water she had the most beautiful lines imaginable in a barge. But she was so lightly built that she wouldn't keep her shape, and had afterwards to be specially strengthened. There was never any doubt, however, as to her speed.

When she first came out, Captain Arthur Coward, a Kentish bargeman, who years later was Master of the mule-rigged *Hydrogen*, raced her for the Goldsmiths, and it was he who achieved everlasting fame on the river by winning the Gold Cup with her. Yet a more modest man it would be hard to find. After the first year's racing *Giralda* was alleged to be too lightly built to carry her cargo. The matter went to arbitration, and although points were decided in favour of both sides, the builders had the barge back again; and after that she raced in other hands under the command of Captain William Mitchell, winning both Thames and Medway Championships many times.

The last race sailed under the old Committee, with Mr Farnfield as Hon. Secretary, was that of 1899. After that year, owing to some internal disputes and difficulties among the Committee and the Trustees of the race fund, which had then reached considerable dimensions, the race was temporarily abandoned. Meanwhile a new committee was formed, and the race was sailed again in 1901 under an entirely separate organisation. The barge *Thelma* (Plate 13) won in that year. The race was sailed in almost a gale of wind. A skipper named Lutchford had her, a man of a noted racing family, who afterwards became master of a schooner on the American Lakes. Among other barges beaten in the race was the wonderful *Giralda*, who broke her cross-trees, and the *Teazer*, sailed by Alf Horlock, who broke her lee-board.

The second series of Thames races were sailed right up to the outbreak of war in 1914.

After that war no race was held until, in 1927, the Farnfields and others representing the original Committee of the nineteenth century worked hard to gain support, and revived the old event. Each year after that it gained ever-increasing popularity. Of all the post-war races, perhaps the hardest racing was seen in the 1928 contest, with thirty-three barges sailing, in which the Coaster Class was won by the *Vigilant* (Plate 52), sailed by Alfred Horlock (Plate 53) and his nephew "Chubb". It was blowing half a gale from the sou'-west and at Southend Regatta the big yachts refused to race. The course from Gravesend round the Mouse Lightship and back measures fifty-six miles, and the return journey had to be made turning to windward over a strong ebb tide. The barges started on the high water and the leading craft had completed the course and were back at Gravesend in 6 hours 11 minutes—or before the ebb was spent. The first six barges rounded the Mouse in under two hours from the start—an average of nearly twelve knots through the water. The *Vigilant* took no fewer than five first prizes; two for the first vessel of all classes to round the outward mark (the Mouse), one for the captain and one for the owner; two prizes, one each to the captain and the owner, for the first barge of all classes to cross the line at the finish; and one prize as the winning vessel of her class. This record has never been equalled, before or since, *Vigilant* having beaten all barges of all classes at every mark. *Remercie* came second, eleven minutes behind, with *Alf Everard* third and *John Bayly* fourth. *Portlight* won in the River Class, with *Queen* second and *Foxhound*, the old Ramsgate barge, third. *Plinlimmon* had the misfortune to break her spreet, and was towed home.

The 1929 race was sailed in a fresh breeze, and *Portlight*, having fought her way to second place, was unlucky enough to lose her main-mast by the board when off Thames Haven on the way back. The River Barge Class was won by *Reminder*, with *Queen* second and *Imperial* third, followed by *Thelma* and *Miranda*. The Coaster Class was won by *Redoubtable*, with *Northdown* second.

In 1930, as a contrast, there was but little wind. There were three classes racing, *Redoubtable* winning the Coaster race, *Reminder* the River Bowsprit and *Fortis* the new class for River Staysail barges. In this new class an interesting competitor was the little *Challenger*, the winner of the 1881 Championship, looking a very small ship among the modern giants. But, for all her fifty-five years, she gave such a good account of herself that she came in third of her class.

Another old craft racing was the *Sara* (Plate 64), an outstandingly fast ship, claimed by some to be the fastest barge ever built, who did very well. Her success was partly attributed to the action of her crew in constantly throwing up water over her sails to make them set better and hold a better wind. But to this story there is an inner history, which unfortunately there is no space here to recount.

The race of 1931, sailed in a nice working breeze, with three classes racing, resulted in a win for the *Redoubtable* in the Coaster Class, with *Phoenician* (Plate 18) a close second. *Sara* won the River Bowsprit Class. But the sensational event of the day's racing, which will make it live long in London River memories, was the wonderful sailing of the little *Fortis*, a river staysail barge, which not only won her own class but was the first home of all classes, outpointing and outsailing every other barge in the race. This is said to be the first time in the history of the two rivers that a staysail barge has been the first ship home, and although if the *Phoenician* had not had the misfortune to misjudge the extend to which the Nore sand had grown, so that she had just touched and been hung up there for some time, the result might have been different, full credit must be given to *Fortis* and her crew for her remarkably fine performance.

Three classes, as usual, competed in the race in 1932; and it might be of interest to recall the conditions. The regulations that year laid down that coasting barges must have not less that 7 feet side, or must have completed three or more voyages either down Channel as far as the Isle of Wight, or in Continental trade, or northwards as far as the Humber, in the six months previous to the 31st March 1932. They might carry not more than seven sails, namely, mainsail, topsail, foresail, mizzen, jib, spinnaker and squaresail or balloon foresail (optional), which must have been in use on that barge on 1st December; a crew of master and five other hands only was allowed.

In the River (Bowsprit) Class, master and four hands only were allowed, and each barge was limited to five sails, namely, mainsail, topsail, foresail, mizzen and bowsprit jib. The River (Staysail) Class was limited to barges which had traded exclusively to the westward of a line drawn from Whitstable to Shoeburyness for the twelve months previous to the date of the race. The crew was not to exceed master and three other hands, and ordinary working sails only were to be used, including topmast staysail, but no jib.

Barges in all classes were not to have had any enlargements to or shifting of the main horse or any alterations in the rudder or leeboards since 1st December 1931; and the masters of all competing craft must have been in the employ of the owners on and from that date. Such, with small variations from time to time, were the rules governing the later barge races on Thames and Medway.

The 1932 race (Plate 49) was sailed over the usual course, with a fresh wind at west-sou'-west. The *Phoenician* failed to hear the gun and made a bad start; *Eva*, in the River Staysail Class, was unlucky enough to lose her topmast in a squall at the beginning and *Redoubtable*, with her immense sails, had gained a lead of half a mile at the Nore over *Reminder*, *Phoenician* and *Sara*. She rounded the Mouse in the almost record time of 1 hour 57 minutes; but in gybing all-standing at the mark, she carried away her weather vang, which, unable to stand the strain of her huge gear, broke off at the lug. She then sagged away a long way to loo'ard, and from then on was out of the race. The wind had westered for the beat back, and a ding-dong race it was, with *Phoenician* and *Reminder* carrying their jib tops'ls in a breeze that carried away *Fortis's* topmast, as they went driving up Sea Reach with their lee decks under water, and often with their hatches swept clean with spray. *Reminder* was griping so badly that she needed two and sometimes three hands at the wheel to hold her. *Sara* meanwhile had worked out into leading place and crossed the finishing line 6 hours 3 minutes from the start, followed by *Nelson* in 8 minutes and *Phoenician* in 9 minutes, with *Reminder* over a minute astern. Thus *Phoenician* won the Coasting Class and Everards' *Sara* the River Bowsprit, while their *Ash* won the River Staysail Class. Lloyd's Cup for the first barge home went to *Sara*, while the Commodore's Prize to the master of the barge showing best seamanship in rounding the half-way mark went to Captain A. B. Finch, master of the *Cambria*.

The race of 1933 was sailed in very light airs and ended in almost a drifting match; but on a sweltering hot day it meant very hard work for the crews, toiling to take advantage of each faint zephyr. It was noteworthy for the reappearance of the famous old *Veronica*, 54 tons, built at East Greenwich in 1906, owned for many years by Clement W. Parker of Bradwell Quay, Essex, and recently purchased by Everards. Thames Champion in 1906, 1907 and 1908 and Medway Champion in 1908, she signalised her return to racing by winning in the Staysail Class on both Thames and Medway in 1933. On the Thames she crossed the line two bowsprit lengths ahead of *Sara* (winner of the River Bowsprit) and was first barge home. The Coasting Class was again won by *Phoenician*.

Fifteen barges started in the 1934 race. The depth of side for coasters was reduced to 6 feet 6 inches; and a new "River Staysail (Special)" class was added, for barges which had traded exclusively to the westward of a line from the River Colne to the Reculvers for twelve months previous to the race, and which had not won a first prize in any class on Thames and Medway since 1927. On a day of lowering skies and freshening sou'westerly wind, the steel-built Mistley barge *Reminder* was both first barge home and winner of the Coasting Class, completing the 56-mile course in the fast time of 3 hours 55 minutes. *Sara* came next, 5 minutes later, winning the River Bowsprits, and *Veronica* again led the River Staysail Class over the finishing line. The new class was won by *Albert*, with the veteran *Challenger* (Champion of the Thames in 1875) second.

In 1935 the number of classes was reduced to three, for Coasting, River Bowsprit and River Staysail (Special) Class. As a result of the change, *Veronica* and *Fortis* both raced with bowsprits. The race was sailed in a light easterly breeze, and the finish was extraordinarily close, *Veronica*, *Sara*, *Queen*, *Phoenician* and *Cambria* being practically in line, *Veronica* winning by half a bowsprit, the rest being close up. *Phoenician* won in the Coasters, *Veronica* in the River Bowsprits; and *Genesta* the River Staysail (Special) Class.

The race of 1936 was also sailed in light airs, calling for the utmost skill and judgment in making the most of what little wind there was. *Phoenician*, racing as a true working barge (she had come straight from trading, and discharged a cargo at Ipswich the week before the race), repeated her success of the previous year by winning in the Coaster Class, bring up her score to ten prizes in eleven races sailed. *Sara* was first of the River Bowsprits, *Veronica* of the River Staysails (she had shed her bowsprit again) and *Princess* of the River Staysail (Special) Class, which had been reintroduced for this year. In spite of the efforts of the Committee to attract more entries, only thirteen barges started; the smallest entry since the race was inaugurated seventy-three years before.

Racing was becoming too expensive. Wealthy owners were able to rig their barges specially for racing in a way that poorer men could not afford. Arising out of this, a challenge was issued by Mr F. W. Horlock of Mistley to race his *Reminder* against Captain Alf Horlock's *Phoenician*, for a stake of £50 or upwards. The challenge was accepted, but subject to a smaller stake, to be devoted to a local charity, and subject to each barge being raced as a true working barge. As the skipper of the *Phoenician* asked, in a statement issued in answer to the challenge, "For what reason does a wealthy man make a high stake when challenging a relatively poor man? I cannot afford to risk £50 if Mr Fred Horlock can. There are also the additional expenses involved by loss of time, payment of crew and possible accidents. I will accept a £10 wager for the benefit of local charity".

The race never took place; but in order to indicate the working of a big coasting barge, as distinct from a rig designed for racing but too powerful for normal trading, the following measurements of *Phoenician* were published, and are worth recording.

Deck to under hounds of topmast, 75 feet 3 inches. Sprit (overall), 58 feet 2 inches. Deck to lower end of sprit, 4 feet 0 inches. Mast (after side) to main horse (after side), 39 feet 0 inches. Headstick (of topsail), hole to hole, 10 feet 3 inches. Mizzen sprit (overall), 28 feet. End of mizzen sprit to centre of gooseneck, 1 foot 6 inches. Hounds

PLATE 48 The Dead Heat on the Medway in 1927

[*Photograph by courtesy of Maurice Gill, Esq*

PLATE 49 Thames Race, 1932. *Fortis, Sara* and *Redoubtable*

[*Photograph by "The Times"*

# A PAGE
## OF
## FAMILY HISTORY

PLATE 50 Captain Richard Horlock, 1868

PLATE 52 *Vigilant*, Champion 1928

[*Photograph by the Autho*

PLATE 51 *Excelsior's* Cup, Barge Race, 1868

PLATE 53 Captain "Alf" Horlock, aboard his famous Champion *Phoenician*

to centre of gooseneck, 16 feet 3 inches. Mizzen boom (overall), 15 feet 8 inches. Bowsprit, 32 feet outside of stem. Lee-boards, 17 feet in length; Lee-boards "Fan", 8 feet. Sail area, 6,000 square feet.

In 1936 there was an additional "Thames to Medway" Race for barges racing on both rivers. *Phoenician* won in the Coasters, and it is interesting to recall that Commander E. G. Martin, author of "Sailorman", sailed aboard her. *Sara* turned the tables on *Veronica* and won in her class. But she had a narrow escape, for she nearly capsized off Sheerness, lying down till the water poured through the cabin hatchway. A master of over forty years' experience said that he had never seen or heard of a barge being pressed so far.

The year 1937 saw the "Coronation Race", and what a race it was! I wish that I had space to quote in full the thrilling eye-witness account by my friend Alan Horlock, published in the "Blue Peter" at the time; but I can only recommend it to those who can find a copy to read. In the first place, the barges were prepared like yachts for the occasion; never have working craft been more resplendent in gleaming paint and shining varnish, their sails the quintescence of perfection. Goldsmith's *Scot*'s whole side was painted in three equal horizontal bands of red, white and blue, the colours of her owner's "bob", and nothing could have been more appropriate. But if the appearance of the barges was outstanding, that was no more than the trimming to a day of wonderful racing. It is not possible to describe shortly all that happened in that thrilling contest; but the wonderful performance of the veteran *Sara* should establish this race for all time as perhaps the most remarkable ever sailed.

*Sara*, sailing in the new Champion Class for unrestricted barges, inaugurated that year, began badly; for she had the misfortune to cross the line just ahead of the gun, and was recalled. To work back over the tide, running strongly at half-ebb against a light wind, cost her dearly; and when she eventually crossed the line she was twenty minutes behind the rest. A hopeless position, be she never so fast; poor *Sara* seemed definitely out of the race. It was a "real Coronation Race", as Mr E. A. Gill wittily remarked in broadcasting a running commentary aboard the Committee steamer. *Queen* had been first over the line, almost arm-in-arm with *King*; while following her royal parents was *Princess*. *George and Eliza* was not long after, and there was also the patriotic *Scot*. What a pity *Coronation* and *Tricolor* were not racing as well!

So the racing craft ran down to the Mouse with a light following wind, which gave poor *Sara* very little chance to make up on the leaders, and although she had passed five of the slower barges she was still twenty minutes astern of the van when she rounded the lightship. But now the wind was freshening, with *Veronica*, "the fastest bit of wood afloat", in the lead for the long beat back to Gravesend. As the race proceeded, however, the incredible happened. *Sara* fought her way by brilliant seamanship and tactics, overhauling and vanquishing one rival after another, until only *Queen* remained. In a final duel *Queen* was met, measured and mastered, and the goal was in sight. "*Sara* made a stirring sight," wrote Alan Horlock, "as she winded close to the *Royal Eagle* (Committee boat): helm down, lee sheets gone, mainsheetman aft to the lee-board winch, jib full, lee-board up and tall planes of canvas heeling the ship down till the chine lifted and the water showed dark under the glaucous sheen of her bottom. What a feat she had done! That dogged Mistley crew should be remembered well. Philip Finch (Master), Harry Finch, Cromwell Horlock, "Chubb" Horlock and Leslie Crix—these are sailormen." Real sailormen indeed, whose names should be honoured whenever barge racing is remembered; days, alas, that never will return in quite this splendid glory.

Of the other barges, *Veronica* won the Coaster Class, with *Princess* first in the Restricted Bowsprits and *Dunstable* in the River Staysails.

The last Thames Race to be sailed was that of 1938; which resulted in two fighting finishes and a disqualification. *Veronica* and *Surrey* fought hard for first and second place on the whole of the run home; *Veronica* crossed the line 50 seconds ahead of her rival, but had the disappointment of being disqualified for having carried a spinnaker as well as a flying jib when she crossed the starting line. *Reminder* and *Surrey* also finished within 35 seconds of each other. With three classes only racing, *Surrey* was first barge home and winner of the Champion Bowsprit Class; *Cambria* won in the Coasters and *Sirdar* in the River Topsail (Staysail) Class. The race was sailed in a light westerly wind, and sixteen barges competed.

In 1939 the threat of war was already upon us, and no race took place; nor has it yet proved possible to revive the Barge Races on the Thames, as has been done, in modified form, on the Medway, thanks to the united efforts of the old Medway Racing Committee and the Marina Club of Hoo, aided by the co-operation of the Thames Barge Sailing Club. Whether a revival on the Thames will ever be possible or not, one thing is certain. For lack of ships and men the barge racing glories of the past are over; and never again shall we see so many working barges fitted out in all their splendour, equipped like yachts and raced with such skill and determination as has never been surpassed in vessels racing under sail.

It appears that no records of the Barge Races on the Medway have been preserved earlier than the year 1895. But as the race that year was the sixteenth annual event, these matches must presumably have started in or about the year 1880, or seventeen years after Mr Henry Dodd originated the Thames event.

In the sixteenth match there was only one class, and the race was won by the barge *Roland*, with *Majestic* second and *Vectis* third. In the race the following year there was also but one class, and only a first prize was awarded, going to the *Clara*. From the next year, 1897, the records seem to have been kept with greater care, and it is possible to trace the history of the races with some satisfaction right up to the present day. The '97 race was sailed on 8th July and was won by the famous old *Satanita*. The race is noteworthy because in it appeared for the first time on the Medway that most wonderful of all racing barges, the *Giralda*, although on this occasion she only came in second, with *Victoria* third. The year '97 was also distinguished by the introduction of a new class for barges of not more than 50 tons register which had not won a first prize in any previous match either on the Thames or the Medway, and this race was won by the *Pastime*.

In the following year the Jubilee Race was sailed, spoken of long afterwards with vivid memories by the older barge skippers. There were again two classes, but the regulations were altered from the previous years, with no tonnage restriction in the larger class, but certain limits on the size of gear, as to length of spreet, etc. This class was won by *Giralda* under her new ownership, with *Lord Nelson* second. William Mitchell, who then sailed the *Giralda*, won a great reputation as a racing skipper, and knew his barge so well that it was truly wonderful to watch what he could do with her. For many years Bill Mitchell and the *Giralda* won the championship of both Thames and Medway, all in hard-sailed matches. Class II imposed a limit of 45 tons on the registered tonnage, and also gear restrictions, and was won, as in the year before, by *Pastime*. The two classes apparently did not prove a success, for the following year there was a reversion to the single class racing, which continued until 1906. In 1899 the race was won by *Centaur*, *Giralda* failing to beat her and getting home second, with *Lord Nelson* third. Next year the barges copied the Thames practice of starting from anchor. As far as one can gather from not very detailed records, the Medway Committee varied the rules from time to time, the barges sometimes starting under way, jockeying for position like racing yachts, and sometimes from stations with anchors down and sails hanging in brails.

In the race of 1900 *Giralda* won again, with *Surf* second, *Mildreda* third and *Centaur*, *Loualf* and *Shamrock* following in that order. The course of these early races seems to have varied slightly from time to time. The start was invariably made from Gillingham, and the barges raced sometimes apparently round the Nore only, but more generally round the Mouse Lightship or round the West Oaze Buoy, finishing at either Gillingham or, in some years, right up at Chatham.

The race of 1901 was won by *Thelma*, whose model is in the Science Museum, and appears in Plate 13. *Marconi* was second and *Mildreda* third. I have not been able to discover whether *Giralda* was racing, or why, if so, she was not placed, either in this year or in the following, when it was won by *Imperial*, *Sara* being second and *Edward VII* third. It is interesting to note that of those barges *Sara* and *Imperial* were still racing regularly in the races after the 1914–18 war. Whatever happened to *Giralda* in the two years preceding, she won again in 1903, *Sara* taking second place and *Genesta* third. *Torment* (Plate 47) had protested against *Genesta* concerning a collision which had occurred between these two barges, but after hearing evidence from both sides it was held that *Torment* was in the wrong and she alone was to blame.

In 1904 Mr E. A. Gill succeeded Mr F. C. Boucher as Hon. Secretary to the Medway Racing Committee, an office he retained until he resigned and was followed by his son, Mr Maurice Gill, in 1928. The order of the barges that year was *Giralda* first once again, with *Genesta* second and *Valdona* third.

The race of 1905 was noted for the incursion of "new blood" from the Essex coast, and it provided one of the most exciting matches on record. The "foreign" barge was the *Verona*, of 55 tons register, built that year by Mr H. Shrubsall and sailed by that well-known Mistley skipper Alf Horlock. The race was keenly contested all the way out, and it was a hard fight from start to finish between the *Verona* and *Giralda* under her old master, Bill Mitchell. There was a grand hard sailing breeze all day. *Verona* early established a lead, and held it all the way out. On the homeward passage she was two minutes ahead at Port Victoria, just inside the entrance to the Medway. *Giralda* then gradually started to overhaul her, and at the finish they were racing side by side with the wind aft. *Giralda*, under *Verona's* lee, kept luffing her and luffing her, trying to force her to pass the wrong side of the mark, until, putting her helm up, she was able to slip by, crossing the line with her bowsprit end two feet ahead of *Verona*, although the latter passed her again just over the line. It was an unfortunate ending to a magnificent race, for there was no possible doubt that *Giralda* had fouled her rival at the finish, by what would be called "boring" on the turf, and the Committee had no option but to disqualify her and declare *Verona* the winner, and had done so before *Verona* even had time to enter a protest. Thus the Essex barge took away the Kentish men's Cup from them in their own river, and Alf Horlock certainly sailed a remarkably fine race on that day. Incidentally, it is worth recording that the *Surge*, a new barge built by Piper that year specially to beat his own *Giralda*, came in last but one. S-U-R-G-E was intended to signify "Sure You Are *Giralda's* Equal", but she never could approach her for speed.

In 1906 two classes were tried again, with a Champion Class, as before, and a Coaster Class, copying Thames regulations, and of a least tonnage of 70 tons. The results were: Champion Class: *Veronica* first, *Verona* second and *Edith* third; and in the Coasters: *Violet Sybil*, followed by *Cambria*. *Veronica* became a noted racing barge, and when she appeared at Mistley some years ago, and her skipper was asked if his barge had won many cups, he was able to reply with emphasis, "Yes—and Saucers too!" Her more recent successes are recorded elsewhere in this chapter.

In 1907 only two entries were received and there was no race. The following year, in an attempt to recover support, a new class was tried, for ordinary working barges, using only their ordinary working gear and carrying a skipper and two hands only. They must never have entered in any Champion Class, nor must they ever have taken a prize in a Thames or Medway race. Another class for coasters was arranged, but for lack of support was never sailed. No fewer than eighteen barges entered in the Working Class, however, and five cups were presented. The race was started under way, and was won by *Maysie*, a fine staysail barge, followed by *Albert*, *Marjorie*, *Golden Eagle* and *Creeksea*, in that order. *Marguerite* was actually fifth at the finish, but was disqualified for putting Horlock's *Marjorie* about in Sheerness Harbour, when outward bound on the wrong tack.

In 1909 again only the Working Class Race was sailed, and was won by *Princess*, with *Sir Richard* second, *Ash* third and *Madrali* fourth. The following year conditions were the same, with the one class only, but three hands were allowed in addition to the master. This year the order of finishing was *Albert*, *Ash*, *Medway* and *Tyne*.

The following year, to attract a maximum entry, there was only one class, open without restriction to barges of any size, whether previous winners or not. This was won by *Ash*, with *Maysie* second and *Thelma* third. In 1912 and 1913 so little support was received by way of entries that as there was no reasonable chance of getting good races none was organised. But in 1914 the race was sailed again, and was

13

made open to all barges of any size, sailed by a master and two hands, and the result was another win for *Ash*, with *Beatrice Maud*, *Albert* and *Sir Richard* second, third and fourth respectively.

The First World War put a stop to all further racing on the Medway, and nothing was done to revive it until the old Committee met again in 1926, and after much preliminary hard groundwork had been put in and proper support had been promised, the first post-war race was held in 1927. It was originally intended to have one class, open to barges of any size, but with five sails only, and for this there were nineteen entries. The Committee then decided that certain of these barges should form a class by themselves, making a separate Coaster Class. The race was noteworthy for producing the only dead-heat that has ever been seen in the barge races. Two barges belonging to the Blue Circle Cement fleet, the *Harold Margetts* and the *Plinlimmon*, in the River Class, sailed up the Medway together, neither gaining nor losing an inch, and finished with their bowsprits crossing the line dead level. The two barges appear in Plate 48, sailing neck and neck. The third barge home in this class was the little veteran *Challenger*. In the Coasters, *Cambria* won, with *Dreadnought* second and *Northdown* third. *Vigilant*, the wonderful Thames winner that year, had sent her entry in six hours too late, and was not allowed to race or she might have won on the Medway also.

In 1928 the minimum tonnage of the Coasters was reduced to 60 tons net, or smaller if the barge possessed a load-line certificate. The order of the first four barges was *Cambria*, followed by *Alf Everard*, *Remercie* and *John Bayly*. In the River Class, with twenty-one starters and a start under way, some wonderful jockeying for position was seen in the confines of the narrow river. The result at the finish was a win for *Portlight*, with *Miranda* second, *Queen* third and *Ash* fourth. *Sara* had actually got home first, but was unfortunately disqualified, on protest from *Miranda*, for fouling when rounding the West Oaze Buoy. This year the Holman Challenge Cup was first presented, to be held for one year by the first barge home, in either class. For the race of 1929 there was a smaller fleet than usual racing, partly owing to the sudden death of that fine sportsman Mr F. J. Everard, with the consequent withdrawal of the Everard barges from the match and also owing to the *Portlight* having been dismasted in the Thames Race, and to other casualties among the barges. *Northdown* won the Coaster, *Reminder* the River Class and the Holman Cup also went to *Reminder*.

In 1930 there were three classes. On the day of the race there was unfortunately but little wind. The Coaster Class was won by *Redoubt-*

*able*, with *Alf Everard* second and *Northdown* third, *Cambria* having been disqualified for fouling *Northdown*. In the River Bowsprits, *Sara* came home first, winning also the Holman Cup for the first barge home and a cash prize of £5 to the first wooden barge home—a pretty record for a barge soon to be numbered among the veterans. *Reminder* was disqualified for trying to force a passage between the *Nelson* and the Mouse Lightship when rounding. *Miranda* won among the River Staysails, followed by *Harold Margetts*, *Haughty Belle* and *Plinlimmon*; the little *Challenger* also raced in this class, putting up a most creditable performance.

The 1931 race, with three classes, resulted in wins for the *Phoenician* in the Coasters, followed by *Redoubtable* and *Cambria*; for *Fortis* in the River Staysails, with *Ash* second and the forty-eight-years-old *Miranda* third; and for *Nelson* in the River Bowsprits, *Sara*, *Reminder* and *Imperial* being next in that order. *Phoenician* led from the start, and maintaining her lead, sailed a splendid race, getting home a long way ahead of all other barges.

The race of 1932 attracted sixteen entries, in three classes, and was sailed in a good westerly breeze. After rounding the mark, *Phoenician* was about to head *Redoubtable* when her bobstay parted. In less than ten minutes a hand had been overboard under the bow, a new bobstay had been rove and up went the jibs again—a smart bit of seamanship, of which I was a close spectator from my own yacht *Cariad*, following the race. In the end *Sara* was the first barge home and winner of the River Bowsprits; *Phoenician* repeated her success in the Thames by winning the Coasting Class; while first of the River Staysails was *Fortis*—a satisfactory consolation for having lost her topmast in the Thames.

In 1933 *Phoenician* was the first barge home, crossing the line four minutes ahead of *Veronica*; Alf Horlock, her master, with eleven Firsts and two Seconds to his credit, having raced her with superb skill and seamanship. She had thus won in the Coasting Class on both Thames and Medway in that year. *Sara* won the Bowsprit Class, and *Veronica* was first of the staysails. An exciting incident in this race was a collision between two of Everard's big coasters. *Will Everard* bore down on *Greenhithe's* weather quarter; *Greenhithe* refused to give way, tried to luff and the *Will*, taking her wind, came aboard, her great bowsprit splitting *Greenhithe's* mainsail to the head rope. By a miracle no man was injured.

For the race in the following year I was one of the party aboard the sailing barge *Quarry*, chartered to follow the race. Conditions were ideal for racing, with a fresh easterly breeze, giving a hard punch dead

to windward all the way out and a fine run home. Sixteen barges
entered, and to quote from another or Alan Horlock's vivid accounts
in the "Blue Peter": "The memory of that splendid fleet beating
down to the Mouse will stand like a bulwark against a winter's gloom.
The sun shone and the bright sea rose all shaking in swells of foam as
the wind drove against the tide. One could see the barges careened
and plunging bows deep as they hit each wave. Leaping on out of a
sea the bow would be lifted clean, the ship's bottom showing black
for an instant before she came down again—boom!—smothered in
white water. On they came in the brilliant light, scattering drifts of
spray under the curved canvas; ships under sail in their glory."

Over the line at the finish, *Sara* repeated her victory on the Thames
and was two minutes ahead of *Reminder* and *Veronica*, followed
closely by *Queen* and *Nelson*—close work after a grim contest. The
Coasting Class was won by *Reminder* (*Phoenician* was not racing this
year); *Sara* winning the River Bowsprits, *Veronica* the Open Staysail; and *Albert*, in spite of losing one lee-board and breaking the
other, won the Restricted Staysail Class; there were four classes this
year, the fortieth event on the Medway.

*Phoenician* was racing again in 1935, and won the Coasting Class, as
she had done on the Thames that year. *Queen* was first home and
winner of the Bowsprit Class, hotly pursued by *Veronica*, with *Sara*
in third place. The little *Dorothy*, 44 tons, built at Rochester in 1885,
was winner of the Staysails.

1936 saw *Phoenician* repeat her double victory of the year before,
winning the Coasting Class on both Thames and Medway; also winning the Thames-to-Medway Race sailed this year. Towards the end
of the race *Sara*, racing in the River Bowsprit Class, did not wind
early enough to enable *Queen* to avoid striking *Sara's* mizzen with her
bowsprit; and although first over the finishing line, *Queen's* protest
was upheld, and *Sara* was disqualified. Thus *Queen* won the River
Bowsprits; *Veronica* was first in the Open Staysail Class; while the
victory in the Restricted Staysails went to *Surrey*. The race was not
without its casualties, for in the later part of the race, when the south-
west wind increased its gusty force, *Princess* lost her topmast and
*Sara's* crew had to jump to master their jib.

The 1937 Coronation Race on the Medway was a day of records,
because the Everard barges again took first prizes in three classes, a
feat unequalled since the races were revived in 1927. The racing
started in light airs, but the breeze freshened as the day wore on, and
on the beat home *Sara* led all the way through the tortuous reaches of
the Medway to the finishing line, which she passed ten minutes ahead

of *Queen* and thirteen minutes in front of *Princess*. Thus she had gained victory on the Medway as she had on the Thames, and was winner of the Champion Bowsprit Class. *Veronica* won the Coasting Class, *Princess* the Restricted Bowsprits and the veteran *Surge* ("Sure You Are *Giralda's* Equal") came home first of the Restricted Stay-sails.

The following year, 1938, saw the slowest match that had ever been sailed on the Medway. Fifteen barges competed in the forty-fourth Annual Race on that river, and the last to be sailed before the war, on a day when there was so little wind that the course had to be shortened to 12 miles each way. The race resulted in a win for *Surge*, who led the fleet over the finishing line and won the Restricted Staysail Class. The winning coaster was *Cambria*, with *Northdown* second ; and *Veronica* was first of the Champion Bowsprits. The surprise of the race was the previous year's winner—*Sara*. Well to the fore at the beginning of the match, she was one of the last to round the mark at Sheerness and was among the last five to finish.

So ended the pre-war racing on the Medway; for in 1939 the writing was already on the wall, and no match took place that year. It was not until 1949 that another race was held, and then it was only a modest affair, organised by the recently formed Marina Club of Hoo, in which the official entrants, with one exception, were all converted barge yachts, of whose owners the membership of the Club was largely made up. No trading barge was entered, so that the race cannot be included in the official sequence of Medway Barge Matches. It was, however, a plucky effort to revive the time-honoured sport, and the Marina Club deserves sincere congratulation for having showed the way and thus inspired the forty-fifth regular match, which was sailed in the following year, 1950.

The Marina Club's Race was held on Saturday, 18th June 1949. Twelve barges were entered, all amateur owned and sailed. These were the *Gladys*, *Winifred*, *Iota*, *Henry*, *Dipper*, *Leslie*, *Petrel*, *Lady of the Lea* and *Dinah*, with the Thames Barge Sailing Club's *Arrow* and the Marina Club's two entries, *Spurgeon* and *Russell*. All but *Dinah* were former trading barges. In addition, an unofficial entrant was the little thirty-foot barge-yacht *Nancy Grey*. Not all crossed the line, however; for the *Lady of the Lea* took the ground on her way round from Milton and couldn't get off; and *Winifred* went ashore at the start.

The barges mustered in Long Reach, River Medway, and crossed the line at timed intervals after the gun, to avoid crowding at the start. Canvas was limited to five working sails, namely, mainsail, foresail, topsail, topmast staysail and mizzen. There was not enough wind for racing, what little there was being easterly to north-easterly, moderate at the start, but soon falling very light. *Gladys* was first away, followed by *Henry* and *Arrow* in that order. Progress was so slow that the young flood made when most of the barges had got no farther than the West Cant buoy, and only *Henry* and the little unofficial entrant *Nancy Grey* were able to round the Nore Towers and so complete the course. *Henry* crossed the finishing line to win at 4.20 p.m., followed by *Nancy Grey*. So ended the match. It was hardly a race, but it was a beginning, and led to the race of the following year.

This was a much more elaborate affair, organised jointly by the old Medway Barge Sailing Match Committee and the Marina Club. A class for working barges was included; and the match has therefore properly been reckoned as the forty-fifth Medway Barge Race. It was sailed on 10th June 1950, on a day when the weather was fine and bright, but with so little wind that until nearly the end the race was largely a drifting match, calling for great skill in the contestants to take advantage of every puff and every eddy. In this game the art and experience of the professional bargemen showed to such advantage that, though the last class to be started, the trading barges were the first home, except for the little *Nancy Grey*, of the small barge-yacht class.

There were four classes in all, the " Bowsprit Barge Yachts " *Venta*, *Thoma II*, *Alice May* and *Petrel* being the first away, in that order. These were followed by the "Staysail Barge Yachts" *Henry*, *Russell*, *Arrow*, *Gladys* and *Spurgeon*. Next came the "Small Barge-Yacht Class", consisting of small yachts, built barge-fashion with hard chines, but bearing little or no resemblance to trading barges. Of these there were four; *Nancy Grey*, *Dione*, *Dinah* and *Macara*. Last to start were the "Restricted Staysail Class" of Commercial Barges. These got away at 11.0 a.m.; *Pretoria* first, followed by *Westmoreland*, *Ardeer* and *Gipping*. *Sirdar*, flying her 1930 Championship Flag, had confused the guns, making what would have been a perfect start had it not unfortunately been five minutes too soon; and she took so long to get back over the ebb that she eventually crossed the line seventeen minutes late.

The course, from Gillingham to the Nore Towers and back, proved too long for the prevailing light airs, and the Committee steamer *Medway Queen* was anchored as the turning mark a mile or so off Sheerness. *Gipping* was first round the mark; but *Sirdar*, by brilliant handling after her late start, was a close second, followed by *Ardeer*, *Henry*, *Russell*, *Pretoria*, *Arrow*, *Westmoreland* and *Alice May*. *Gladys*, who was racing stumpy-rigged, having lost her topmast when she was run into at anchor just before the race by a power craft, and *Venta*, who had got foul of a buoy and picked up a telephone cable with her rudder, both retired; as did *Dinah*. On the way home the breeze that all had been waiting for sprang up, and there was a fine spirited finish. The little barge yacht *Nancy Grey*, with her designer and builder, Frank Shuttlewood aboard, was first home; with *Sirdar*, first of the traders, only a minute astern. *Henry* won the Staysail Class for Barge Yachts, with *Arrow* second; and *Alice May* was first home in the Bowsprit Class. Altogether, it had been a most successful day, encouraging one to hope for another race on the Medway in 1951; and, dare one add, for a revival also on the Thames?

The Thames and Medway were not alone in providing barge races, however, for the Blackwater also had its own course, confined to barges owned locally in the Maldon district. From Dr H. Reynolds Brown of Maldon I received such particulars as were available of the Maldon Barge Races. It is difficult to obtain any certain information, as no records have been kept, and when the office where programmes were printed unfortunately changed hands some years ago, quantities of old matter, bill-heads, programmes and the like, were destroyed. But the race was certainly held as early as seventy-five to eighty years ago, and can thus almost rank with the Thames and Medway events in antiquity. It has been held at irregular intervals, as often as funds could be raised, and generally about every two or three years. Usually three or four barges started, although five starters have been known, which must have needed very careful sailing in so narrow a river. The race was a single-class match for trading barges registered at Maldon. All started from scratch, and there were no other restrictions. No list of winners is to be found, but *Saltcote Belle* won the cup outright once by virtue of three consecutive wins. *Mermaid* won the race held in 1929. The last race was held in 1936, and was for the "Ebenezer Richard Keeble Memorial Cup", presented by the Cement Marketing Co. It was won by *Emma*, Captain R. Flint, with *Ethel Maud*, who had won most of the earlier races, second.

Before leaving the fascinating subject of barge racing it is worth noting that the expense of fitting out a barge for the race was much greater than is generally imagined. Although only working sails and gear might be used, which had to be part of the barge's ordinary equipment some months before the race was sailed, the expense of preparing the barge, treating her bottom, overhauling her rigging and so on was very heavy. Not only was there an actual considerable outlay, but the barge was not earning any freights for some weeks before the race while the fitting out was proceeding. It actually cost anything from £150 to £300 to race a barge if she were properly prepared, and this high cost was bound to affect the number of entries when barges were passing through lean days, as they were for many years between the wars.

Since the first edition of this book was published, Mr Philip Kershaw has called attention to the fact that many years ago a race for local barges was an important event in the Regattas at Southend ; and, after painstaking research, he wrote a detailed account of them which was published in the Summer number of "Spritsail" in 1949, from which the following information has been extracted by the courtesy of the Editor.

The annual regatta, which at first was a purely local affair, was first organised in the eighteen-sixties ; and in the early years most of the races were for working craft—bawleys, cocklers and shrimpers, with rowing matches for watermen and coastguards. A few years after its start, barge races formed a regular part of the programme. Southend then had a barge fleet almost rivalling Maldon in numbers. All possible craft entered for the race, sailing as they were, with very little special preparation. Most were slow, battered old river barges ; but the hoy traders—"goods barges" to the locals—which ran on regular weekly services from London, were smarter and better kept.

The Vandervords were the best-known owners, and their best-known barge was the *West Kent*, whose skipper for thirty-nine years was Joshua Brand. She was famous locally for smashing through Southend Pier in the great gale of 1881, and survived until the nineteen-twenties. The Brasiers also were a barge-owning family, with some incredibly old craft, such as the *Two Brothers*, built in 1795, and the *Gregory* of Maldon, built in 1797 ; both continued trading for ninety years—two more examples of the longevity of barges.

The first really definite racing records are for the year 1876, when seven barges entered, in two classes. The winner was Burford's new *Conqueror*, winner of the Thames Race that year ; with *Challenger* second. In the swim-headed class, Howard's *Catherine* won, with his *Quartus* second. Next year, *Challenger* gained the victory in the first class, while the winning swimmie was the delightfully named *Rogue in Grain*, a very old Maldon-built barge. There was no race in 1878, but in 1879 four swimmies raced over a course of some 10 to 12 miles. *Rogue in Grain* was the first to get her anchor, but *John and Jane* soon took the lead, and finished 10 minutes ahead of *William and Mary*. In the round-bowed craft, *Matilda and Amy* led at the start, to give place to *Henry and Annie*, who eventually won by 5 minutes from *West Kent*, carrying off a cup as well as champion flag and prize money. The following year *James*, *Three Friends*, *Mary Ann* and *Joseph and John* started in the first class, in which the barges were required to make two rounds of the course; the winner was *Three Friends*. In the second class, with three starters, *Maid of the Mill* was winner, *Gregory* second and *Two Brothers* third.

The event in 1881 was limited to local barges (Kentish craft had been admitted in 1880). *Three Friends* of the round-headers was first home, with *Lord Palmerston* a bad second, half an hour later. *Royal William* was disqualified for passing the wrong side of a mark boat. First of the swimmies was *Sarah and Elizabeth*, with *Jane and Sarah* second and *Gregory* third. It was this year that, in pursuance of the policy to exclude "foreigners", it was decided to fix a separate match for Maldon barges. This was probably the beginning of organised barge racing on the Blackwater. There was no race in 1882, and the records for 1883 (when there was an open race) and 1884 are missing. There was only one class in 1885, and all the entries were "locals". Vandervord's *George and Alfred* was slow getting her anchor at the start, and the race was won by *West Kent*, *Lord Palmerston*, second, coming in 35 minutes later, and *James* 24 minutes after her. *Alfred and Elizabeth* was unlucky, first losing her topmast and then breaking her sprit.

The 1886 regatta, sailed in light airs, was badly advertised and rather a "flop". *Alfred and Elizabeth* won in 3 hours 20 minutes, in a fairly close finish, with *Alfred* second and *Emily* third. There was no race for barges in 1887; but in 1888 five barges entered, in only one class, being *Alma*, *Essex Farmer*, *Walter Hawthorn*, *Factor* and *Ness*, who finished in that order. A long gap followed 1888, and if there was a race in the next ten years it was not part of the local regatta. Southend was becoming more "yachting-minded" and the tradesmen's interest in barge racing was on the wane.

1900 seems to have been the next race for local traders. Winner of the race that year was S. J. Peters' *Mary Jane*, with the well-known "Tubby" Blake aboard as third hand. She was a nice little 42-ton barge, built at Milton in 1877; she was followed by Luddesdown second and *Gannet* third. "Tom White was her skipper in the nineties," writes Mr Kershaw. "One year she was off the Pier on the last lap when her topmast came down, just as the mate was going to climb the weather vang with the champion flag wrapped round him to put at the peak. Tom White called to him to wait till she'd won. Anyway, she *did* win. *Mary Jane* was like a yacht, black-leaded and polished up—even the anchor was blacked for the race. She was built to carry 40,000 bricks; sold in the twenties, she is now a house-boat at Benfleet."

Mr Kershaw records that the last Southend race seems to have been held in 1904. The barge race that year was sailed by "Old Towners". *Ethel Ada*, Underwood's fine new barge, built at Paglesham the year before, won, in spite of losing her topmast, brought down by a huge racing spinnaker. Vandervord's *Jane* took second place, with Goldsmith's old iron pot *Bras de Fer* third. Gundy's brickie *Luddesdown* had been entered, but could not be got ready in time.

Since then, although barge yachts have raced in Southend and Westcliffe regattas, there have been no races for working barges. There was one entry from Southend in the 1935 Thames race, the *Percy*, but no one expected her to do very well. The Brasiers and Vandervords had sold their barges before the 1914–18 war. Barge racing at Southend was never more than an event in a local regatta, but it provided good sport while it lasted.

Much the same may probably be said about barge racing at Harwich, where organised matches would appear to have been held some years before Mr Henry Dodd promoted the first race on the Thames in 1863. I have long heard tales of organised barge racing at Harwich in the middle of the nineteenth century, but only recently was I able to find any contemporary account or other evidence. It was, therefore, with the greatest of interest that I heard from Mr Frank Hussey of Ipswich, of his researches into the old records of the Royal Harwich Yacht Club, which produced two references of pertinent importance, both in the year 1856.

Of them, the first appears in the Minutes of a meeting of the Regatta Committee on 28th May 1856; where it was recorded that "the Committee are desirous to get up a Purse to be sailed for by the Barges employed in the Stone Trade". A month later, at a meeting of the Royal Harwich Yacht Club held on the 29th June, it was agreed that a small bill should be printed announcing that "A Prize will be given for Spritsail Barges belonging to Harwich and Ipswich".

These references started me off on the scent, and I then found, from "Hunts' Yachting Magazine" for August 1856, that the barge race duly took place as part of the Royal Harwich Regatta. It also appears that the barge-racing event was by no means the first at that port. The report describes it as "a race for Sprit-sail barges for five guineas, given by Sir George Brooke, Bart. This race is almost of a novel character having been introduced into the regatta at Harwich a few years since, but not having been paid much attention to of late. The kindness of Sir George Brooke this year enabled the Committee to renew this description of race."

Three barges started, the *Levanter*, owned by L. Richmond; *Alacer*, belonging to J. Gall; and J. Watts Junior's *Rapid*. The start was even and they were together for a little time; then the *Alacer* took the lead, and never lost it, winning the race by a considerable distance. "The *Rapid*," says Hunt, "*belied* her name, and was passed by the *Levanter*, who came in second."

A race for barges was also held in the Harwich Regatta of the following year, 1857; with a prize of fifteen sovereigns. Four barges entered, the *John Etherden*, *Levanter*, *Rapid* and *Charles Napier*; and the race was won "by the two first" (did that mean a dead-heat?) over the same course as the larger yachts, once round. This was from abreast the starting vessel, out to the Cork Lightship, thence to a mark boat at the Stone Banks, back into the Harbour, thence to Ewarton Bay mark boat, in the Stour, and so back to the starting vessel. The total distance was about 20 miles.

Unfortunately, after this year the barge race seems to have been abandoned; but it seems clear, from the foregoing evidence, that to this ancient port of Harwich must be given the honour of providing the first race for working barges ever to be recorded.

A much later race, sailed at Harwich in 1897 or 1898, has been described by Hervey Benham in his delightful book "Down Tops'l", published by Harrap in 1951. This was won by *Centaur*, with *Orinoco* second and *Consul* third. Other barges sailing were *Primrose*, *Ida* (who broke her bowsprit), *Petrel* and *Iverna*. Each barge was allowed five hands, and the course was round the Cork lightship and the Stone Banks buoy, to finish round a steamer at Harwich.

A private challenge match from Maldon round the Cork and back is also recorded in the same book. This was between *Mermaid* and *Hyacinth*, and won by the former, sailed by Sim Staines.

There were also races in the Colne, but these, says Mr Benham, were "occasional, irregular, and unrecorded." He mentions Marriage's *Fleur-de-lis* sailing against the Maldon *Violet*, but the result has been forgotten. On another occasion, *Fleur-de-lis* was beaten by *Ready*, who also beat *D'Arcy* in yet another half-forgotten race. There must have been many such, formal and informal, all through the years of bargeing. No true bargeman could ever resist a contest!

# CHAPTER XII

## *Some Famous Bargemen*

In the pages that follow I have endeavoured to gather together a number of yarns, pen-and-ink studies and personal sketches of some of the better-known bargemen of past and present days. I am only too conscious that in this there have been many omissions of well-known names that ought not to have been left out. The stories themselves, it may moreover be objected, are sketchy, their order indiscriminate. But let it be remembered that I have set them down just as they have been told to me over a period of several years : some at sea, with the song of the wind in the rigging ; others over a pipe and a glass of beer in some snug riverside tavern ; and not a few in the cabins of barges, or in the cabin of my own little ship with bargemen guests aboard, sitting gathered round the fire, and the air about all thick with tobacco smoke. As I have heard them, so have I written them down ; and from the pages of many notebooks I have made this chapter.

The first barge I sailed in was the *Phoenician*, a fine modern vessel built after the First World War, and described in Chapter VI. Her skipper, the late Captain Alfred Horlock of Mistley, who owned a half-share in her, was one of the best-known racing skippers of all time. At his home at Mistley in Essex he had a collection of cups of which any man might well be proud. He was sailing his barge *Vigilant*, of which his nephew "Chubb" Horlock was skipper when she won the Thames Barge Race in 1928. He also won the last two races sailed before the First World War. His many triumphs between the wars are recorded in the chapter on the Barge Races. A fine, powerfully built man, he was a splendid specimen of a sailorman, a man of iron nerve and great determination. He made up his mind quickly, and once decided, never went back. Woe betide the lighterman who held him up in a dock ! Yet for all that there was a genial twinkle in his eye which put one at one's ease immediately. His physical strength was enormous. On one occasion, having loaded his barge at Mistley, humping sacks of wheat on his back all day, he sailed her down the river about five miles and anchored ; rowed the heavy barge's boat back to Mistley over the ebb tide to go to a dance ; danced until early in the morning ; rowed back to his barge over the last of the flood, got under way at once and sailed to London. As a young man he was a very strong swimmer, and held medals from the Royal Humane Society for life-saving. He was a keen oarsman and a member of the Four which won the Orwell Challenge Shield outright in 1897. In single sculls he won the championships of both Orwell and Stour. He was also a great reader in his spare time, and named his barge after the ancient Phoenician traders to Cornwall.

What Alfred Horlock didn't know about making a barge go was simply not worth knowing. He had a great knowledge of the proper setting of sails. Many and many a time while I was aboard other barge skippers would visit us to ask him about the set of their sails. "Wish you'd have a look at that new mains'l of mine, Alf," was the usual request. "The one so-and-so made me. That doesn't set right some-how, and I thought that you . . ." and invariably, seeing the sail set, with a little wind in it, Alfred Horlock could spot the reason. He was a member of one of, if not *the*, greatest of barge-racing families. From his grandfather, who owned the *Excelsior*, winner of the biggest class race in 1868, to his nephew "Chubb" Horlock, who raced in the *Vigilant* in 1928, four generations of the Horlocks have won the Barge Race, not occasionally, but many times.

When he died suddenly at his home "Fairwinds", Mistley, on 7th October 1940, at the age of 67, he was mourned not only by his family, but by a wide circle of friends and acquaintances who had learned to value and honour him for his sterling worth, both as a sea-man and a friend. He had won notable distinction as designer and master of sailing barges. He first won the Thames championship in 1905, and this was followed by a long series of successes in barges built to his design, including *Vigilant* and *Phoenician*. In all, he won championships of Thames and Medway nineteen times out of the twenty-one contests he entered; a record which has never been equalled.

The late Commander E. G. Martin, R.N.V.R., relates in his "Sailorman" (a real classic of bargeing) that it was to Captain "Alf" Horlock he first went when he wanted to learn how to sail a barge. "Alf" was able to arrange for him to sign on as mate of the *Vigilant* under his nephew "Chubb"; and his experiences are recorded in that delightful book, published by the Oxford University Press in 1933.

His love for sailing was not confined to barges, for he took a keen interest in the Stour Sailing Club at Mistley, of which he was Vice-Commodore when he died. During the First World War he was the first Mistley captain to trade across the Channel, which he continued to do throughout the war. He held both the British War Medal and the Mercantile Marine Medal. In the Second World War he was on duty with the Observer Corps up to the day before his death.

I am proud that I was privileged to enjoy his personal friendship; and it is with a heavy heart that I record that he has now made his last port. I can but pay my humble tribute to a splendid sailorman, for whom I had such high regard and admiration.

Robert Richard Horlock, father of Alfred Horlock, was also a well-known and able skipper in his day. The *Volunteer*, the first barge ever to have advertisements on her sails, was built for him. The advertisements were of "Beecham's Pills". She was afterwards converted into a yacht with auxiliary engines, and a very comfortable old ship she made. At one time large advertisements used often to be painted on barges' sails, and Plate 54 shows the *Millie* in the creek at Stone's yard, Brightlingsea, with her sails like a travelling hoarding. Among many relics collected during his days at sea, R. R. Horlock used particularly to cherish a bottle of Bass from the bar of the excursion steamer *Princess Alice*. This he had picked up floating in the Thames after that ill-fated vessel had been run down near Woolwich with a loss of nearly six hundred lives. He was a far-sighted man and foretold both aeroplanes and speedboats, maintaining that if a flat-bottomed craft like a barge could be made to rise and skim on the surface, she would need little power to drive her, and would travel so fast that she would remain on the surface. Similar planing conditions would also apply to the air.

"Chubb" Horlock, for many years skipper of the *Vigilant*, a fine, fast barge built by Orvis at Ipswich and owned by his uncle Alfred Horlock, is perhaps one of the best-known of a younger generation of skippers, and few men are smarter at handling a barge. He sailed as skipper when little more than a boy. To him I am indebted for much of the up-to-date information contained in this edition; and I have also to thank his cousin, Alan Horlock, of Mistley, Captain Alfred Horlock's son, who has compiled many notes, largely from the recollections of that veteran bargeman Captain James Stone.

Alfred Horlock's mate, Fred Bloomfield, brother of Ernest Bloomfield, then skipper of the *Jock*, one of Paul's barges, was a very cheery soul and a terror for work. He could be a gay lad when he liked, for he believed that it is a poor heart that never rejoices. He and I shared the foc's'le, and a right good companion he proved. He also was a powerful man, and he needed to be. Although the *Phoenician* could load 180 tons, she carried only two hands. By the time one had hove in fifteen or twenty fathoms of chain, wound up the tops'l (for it was hoisted by a winch), hoisted the foresail and sheeted home the mainsail, one wanted to sit on the hatches and gasp before tackling the setting of the jib. It was hard enough work when I was aboard to lend a hand. For two hands it must have been a very severe proposition. At one time Fred had been master of a small barge, the *Hilda*, one of Paul's fleet. But she had her gear blown out of her somewhere off Harwich; there was a bit of trouble over it and Fred Bloomfield left her.

Among the long-distance bargemen, Thomas Strange, skipper and owner of the *Davenport*, in which I sailed to Antwerp as mate, and his brother Harry, were among the most famous. Tom Strange was the first man ever to take a barge to the Shetlands, and a great stir she created when she arrived. The natives could not understand her at all, for they had never seen a ship that could sail without ballast when light. On one occasion he sailed a barge into Dunkirk with the rudder unshipped, steering her with a sweep, which proves what a handy vessel a barge can be. It happened in this way.

Somewhere about the year 1909 or 1910, when he was skipper of the old boomsail barge *May Queen*, he came away from Dort in Holland. The *May Queen* was a beautifully shaped old thing, loading about 165 tons. She could load with 3 feet "odds", that is, difference of draught forward and aft, and liked it. Some barges have to be trimmed within an inch or two. The previous night he had come away out of the Roompots bound for London, with a nice breeze north-easterly. When they got to the North Hinder light-vessel, however, the wind flew round to the west-nor'-west, which was no good to them, so they turned in to the land on the starboard tack. Next morning, when breakfast was ready, they went down to eat it and left Dan, the third hand, steering. They were in sight of the land, and steering in towards Dunkirk.

About halfway through breakfast, she touched. Skipper Tommy ran up on deck and found that when she had touched—on the Dunkirk Banks—she had sat down with the swell and unshipped her rudder. She lay there for three hours. Several times, as she bumped, she re-shipped the rudder of her own accord, but always unshipped it again, and did so the last time she bumped. Although they were in sight of the shore all the time not a soul came near them. The skipper then decided to take her into Dunkirk, and shipped a big oar aft, with which he steered her over the stern. He told me that she steered like a boat; and when they fetched Dunkirk, he shot her into the harbour and at once got the boat out. The boy got into the boat and sat and sheered her against the barge as she towed alongside, to help the steering. In that way she was sailed right up to the old dock, and no one knew that she had unshipped her rudder until she was lying alongside by the lock gates. She went into the dock that day, and by topping up the mizzen boom the rudder was raised a little and the weight taken. Next day she went alongside, grounded in a good berth and the rudder was reshipped at low water.

Tom Strange made many voyages to Ireland with his brother Harry, who was at one time skipper of the well-known old *Cock of the Walk*, built by Surridge. She was Harry Strange's last ship, a very pretty vessel, and she was eventually sunk by the Germans in the First World War. Harry Strange was said never to have been surpassed in handling a barge. He was a very quiet man, always even-tempered, never flurried ; whether in a calm or a gale of wind, he was quiet and self-possessed. He was known as "The Toff", for he was always very smartly dressed and wore a neatly clipped beard. He once went into Bantry Bay, on the south-west coast of Ireland, in a barge called the *Moss Rose*, with his brother Tom as mate.

An amusing story was told to me by Tom Strange, of the Ratcliffe Highway in the old days, when it was perhaps the warmest corner of London and sailormen were often drugged and robbed of even the shirts from their backs. Early one morning, his brother, then a young lad, was returning to his barge when he met a sailorman running down the street with nothing on but the morning newspaper wrapped round him amidships. "Morning, mate!" sang out Strange. "Bit close reefed, this morning, aren't you?"

The man looked across at him and grinned. "Well, I am a bit snugged-down like, you might say. But you wait a minute—there's a beggar running up astern of me under bare poles!" True enough, a few moments later a fellow followed him with no "sail" at all!

Another famous long-distance trader, and a great friend of Skipper Thomas Strange, was Simeon Stanes. At one time he had the *Emma*, a Maldon barge mentioned elsewhere (Chapter XIII). He used to trade regularly to Newcastle, with a young lad as his mate and sole crew. On one occasion, when near Newcastle, and brought up to wait for the tide, he was visited by a yachting party. He showed them over the barge and made them a cup of tea. Before they left they expressed a desire to see his crew.

"Certainly," said Sam, and going to the foc's'le hatch, called below. "Come up a minute, Fred!"

"But aren't you going to call up the rest of your crew?" asked his guests.

"This *is* my crew," replied Sam, to their extreme astonishment.

Sim Stanes afterwards had the *Record Reign*, also of Maldon, the barge used as a Q-ship during the 1914–18 war.

PLATE 54 Advertisements on Sails: *Millie* at Brightlingsea

[*By courtesy of Douglas Stone, Esq*

PLATE 55 The *Seapoy* ashore off Cromer, 13 December 1933

[*Fox Photos*

PLATE 56 Light and Shade among the Barges: *Northdown*

[*Photograph by " The Times "*]

Another well-known long-distance skipper was a man named Grant, who had the reputation for being a very "hard case". For he went to sea in all weathers and frightened skippers of big schooners by his intrepid sailings. At one time he was trading regularly to Wexford in the *Elsie*.

To my old friend the late Mr Harry Ward, a retired bargeman who lived at Pinmill, I am indebted for much information about well-known barge skippers, and particularly about his elder brother, Walter Ward, whose reputation sixty years ago was second to none. It was said of him that "he could take a plank to sea". He was skipper of the *Opal*, when he was only seventeen, trading to Newcastle. He also had the *Cock of the Walk* for some time. Walter Ward it was who, when skipper of the *Arundel Castle* about sixty-five years ago, cleared from Antwerp loaded for Christiania (now Oslo) in Norway. He was the only man ever to do so. The mate was a man named Joe Palmer, who afterwards kept an inn at Salcot. From Oslo he brought back timber for London, loading a 6-foot stack on his deck. On the voyage home they struck heavy weather and were hove-to for three days off the Dogger Bank. The crew spent the time below "turned in", and playing cards in the cabin, as "happy as sandboys". "There was nothing else to do!" they said when they returned. On that trip he brought home a little Norwegian pram dinghy of which he was very proud, calling her *My Fancy*.

He eventually lost the *Arundel Castle* in fine weather in the Channel. She had come out of Guernsey loaded with stone for Shoreham. In Guernsey she had been compelled to lie in a round-bottomed vessel's berth, which was quite unsuitable, and strained her badly. When off the Casquets the boy went below to get dinner ready and found the water up to the cabin stove. They at once tried the pumps, but the water gained on them so rapidly that she went down within ten minutes. They had only time to jump into the boat, cut the gripes holding her down and let her float off the hatches as the barge settled under them. It was a gloriously fine day, and she sank with every sail set, mizzen-topsail, boom-jib, flying-jib and all. His son, Dudley Ward, was mate with him at the time. The most likely explanation of this extraordinary foundering was that, sitting in the bad berth, a boulder had been forced into her bottom, which had dropped out when she began to work a bit in the swell outside. The *Arundel Castle* belonged to Walker and Howard of Tower Street, London.

Walter Ward then went master of the *Gem of the Ocean*, and did very well in her, until she was lost with all hands off Dungeness in a gale of wind on 8th December 1890. She just failed to weather the

14

Ness. Harry Ward was boy in the old *Davenport* at the time. The *Davenport* was then a "spreety", and one of the fastest "bits of wood" afloat. She was brought up in the Gore, above Margate, the night the *Gem of the Ocean* was lost, and next morning, running round the Foreland with the wind nor'-easterly, they met the *Francis* bound the other way. Her skipper, Captain Cowey, sang out that the *Gem* had been lost with all hands, not knowing that her skipper's little brother was aboard. It was certainly a shock for the lad, for this was his first news of it. His skipper tried to comfort him. "Don't you take no notice of what he says, boy," he said. "He'd tell you any old yarn." But it proved to be only too true. Dudley Ward, the mate, a very powerful swimmer, managed to reach the shore alive, but died soon afterwards. The others were eventually picked up, Walter Ward at Gravelines, the third hand a long way down the English coast, at Poole. Such is the fate of bargemen.

Some years later Harry Ward went to Pembroke in the *Alert*. She was the first East Coast barge ever seen there and was dubbed locally a "London Flat". The lee-boards were a particular puzzle to the dockers there. One day a boat-load of dockers rowing by hailed them.

"Heigh, master," they called, "we want you to settle a bet we've got on. Which board do you use—the weather or the lee one?"

An old friend of his, Mr Harold Cox, a retired coal merchant, living at Woodbridge, was at one time mate of the little Yorkshire billyboy *Brilliant*, of Goole. She was only about sixty feet long, tubby, round-bottomed and round-sterned. She was ketch-rigged and used to wallow along with about a foot of list, being steered by a stumpy little tiller only $4\frac{1}{2}$ feet long. Steering was very hard work; she went off her course in a moment, and it was "hard up" and "hard down" all the time.

One day, coming out of the Humber and running across the Boston Deeps, the skipper, who had been below, came up and put his head out of the cabin hatch.

"How's she going?" he said to the mate, meaning how was she heading by the compass.

The mate, running across the deck to loo'ard on one of his "hard down" expeditions, sang out: "Don't know, skipper, but I'll tell you when I come back!"

In the same ship was a boy who thought one day he would catch some mackerel. He made up some sort of hooks, and hung them over the side on a piece of rope-yarn. The *Brilliant* wallowed on slowly.

Presently the skipper came on deck. "What have you got that rope-yarn over for, boy?" said he.

"Thought I'd catch a fish, skipper."

"Do you know that's stopping her a knot an hour, boy?"

"How fast do you reckon she's going, then?"

"Oh, about three knots."

"Well then, skipper, I'll hang a couple more over and stop the old —— altogether!" was the ready answer.

Harry Ward also sailed with David Garnham, another Pin Mill man, when the latter was in the *Eastern Belle*. (See page 80.) Garnham was a fine long-distance bargeman, and went out to Lisbon with her. On one occasion, when Harry Ward was aboard, they were coming down from Totnes on the Dart in a flat calm, and had the boat out with four men in her towing ahead to give steerage way. The skipper went below to light his pipe and the barge was caught by the tide and went slowly on in a bend, right up to the shore. There she pushed her bowsprit through the bedroom window of a house built on the waterside, to the considerable indignation of the house-holder!

On another occasion, David Garnham lost his mate in Antwerp by a "pier-head jump". The mate wanted to take a job which had been offered him on a deep-water ship. The skipper couldn't spare him and wouldn't let him go. The mate said nothing, but waited until the barge was being towed out of the dock by a tug. He stood watching the gradually widening gap to the pier-head, and eventually, with a cheery, "Well, so long, Master Garnham", he leapt overside and swam to the shore.

It is with the greatest regret that I have to record the death of Mr Harry Ward, senior, on 25th March 1945. We had known each other for more than twenty-one years, ever since the day when I acquired my first sea-going yacht, the little *Lily*, of 5 tons, which he looked after for me. Afterwards my Bristol Channel pilot cutter *Cariad* was in his charge. Acquaintance had ripened into friendship with the passage of the years. It was through him that I was first introduced to the world of barges; and to him I owe innumerable stories of the ships and men of years gone by. He was a fine waterman, too, and could do anything with a boat.

When he died he had been in failing health for some time; for he never got over the loss of his elder son, Harry, who was drowned at the end of Pin Mill Hard in a winter's gale and blizzard on 18th January 1940, as recorded elsewhere in this book. In his last illness, before he was removed to the hospital where he died, he would lie on his bed, which had been moved down to the sitting-room of his house at Pin Mill, looking up at his painting of the old *Septimus*, which hung

over his head ; and repeatedly insisted that it was to be for me after he
had gone.

He was always proud of that picture, as I am proud to have it now,
in memory of an old, true and valued friend. Fond as I still am of Pin
Mill, it can never mean quite the same to me without the two Harry
Wards, father and son.

To turn again to a sadder side of life in the barges, one of the greatest risks run by bargemen, during the winter especially, is the danger
ever present of losing a man overboard. This may happen in a
moment, and if it should happen at night the chances of picking up
the lost man are small indeed. More than one bargeman has had the
agony of seeing a comrade snatched from him by the relentless sea.
Perhaps the bitterest and cruellest case I know was when one of the
ablest young skippers, a man still in the early twenties, had the misfortune to lose his mate overboard in circumstances which make the
story one of the most intense dramas of the sea that I have ever heard.

This young skipper and his mate had been together since baby-
hood. They went to school together, grew up together as inseparable
companions. Where his mate was, the other would always be. So from
boyhood to manhood they grew together, and went to sea as mate and
cook in the same barge. When the elder himself got a barge and went
skipper of her, he took his friend as mate. There were just the two of
them, and a happy ship she was.

Then, one night, running down out of the Wallet past Harwich,
bound for somewhere in the Broads district, a fresh breeze turned into
a strong, hard wind. Tearing at the water, it soon raised a short and
angry sea. Sail had to be reduced. Came a sudden, furious squall,
with driving, stinging rain. The mate ran forward to take in and stow
the jib. Just as he was doing so, the laden barge dived deep and took a
drink over the bows. She rose again, and as she rose the lad was torn
from his hold and swept overside past his horrified skipper. The
latter lost not a second ; he flung a lifebuoy at once and in that brief
instant as the lad flashed by, saw that his aim was true and that the
buoy had landed near him. He took a quick glance at his compass,
noted his course, put his helm hard down and as the barge came
round into the wind, started frantically to heave in the main sheet. He
got it fast and then, with admirable coolness and judgment, worked
the barge back in short tacks of about a minute and a half each way,
back over the course she had come. The quest was almost hopeless :
alone in a large and heavily laden barge, with half a gale blowing and
a wicked short sea.

The night was dark as the grave, no moon, not a star, nothing but the blackness of the streaming heavens above, and the white flashes of the foam-flecked sea around him. Yet, impossible though the task seemed, he found him. Sighted him, and threw him a line. The boy caught it as the barge surged by, and his skipper began desperately to haul in the rope, hand over hand. Then, on the verge of victory, he lost him. The barge had a non-reversing screw steering gear, which of course remained fixed, so that she tore on with speed unchecked. As the skipper hauled his mate towards him the boy was being choked and drowned by the water forced down his throat. Even so he hung on valiantly, while the skipper got him to the rail and leaned over to haul him in. But the boy's strength was gone. His skipper touched his hand, actually touched his hand, as his strength failed. Gasping his friend's name, the boy disappeared into the blackness astern.

Alone on the barge, after a fruitless search, the young skipper worked her back into Harwich. In the early hours before the dawn the wind fined right away, and he dropped his hook in the harbour. Leaving his sails flapping idly in the still air, he paced the deck like a man in a dream. So the Customs found him when the day dawned and they came off to the barge. But all that he could think of was—he had touched his hand—and lost him. He had actually *touched his hand*.

It is perhaps unnecessary to stress the remarkable feat of seamanship which the finding, and almost recovering, of the lost man represents. It was an astounding achievement. But I do want to emphasise that this risk of losing a man overboard from a laden barge is one that is always present. Yet it is one that the bargemen have to face, in all weathers, as part of their daily work. They face it cheerfully and without a qualm.

Another story of a man overboard has a less tragic ending. It concerns another East Coast bargeman known as "Coddy" Polly, a Harkstead man, skipper of the barge *Orinoco*. His brother sailed as mate with him, and a wonderfully smart pair of hands they were. I once saw the *Orinoco* on the hard at Pin Mill, near Ipswich, refitting. She was having a new mainmast, and in the evening "all hands" at Pin Mill were engaged "parbuckling" the new mast aboard and shipping it in the mast-case. Nothing else was done. Yet, next evening, by the same time, the barge was rigged and ready for sea, with sails bent and the brothers touching up the blocks with aluminium paint. The two alone had done it—put the rigging over, set it up, bent the sails and completed the job in the single day, working from dawn to dusk without a break even for a meal. Scarcely a word was spoken ; the brothers had been together so long, words were not necessary.

But the story I was about to tell was of a day when, as the mate was "swigging" on a stack lashing to tighten it, the lashing parted and he fell backwards overside.

"Throw us a rope, Coddy!" he yelled, coming up for the first time. "Coddy" took no notice, but went on steering the barge.

"Throw us a rope," he yelled again. "I can't swim."

"Well," replied his brother, "now's your time to learn, mate!"

Fortunately the mate caught hold of the dinghy painter, and scrambled aboard, so the end of the yarn was comedy merely.

The hero of this story, "Coddy" Polly, is still bargeing; and is now skipper of Cranfield's *Beric*.

Yet another "overboard" yarn, which was told me by a retired barge skipper named Fred Knights, who also lived at Pin Mill, illustrates the extraordinarily shallow water in which an empty barge can sail. A barge, whose name I have unfortunately forgotten, was sailing into Wakering Haven, just below Shoeburyness. The course in crosses the Maplin Sand, and there is very little water. The mate, who was alone on deck, was heaving up the lee-board to lighten the draught, when the handle slipped off the winch and he stumbled and fell overside. The water was only up to his waist, so he picked himself up and *ran* after the barge, yelling to the skipper to come on deck to turn around and pick him up. A ludicrous sight he must have presented, leaping through the water like a dog in long grass, and the barge gaily sailing on without him!

An amusing story is told of a mate, who must be nameless, given to celebrating too luxuriously when he went ashore. His skipper could never get rid of him, however, as, though often "sacked", he was such a likable fellow that he generally got himself reinstated the next day. On one occasion he had come back more than usually "merry", and next morning was told to pack his traps and clear out. "Oh, no!" was his tactful answer. "I'm not going to go, for if you don't know when you've got a good mate, I know when I've got a good skipper!" He stayed.

There is also a well-known yarn of a mate who, having spent a very trying night at sea, eventually lost his temper and let go the anchor. "There," he called out to his scandalised skipper, "I've brought up my end of her, and you can do what you like with yours!"

A skipper named Ben Keeble held a wonderful record in the hay barges. He used to be master of the *Farmer's Boy*, a stack barge belonging to Wrinch of Ewarton, Suffolk. He is said to have carried no less than 52 cargoes of hay from Harwich to Vauxhall, and brought back 52 cargoes of manure within 52 weeks; of which period a fortnight was spent on the shipyard painting and refitting. This was a remarkable achievement, for it must be remembered that it meant regular passages at sea in the depths of winter with 12 feet of hay on deck. It meant "shooting" bridges up to Vauxhall, and before the gear could be lowered space had to be cleared in the stack, and the hay moved aside, to enable the mast and spreet to come down. If a huffler was available to help, so much the better. If not, Ben Keeble took the barge through without. The barge had then to be unloaded, re-loaded and to return to Harwich. This record was never equalled.

I wish that I had space to spin many more yarns of famous bargemen, past and present. Of Skipper Bill Leaks of Pin Mill, for example, who took the *Matilda Upton* into Southwold in the dark, sending his boat ashore with his sidelights and hanging the port light on one pier-head and the starboard on the other to steer in by, as the port is otherwise unlighted. Of my old friend "Schoolmaster" West who was for so long skipper of the barge *Arrow* belonging to the London and Rochester Trading Company. "Schoolmaster" West earned his nickname because all the new hands in that firm were sent to sea under him first to be trained as mates. In 1931 he was almost "The Father of the Fleet", having been employed with the firm for so long, although this title was then actually held by Captain William Watson of the *Pudge*.

Typical of the older type of river barge skipper were two of the skippers who were employed by the Associated Portland Cement Company in their once famous "Blue Circle" fleet of sailing barges— now, alas, all replaced by more modern craft—who were all alive in 1931, when the first edition of this book was published. One of them, Thomas Shields, had sixty years as captain and mate of the firm's sailing barges, and as lighterman, and was a member of a family of father and three sons who had given a total length of service of 150 years to the same firm. Another of the skippers, Captain Frederick Butler, didn't want to retire on a pension at the age of eighty-four— he thought he was only seventy-four, until he got his birth certificate. He was still hale and hearty, and, at the advanced age of ninety-one, in perfect health and spirits.

In closing this chapter I cannot resist telling this story of a Suffolk bargeman's little son, who did a trip with his daddy in the barge to London. Before he left home, his mother had impressed upon him the importance of remembering to say his prayers while on board. On his return, however, he silenced her inquiry as to whether he had done so by saying, with great dignity, "But, Mummy, bargemen don't say *prayers*!''

# CHAPTER XIII

## *Light and Shade among the Barges*

THIS chapter, like Chapter XII, is but a collection of yarns. Here, however, I am concerned more with the ships than with the men. It is one of the mysteries of the sea that ships have characters, just as do people. Some barges are notoriously lucky; others exactly the reverse. And it does not follow that two barges, apparently almost alike in every respect, built may be at the same yard and even at the same time, will put up similar performances under sail. One may be definitely fast; the other may never "go" at all; and there is no apparent reason. It is my own belief that something of the spirit of the men who build them enters into the barges as they are built; and that ships, though they may not have souls, are yet something more than the mere wood and iron of which they are constructed. The barge-men themselves seem to feel this, for they speak of a barge as "living" so many years, and will say, on hearing of an old barge still at work, "Oh, is she still *alive*, then?" Some barges, lucky ships, seem to take care of themselves in an almost uncanny way. Perhaps one of the most extraordinary examples of this was the adventure that befell the *Lady Daphne* in the winter of 1928.

It is a far cry down-Channel to the Scilly Isles, and they are no place for a spritsail barge to be nosing around in the depths of winter. Yet on the evening of Boxing Day in 1928, the *Lady Daphne*, without a soul on board, successfully negotiated the dangerous and rock-infested entrance through Crowe Sound and picked herself a safe berth on a sandy beach on the Island of Tresco, where she grounded and lay undamaged until she could be towed off and taken to Hugh Town, after the weather had moderated.

The *Lady Daphne* was on a voyage, light, from Weymouth to Fowey, when she got caught out in a hard north-easterly gale, thick with snow and bitterly cold, and described locally by an old blue-water sailorman as a "regular Cape Horner". Early on Christmas night the captain was washed overboard, and the barge became unmanageable, driving down-Channel before the gale. From time to time the two remaining members of the crew burnt flares as signals of distress, but they were not seen owing to the thick snow, till they drove past the Signal Station at the Lizard. The lizard lifeboat was at once called out, and one can imagine with what heart-felt relief the two half-frozen men in the barge saw the rocket that told them the lifeboat was on her way. The story is told in "Sea Breezes" for April 1928.

Soon after getting afloat the Lizard coxswain showed an electric flare-up. This was seen and acknowledged by the barge, and afterwards the lifeboat got close to her at 12 miles W. by S. of the Lizard. Now came the most difficult task, that of getting the two half-dead men off the wreck. The boat was very ably managed, and after a good deal of most careful handling got close enough to enable the two men to jump on board of her. They told the coxswain that when they saw his flare-up they had only a drop of paraffin left. They soaked an old coat in this and fortunately managed to set fire to it.

All this happened in the early hours of Boxing Day. The next part of the barge's adventure is told in the following eye-witness account of her arrival in the Scillies, which reached me in a letter from 2nd Lieutenant Bernard Fergusson of the Black Watch, now Brigadier Fergusson, who was staying in Tresco at the time, and saw it all. Here, in his own words, is the story.

"I was staying at Tresco Abbey that Christmas. It blew like the devil and I was five days in Penzance Harbour waiting for *Scillonian* to sail. If I remember right, it blew very hard from the S.W. for a week, and we got out and across on Christmas Eve; it was a week before *Scillonian* got back to Penzance. There were two wrecks in the islands that week-end and two the week before, and it was in the afternoon of Boxing Day (blowing hard from the S.E.) that Major Dorrien-Smith, the Lord Proprietor of Scilly, came into the smoking-room at Tresco and said, 'There's a small vessel coming in through Crowe with her sails in ribbons.' We went up to the top of the watch-tower and had a look at her through glasses. She was driving on very hard about a mile outside Crowe, under jib only, as we afterwards saw. We rang up the St Mary's lifeboat—I remember the gale made it very hard to make ourselves heard—and told them, as she wasn't visible from Hugh Town. Ten minutes later we saw the spray fly up as she took the water, two miles away. It was most exciting watching them racing in, as we could see both barge and lifeboat, and neither of them could see the other. As the lifeboat (which had already been out the previous day to a French schooner off the Seven Stones) got well out from St Mary's, she ran fairly into it.

"We couldn't make out what *Lady Daphne* was doing as she stood straight on for a sand bar that runs out from St Martin's half-way to St Mary's. Even light, as she was, it was very risky to come through

Crowe Sound at that state of the tide, and breakers were clearly visible on the bar. She stood clean over them—and we breathed again. Then, instead of turning south to shelter in St Mary's Pool, she stood straight on for the Hats, which nothing has ever got over. It wasn't till then that we had any doubt but that she had a crew, and even then there was a ruckle of gear just forward of her wheel that we decided was somebody lashed to it who was probably 'out'.

"She reached the Hats, struck, lay on her lee bow twice as the seas struck her, then right over and slid into deeper water on the hither side. (The Hats are about half a mile from the Tresco shore.) Three hundred yards from the shore the lifeboat reached her, came alongside to leeward and several men swarmed up (I think) her davit falls, though I don't see how, as they would probably run out on the blocks. However, they got aboard and ran aft, two fellows getting to the wheel. They put it hard down and she swung for a moment; and we all thought they had her, but there was a crack like a gun, which we heard half a mile up the shore long after we saw it happen, and the jib split. She paid off again and drove the hundred and fifty yards ashore under bare poles.

"The beach she stranded on was on Tresco. I only know of two other vessels piling up on Tresco in all history: one about forty years ago (i.e. c. 1890), and the other, one of Sir Clowdisley Shovel's ships in 1707, the night he was drowned in the *Association* and four of his other ships were lost. Tresco is the inmost of all the islands, and surrounded with ledges and shoals on almost every side."

Brigadier Fergusson sent me a rough chart, showing more or less exactly the tracks of the barge and lifeboat, and the positions where the various incidents took place. He then continued: "She sank in two or three feet of water, it being about half-tide, if I remember right. She lay there two or three days, and then was towed over to Hugh Town. When I left the islands some weeks later I passed her under tow back to the mainland."

I had heard the story myself when I was in the islands in my ex-Bristol Channel pilot cutter *Cariad* in 1929; but some of the details then told to me, as recounted in the first edition of this book, were in error. But what had impressed the island boatmen most had been the uncanny way in which the barge had brought herself in, until she struck on the Hats. Only then did she fail to make the small alteration of course that would have avoided them. In fact, so accurate was her navigation that I was told those who saw her first thought she must have a local man aboard, piloting her in. Judge then of the astonishment of the lifeboatmen who boarded her to find that the only living creature aboard was the Captain's canary! If there are lucky ships, truly the *Lady Daphne* had made her claim to be included in that happy company. But only those who have themselves sailed in by Crowe Sound can realise how lucky indeed she was.

The *Lady Daphne* was, of course, a fine barge. She was built off lines by Shorts of Rochester, the foreman in charge of her building being a man named Parker. She loaded about 220 tons, and was reckoned by many to be "the fastest barge in the three Channels". Skipper Tom Harker, who at one time had the *Challenge*, a noted fast 160-ton sea-going barge, tells a story of how she passed him once when they were both coming up-Channel loaded with Portland stone. At sunrise one morning he saw a barge as far off as he could see, dead astern of him. At eight bells (four o'clock) that afternoon, she passed to wind'ard of him, close-hauled off Dungeness, and by sundown she was miles ahead and almost out of sight. The barge was the *Lady Daphne*, and Captain Tom Harker was so sick at being passed that he went below and stayed in the cabin until she had gone by; for the *Challenge* herself was admittedly a very fast barge.

I mention the fact that *Lady Daphne* was built from lines, because this is so unusual as to be hardly known in barge building. Barges are generally built by eye alone or from a wooden half-model. The *Lord Haig*, built by Shorts, and the *Lady Jean* were other barges built from lines.

The *Lady Daphne* is still trading, and is now owned by Messrs R. & W. Paul of Ipswich. She had an auxiliary engine installed in 1936. In that same year she was one of the barges employed in salvaging the cargo of the wrecked *Herzogin Cecile*, when that famous old sailing ship was lying beached near Salcombe. The *Lady Jean* is also still at work, and she, like her sister, now has an auxiliary. *Lord Haig*, however, has been lost, having been run down in the Humber some years ago.

The story of the *Lady Daphne* proves what bad weather a barge can go through safely even if left to herself. The loss of the Rye lifeboat with all hands will still be remembered. Yet on the night she was lost, the Maldon barge *Emma*, bound up-Channel, was running round Dungeness in perfect safety about an hour before the lifeboat was swamped. She is not a very large barge and had aboard a full load of 140 tons of Portland stone at the time. The skipper who then had her, Fred Morton, afterwards landlord of "The Three Cups" at Maldon, was lashed with lines to the mizzen rigging, as was the mate, Frank Parkes, later in the *Record Reign*. The mate was washed overboard by one heavy sea she shipped. He managed, however, to catch the lee vang as he was swept overside, and hung on. That saved him, and the next sea washed him back aboard again. The barge's decks were, of course, continually full of water, but the hatches kept on, her gear was good and she didn't so much as lose a sail. When I was last aboard her, indeed, in May 1931, she still had the same sails that she had carried through that historic gale. But the *Emma* was always a good barge to steer off the wind, and that contributed greatly to the safety in which she made the run.

It is the ability of the barge to go through bad weather at sea that has enabled her to make the amazing long voyages referred to in an earlier chapter. The voyages of the *Eastern Belle* and *Arundel Castle*, there recounted, were perhaps unusually long, but many barges were regular long-distance traders. A famous example was the *British Lion*, an ordinary "spreety" barge still afloat. About twenty-five years ago she used to trade from Guernsey with stone. She has come out of Guernsey, deep loaded and bound for London, in weather that kept the deep-water schooners in port, although bound for the same place with similar cargo. It has come on to blow really hard when she was in the Channel, and the masters of the schooners have been very anxious about her. They have indeed given her up for lost. Yet she has been to London, discharged, loaded again, and while sailing down-Channel has met those very schooners she left in Guernsey only then on their way up. This happened not once but many times.

When Captain Bill Hammond had her she had the reputation of going up- and down-Channel when nothing else under sail would look at it—with the skipper lashed to the wheel, very often. She was built by Gill at his Chatham Yard in 1879 for Sam Burford, who kept the "Gibraltar" public house, near Chatham station. She was a fast barge, and beat the same owner's *Challenger* in the barge races. Of 43 tons net, she loaded about 100 tons; and among fast passages was credited with one of 32 hours from the Medway to Portsmouth.

In July 1947 she was sold for conversion to a barge yacht, and the work was carried out at the Whitewall Yard in the following year. She had bad luck in her first passage as a yacht, getting caught in dirty weather off Margate and losing her mainmast. She was soon refitted, however, and completed her passage to the South Coast, where she spent the winter of 1948–49 at Chichester.

The barges will also ride out extraordinarily bad weather in open or semi-open roadsteads. In the winter of 1929 the barge *Ironsides*, 78 tons, one of the older iron barges, built at Grays in 1900, was caught out in a gale of wind when lying in Dungeness East Bay. She started to drag, and the Dungeness lifeboat put off and took the crew out of her.

Nevertheless, she rode it out safely with no one aboard, and two days later the crew were put into her again and continued the voyage up-Channel. I saw her a few days later at Rochester, looking none the worse for her adventure. But she also was a lucky ship. For some years she was employed in the ballast trade, and is still working, though as a fully powered motor barge, with all her sailing gear removed.

Barges will live through almost anything if only the hatches can be kept on, and many of them have been knocking about at sea for days, after having been abandoned, and then picked up and towed safely into port. The *Ardwina*, 60 tons, one of Goldsmith's barges, built by Orvis at Ipswich in 1909 and a very good ship at sea, was caught out in dirty weather in the Channel, and the crew were taken out of her by a steamboat. A man named Dines was skipper of her. She then continued knocking about the Channel for three days. The mail-boats kept reporting her, and she was a great danger to shipping until she was eventually found and towed into port. She has since been sold, first to Metcalfe Motor Coasters Limited, and then to Mr L. Vandersyde and Daniels Brothers; and is still trading. She was in collision in the Thames towards the end of 1948, but was not seriously damaged.

Another barge that had to be abandoned by her crew was the *Venture*, and she was in the end picked up by French fishermen and taken into Boulogne. *Venture*, built by Shrubsall in 1900, carries about 140 tons, is still trading under sail alone and is owned by Cranfields. She was on powder work at Strood during the Second World War, and was afterwards partly rebuilt at Lowestoft in 1947–48. She turned up later at Ipswich, looking very smart, and is a very good type for the Yarmouth and Ipswich trade.

The barge *Lord Nelson* had a curious adventure. When in dirty weather, blowing very hard, but thick, she went foul of the Cockle lightship off Yarmouth. Thinking she would undoubtedly be stove in and sunk, the skipper, a man named Tom Dorrel, sang out to the crew to jump for their lives and hang on to the lightship. This he succeeded in doing himself, getting hold of one of the great mooring chains as the barge swept by, and so scrambled aboard. The rest of the crew failed to do so, however; and the damaged barge kept afloat until, after having been given up for lost, she was eventually picked up by Ramsgate fishermen and taken into that port.

A more tragic story is that of the "boomy" *Lord Hamilton*, another of the famous "Lord" barges. On a dark winter's night a few years ago, when it was blowing a howling gale of wind and freezing hard, she drove ashore on the dreaded Goodwin Sands. Flares were lit and sent up, but the barge started to go to pieces at once, and settled down so that only the mast was above water. The flares were, of course, extinguished almost as soon as lit. The third hand and the cook, both nephews of the skipper, were swept away by one huge sea ; nothing could be done to save them, and they disappeared into the black turmoil of seething waters. The skipper and mate succeeded in scrambling up the rigging of the mainmast, and there crawled into the folds of the heavy topsail, which protected them somewhat from the icy blast and freezing spray. Then began a weary vigil waiting for the dawn and, please God, the lifeboat.

The lifeboat came, but in the blackness of the night she could not find the wrecked vessel ; so stood by to await the coming of day. When the sun rose, she ran down to the barge, of which only the mast was visible in the tumbling waste of yeasty foam. Not a soul could they see aboard her. Yet the skipper and mate were there all the time, lashed up in the tops'l waving their arms and making such feeble shouts as they were able, all without avail. But they were too weak from exhaustion and numbed with cold to extricate themselves from the iron-hard folds of the frozen sail, and to their dismay the lifeboat left them, to go to another wreck on a different part of the sands. Then it was that despair almost descended upon them. The barge seemed likely to go to pieces at any moment, and the mast shuddered and swayed with every shock. When it fell, a certain death awaited them.

Yet in spite of their peril, the indomitable spirit of the English seaman kept them cheerful, and Davies, the mate, kept up a running fire of jokes with the skipper about "What time he should put the kittle on?" and "What are we going to have for dinner, skipper?" So the day passed, and a second night as bitter as the first. But on the morning of the second day, when the two men realised that a few hours only would see the end, from cold and exhaustion, if not from the fall of the mast, help came to them. Someone ashore with a telescope, watching the wreck, reported something moving in the tops'l of the barge. The lifeboat needed no further bidding. She put off at once, and thus, at last, the two men were rescued, after thirty-six hours' exposure to the bitterness of the gale. They were almost dead when picked up, and the mate's feet were so severely frost-bitten that he spent months in hospital. He never properly recovered, and was never able to wear boots again.

When one considers the amount of sail they carry and the fact that they draw so little water and sail without ballast, it is surprising that so few instances are known in which barges have turned over under way. When they have done so, on rare occasions, it has usually been caused by the lee-board touching the sand when sailing in shoal water. This once happened to the *Anglo-Dane*, sailing in a race with a schooner yacht, when she capsized off the "Hooks and Eyes" at Blackwall Point from her lee-board catching the sand when standing in too close to get out of the tide. The turning over of the *Victoria* in a match with the *Satanita* is described in Chapter XI.

I heard a vivid account of the turning over of another barge, the *Formosa*, off Maplin Sands, from the skipper who then had her, Captain William Bournes of Rochester, augmented from other sources. He came out of the River Colne one Easter some sixty years ago. He had been up to Colchester with broken granite from Rochester for road-making. The wind was blowing hard nor'-westerly, but the crew were anxious to sail. "Let's go down into Colne, skipper," they said, "as we've got a fair wind down."

Having reached the Colne, they decided to carry on, and with any luck they would be able to get home and spend the evening at Gillingham Fair, which always took place on the Monday and Tuesday after Easter. As they were standing along the Maplin edge, between the old Maplin pile lighthouse (now removed), known to all bargemen as the "Sheers", and the Blacktail Spit buoy, there came a sudden hard snow-squall, causing the barge to lay over sharply. The skipper was below at breakfast, and the mate, feeling her hard pressed, called out to him, "What are we going to do about it, skipper?" As he did so, the barge turned over, and was on her beam ends before the skipper reached the deck. Fortunately the boat, being on the starboard quarter, was undamaged, the sail being over the port side, and they managed to get away in her safely. The barge then turned bottom up and shot her loose cable, which was on deck, overside, so that this brought her up, aided by the spars, hanging downwards, dragging on the bottom. The crew were picked up by a steamboat bound for Boston. Their adventures were not over, for she got into Lynn Well, had to turn back because of heavy weather, and they were eventually landed at Yarmouth. They did *not* get to Gillingham Fair!

Another barge, the *Alice*, belonging to the same owners, and bound also for Rochester, left the Colne later on the same day, went through the Raysand Channel and brought up off Shore-ends. She then went "overland" across the Maplin, when the tide served, and got into Gillingham that night. They were surprised that the *Formosa* had not arrived first, when almost at that moment news of her capsizing came through.

Next day the *Alice* went down to look for her. Near the Blacktail Spit they saw a small tops'l barge made fast to what they thought at

first was a whale. On a nearer approach, however, the object proved
to be the *Formosa*, bottom up. Her grey bottom, well scrubbed and
black-leaded, gave the whale-like appearance. The small barge was a
little sharp-sterned craft called the *Hector*, of which Alf Stevens, of
Pin Mill, was at one time master. She belonged to Kirby, up above
Landemere in Hamford Water, and used to carry about 40 tons of
cement. She was mounting guard over the wreck. She had a rope
through the staple in her rudder, and was vainly trying to tow her,
intending to claim her share of the salvage, and a free fight nearly
ensued when the *Alice* put in an appearance and wanted to cut her
adrift. Presently, however, one of Paul's steamboats, of Ipswich, came
up, got a wire round the *Formosa* and towed her bottom-up to the
Sheers, tearing all the gear out of her. Her anchor cable, I was told,
was burnished as bright as a silver watch-chain by the friction on the
sand. They then grounded her on the sand, got a wire right over her
and pulled her upright. They baled her out, as the pumps were all
smashed, and when the tide made, she was towed into Harwich, salvage, of course, being claimed and awarded. The *Alice's* crew helped
in the baling out, and that was the only part they were allowed to play.

What must be one of the most extraordinary adventures a barge has
come through without injury was that which befell the *Mermaid* at
Maldon some twenty years ago. On the top of a very high spring tide
she drifted over the edge of the quay, and as the tide fell her one chine
remained on the quay, while the other sank until it rested on the mud.
The barge was left lying over on her side, with her mast some 45 degrees
from the horizontal! It is amazing that she did not fall over on her
beam-ends, and it was obvious that only a slight push was needed to
throw her over. But planks were carefully worked under her, and at the
next high water she was successfully launched sideways, none the
worse for her experience.

The *Mermaid*, of 49 tons net, was built by Howard at Maldon in
1888, and was one of that fine builder's best. She was a good barge for
stack work, but also had a strong claim to be considered the "beauty
queen" of that beautiful little fleet of Maldon-built barges. Winner of
the Maldon Barge Race in 1929, she has now been sold for conversion
to a yacht. She was seen at Pin Mill in 1948, looking very smartly kept.
During the winter of 1948–49 she was berthed at Conyer.

While some barges have perished by sea, a few have perished by
fire. The *Foxhound*, a barge laden with petrol, was burnt down to the
water's edge in Woolwich Reach rather over twenty years ago. She
was rebuilt, however, and sailed in the Medway Barge Race in 1929;
and a few years later was chartered, together with the *Greta*, to follow

PLATE 57 *Davenport*: Captain Strange by the Heel of the Bowsprit

[*Photograph by courtesy of the late Captain T. Strange*

PLATE 58 A Fresh Breeze and the Open Sea, aboard the *Squeak*

[*By courtesy of Roger Finch, Esq*

PLATE 59 In the Hold, Sailing Barge *Squeak*

[*By courtesy of Roger Finch, Esq*

the Race of 1933 with a party of sailing barge enthusiasts—myself among them—on board. Another, many years back, called the *Lankaster*, was burnt out at Shell Haven. She was a nearly new barge at the time, and her bottom, which was not damaged, was so good that a new barge was built on it, and the rebuilt barge was still at work until recent years. She is still afloat, belonging now to Clarke's of Erith; but she is no longer trading, being used only as a "roads barge" in the lighter roads there.

The long voyages made by the Thames barges used to occasion no little surprise to the steamboats that sometimes would meet them far out at sea. A story is told of the *Havelock* of London, a spritsail barge carrying 100 tons and built at Nine Elms in 1858 and still afloat in 1939, that used to trade regularly between Liverpool and Rotterdam. On one occasion, when she had left Liverpool, she was hailed by a steamboat somewhere in the middle of the Bristol Channel and asked where she was from.

"Liverpool," replied the mate, James Marshall, who was at the helm.

"And where are you for?" asked the steamship, somewhat incredulously.

"Rotterdam."

"Oh, Rotter-hell, you ——!" And the steamship made off. This story became a standing joke among the bargemen, for the steamship master evidently did not believe such a voyage possible in a craft with lee-boards and a freeboard of inches only. The *Havelock* was afterwards one of Wrinch's "stackies", and later owned by J. O. Robson, who employed her in sand and stack-work, the revived post-war stack-work that has been described elsewhere.

There are a number of standing jokes among the bargemen, some of which are worth recording here. One of the favourites is that of the barge that shot Herne Bay Pier in mistake for a bridge. It was first told me by a barge skipper as we were sailing past Herne Bay.

A London river barge on one occasion got a cargo for Margate. The skipper, never having been below the Nore before, inquired the way from the skipper of a coasting barge.

"Well," said this skipper, "that's quite easy goin' dahn to Mawgit. Yew knows the way down to the Nore, don't yew? Well, when you gits to the Nore, yew keeps on, see, running down along the land to the east'ard. And ef yew goo dahn jest after the high water, yew'll have plenty of water, an' yew can keep the land fairly close aboard all the way." He went on to tell him about crossing Swale and passing Whitstable and Herne Bay, but mentioned nothing of the pier there.

15

He then described the Reculver Towers, and, having left those astern, "Why then you sees Mawgit stickin' aht ahead. Cawn't miss it, mate. Yew want to be keerful of the Nayland Ledges on the west side, an' not go in too close till yew gets by the head of the jetty. Only yew can't go wrong, drawing nothing much, like what yew river barges dew."

The river barge set off, and passed the Nore in the early dawn. It was hazy as she crossed the Swale, and passing Herne Bay the skipper kept close along shore. Presently, to his astonishment, he saw the pier stretching out across his path. The shoreward end he could see, but the seaward end was lost in the fog.

He rubbed his eyes and looked again. But there was no doubt about it. He called the mate, who was cooking breakfast, on deck.

"D'yew see that bridge ahead there, Garge? That is a bridge, ain't it? But ole Bill never said nothing abaht no blarsted bridge goin' dahn to Mawgit, did 'e?" "No, I don't remember nothink abaht no bridge." "Why didn't ole Bill tell us there was a blarsted bridge then, goin' dahn to Mawgit? We shall 'ave to lower our gear, that's all. Yes, that's all there is abaht that. Git our stay fall up, Garge."

So the gear was lowered in the usual way, and the barge shot through under the pier. And as they were laboriously heaving up again on the other side, the skipper kept muttering to himself:

"Well, I dew think ole Bill might ha' towld us there was a bridge goin' to Mawgit. Yes, 'e might ha' towld us that!"

Another favourite story, of which the cream of the jest is directed against the yachting fraternity, concerns a small yacht that followed a barge by what she imagined to be a short cut across the Pye Sand into Walton backwater. The wind was from the north-east, and the yacht, coming from the westward, would be saved a long turn to wind'ard. It is true that the short cut was not marked on the chart, but where the barge could go, the yacht could surely follow.

All went well for a time, until the barge eased up and stopped. The yachtsman hailed, in some alarm.

"Hi! Barge ahoy! Do you know you're aground?"

The old skipper looked round. "Yus," he shouted dryly. "An' what's more, so are yew! I come 'ere to load sand. What 've yew come 'ere for?"

It was only too true. The yacht went ashore very thoroughly, and spent some ten hours on the Pye sand before the tide floated her again.

Perhaps I am treading on thorny ground in telling this story of an inefficient yachtsman and am in danger of giving the impression that bargemen as a whole are contemptuous of the abilities of the yachting fraternity generally. If so, I would hasten to dispel such an illusion. For the keen practical yachtsman, who is fired with a true love of the sea and sails his own ship with an ardent desire to learn all he can of seamanship, the bargeman has a genuine admiration. He is always willing and anxious to help with practical assistance, or with advice when asked. It is true that he is shy of offering advice unasked, but merely because he fears it may be resented. Not for the keen yachtsman is he lacking in respect. It is rather for the many fools, unfortunately increasing year by year, who, knowing next to nothing of navigation and even less of seamanship, set forth in small, unsea-worthy craft, utterly regardless of wind, tide and weather. It is for men, and unfortunately women too, such as these, that the bargemen have a hearty contempt. They are a danger not only to themselves but to every other small craft afloat. The bargeman has learnt to treat the sea with profound respect. It is a good servant, but, give it the least chance and it will prove a most cruel master if it can once get the whip-hand.

As an example of this type of yachtsman—with whom fortunately yachting is usually a temporary craze—I quote the following yarn told me by Captain Alfred Horlock, of the barge *Phoenician*.

One day, in very thick weather, several years ago, he left Harwich bound for the London River. There was a pleasant breeze nor'-westerly, but the fog held. Using the lead, they stood up the Wallet, picked up the Wallet Spitway Buoy, and went over into the Swin. They used the lead carefully all the way to Southend, feeling along the edge of the Maplin Sands; and the first definite mark they saw was the end of Southend Pier. A fine piece of navigation in a fog as thick as a hedge, but of such the bargemen think nothing.

As they had just come over the Spitway into the East Swin, and were somewhere between the Swin Spitway Buoy and the Whitaker Spit Buoy, a small yacht loomed up through the fog ahead. She hailed as the barge passed.

"Barge ahoy!" they shouted. "Can you tell us the way to Burn-ham?"

Chartless, compassless, adrift in a thick fog in a network of sands, with strong tides setting in ever different directions through narrow channels, she wanted to know "the way to Burnham"!

As the skipper said, what could he tell them? "It's not like being ashore, you know," he shouted, "first on the right, second on the left, and mind the step!" But he gave them such directions as he could, and left them to it. As no news was ever heard of a yacht in trouble at that time, presumably she found her way in somewhere safely. But truly, there must be a very benign little cherub sitting up aloft to look after the lives of some make-believe yachtsmen.

A barge belonging to Rochester, called the *Sunrise*, was the subject of another bargeman's joke. Someone in a local tavern claimed to have seen "the sun rise in the middle of the night." Bets were offered, and taken, that he hadn't, and that he couldn't prove it, as he claimed. Having made as many bets as he could, he took the company outside, and, leading them some distance along the quay, showed them the *Sunrise*, then a new barge only just out, serenely lying in the glow of a street lamp!

The longevity of some of the barges is really amazing, when one considers the hard work they are called upon to perform and the little time they are allowed for the refitting, painting and general titivating so necessary for the proper upkeep of a sailing ship. In 1926 no fewer than 112 vessels built before 1870 were still in commission, of which twenty-two were built before 1860. The oldest of all was the little *Defiance*, a 40-ton barge built at Maidstone in 1789! She was employed in stack-work in her later days, and continued trading until 1928. Another of 44 tons, built in 1800, had been rebuilt after 114 years' service. Yet another, launched in 1803, was rebuilt in 1898. The *Eastwood*, 43 tons, built at Southwark in 1822, was "still alive", as was also the *Hamlet*, built at Lambeth in 1829.

What was believed to be the oldest barge still in service in 1929 was the *Favorite*, belonging to Messrs Smeed, Dean & Company Ltd. of Sittingbourne. I am indebted to Mr George Andrews, who had a long connection with that firm, for the following detailed account. She was in many respects the most interesting sailing vessel then under way.

She was built in 1803, yet in 1929 was still in first-class condition, and larger and more valuable than when originally built. She was at first a "swimmy", both head and stern, but after a collision she was rebuilt aft in about 1870, and had a rounded stern of the ordinary modern barge pattern built into her. Many years later, in 1898, she was sunk by a steamer, which cut away her swim-head, and when raised she was rebuilt with an ordinary round bow. Quite a considerable part of the original hull remained, however, in the middle of the barge. Being in such excellent condition, she continued to be engaged regularly in the cement and dry goods trade, where it is essential that a barge shall carry her cargo without any risk of wetting it.

When under way in a stiff breeze, she was the most upright barge of any fleet, for her width of beam above compared with the width across her bottom from chine to chine prevented her from lying over under wind pressure as most sailing craft do. In 1929 this wonderful veteran was actually entered in the Thames and Medway Barge Races as an exhibition barge, when she was the centre of a lively interest.

Her history has been as eventful as it is long, but space permits of giving only a few outstanding details. As a small swimmy she was of about 70 tons only, and traded in and out of Milton Creek and to and from London. When enlarged, she traded coastwise, and made several voyages to the Tyne among other places. Her most eventful trip was when the late Samuel Gorf was master. On the particular voyage referred to, she was laden with blocks of stone which were used for and may still be seen in the façade of the Windsor Hotel in Victoria Street, London. While at sea, the mate, who was the only other member of the crew, developed mental trouble, which later made him an inmate of the Chatham Asylum. The passage from the Yorkshire coast across the Deeps and round the Norfolk coast was a terrible ordeal for Captain Gorf. He had locked his mate in the cabin below, and for forty-eight hours he was unable to leave the helm. From Yarmouth, working his tides, he was able to navigate to Sheerness. During the whole passage he was virtually single-handed, and had the added responsibility of having to look after his mate and to keep him under control.

During the many years that Sam Gorf had the *Favorite*, he did much beach work with her. He would place her on any shore from Southwold to Brighton with cargoes of bricks or of road materials; the conditions required that the cargo must be cleared in one tide. She freighted hundred of cargoes to such places as Walton-on-the-Naze, Frinton, Clacton, Herne Bay, Deal, Hythe, Dymchurch, New Romney, Brighton and Hastings, to mention a few at random, and although occasionally washed up on the beach, was always able to sail away for home at the earliest opportunity.

As a wreck salvage craft she did truly wonderful work, saving the cargoes from wrecked vessels off Dungeness, a dangerous trade which always involved the risk of getting badly caught on a lee shore. She rode the shallow seas like a bird, and in her old age, although she was keeping within the rivers and their estuaries, she was still the same stiff, strong, useful craft. Her master in 1931 was William Chapman, whom one of the great London papers has described as the "Old Bill" of the Thames. "Long may she live!" wrote Mr Andrews. And who can fail to agree with him in that sincere and earnest hope? Long may she live indeed!—for she is still "alive", though no longer trading. When over 130 years old, she was converted to a yacht. She spent the last war lying above Hammersmith Bridge. Although she has now lost her gear, and is at present used only as a houseboat, it says something for the men who built her that she should have reached the very respectable age of 148, "not out".

## CHAPTER XIV

# A Voyage to Antwerp

"CAN you go Mate of Barge to Antwerp—join ship to-night?—Ward."

Such was the text of a telegram that reached me from my boatman, the late Harry Ward of Pin Mill, on the afternoon of Monday, 26th March 1928. I was then at Cambridge, starting work for an examination taking place in the far-too-near future. But I was sick of the shore, and the call of the sea was strong within me. With luck, I should yet be back in time to do the necessary amount of work. I took a sporting chance and the next train, and joined the barge *Davenport* of Ipswich, master and owner, Captain Thomas Strange, at Pin Mill that same evening. Next morning the voyage began.

We "mustered" at about 7 a.m., broke out our hook and got under way with the wind sou'-westerly, moderate; but the sky was bad and the dawn dirty. So that we progressed no farther than Harwich, where we anchored just within the breakwater to wait for more favourable conditions. And, as we lay there, I had my first opportunity to examine the barge with some thoroughness.

She was an interesting ship. Built over seventy years ago at Ipswich, she had been a ketch in her earlier years, as she appears in the photograph, Plate 57. But her skipper had recently, when buying a new mainsail, altered her rig to make her somewhat easier to handle. The main-boom had been discarded and the gaff rigged permanently aloft and fitted with vangs, or "wangs", like an ordinary barge's spreet. The sail was then fitted with brails and set loose-footed, in the same manner as a spreety's mainsail. It was, in fact, the old half-spreet of the seventeenth and eighteenth centuries. There was at that time only one other barge on the East Coast rigged like the *Davenport*, and that was the old *Britannia*, a barge once well known on the Kentish coast, lost on the beach at Gorleston in the winter of 1928–29. The rig had certain advantages in doing away with the great weight of the spreet aloft, but on the other hand this advantage was lost in some added difficulty in brailing the sail, owing to the fact that there was no spreet to prevent its blowing out and taking charge when reefing or stowing by brailing. And from experience of both rigs, I am inclined to think that the gaff mainsail does not set so well.

The mizzen set in the same way, but carried a boom, and was sheeted to the outboard end of the rudder, in the usual way, for help in bringing the head round when wending.

She carried moderately high bulwarks with wooden stanchions, much more solid altogether than the rails fitted to modern barges. In many ways her gear was archaic, which threw a good deal more labour than was pleasant on the muscles of the crew. But she had the advantage of the wide decks and small hatchways of the old timers; and, whatever their limitations for handling or trimming cargo with modern machinery, the added comfort and safety they gave at sea was very much to be appreciated.

Her cabin aft was small but comfortable, with a cheery coal stove set in the forward bulkhead and a horseshoe-shaped settee running round a table at the after end. The skipper's state-room was on the starboard side. How he and his wife managed to stow themselves away in the microscopic space available remained a mystery to the end.

The fo'c'sle was low and rather dark, but otherwise roomy. It contained a galley range of undeniable efficiency, though the cooking heat it gave was by no means confined to the oven, nor was the smoke to the chimney. The mate's folding berth was on the port side, the boy's on the starboard, partially overhanging the stove, with its frequently red-hot top. As the canvas of the boy's cot was in a most precarious condition, so that Jack's legs hung perpendicularly downwards, he had little chance of suffering from cold feet when turned in.

Our ship's company numbered four all told. The skipper, a fine old seaman of the coaster type, slightly built, but tough and wiry, and skilled in the handling of small craft as only a lifetime spent at sea could make him. With him was his wife, the daughter of a Belgian pilot. She was responsible for the catering, which she managed very well. But having broken her leg some short while back, and being heavily built withal, she still had considerable difficulty in getting about. In consequence she took no part in the handling of the vessel. The mate was, as already explained, the author, and the "boy", "cook", "third hand"—call him what you will—was a gardener's boy from a Suffolk estate on his first voyage to sea. He frankly hated it. He had never been away from home before, and, deciding he was not cut out for a sailor, returned to his gardening job at the end of the cruise.

So much for the vessel and her crew. Now for the voyage.

All that day we lay in Harwich, and in the afternoon I went ashore in the boat to collect some odd supplies and a magazine for the skipper's wife. While I was about this business it breezed up from seaward and looked like raining hard. So to avoid getting wet I left at high water without waiting for the ebb, and had a very hard row back. Nor did I escape a soaking, so that I might as well have waited and saved my labours. The following morning, however, we left at daybreak, with the wind sou'-westerly, but the weather looking very unsettled. We worked up the Wallet, over the Spitway, and were just by the Admiralty buoys on the Maplin Edge when the tide turned against us. It was a trying day, with fickle light airs that fluked about and headed us at every turn.

In the morning we got under way again and had better fortune, for we had a good hard wind sou'-westerly; and having worked over to the Kentish shore, stood along the coast and into the Gore, where we brought up in a sharp squall and driving rain. The ease and quickness with which a barge can be "hooked" and her sail stowed is a feature greatly to be appreciated in this class of vessel.

It came on to blow harder in the afternoon, and I went aloft to pass the gaskets round the tops'l and make all snug for the night. We rolled somewhat, and the cook was sick. We lay in the Gore the whole of the following day, Friday, waiting for conditions favourable for making a passage.

Next morning we went on to Margate Roads and brought up again; the weather still looking doubtful. A barge has to await her chance for a slant across at this time of year. With so little freeboard and gear that is often far from trustworthy, to say the least of it, few risks must be run with the weather. "It's better to be safe than to be sorry" is a saying whose truth has been proved in the barges times without number. But we hoped for an opportunity to get away on the night's tide.

Having dropped our hook, we went ashore with the bread bag, picking up on our way the skipper of an old Whitstable ketch-barge that was lying in the Roads. She was a fine-looking vessel, with a counter-stern and ample bulwarks, a type of which very few were left even then. She had met with a series of delays, and was already six weeks out from London bound for Shoreham. She had lost her anchors in a bit of a blow, and these had been replaced by a couple of little kedges that would scarcely have held an oyster-smack. As her last passage had taken four months, bound from Portland to Hull with stone, it is hardly surprising that her owners were a trifle annoyed. Which perhaps explains the fact that her crew of four hands could only muster between them the grand total of five shillings wherewith to buy stores. But as they had eaten their last loaf and hadn't a scrap of food of any sort left, the skipper was going ashore to try to "raise the wind". He tried our "old man" first on the way, but the latter was too wary to be caught. He sent the hungry one to Lloyd's Agent, from whom a couple of pounds was raised. We then re-entered a handy tavern and celebrated the fact. It was there that I learnt that Cambridge had won the Boat Race, and was promptly thought to have gone mad! But sufficient beer to celebrate this further cause for rejoicing caused my temporary insanity to be forgotten, or at least condoned. And so we went aboard again.

At dark the wind came from easterly, which was of no use to us. But our Whitstable friend got under way on the turn of the tide, beat round the Foreland, and we saw him no more. As this wind held for some days, she doubtless reached Shoreham before the two pounds were exhausted. We, however, spent an uncomfortable night, for it breezed up fairly fresh, and Margate Roads is not a quiet anchorage. So in the morning, the weather looking beastly and the wind still no good to us, we hove up our hook and ran back to the Gore. It being Sunday, we had a roast for dinner, and I sampled for the first time the excellence of the skipper's plum duff. I could write an essay on that duff! It melted in the mouth. Eaten with gravy before the meat, this is always the *pièce de résistance* of the bargeman's Sunday dinner. In the afternoon, the weather still looking foul, after a shouted conversation with the skipper of another barge, the *Alderman*, also lying in the Gore, we ran back for the Swale, and brought up for the night just below Faversham Creek. Going in after about an hour's flood, we grounded in mid-channel between the Pollard Spit and Ham Gat buoys where the chart shows a depth of two fathoms. The *Alderman*, being light, sailed over it, but we had to wait for the tide to float us.

Monday was a day wasted—in search of coal! Bad luck had dogged us all the way, for we were down on "bunkers" and not a single "coalie" had we met. To a bargeman that was a real misfortune. The weather was perfect—too perfect—for there was no wind. Sky hard and clear, and distant craft "looming" most noticeably—a sure sign of further easterly weather. The skipper and I, with Captain Flory of the *Alderman*, took the boat and rowed into Faversham Creek on the flood. Acting on the advice of some oystermen, we went up Oare Creek as far as the village, being told that coal could be obtained from the local stores. This proved to be a myth, but it was said that "the coalman gener'lly come by Mondays". So we lounged on the bridge and waited for a coal-cart that didn't arrive, with an occasional visit to the local inn, as it was thirsty work. Eventually, however, we had to leave, for the Creek dries out and tide waits not for any coal-man. It was, of course, too late to get up to Faversham that day, so we returned aboard to meet the wrath of the skipper's wife, who made some pointed remarks on the subject of what she called "boozers".

The following morning we rowed up to Faversham against a strong head wind. The distance is short as the crow flies, but with the ex-cessive winding of the creek we found it a long pull. The Faversham barges turn up here in head winds, as sometimes on the Colchester River. It is marvellous that so large a vessel can turn in so narrow a channel, and the marks gouged out by their lee-boards scored the mud on either hand. One, that had apparently cut things too fine, lay beneaped at the mouth of the creek, and her crew were improving the awaiting hours by getting all gear down, scraping masts and refitting, etc.

At Faversham we had no difficulty in getting coal, and spent the time waiting for the ebb in exploring the rather fascinating old town. We intended to sail back, but a friendly launch throwing us a line, we towed down to Hollow Shore, where we filled our water breakers and sailed the last part out to the barge. In the evening we discussed oysters. But enough of that! My bargemen friends will know what I mean. Shortly before midnight the *Alderman* sailed, her skipper believing that if he got down to Margate he might find the wind going round into the sou'-west and giving him a chance to slip across to Dunkirk.

Next morning we left the Swale just after high water, and sailed with the ebb down to Margate. The wind was light from the sou'-west, and we brought up in the Roads to wait for the evening's tide before striking across for the other side. I spent the afternoon studying Roman Law in the fo'c'sle, with occasional "musical" (?) interludes on the tin whistle. In the evening we sailed. The wind was light from the sou'-west, and the old *Davenport* slipped past the light on the North Foreland and shaped a course for the Nor' Sand Head. The skipper and I relieved one another at the helm. Jack was allowed to spend the night turned in. At midnight we brewed steaming hot cocoa, and very good it was, for the wind had a nip to it. Towards dawn it freshened, and by daylight was blowing a strong breeze, before which the ship surged on. A lumpy swell rose, and the *Davenport* bucked and lurched and plunged, and needed much hard work at the helm to hold her on her course. So we continued, until we had passed the great West Hinder lightship, looking like a mighty steam-ship with her light tower and high slab sides, and in the afternoon as we were raising the Belgian coast, the wind fell away. Slowly we closed with the land. The towers and houses of Knocke, Middlekirke and Zeebrugge rose higher out of the sea, and the low-lying coastline appeared. For an' hour or two in the late afternoon there fell a flat calm, and the barge rolled in the swell, with her empty sails banging and booming and the rudder chains clanking a dismal dirge. But as it was getting dark a light air sprang up, and just carried us past the end of Zeebrugge Mole before it died away. There we let go our hook, and the barge lay to the ebb, which within half an hour was sluicing past our sides so that we raised a wash like a steamboat's, and the chain tore out an extra ten fathoms over the drum of the windlass by its own unaided efforts.

We were away early next morning, on the first of the ebb—partly because the wind was very light and we were anxious to make the most of our tide, but also because we did not want the harbour authorities out trying to prove that we were liable for harbour dues. The wind continued light all day, but our good friend the tide helped us along, and the ebb having carried us to the mouth of the Scheldt, we went into the river on the flood. The wind then failed completely, and a little above Flushing, on the Island of Walcheren side, we let go the anchor. For the tide was setting across one of the many shoals that encumber the entrance to the river; there was no wind; and we were unable to "drudge" her clear with the anchor dragging on the bottom. There we remained for the night.

The morrow was a day of sunshine varied with cloud, which I remember chiefly for one of the loveliest sights I have ever had the good fortune to see. The three-masted topsail schooner *S. F. Pearce*, a steel vessel of about 300 tons, flying the British flag, had come in during the night, and was ahead of us when we weighed anchor and started to turn up the river against a south-easterly wind. We were, perhaps, half a mile below her, and throughout the morning we neither gained nor lost anything of our distance, so that we crossed the river back and forth, tack by tack with her. She had at that time no auxiliary power, and her master turned her up the river with consummate skill, scorning the services of a tug. As she tacked, we could imagine the inward curses of her crew as they manned the braces and swung the heavy yards round by hand. Never once did she miss stays. On the one tack her white sails gleamed in the sunshine; on the other they were black with shadow. She made a wonderful picture, and all the morning I could do nothing but feast my eyes upon her, until she anchored off Walzoorden, where the channel narrowed. There we left her, for the flood was not yet done, and we sailed on until, when the ebb began, we anchored off the edge of the mud, just below Bat.

The river was black with traffic. The bluff-bowed Dutch and Belgian barges, with their baggy brown sails, looking much as they must have looked three hundred years ago, were dodging in and out among great ocean steamers and modern motor freighters. And the ebb and flow of the tide went on unchanged as it has done for thousands of years, caring nothing for the changes wrought by man in the shipping it carried.

It was a trying beat up the river bound for Antwerp. The wind continued foul and light, and next day we got no higher than just above Lillo. Here we were in Belgian territory. The following Sunday morning we drifted up with the flood in almost a calm, until on the last of the tide we rounded the bend and opened up the long quays backed by the lofty spires and pinnacles of Belgium's greatest seaport. But the tide was done, and within a cable's length of the gates of the old dock by which we must enter, the tide began against us. Not a tug appeared. They pass three to the minute when they are not wanted. Not a craft came in sight that could have given us a tow. The slightest breath of wind would have carried us home. But never a zephyr ruffled the oily surface of the Scheldt, until we had the mortification of seeing the gates close against us, and then came the wind, too late. We sat upon the hatches and cursed bitterly. But this helped us not at all ; and as mooring is prohibited opposite the port, we had to sail back over the last hard-won mile, and anchor in the river below.

Next morning we entered the old dock, and tying up alongside the quay, the skipper sought out the agents, and found where the ship was lying for which we had brought our cargo. It was not until the following day, however, that we were taken in charge by a fussy little tug, which, lashed alongside, towed us through a labyrinth of docks, narrow cuts and swing bridges, until we were berthed alongside our steamship.

For eleven days we remained within the port, and at the end we had discharged our cargo and taken on board a full load of 140 tons of bog ore for the gasworks at Ipswich. We had precisely 6 inches of freeboard amidships, and we battened down our hatches with care for the passage home. Six inches was not much if the North Sea should be in boisterous mood during the voyage. Among the many interesting small craft in the port was an ancient English West Country ketch, the *Lolly*. She was a real old-timer and was manned by her owner, his wife, two sons and a daughter. The daughter wore trousers, worked

aloft, was powerful as an ox and as good a man as any of them. She
had the reputation for being able to hold her own with any bargeman
afloat in the manner of repartee. This ship was loading a general
cargo for the Channel Islands, where she was trading regularly.
Among other things, she loaded 40 tons of dynamite and a quantity
of sheet iron. As the iron was dumped unceremoniously into the hold,
so that the sparks flew in all directions, I was not too keen to investi-
gate her thoroughly until loading had ceased for the day.

In the evenings, when the work of the day was done, I was able
systematically to explore Antwerp's sailor-town with a couple of other
English bargemen. Ernest and Douglas, two brothers, were mate and
cook of the Brightlingsea barge *Major*, then in the port. Their skipper
was away, for his wife had been taken seriously ill. And the two lads,
as shipkeepers, worked hard all day on the barge, scraping her spars,
painting and making her look almost yacht-like in splendour. They
were proud of their barge, those lads. We soon became firm friends,
and keeping together, we explored every haunt in "Schipper Straat"
—the "Ratcliffe Highway" of Antwerp—with most of the amenities
of that famous (or infamous) sailors' haunt of old-time London. The
street was full of dance halls, gin palaces, gambling dens and the like,
such as one imagines exist only in film-producers' minds, and was
thronged with tough customers from every quarter of the globe.
Coloured firemen, flashy South American seamen, Dutch bargees, all
hob-nobbing together in an atmosphere of coarse tobacco and strong
liquors. Beautiful young girls sat in the windows to entice the sailor
within. These girls received a commission on all drinks they sold, and
it was in their interests to make their clients drunk. Robbery was
common. Once in a café I was asked by "Madame" to replace my
sheath-knife, with which I was cutting up my tobacco. They had had
a man knifed there a few days before, she explained. The girls all
spoke Flemish and English. French was hardly spoken. When they
thought they had got all they could from one, and a new client came
in, fresh from a long voyage with money to burn jingling in his
pockets, they would slip off with a farewell kiss. "Good-bye, darl-
ing", is the usual formula. "You onderstan'—yes? Love is love,
but—beesness is beesness!" I received my only leap-year proposal
from a girl in one of these cafés. She suggested that I should leave
seafaring, marry her and that we should keep a café together! Such
were the trivialities with which the English bargeman might spend
his evenings ashore in a foreign port twenty years ago!

On the afternoon of Thursday, 19th April, we towed out of the old
dock in company with the *Major*, and being slipped by the tug a mile

or so down the river, we brought up for the night off Doorne. For the
next two days the wind was foul, and we turned down the river to
Flushing, where we anchored just above in the Rammekens, waiting
a chance for a slant across. The *Major* broke her bowsprit short off
by the gammon-iron in a squall on the way down, and on the Sunday
we lay in the Rammekens all day while she rigged the longer portion
of her broken spar. The wind was westerly, and we could not sail. On
the Monday, however, which was my birthday, a slant of wind came
out of the south-east, and we sailed in company with the *Major* and
*Lolly*. The wind came ahead and fell light, so we had to bring up for
a tide. But that night we anchored within the shelter of Zeebrugge
Mole on the anniversary of the famous attack of 23rd April 1918.

The following morning we left almost before dawn, and had a light,
fair wind all day; so we hauled a tattered mizzen staysail out of the
sail-locker and rigged a big light staysail as a spinnaker. Next morning
we sailed past Margate, looking very clean and refreshing in the sunshine, before the sands were blackened with people; went up through
the Horse and Gore Channels; and at the West Last Buoy we laid our
course for the Girdler light-vessel. A submarine passed us travelling
at full speed on the surface. The day was warm and sunny, and the old
*Davenport* slowly ambled on her way. We washed and shaved, removing a week's growth of beard. But the wind failed us in the end, falling
very light, so that we did not get into Harwich until after midnight.

When daylight came, the Customs boarded us, and, after the usual
formalities, we were allowed to proceed up to Ipswich. There we tied
up outside the lock-gates, and later in the day entered the dock and
sailed to our berth at the Gasworks Quay. So we brought our voyage
to an end, and with genuine regrets I signed off, received my wages,
packed my kit and returned to Cambridge, leaving the old ship lying
lonely in the shelter of the gasometers.

The old *Davenport* survived for nearly eight years. Tommy
Strange sold her two or three years after I left her, and retired from the
sea to live at his house in Ipswich, where he died on 19th November
1936, and was buried in the New Cemetery, Ipswich. Kind, generous,
warm-hearted Tommy Strange. He was a fine seaman and a true
friend.

The *Davenport's* end came in 1936. On 19th February of that year
she left Plymouth under Captain Rands, laden with bricks and fire-
clay for Ridham Dock, Sheerness. When she was off Newhaven, she
started to leak, and passing Beachy Head the port pump choked. The
skipper therefore let go his anchor in Eastbourne Roads about 1½
miles E.S.E. of the pier at 10 a.m. on 27th February to pump her out

with the starboard pump. While she was being pumped out, the wind backed to S.S.W., and wind and rain increased so much that the old ship dragged and a heavy sea stove in her fore-hatch. The crew burned flares for assistance, but the *Davenport* continued to drag until she got into broken water off the pier. The water then gained on the pumps so rapidly, while the seas broke all over the barge, that the crew had to take to the rigging, whence they were taken off by the Eastbourne lifeboat. The Newhaven tug *Foremost*, which had been sent to the rescue, stood by, but it was not possible to get the old ship off, and she eventually broke up. A local yachtsman sent me the hub-cap of her wheel as a souvenir. It makes a fine brass paperweight, and it lies before me as I write.

# CHAPTER XV

## The First World War

THE English barges played no mean part in the Great War of 1914–18, and right from the beginning to the end of hostilities the coasting barges were employed in carrying supplies from this country over to the Continent. The bargemen were exempt from all other forms of war service, for the importance of their work was fully recognised. With their shallow draught, barges supplied a form of transport peculiarly suitable for avoiding the dangers of cross-Channel navigation at that time, for they could sail over anchored mines, which were generally too deep to hurt them. As for submarines, barges were too small a target to justify a torpedo. Thus, in spite of the large numbers of barges crossing the Channel, very few of them were lost through enemy action. Yet as many as 180 English barges were seen in Tréport at one time. Many of the barges, however, had thrilling adventures and not a few "narrow squeaks", and the risks run by the bargemen were, without doubt, considerable.

On the other hand, the war-time work across to the Continent had the advantage of being highly profitable. Towards the latter part of the war, when scarcity of shipping tonnage sent freights soaring sky-high, the profits made by some of the bargemen were really large, and those among them who were provident enough to save and fore-sighted enough to realise that the time was coming when the golden eggs would cease, were able to feather their nests very well, and a few retired with small fortunes. As an example of the quick way in which money was earned, I will quote only one instance. A barge skipper known to me, who was half-owner of his own barge, loaded a full cargo of coal for Calais, at Goole, up the Humber. He was loaded the day he arrived at Goole, was four days on the passage, and discharged the day he reached Calais. His barge carried 200 tons and the freight was £6 per ton, so that his half-share of the total was nearly £600 for a week's work! This was, of course, much above the average freight, but was not exceptional. The cost of new gear, etc., and all running expenses were extremely high at the time; but even so, it did not take a great number of successful trips to make the price of the barge her-self.

Not many of the bargemen, however, saved much from their war-time profits. It was only the barges running the risk of the cross-Channel passage that made the "big money", and with most of their crews it was "easy come, easy go" with it. There was always the very real risk that the next trip might be their last, and they were gambling for big profits with their lives as the stakes. Why save when they might never live to enjoy it? Some never even bothered to think about it at all. One skipper, Douglas Bartlett, of Ipswich, when he used to turn in at sea on a passage across, always threw his coat up on deck with his wallet in it, containing sometimes as much as £80, saying to his mate, "If anything happens, you can have a good time on that".

The cargoes carried by the barges during the war consisted mainly of foodstuffs and large quantities of coal, coke and pitch. In addition to the fleets of fine coasting barges which firms like Everards, Gold-smiths, the Associated Portland Cement Manufacturers, the London and Rochester Trading Company, Albert Hutson and many others were able to put into this service, there were large numbers of old barges owned by their own skippers which entered upon a new lease of life and found plenty of work to do. There were not enough ships to go round, and the barge trade "boomed" just like the larger ship-ping interests. The profits made in the coasting trade were less than in the cross-Channel work, for the risk the barges ran was not so high. But it must be borne in mind that the rates for freight were high merely in correspondence with the risks run; and, with the shortage of ships, were governed by the law of supply and demand.

Towards the latter part of the war, navigation in the Channel was becoming increasingly dangerous from submarines and more par-ticularly from minefields, and the barges were kept under very strict supervision and restricted in their movements to certain specified routes. An elaborate system of patrol was in force, and barges would sometimes lie for days or even weeks off Southend, in Margate Roads or in the Downs, before being ordered to proceed on their voyage. They would be given a special code flag to fly, which was changed from day to day. A barge flying the wrong flag or the flag of the pre-vious day, would at once be challenged and sent back where she had started. This infuriated the bargemen, for often it meant losing a fair wind across and a hard beat back over a foul tide, with perhaps days of delay before it was possible to get another slant over.

The patrol-boat officers, though no one has ever doubted the efficiency with which their difficult work was done, yet showed the usual steamboat man's incompetence where sails are concerned, and many a time the barges were ordered to steer impossible courses, having regard to the conditions of wind and tide, or the absence of wind, at the time. Or barges would be required to drop their anchors down where they were, in open roadsteads, even in bad weather, where it was impossible for them to lie in safety or to clear out from if the wind should freshen and come on shore. A patrol boat would come tearing up to a barge under way. "Put up your flag and let go your anchor."

"But I can't let go here, Captain!" the horrified skipper would protest. Useless his remonstrances—"Do as you're told," was the only reply.

The *Flower of Essex*, under Captain Keeble of Ipswich, who afterwards had the *Olive Mary*, one of the finest wooden barges afloat, had to lie in the Downs off Deal in a gale of wind, with two anchors down, and wasn't allowed to get out of it into safety. She was rolling so violently that the crew couldn't keep in their bunks, and had to have their food on the floor as nothing would keep in place. It says much for her ground tackle that she rode it out in safety. Barges laden with an open stack of coke on deck would be compelled to anchor off the tail of the Brake Sand, off Deal, for example, and not allowed even to sail the extra cable's length or so which would take them into the comparative safety of the Small Downs. Barges are, of course, wonderful ships for riding out gales of wind with one or two anchors down. The *Britannia* and the *Sussex Belle*, both then "boomies", of which the latter was the faster, were trading all through the war with coal from Hull, and rode out many a gale of wind in Yarmouth Roads. The skipper and owner of the *Sussex Belle* at that time, who afterwards retired from bargeing to become the landlord of the "Foresters" at Pin Mill, had to lie for weeks at a stretch off Yarmouth, and always held that his barge would ride out anything.

Other barges were not always so fortunate, however, and occasionally got into trouble through having to lie in the open in bad weather. The *Intrepid*, for instance, was anchored off Margate when it came on to blow very hard, and she had the misfortune to part her cable. Immediately following on this disaster, she broke her spreet, which came crashing down on deck. It just missed smashing the boat, which was on top of the main hatch. Captain Bill Leaks, her skipper (later of the *Matilda Upton*, see page 215), then set the foresail and let her go as close as she would fetch on the port tack. In this way she managed to fetch the Cockle lightship, off Yarmouth, and was picked up and towed into that port by fishermen. The weather was exceptionally bad, and she had been given up for lost at Margate. But the *Intrepid* proved herself to be a splendid sea-boat and made wonderful weather of it. She was bound for Dover at the time, carrying 100 tons of flour, and in all that adventure she did not damage a single bag. Having rigged a new spreet, she was able to proceed at once to her destination.

The result of the often impossible and stupid orders which it was attempted to make the bargemen carry out was that the bargemen, whenever possible, took matters into their own hands and cheerfully ignored every regulation as soon as they were out of sight of the patrol boat. Their attitude was well summed up in the words of Skipper Tom Harker, who had the *Oxygen*, a 140-ton spreety barge trading across during the war. Tom was reputed to be a very "hard case". Fearing nothing and damning all official routes, he would set a straight course for the port he was bound to, over minefields or anything else. "Mines?" he used to say. "They won't hurt a barge. If you're going to be blown up—you'll be blown up; and if you're going to be drowned—you'll be drowned!" He was drowned too, poor Tom, but not until after the war was over. Then, on a pitch-black night he was run down by a Norwegian ship that didn't see his stern light. The barge went down, and the skipper and his wife, who was sailing with him, were drowned, only the mate being picked up.

The following extract from a letter from Captain Simeon Stanes (see page 208), who had the *Emma* during the war, gives a very fair idea of the sort of difficulties the bargemen had to face. "I was trading to France during the war," he wrote, "and as you know, it was rough in times. We went through the Gateway, as we called it, that was between two lightships at Folkestone, the morning after one of R. & W. Paul's boats was blown up.* It came thick with fog, and the patrol boat came to us and told us to keep three miles farther westerly, as they had found another minefield. But as soon as we lost sight of them we kept our course, and during the day passed one mine on top. We did not get into Boulogne that night. Brought up nine miles off. When Ned Frances (another barge skipper) pulled his light up, I thought it was the wrong thing to do, and told him so, as I said we might have Jerry round after us. Ned said yes, and he would have a blinking fine haul for him. . . ."

My old friend Captain Tom Strange not only ignored patrol boats' orders whenever he could, but also made use of the vessels themselves as tugs against their wills on more than one occasion. If the wind fell light when he was returning across the Channel and he was anxious for a tow to get into the Downs and have a good night's sleep, the method he employed, with considerable success, was to use

* The *Seagull*.

the last of the wind to steer as far as possible into the nearest known minefield. Before long a patrol boat would come steaming up. "Hi! Captain! You mustn't go there, you're entering a minefield, and you've got to get out of it."

"Ha!" replied Strange. "That's all right, that is. Get out of it? Ha! How d'you think I'm goin' to get out of it, eh? No wind and the tide taking me atop of it. I can't *make* the wind blow, can I?"

"Well, I don't know about that, Captain. But you must get yourself out of it somehow, for you can't go there."

Then off would steam the patrol boat; but not too far to keep an eye on the barge. And in every puff of wind "Strangey" would edge her farther and farther into the forbidden area. At last the patrol boat would return in disgust, and without saying a word, pass a line to the barge, tow her out of the minefield into the Downs, and drop her in above Deal pier.

Some of the barges had strange and often exciting adventures during the war. The *Dunkirk* was up the Rhine in German territory when war broke out, and in consequence there she remained, with her crew, until peace was declared and she was ultimately returned. Ike Garnham of Pin Mill was in her, brother of the David Garnham referred to in Chapter V. A more interesting story is that of the boarding of the *Ivernia* and the capture of her crew. In company with a fleet of English barges, all bound back from France light to reload again in English ports, she brought up one night to wait for the tide within a quarter of a mile of the guns of the North Foreland. In the middle of the night the skipper heard someone moving in the cabin. Thinking it was the mate, he called out, and at once a torch was flashed in his face, and he found himself looking into the muzzle of a German naval officer's revolver!

The officer belonged to a German destroyer, one of a flotilla then lying off the Foreland. It had been hoped that the barges were all laden with food, and it was intended to tow them back to Germany. On learning that they were all empty, however, this plan was abandoned, and only the master and mate of the *Ivernia* were taken, together with the ship's papers, as proof of the raid. The crew of the barge were fairly well treated by the Navy. "You'll be all right while you're with us," they were told; "but God help you when you get ashore." In point of fact, as prisoners of war in Germany the bargemen did have a very bad time.

A barge called the *John Evelyn*, one of the first iron barges belonging to the London and Rochester Trading Company, and built in 1885, was bombed when lying in one of the docks in London during an air raid; an incendiary bomb dropped right through the skylight into the cabin, killing both her crew, who were sitting at the table. The *Centaur*, another Kentish barge belonging to Rochester and winner of the Medway Barge Race in 1899, had an adventure of rather a different kind. Sailing gently along in a light air and thickish fog one day somewhere in the Channel, the skipper heard the roar of a coastal motor boat's engine drawing uncomfortably near. Nothing could be done about it, however, and in a few moments the sleek hull of a C.M.B. travelling at speed shot out of the mist alongside, and, striking the barge at right-angles amidships, leapt on deck and there settled down comfortably plumb across the middle of *Centaur's* main hatch! It was a shock for the masters of both craft, but the old *Centaur* made port quite comfortably, and there discharged her novel cargo.

While writing of the *Centaur*, it is perhaps worth recording that she was actually built in six weeks specially for the Barge Race—launched one day and in the race the next!

Moonlight nights were the bargemen's chief fear during the war; for it was then they ran the greatest risk of being shelled by enemy small craft or submarines out on the prowl. But as against this, the moonlight gave them a sporting chance of spotting floating mines and altering course in time to avoid them. Spotting and avoiding mines was an important part of the day's work all through the war for the bargemen.

One skipper I knew, Captain Bert Wright, who afterwards had the *Pride of Ipswich*, had a narrow escape from being shelled when the Lowestoft fishing-boats were attacked while working inshore to the nor'ard of Yarmouth. He had just passed through the fleet, bound down to the Humber, and had had several close risks of collision, in the absence of lights until flares were shown at the last moment. The night was exceptionally dark and he was congratulating himself on having got through successfully when he heard the sound of firing and saw the flash of guns just astern of him. He at once altered course close inshore. "If they follow me," he thought, "it will be into mighty shoal water"; and, in the last resort, there was always the beach to put her on. But the barge escaped unscathed, although thirty fishing-boats were sunk that night.

So far I have dealt only with the war service of the ordinary working barges. But pride of place for distinction in war service must be given to two barges which had the honour of being chosen and fitted out as Q-ships for submarine-hunting during the later days of the war.

Of these, one was the Maldon barge *Record Reign*, a particularly

interesting ship ; and her late owners, for whom she was built, Messrs
John Sadd & Sons of Maldon, have kindly supplied me with detailed
information about her. To them I am also indebted for the fine picture
of her which appears in Plate 33. She was built by those well-known
builders Howard & Son, at Maldon, in the year 1890. The picture,
taken from an oil painting made in the early part of the present century, shows her in her original rig. It will be seen at once on what
lovely lines she was built, with clipper bow and counter-stern ; she
was boomy-rigged, with the addition of squaresail, square topsail and
to'gans'l. With her black rails and light topsides below, and her
white canvas straining at the bolt-ropes in a fresh breeze, she makes
a splendid picture, and illustrates far better than any mere description
can do the rig of those few fine barges which carried square canvas.
But some time before the outbreak of war, the square canvas was
removed, although to the end of her days she was boomy-rigged.
When built she was designed to be of the largest dimensions to allow
her to pass through the lock at Heybridge Basin, being intended for
the timber trade there, where the timber had to be unloaded into
small barges in which it was towed up the canal to Chelmsford. But
when she first entered the lock it was found that, although she was the
right length between stem and sternposts, due allowance had not
been made for the overhang of her beautiful counter-stern, and the
lock gates would not close beneath it when she was deep loaded. Thus
it was only on exceptionally high spring tides that she was able to
enter the basin with a full cargo.

She was certainly a large barge, having carried as much as 282 tons
of stone, and full particulars of her appear in Appendix IV. After
being taken over by the Admiralty, her two 40 h.p. Bolinder engines
were installed in 1915, to equip her for her special secret work. The
Admiralty led the exhaust into a hollow mizzen-mast with the outlets
near the hounds, and to all appearances she was merely an innocent
and inoffensive sailing barge.

The following is the account of her sent to me by her owners, and
some of the remarks on the behaviour of flat-bottomed ships generally
are of such interest that I have included them here :

"The Admiralty spent a lot of money on her, fitting false deck-
houses and steel topgallant bulwarks to fall down ; the keelson was
boxed with steel plates ; and iron bulkheads and wood-covered deck-
houses were fitted throughout. So far as we are aware she was never in
action, but frequently in the dockyards for alterations, engine repairs
and so forth. We much regret we are unable to state the armament.
The deck-house aft, containing most commodious captain's quarters,

closet and galley, was fitted when the after accommodation below decks was turned into an engine-room.

"The writer is given to understand that the vessel with her original rig was very handy and quite reasonably fast for a flat-bottomed ship. The main disadvantages of a flat bottom at the present time in coast-wise vessels is that so many of the mud berths have previously accommodated round-bottomed steamers and barges, and it throws a great and uneven strain on a flat-bottomed vessel to follow them. From the point of view of seaworthiness, a flat bottom seems to improve the ship rather than otherwise, and all hands who have sailed in the *Record Reign* agree that she was one of the finest sea boats in the coasting service and would live in any gale of wind.

"Her figure-head was originally the head and bust of Queen Victoria, but this unfortunately was damaged and knocked adrift by a trawler during attempted salvage operations some years ago.

"The vessel eventually went ashore in Holland during a full gale of wind, but owing to her flat bottom and it being high water at the time, she was swept up on the stone dykes, the damage being very little indeed; but Captain Stanes, who was in charge of her at the time, can spin this yarn far better than we can.

"So far as we can trace, the captains of the vessel have been successively: Captain N. Handley, Captain J. D. Sullivan and Captain S. H. Stanes."

Captain Sullivan, who was in command of the *Record Reign* until she was taken over by the Admiralty, and who took her over from them when her war service was completed, kindly supplied me with information as to her armament. She was quite a little warship, for she carried no less than five guns. Of these, four were small guns, about 12-pounders, mounted on folding or collapsing mountings hidden beind collapsible steel bulwarks and placed one on each bow and one on each quarter. Amidships she carried a much larger gun, probably a 7·9, about 14 feet long and mounted on a very strong mounting arranged about in the middle of the main hatch, which had raised dummy coamings. This gun was very cleverly disguised by being completely enclosed in a dummy barge's boat, apparently resting in chocks on top of the hatch. The boat was, however, cunningly divided amidships, and the two halves could be parted and slid along the deck away from each other in a moment, thus exposing the gun.

That, briefly, is the history of the *Record Reign*. Although it is a popular tradition among the bargemen that she had more than one submarine to her credit, I have never been able to obtain confirmation of this story. Captain Sullivan told me that he met an officer,

Captain Butters, who was in her during the war. Although she had sighted a submarine once, as far as can be discovered she was never in action.

The *Record Reign* continued trading as a motor ketch until she went ashore in thick fog at Littleham Shute, about 2 miles west of Branscombe, near Beer in Devon, on the morning of Friday, 8th February 1935. She was then holed below the water-line on the starboard bow; and at low water was high and dry, with 3 to 4 feet of water in her hold. It was found that she was firmly wedged between two rocks; and although the Brixham tug *Dencade* arrived on the following day, the barge was leaking badly and all efforts to get her off failed. She was already starting gradually to break up, and salvage work on her cargo was greatly hampered by a heavy swell on the beach. Two days later it was unhappily realised that the end of the *Record Reign* had come at last.

The other barge with a record as a Q-ship in the First World War was the *Sarah Colebrooke*, now *Bolham*. She was built at Rye in 1913 by Messrs G. & T. Smith Ltd., to the order of Mr W. E. Colebrooke, and named after his wife. In 1931 she was owned by the Lumley Shipping Company, of Emsworth, Hants, of which the Chairman was Mrs M. Marshall-Hole. She was then an auxiliary barge with a 90 h.p. semi-Diesel engine, and her mizzen-mast had been removed. From one of the directors, Lieut.-Commander (as he then was) G. H. Gardner, R.N., I received a full account of her war-time activities as a Q-ship, together with a record from the Admiralty of her Service career, and a description, from her commanding officer at the time of her engagement with an enemy submarine.

The *Sarah Colebrooke* was a ketch-rigged, chine-built sailing barge, with a D.W. capacity of 250 tons and gross registered tonnage of 158. She was 102 feet 6 inches in overall length, with a beam of 24 feet 6 inches and a depth of 8 feet respectively. The Admiralty statement says that she was commissioned at Portsmouth on 3rd May 1917, under the name of H.M.S. *Bolham*, as a decoy ship carrying a concealed armament. A month later, on 3rd June 1917, about 20 miles south by west from Beachy Head, a submarine fired on her, the fourth shell shattering the gun house. The *Bolham* then opened fire with her foremost gun and the submarine disappeared, apparently in a sinking condition. The commanding officer of the *Bolham*, Lieutenant C. W. Walters, R.N.R., was given the Distinguished Service Cross for this action, the Distinguished Service Medal being awarded to two of his crew. Subsequent information, however, showed that the submarine had not been seriously damaged.

The *Bolham* was based in Portsmouth between June 1917 and May 1918. From May 1918 till 7th October 1918, when she was paid off, she cruised in the English Channel. There is no official record of any second encounter with a submarine although her commanding officer states that on two subsequent occasions he engaged a submarine, though without result, other than the shelling. His own account is so interesting that I quote it in full.

"I fitted out *Bolham* in the spring of 1917," he writes, "as a special service vessel or 'Q'-ship, as they were commonly called, and commissioned her at the beginning of May with a specially selected volunteer crew. It was on our maiden cruise that we were in action with an enemy submarine about 15 miles south of Beachy Head. *Bolham* was heavily shelled and rather badly damaged. The submarine was also badly damaged, if not destroyed, but as we had no actual proof to take back to Portsmouth the result of the action was doubtful. We were very fortunate in having no casualties. After a long refit at Portsmouth we resumed our work of decoy, and although I engaged two more submarines there was no actual result other than shelling. I left her early in 1918 to fit out another vessel and she was then commanded for a short period by Lieutenant A. T. Sellers, R.N.R., who had previously served with me as first lieutenant. Nothing happened during the period he was in command, and she then returned to Portsmouth to pay off and recondition. She had become so well known to the enemy submarines that she was of no further use as a decoy.

"The English Channel was the general hunting ground and Penzance was the most western port used. On the occasion of the Beachy Head action our name was *Worrynot* of Littlehampton. We used several other names, but never sailed under *Sarah Colebrooke* of Rye. Below the main deck we had accommodation for 4 officers, 3 engineers, 2 wireless operators, 3 petty officers, signalmen and a number of other ratings and guns' crews. We carried two fairly large guns, depth charges, bombs of all kinds, machine guns and many hundreds of rounds of ammunition, large and small. The hull was sand-bagged inside in way of vital parts and her lee-boards were fitted with steel plates on the inside. The lee-board on the port side was the saving of the ship at Beachy Head. A direct hit from the enemy struck and shattered the lee-board and damaged the hull, but did not quite penetrate. Had the lee-board not been there, and up at the time, *Bolham* would no doubt have been very badly holed, and the fact that our ballast consisted of scrap iron and lead did not improve our chances of remaining afloat. Although *Bolham* has not a long list of submarines to her credit, she did quite good work, and Admiral Sir Stanley Colville, who was my Commander-in-Chief (Portsmouth Command), was very proud of her. During the time I served in command she was inspected by Royalty, our most famous Admirals and Generals, the Lords of the Admiralty, the U.S. Naval Commander-in-Chief and the C.-in-C. of the South African Army. It may also interest you to know that a steel tube was fitted into the forward end of the main hatch down through the ship and fitted to a steel shoe in the bottom. Through this tube I towed a submarine submerged, and in a fair breeze made four knots under sail power alone. This was not satisfactory as the weather was so seldom suitable, and during the winter it proved quite a hopeless task. However, we gave it a good trial. Our largest guns were two 3-inch high-velocity of the latest type then in use, and it may interest you to know that the guns' crews were so well trained that at the order "Action" we could mount the gun, load it, train it on the object and score a hit at one thousand yards' range in *five seconds*."

He added the comment: "I was brought up in large sailing vessels and I must say that *Sarah Colebrooke* was the queerest craft I ever handled. I never could remember the lee-boards when going about."

When she was being refitted at Rye after her war service, sundry nameplates of ordinary coasting vessels were found on board, as her name was constantly being changed when she went seeking the enemy, so that she should not be identified.

After her release from the Service, she was fully reconditioned at Rye. Freights for some time after the war were exceptionally good, and for about twelve months she was on charter running coal between Dover and Boulogne at 20s. a ton F.I.O. She also made one round trip from London to Rouen and back for £450—not bad going; and after that she went into the Continental trade, running a lot to the Thames. Large sums of money were spent on her, following collisions and other damage at various times; and at Great Yarmouth she had a rider keelson put in and was doubled to her chines. She also had a succession of engines installed—at least three by 1931. Many of her voyages were to the east coast of Scotland and back to Rye with coal.

Between the wars *Sarah Colebrooke* had several owners, including the Lumley Shipping Company. She featured prominently under a disguised name as *Jane Peake* in Joan Grigsby's book "Longshore and Down Channel", published in 1932; and Miss Grigsby gives a graphic account of a passage in her when trading to the Continent. She survived the Second World War, and is still alive under her war-time name of *Bolham*, to which she reverted in 1932. She is now working in and out of the Mersey, trading to such places as Point of Ayr, the River Dee and the Isle of Man ports. Although classed as an auxiliary cutter (she was originally shown in the Merchant Navy List as a ketch), she is in fact working as a fully powered motor vessel. Her one remaining mast is little more than a derrick-pole. *Sic transit*— but it is good that she is still alive. Her present owners are Messrs Coppack Bros. of Connah's Quay.

In writing the story of the barges in the First World War, it would be a grievous fault to omit the important part played by the barge-men's womenfolk. Many a skipper's wife rallied to her husband's aid and helped with the working of the barge, often sailing as only mate, and releasing an able man for other work at a time when the shortage of able men was being keenly felt; and credit and honour are due to the bargewomen for the readiness with which they faced the hard-ships of life at sea and ably performed men's work in the nation's cause.

Although there were many women mates of barges during the war, Mrs Charlotte Whale of Collis Street, Strood, claimed to be the only woman entitled to wear the Mercantile Marine Medal. In 1914, when barge crews were much in demand, and many of the men had joined up on active service, she volunteered as barge mate and satisfactorily passed her tests. She was examined by Mr Ernest Gill of Rochester, and had a very sound knowledge of barge work. But she found the examination a trying ordeal, although she sailed through with flying colours. "I *know* all right," she would answer to a question, "but when you look straight through me like that, I can't seem to tell you anything!"

Mrs Whale then made many an exciting voyage on a sea-going barge, and on one occasion her barge was nearly struck by a bomb when lying in Ipswich. She was destined, however, to survive all her bargeing adventures unscratched, and by the queer irony of Fate was ultimately wounded by shrapnel during the last Zeppelin raid of the war!

# CHAPTER XVI

# The Second World War

THE story of the barges in the Second World War is one of hard work and hardship in conditions infinitely more hazardous for ships and men than anything they experienced in the earlier conflict. From the evacuation of Dunkirk to the last days of the war, the Thames Estuary was right in the fighting line, and the port of London the target for every infernal means of attack that a ruthless enemy could fling at it. Mined, machine-gunned, bombed and burned, over-routed, unprotected, the barges carried on; quietly, efficiently and with superb courage. There is little sensational in the story; the high-lights were few, though the perils were endless. It is a story of the unflinching courage and relentless determination of the bargemen, who sailed their craft from one target area to another, running the gauntlet on every passage as they shuttled to and fro between the frying-pan and the fire. Yet through all those cruel years, to their undying glory, the barges went on sailing. Through all the hell of total war the barges *sailed*.

Take, for example, the *Will Everard*, last of the four big steel-built sister ships to continue trading under sail alone. Her skipper through-out the war was Captain J. A. Uglow, M.B.E., of Gravesend, who was, I believe, the only bargeman to receive this decoration, awarded for gallantry, devotion to duty and meritorious service during those six long years. At my request, he has been kind enough to send me a short account of the *Will Everard's* war-time career, for which I here record my thanks.

Captain Uglow has always been a bit of a "lone wolf", sailing his own ship and not bothering overmuch about others. His job in the war was to take the *Will Everard*, laden or light, wherever she was wanted, and, apart from an occasional tow, he did it under sail alone. On the Thursday before war was declared, being the 28th August 1939, the *Will* loaded in London a cargo of cement for Southampton. She arrived at her port of discharge on the Sunday morning, 1st September, in time to hear the declaration of war broadcast by the B.B.C. on that momentous day. From September 1939 to May 1945, the *Will* actually completed 147 coasting voyages, and carried 38,345 tons of various commodities such as grain, sugar beet, oil cake, fertilisers, flour, sugar and cement. This, it will be appreciated, was carried without any cost of fuel to the nation. Her voyages were mostly between London and Ipswich or Yarmouth, as well as down-Channel between London and Southampton. I am indebted to Mr W. J. Everard, and the staff of Messrs Everard's Greenhithe office for abstracting the figures quoted above. Mr Everard also tells me that the *Will Everard* had several narrow shaves whilst trading during the war. She was lifted off her berth by a bomb explosion at Southampton, severely damaging her bottom, as related below by her skipper. She was attacked by enemy aircraft on several occasions. In one instance her sails were absolutely pepper-boxed with machine-gun fire; and eventually she was fired upon by our own battery at Shoebury.

To continue with Captain Uglow's story of her adventures, there was an occasion in May 1940 on which they were two miles off Southwold, bound for Yarmouth, when a British destroyer dropped a pattern of depth charges only about 300 yards from them—"Presumably," as Captain Uglow writes, "to flush a submarine." Whatever its effect on the supposed "sub", it was certainly close enough to the *Will* to give her a bad shaking.

An example of the sort of difficulties bargemen had to face from the sometimes impossible instructions of well-meaning but occasionally unseamanlike naval officers, lacking understanding of small sailing craft without engines, is illustrated by another experience. In May 1940 the *Will* was bound from London for Southampton and had not at that time been "wiped", that is, given electrical treatment to de-magnetise the ship, affording, while it lasted, some protection from magnetic mines. She had been routed off to the North Goodwin Light-vessel. The wind was strong, easterly. Near the North Goodwin several fairly large ships lay at anchor. The *Will Everard* was then ordered three separate times to do the same. Captain Uglow resolutely refused to obey any such order, pointing out that the *Will* was a small vessel and that it was quite impossible for her to anchor in 14 fathoms of water and a nasty breaking sea. The Navy either could not or did not think of any answer to that, so he proceeded through the Brake Channel and anchored in the Small Downs, off Deal. There they rode heavily for three days, awaiting permission to proceed. No one came near them or communicated any message.

On the third day they saw the steamers getting under way. The skipper was watching them through binoculars, and swearing to the crew because these ships had permission to go on and he had not,

when he saw two of them blown up by mines. "Half and hour later,"
he writes, "a launch came off to me, and I was told by a Naval
Lieutenant that I could proceed, as it was an unhealthy spot—as if I
didn't know!" They got under way, and continued their voyage without further incident.

After the collapse of France, the *Will* arrived at Southampton on
28th June 1940; and from then until 29th July 1941 she was confined to local trading between Cowes, Newport (Isle of Wight),
Southampton and Poole. In August 1940 she was machine-gunned by
enemy fighters on two days in succession, when lying at the Medina
Cement Mills, up the Medina River. A few weeks later, on the 26th
September, she was at the Phoenix Wharf, Southampton, when she
found herself in the centre of a concentrated daylight raid on the
Supermarine Aircraft Factory. One hundred and fifty-three bombs
were dropped in a straight line, on both sides of the river, in a length
of 600 yards. The *Will* was partly loaded at the time; and the vessel's
bottom was hogged through being partly lifted out of the water and
then striking the ground. The fore hold was filled with debris from
surrounding buildings, the hatches were blown over the side and the
skylight blown in. The crew all had narrow escapes, and Captain
Uglow helped to tend the injured.

On the 29th July 1941 *Will Everard* was towed from Poole to
Southend in a 7-knot convoy, on the understanding that, if she broke
adrift from the steamer towing her, her skipper would be left to his
own resources. They ran the gauntlet of the big guns in the Pas de
Calais, but came through unscathed, and started again in the East
Coast trade. The *Will* was sailing in company with the barge *Britisher*
in November 1941 when the latter was blown up on a magnetic mine.
She was about 500 yards away at the time, and simply disappeared,
blown to atoms, with no survivors. The *Britisher*, also owned by
Everard's, was a spreety of 68 tons net, built at Greenhithe in 1902.
Skipper and mate both perished.

During one voyage in the winter of 1942, when bound for Norwich,
Captain Uglow endeavoured to sneak down a few miles in the dark on
a night of dense fog. They drained down with the ebb until they were
abreast of Harwich, and about one and a half miles off. They could
hear several M.T.B. engines not far off, so decided to anchor to avoid
detection—barges were not supposed to be under way after dark in
those waters. One M.T.B. circled round them for about ten minutes,
but failed to find the *Will*. They then heard continuous fire from
light guns at Harwich, continued later at sea; and presumed that this
was some sort of exercise—a mock attack on Harwich. It was not until

they reached Yarmouth on the following evening that they discovered enemy E-boats had carried out a very lively attack on the harbour at Harwich, while another flotilla farther north was attacking through the Stanford Channel off Lowestoft.

In the following year, on 9th March 1943, at 7 a.m., when off the Whitaker, the *Will* was attacked by a Fokker-Wulf 109, who managed to put 1,000 holes in her mainsail and generally spray the decks with "cannon fire". All members of the crew were on deck at the time; but although it sounded like hailstones pattering around, nobody was injured. "After that," writes Captain Uglow, "there was nothing particularly exciting apart from the raids, 'doodle-bugs' and rockets generally experienced by everybody in the south-east corner of England."

Captain Uglow's experience of attentions from the enemy was not limited to bargeing, however; for when he was staying at his home in Gravesend, on 3rd March 1943, the roof was blown off the house, among other damage. His family all fortunately escaped injury.

For another account of work in the sailing barges during the war I have to thank my friend Captain "Chubb" Horlock, skipper of the *Vigilant* when Commander E. G. Martin was his mate in the early 1930's. "Chubb" had the *Oxygen* all through the war, owned by Sully's firm, and now an auxiliary, but working under sail alone until 1947. She is a fine barge, though smaller than the *Hydrogen*, of which the late Captain Arthur Coward was the skipper, and she was built at Rochester in 1895. Of 69 tons net, she would carry 150 tons, and was in the Humber and Channel trade before the war. Both she and *Hydrogen* were built originally by Gill as tank barges, but the tanks were later removed.

"I was trading to Ipswich and Yarmouth all the war," Captain Horlock writes, "and nothing very exciting happened to me, except once, when I think the vibration of the bobstay set off a mine—unless it was a time mine—about fifty yards astern of us." On another occasion they were coming down on one trip, knowing there were magnetic mines about, when two went off on the port bow. The skipper therefore altered course a little, and then two or three more went up ahead; so he altered course again. More mines went up ahead of them. "So," the skipper said, "I got fed up altering course and we continued on our proper course, and counted twenty-three mines in the space of half an hour." Nothing very exciting, forsooth! But quite enough, one might well be excused in thinking, for one half-hour.

During the first week or so of the magnetic mines, sailing barges

were used to take stores to the craft at the naval base at Southend, as
so many power craft were blown up then, and it was thought that
sailing barges stood a better chance.

To combat the menace of mine-laying by enemy aircraft in the
Thames Estuary, a considerable number of barges was requisitioned,
and these craft, about sixty in all, had their gear taken out and were
then moored in strategic positions with mine-watching crews aboard,
whose duty it was to spot and report the activities of aircraft laying
mines and the positions where the mines were seen to come down.
Among barges taken up for this work were *Lord Roberts*, *Haste Away*
and *Eureka*.

Other barges were requisitioned as balloon barrage ships, and spent
the war at anchor, flying balloons with steel cables to help in the
defence of London. One of these was the *Katherina*, a steel ketch
barge, built foreign at Stadskanaal in 1910 and sharing with the *Olive
May* the distinction of being one of the last two sailing coasters
owned in Rye. She was sold to West of Gravesend in 1937, and was
condemned just before war broke out, her masts and decks being
unsound. Her hull was quite good enough, however, for her to serve
as a balloon barrage vessel, and she was requisitioned and used for
that purpose.

Unfortunately, the barges requisitioned for mine-watching and
balloon barrage service suffered more serious damage than any others
—not from the assaults of the enemy, but by the attacks of those
insidious little borers, the marine worms. Lying about as these craft
did for years, never under way and moving through the water, never
on the blocks for scraping and tarring, their neglected bottoms grew
a crop of weeds that would make the hanging gardens of Babylon look
like a freshly mown lawn, surmounting a culture of barnacles like a
rough-cast wall. As a result, the worms enjoyed a banquet of gar-
gantuan proportions; and when the barges were returned to their
owners by the Ministry of War Transport, many of them were so
eaten up and riddled as to be beyond repair. It also taxed the patience
of the unfortunate owners beyond the limits of endurance to explain
to the unilluminated official mind that barges weren't just naturally
eaten up by worms in a few years anyway—in spite of the unimpeachable evidence of such old stalwarts as the *Favorite*, born 1803 and still
"going strong". *Res ipsa loquitur* can be a two-edged weapon in
official hands.

Among barges which suffered badly in this way was *Sir Richard*,
belonging to the London and Rochester Trading Company, a barge
of which many of us have pleasant memories as one of the craft

PLATE 60 *Cambria* and *Reminder* racing

*[Photograph by courtesy of "The Times"]*

17

chartered to follow the Medway Barge Race with a party of enthusiasts on board. She was one of several barges requisitioned by the
Ministry of War Transport for the conveyance of ammunition and its
dispersal in the naval port of Chatham. She was laid up for long
periods in the lower creeks of the River Medway, with the inevitable
result that the worms had a banquet. *Wouldham Court*, a stumpy
belonging to the same owners, was requisitioned for mine-watching.
She was seriously damaged when a German bomber crashed on her,
as recorded on page 88.

The London and Rochester Trading Company affords a good
example of the extent to which the barges were taken up by requisition during the war. When hostilities began, the company's fleet
numbered 160 craft, which included sailing and motor barges, lighters
and motor coasters. Of these, 108 were requisitioned, chiefly for mine-
watching and powder work. The ravages of neglect were far more
destructive than the efforts of the enemy, and the fleet suffered severe
losses as a result. For the following notes on the part played by
individual barges, I am indebted to Mr E. A. Gill, M.I.N.A., who is
not only a director of the company, but also a great enthusiast for
sailing barges.

*Alderman*, who had been converted to auxiliary power before the
war, was ordered by the Ministry of War Transport to proceed
through the Caledonian Canal to the Clyde. She made the passage
round under her own power, but was afterwards run down and sunk
while still in Scottish waters. She was a fine barge, of 73 tons, built by
Shrubsall in 1905 for Groom of Harwich. She was one of the barges
taken over from his fleet by the London and Rochester Trading Company in 1924, with a number of older barges, since broken up. The
*Arrow*, once well-known as the barge of which the famous "Schoolmaster West" was skipper, and now, by the generosity of the company, the Club barge of the Thames Barge Sailing Club, was requisitioned by the Ministry of War Transport and used under sail for the
transport of stores for the balloon barrage in the Thames Estuary.
Although only under sail, she performed admirable service amongst
the mines which were continually being dropped, for, having no
engines to cause vibration, she had no effect on acoustic mines.

*British Lion* was employed for the storage and delivery of ammunition to ships coming into the naval port of Chatham. *Imperial* and
*Queen* were both requisitioned for similar duties. *Imperial* is now
being reconditioned and fitted with an engine. *Queen* is being converted into a motor barge, with all her sailing gear removed. *Whimbrel*
was trading under ordinary conditions during the war, but was badly

17

damaged in a collision in 1944, and afterwards broken up. *Pudge* went over to Dunkirk in 1940, and brought back crews from tugs and barges and men who had been picked up off the beaches, as described later. *Ironsides* was slightly damaged by bombs in the London docks during the big raids of September 1940. *D.E.F.*'s war service was rather different. She was sold in July 1939 to the British Council, who installed engines in her for special work during the war period by the Salvage Corps in London. The little stumpy *Jim Wigley* was found to be beyond repair to fit her for active service, and was used as a store barge.

This record, taken at random, gives a fair cross-section of the kind of work done by the barges during the war. Though it only represents a few of the ships of one company, it is reasonably typical of all. Messrs R. & W. Paul Ltd. of Ipswich had all their barges trading between London and Ipswich and other East Anglian ports throughout the war period. *Aidie*, *Barbara Jean* and *Doris*, of their fleet, were lost at Dunkirk, as described later; while their *Ena* and *Tollesbury*, which were also there, returned safely. They afterwards lost *Bijou* (always pronounced "*By Joe*") by enemy action, and *Audrey* was run down in the River Orwell. Messrs Goldsmiths of Grays also lost a number of their barges during the war.

It must be remembered, too, that the barges still had the ordinary navigational dangers to encounter, as well as the attentions of the enemy; and the hazards of fogs and gales and suchlike commonplace difficulties were rendered much more perilous by the restricted channels, wrecks, mined areas, limitations on navigation by night, prohibited anchorages and all the other unpleasant conditions which added to the bargemen's troubles. They were, moreover, limited as to the area in which they might trade. Admiralty restrictions prevented them from trading as far north as King's Lynn or the Humber, and Harwich and Ramsgate were the usual limits; although barges with special routing instructions were allowed to proceed as far as Yarmouth. "Confidential Instructions" were printed and issued to wooden sailing barges, and to iron and steel barges that had been "wiped", which were trading within these limits, and in the tidal waters of Thames and Medway, Crouch, Blackwater and Colne. They were also given the positions of the scores of wrecks which littered the shallow waters.

When, in the later years of the war, some limited navigation at night was permitted in certain areas, every barge trading between the Thames and Medway and Harwich or intermediate ports required a signed Certificate of Identity for each voyage, from the Sailing Barge

Owners' Committee; and she was then allowed to be under way at night within the coastwise channels of Swin and Wallet, nearest to the Essex coast, and including the Rivers Colne, Blackwater and Crouch. There were, however, conditions attached to such voyages. Auxiliary barges were not to use their engines outside river entrances. All barges bound for Harwich had first to be routed to the Colne, and then on to Harwich. No barge was allowed to enter Harwich after dark, except in stress of weather; and then only with permission from the Flag Officer in Charge, Harwich. One can imagine how easy it was for a sailing barge in a howling onshore gale to ask the Flag Officer in Charge for permission to enter! Finally, barges should pass outwards through the Yantlet Gates at 5.0 a.m. (I wonder whether anybody but sailing bargemen ever thought of the tide?); but were allowed to enter at any time between sunrise and sunset.

By a later amendment, the area in which they might be by night was even more restricted. No doubt such regulations were considered essential or they would not have been imposed. But the official mind seems quite incapable of appreciating the fact that no regulations will control the wind and tide at sea, and these are all the sailing bargeman has to take him to his destination.

Goldsmith's *Esterel* came near to being lost through stress of weather during the war years, when she struck on the Cork Sand in a fierce easterly gale; but she re-floated, with her spreet carried away, and drove ashore on the Essex coast. She was subsequently recovered, and continued trading until she foundered off Clacton in the winter of 1948–49; her crew of three were landed by the local lifeboat. *Esterel*, 67 tons, built at Southampton in 1899, was then laden with wheat for Ipswich from London, and sank in fairly shallow water about three-quarters of a mile off the shore. Among barges lost by what I might call "natural causes", namely, stress of weather, were *Evening*, lost off the Blacktail Spit, and *Tam o' Shanter*, laden with wheat, which came to grief in the Spitway, off Clacton.

Other hazards included the ever-present danger of striking a wreck. The Ipswich-built *Castanet* was lost in this way, by striking a wreck in the Wallet, when laden with wheat, in February 1943. Everard's boomy *Martinet*, of Goole, was lost by springing a leak. Built at Rye in 1912, she was quite a big barge, of 99 tons net, and was the last boomy actively trading, until she foundered in Hollesley Bay, near Aldeburgh, in February 1941. *Chieftain*, of 59 tons net, a London-built barge, launched in 1893 and owned by the London and Rochester Trading Company, although she had once belonged to Covington's fleet, was lost in the Barrow Deep by being towed under by a powerful Government tug, while under requisition. *Enchantress* of Rochester, another barge owned by the same company, a craft of 56 tons net built at Maidstone in 1908, was lost in the Royal Albert Docks, London, during the blitz, when Rank's Mill fell on her.

The little *Emma* of Maldon, mentioned elsewhere in this book as winner of the Maldon Barge Race in 1929, was at Bellamy's wharf, Rotherhithe, waiting for an ocean-going steamer to tie up, and when the latter had reached within about seven feet of the quay she exploded a magnetic mine, which blew off the bows of the ship and seriously damaged the stern of the *Emma*. Both skipper and mate fortunately got away unscathed, in spite of being in the cabin at the time. The incident occurred on 29th March 1941; and the wreck of the *Emma* is now lying alongside at Messrs John Sadd & Sons' yard at Maldon.

Another of the barges lost in the London River was the little *Spider*, one of the old nipcat barges, which was bombed as she was finishing her days as a mooring lighter on Woolwich buoys.

Mention has already been made of the use of barges in powder work on Thames and Medway during the war years. The War Office also used spritsail barges to carry military stores in the Thames, and were still doing so in 1946. Among barges in the powder work was the *Major*, of 67 tons, originally a boomy, built at Harwich in 1897, and once one of Groom's barges. She was skipper-owned before the war, with her mulie's mizzen removed and a small third hatch fitted to give easier access to her big cupboards. A small sprit mizzen was put into her. She survived the war, but afterwards broke her moorings at Whitstable, in a gale at the end of September 1946, and drove up on the beach, where she had to await the spring tides to get afloat again. She was then practically rebuilt at Anderson's Yard, Whitstable; she was doubled, and had an auxiliary fitted. The job took nearly two years, and was completed at the end of 1948. A fine barge, of 81 tons gross, she had been in the Channel and Humber trade in pre-war days.

Other barges in the powder work were *Verona*, built by Shrubsall for the Thames Race in 1905; *Sam Weller*, owned by the London and Rochester Trading Co., and once one of Covington's barges; and *Venture*, built at Ipswich in 1900, and employed carrying ammunition on the Medway. *Fred Everard* had already been converted to full power before the war, and as a motor barge she was one of a number of Everard's craft employed as ammunition store issuing ships, and was attached to the Home Fleet at Scapa Flow.

The little *Marconi*, 43 tons, built by White at Conyer in 1901, and a noted racing barge, was in use by the Services at Ramsgate, where she was bombed; and she was eventually broken up there in 1947.

A number of barges were employed on Government work outside the Thames Estuary during the war. Reference has already been made to the *Alderman*, but there were several others. Most of these went to the Clyde, among them *Marie May*, a big auxiliary of 83 tons net, built at Maidstone in 1920 and owned by the London and Rochester Trading Co. Some auxiliary barges had their sails landed when they were requisitioned, and they rotted ashore during the war. The skipper of the *Marie May*, however, kept his nailed up in the fore cupboard, and she was carrying the same suit in 1949. *Knowles*, also belonging to the London and Rochester Trading Company, built at Frindesbury in 1910, of 63 tons net, with an auxiliary fitted before the war, was another that went to the Clyde, where she was lost as the result of a marine casualty. M. F. Horlock's *Resourceful* was also working on the Clyde, though as a pure motor vessel, to which she had been converted in 1933. So was *Success*, a big iron barge, carrying about 250 tons, once a mulie, but converted to full power.

*Lady Gwynfred*, built at Gravesend in 1904, was working not only on the Clyde but as far as the Outer Hebrides, under Captain George Barker, who now has the *Major*. The London and Rochester Trading Company's *Cabby* was likewise trading from the Clyde to the Islands. She was built at Gill's Lower Yard on the Medway for that company in 1928, and will probably remain for ever distinguished by being, with the exception of the little stumpy *Lady of the Lea*, the last wooden barge built. She raced in the Coasting Class in the barge race, but had had an engine installed before the war. *Arcades*, *Saxon* and Sully's *Raybel*, all auxiliaries, were also on the Clyde; as were *Hydrogen* and *Leonard Piper*. On the subject of barges trading in Scottish waters, Roger Finch writes that he will never forget going into Campbeltown when he was in the Fleet Air Arm, stationed at Macrihanish, and seeing, to his astonishment, three topmasts and sprits rising up above the "puffers" and fishing craft. They were the three auxiliary barges *Lady Gwynfred*, *Leonard Piper* and *Hydrogen*, en route for the Thames after their war service on the Clyde. They were bound home by way of the Caledonian Canal on the next leg of their journey. The crews he described as "looking very fed-up and far from home", surrounded by dour Scots fisher-folk. Later he learnt that they had a "real dusting" off the north-east coast on the passage south.

It will be noted that all the barges going to Scotland or to the Bristol Channel were either auxiliary or pure motor barges. They were assisted there by the Navy; but most of them returned unassisted, brought back by their skippers.

It is perhaps worth mentioning here that one of the barges requisitioned for war service, although she never visited her native land, was built in Scotland. One of the very few barges to be built in that country, the appropriately named *Thistle*, of 79 tons, was launched at Port Glasgow in 1895. Up to about 1930 she was ketch-rigged. Once owned by Covington's, she became a spreety, and was acquired by the London and Rochester Trading Co. She is still going strong.

Two barges, on requisition as motor vessels, went to the Bristol Channel to work. These were the *Beatrice Maud* and the *Shamrock*, and they were employed between Milford Haven on the north and Bideford on the south, and to all the ports to the eastward of that line. They were working for the Ministry of Food, and, as far as is known, were the only barges to carry beef-steak-and-kidney puddings! What memories this must recall of lavish rations in war-time days, before we enjoyed the benefits of peace. *Beatrice Maud* is a big London barge, of 102 tons, and she continued trading in the Bristol Channel well into 1946; though she was back at work between London and Ipswich in July of that year. *Shamrock* (not to be confused with the craft of that name which became the barge-yacht *Black Swan*) is still in the Bristol Channel, working from Appledore in the sand trade, as a pure motor barge. Roger Finch saw her at Barnstaple in 1946, and reports that she had then been fitted with a grab.

No record of the barges' work would be complete without a reference to the many who were blown up by mines, an ever-present hazard in the waters where they were trading. Reference has already been made to the loss of the *Britisher*, but the full list of such casualties is a long one. Among them were several of the barges owned by M. F. Horlock of Mistley, including *Resolute*, 60 tons net, a spreety built at Harwich in 1903. She was lost in 1942 near the No. 2 Wallet buoy, and was laden with wheat at the time. The mate was drowned, but the skipper was rescued. The same firm's *Blue Mermaid*, a new barge, built in 1930, was blown up by a mine near the West Hook Middle Buoy on the 9th July 1941, also laden with wheat. Both master and mate lost their lives. *Rosmé*, another modern barge, of 67 tons net, built at Maidstone in 1927, and owned by the London and Rochester Trading Company, was mined off the Blacktail Spit, and was carrying wheat at the time. Her stern was blown off, but her skipper, Captain Frederick Smy of Ipswich, was able to save his mate, who was down in the cabin at the time. He was later

awarded the British Empire Medal for his gallantry, and is now
master of the London and Rochester Trading Company's steel motor
barge *Wyvenhoe*.

Another of the mined barges was the *Bankside*, an auxiliary spreety
of 60 tons, built at Milton in 1900, rebuilt in 1927, and owned by
Colonel R. C. Bingham, with Francis and Gilders. She was blown up
off the Maplin Spit, laden with flour; both skipper and mate perished
with her. *Globe*, a small barge of 46 tons net, built at Frindesbury in
1884, was mined off Garrison Point, Sheerness. *H.K.D.*, formerly
*Jewish*, was also blown up by a mine off Sheerness, by the Outer Bar
Buoy, on 19th January 1942, but her skipper was saved. She was making
passage light at the time. *Ailsa*, a barge of 67 tons net, built at Deptford in 1898, was another casualty from mining, and was lost near the
N.E. Whitaker Beacon when crossing the Whitaker Spit; her crew
was saved. *Gertrude May* was mined off Clacton in July 1941. Her
mate, a Norwegian, was lost, but her skipper escaped alive. Yet
another victim was the *Ash*, built in 1907, mined near the Red Sand
Tower; and the *J.B.W.*, a big spreety built at Millwall in the same
year, went up on a mine off the Maplin Edge. She was carrying a cargo
of rubble, and was lost with both her crew.

Such were the hazards run by the barges in their everyday work
throughout the war; but, though every voyage was fraught with peril
and dangers lurked both in the skies above and the waters beneath,
they carried on. Nothing the enemy could ever do could stop the
barges sailing. All honour to the men, and ships, whose record was so
truly glorious; and if it was at Dunkirk they saw their finest hour, this
is but the highlight in a splendid picture of years of selfless devotion
and undaunted courage.

The story of Dunkirk has been told many times and will doubtless
be told again with pride as long as any British people are left to
inhabit the earth. I shall not attempt to tell that story, for I am only
concerned here with one part of it, a part that has not so far been
more than briefly touched upon—the part played by the sailing barges.
It began in the middle of the Dunkirk evacuation, when the Admiralty
put out an urgent appeal for sailing barges to carry stores and
ammunition to the beleaguered troops. The Thames barge, with her
big hold and flat bottom, and made to take the ground, was ideal for
the purpose. Sixteen barges in all crossed the Channel, some being
towed over, and they brought back large numbers of troops. Keble
Chatterton in his "Epic of Dunkirk" calls attention to the fact that
this was the first time that spritsail-rigged craft had taken an active
part in hostilities since the Anglo-Dutch Wars, although there were

armed barges fitted as gunboats in the Napoleonic Wars, which did not actually take part in active operations.

The sixteen barges were *Pudge, Lady Rosebery, Doris, Duchess, Thyra, H.A.C., Glenway, Lark, Valonia, Ethel Everard, Royalty, Tollesbury, Beatrice Maud, Barbara Jean, Ena* and *Aidie.* Heavy losses were sustained, however, and many who failed to return ended their days on the beaches of that hellish Armageddon. Among those whose names should be inscribed upon the Roll of Honour were two of Everard's fleet, *Ethel Everard* and *Royalty. Ethel Everard*, one of their four big barges of 158 tons net, built at Yarmouth in 1926 and mulie-rigged, was towed across with food, drinking water and ammunition, and ordered to beach herself at La Panne, about four miles to the east of Dunkirk. Frank C. Bowen has told her story in "Sea Breezes" for June 1946, in the following words:

"The military working party which had been promised to get out this cargo did not appear, but the Germans were rapidly approaching. A naval officer borrowed her boat and two of her hands to row him to his ship for orders, but did not return, as it was immediately used for evacuating the troops. Captain Willis and six soldiers were therefore marooned on board, but early in the morning they were taken off by another vessel's boat. They were informed that all the beached ships would be destroyed, although captured German photographs showed the *Ethel* still ashore a considerable time afterwards, and claimed as a German victim."

As postscript to this, I well remember seeing published at the time of the "invasion fever" later in the year, in one of our leading and more respectable daily papers, a photograph of what purported to be the effects of our destructive bombing of the German barges assembled to transport Hitler's armies to England. Prominent among the craft "destroyed" by the R.A.F. was the *Ethel Everard*; and other English barges on the beach showed quite clearly, to all who knew what Thames barges and lighters looked like, that this picture of Dunkirk beaches was being issued for propaganda purposes, to show how well we had smashed the Führer's fleet! I had—and have— no doubt that the Führer's barges were even more roughly treated than ours ever were; but I was sorry to see the sacrifice of our gallant little ships used as a cheap propaganda trick.

*Royalty*, the other barge lost from Everard's fleet, was a smaller craft, of 85 tons net, and had been built at Rochester in 1898. Her story too has been told by Frank C. Bowen in the same number of "Sea Breezes". "She was loaded at Dover " he writes, "with some 50 tons of military stores, as well as drinking water in cans, and was towed across on 1st June. Captain Miller beached her to get his ammunition ashore as quickly as possible and to embark evacuating troops and float off with them on the rising tide. Unfortunately things happened too rapidly for that to be done, but her three men and half a dozen soldiers already on board got away in her boat; although repeatedly bombed and machine-gunned from the air, they reached a tug and were taken home." Captain H. Miller was later awarded the British Empire Medal for his services.

Messrs R. & W. Paul of Ipswich had five barges at Dunkirk, and lost three of them, including the two big iron barges *Aidie* and *Barbara Jean*, both built at Brightlingsea, and loading about 280 tons each. *Aidie* was beached, and set on fire, on 1st June; Captain Harry Potter, her master, was taken off with his crew. *Barbara Jean* had to be blown up and abandoned on the same day; but before that, her skipper had sailed up and down through Dunkirk Roads which as my friend "Chubb" Horlock to whom he had described his experiences said "must have been rather a strange sight, under those conditions!" The third barge lost by Paul's was the *Doris*, a spreety of 62 tons, built at Ipswich in 1904. The same owners' *Tollesbury*, 71 tons built at Sandwich in 1901, successfully evacuated 270 troops from Dunkirk to England. She is still trading. Their *Ena*, anchored and abandoned in Dunkirk Roads, took such a strong personal dislike to her position that she sailed herself home, alone and without a soul on board, and was later found empty and comparatively undamaged on Sandwich Flats!

Two barges from the London and Rochester Trading Company's fleet were there: *Pudge* and *Thyra*. Both brought back survivors. *Pudge*, of 80 tons net, launched at Rochester in 1922, was one of the few wooden barges built after the 1914–18 war. She had an auxiliary engine installed in 1933. She was towing out of Dunkirk, with two other barges, when the tug went up on a magnetic mine. The two other barges, Paul's *Doris* and the *Lady Rosebery*, were both lost; and *Pudge* picked up the survivors and brought them home. *Thyra* the other London and Rochester Trading Company's craft, a 70-ton spreety, built at Maidstone in 1913 and now an auxiliary, brought back 250 soldiers. *Lady Rosebery*, who was lost, was a fine Channel barge, not unlike the famous *Lady Daphne*.

Captain "Chubb" Horlock tells me that three barges returned from Dunkirk *under sail*, not under their own skippers, who had been taken off by the Navy, but sailed by fishermen and soldiers. One of the three was the *Beatrice Maud*, which afterwards went to the Bristol Channel, where she worked for the rest of the war, as recorded earlier in this chapter. Edgar J. March was mistaken in his "Spritsail Barges of Thames and Medway" in stating that she was among the barges lost at Dunkirk. She was certainly in need of repairs when she returned, but after her Bristol Channel service she is still trading to this day, back on the East Coast. Another was the *Glenway*; beached and also abandoned, she was refloated and sailed to safety by some 200 soldiers. Two more barges that were lost, however, were the *Duchess*, a 55-ton spreety built at East Greenwich in 1904, and once flying the well-known blue "bob" with the red heart on the white hand of Clement W. Parker's fleet, owned at Bradwell Quay, on the Blackwater; and the *Lark*, 54 tons, built at Greenhithe in 1900, and owned by T. Scholey of Greenwich.

*Valonia* was also a casualty at Dunkirk, though not by enemy action. She was a big 90-ton spreety, built at East Greenwich in 1911 and owned by Horace Shrubsall. Captain Battershall had had her since before the war, and she was the last barge to trade to Portland in pre-war days. The usual work was with cement to Penzance outwards and stone from Portland to London home. *Valonia* was already in Dunkirk about her lawful business when the evacuation began, for she had arrived there with a cargo of pitch from Aylesford and had completed discharging by noon on the Saturday. She was due to load wheat on the Monday, but, as her master told me, "Jerry got there first". She was held in the port, to bring back survivors; but when she was waiting to leave the dock on the Sunday, an oil tanker in a hurry, in charge of an impatient Belgian pilot, came ahead too soon, without waiting to straighten up, and struck her on the starboard lee-board. A hole six feet long was knocked in her side, and she had to be abandoned. Her skipper, Captain Battershall, was saved, and looks back with pride on the fact that *Valonia* was the last sailing barge ever to trade to Dunkirk. On his return, he went as captain of the *Veravia*, and in 1948, after nearly twenty years in Shrubsall's barges, he took over the little 100-ton *Henry*, owned by Cole and Lecquire, who ran her principally in their own trade to and from Gray's just after the war, and thereafter in the East Anglian work. At the age of seventy he was finding the bigger *Veravia*'s gear a bit heavy. After the *Henry* was sold to Arthur Bennett for conversion to a yacht, he became for a short time Captain and Instructor to the Thames Barge Sailing Club, as Master of the *Arrow*, thus following in the footsteps of "Schoolmaster West".

I do not think I could conclude this chapter better than by quoting from an eye-witness account of the barges going to Dunkirk, from one who had just been rescued. Mr F. S. Fullar, who had served in the barges until he was called up for military service in September 1939, described in "Sea Breezes" for July 1947 the heartening and inspiring scene which he saw when he was returning from Dunkirk in June 1940 as an evacuee.

"I was profoundly impressed," he writes, "to see a string of sailing barges go past in tow, bound for the hot spot which I had just left. Realising the courage needed to man such a craft on such an errand, they made, to me, an unforgettable picture. At the wheel of each barge stood the skipper, as imperturbable and as solid as those I had served under, apparently unmoved by the somewhat fearsome danger awaiting in and above those troubled waters."

# CHAPTER XVII

## *Barges as Yachts*

IN the preceding pages I have endeavoured to show that the modern sailing barge has many virtues. She has elegance, seaworthiness and speed; she can float in the shallowest water; and she can be handled with an absurdly small crew. But her good qualities do not end here, for she has in her an enormous hold, of which the bottom is flat, the sides almost straight and the hatches large and roomy. The impression gained by any lady to whom I have ever shown the open hold of a tolerably large barge has made her exclaim, "Why—you could build a house down there!" Then why not?

This idea of turning a barge into a house has, indeed, appealed to many, and numbers of old barges have been bought, converted into comfortable houseboats and now provide houses for happy owners who pay no rates and fear no doctor's bills. Among the old barges which were treated in this way is the *Garson*, for many years between the wars the home of the Erith Yacht Club. She was originally a fairly big boomsail barge, with deep hold and high and massive bulwarks. She was said to be the fastest barge ever built at Yarmouth. When Captain Harry Stone of Mistley had her as a "boomy" she was really dandy-rigged, with a little mizzen stepped on the rudder. She lost the mizzen overboard once on a voyage to Caen. During the First World War she was trading regularly to the other side, and when peace was declared she was sold and converted into a houseboat. For a time she was in the hands of a doctor who was a keen vivisectionist, and was filled with rabbit hutches, cages, kennels and so on, for the accommodation of the livestock. Some time later she was bought by the Erith Yacht Club and towed down from Chiswick Dock, where she was then lying, to her present berth in Anchor Bay. There, with a causeway over the marshes, telephone laid on from the shore, and other amenities, she provided in her two-storied house ample accommodation for the Club, for which no rates were payable. Near her was the old swim-headed barge *Orient*, turned into locker stores where members could keep their gear.

Barges make admirable houseboats, and barge-houseboats may be found in considerable numbers in many places where the barges themselves are wont to trade. But if a barge makes a roomy house-boat, why not make her a *movable* houseboat? That is to say, retain the barge's gear and let her be ship as well as house, yacht as well as home. When this is done, the result is a barge-yacht. Of recent years, and particularly since the Second World War, the number of yachts-men fired with this idea has increased enormously and is still increasing.

Perhaps the most famous of all barge-yachts is that described in Mr Cyril B. Ionides' delightful book, "A Floating Home". The real name of this vessel is disguised throughout the book, where she is called the *Will Arding* before conversion and the *Ark Royal* after-wards. She was still in existence between the wars as a houseboat up some obscure Essex creek. But the tale of her coming into being and the causes thereof points a useful solution to many problems of post-war existence, with its high taxes and small incomes, and a relentless Chancellor of the Exchequer squeezing the last penny out of the unfortunate taxpayer.

Briefly, Mr Ionides' problem was to give a growing family a public-school education on a small and inadequate income, without giving up his sport of yachting. He solved it by selling both his house and yacht, buying a barge and converting her. In this way he was able to obtain within quite a small vessel more room and greater comfort than could be found in a small London flat. Here he was able to live rent-free and rate-free, while mooring her within easy daily access by train to town. When holiday time arrived, he had only to cast-off his moorings and sail wheresoever he listed, taking home and family with him. All travelling and hotel expenses were saved. There were no large tips to be provided. While as for general upkeep, barges' hulls are tarred, and tar is cheap. The amount spent on paint and varnish is very small. And whereas one cannot scrub one's own doorstep or paint one's front door without exciting unpleasant comment, one may scrub down one's decks or varnish one's rail in front of the Squadron Castle itself. When the children came home for their holidays, they had a delightful vessel where they could invite and entertain their friends. Finally, as Mr Ionides points out, no one was to know whether they were eccentric millionaires or paupers only just keeping to wind'ard of the workhouse.

Many keen sailing folk in the early 1930's followed Mr Ionides' example. Small barges were absurdly cheap to buy in those days. The smaller barge, because her hatches could not readily accommodate modern cargo machinery, and because, with less carrying capacity, she still needed the same crew as a larger vessel, found it increasingly difficult to pay her way. By a little careful looking around, a sound barge could then be obtained for between £100 and £200. Sometimes they could be picked up for even less. I remember, some twenty years ago, two perfectly sound barges, with anchors, cables and all their gear, which could be bought for £15 apiece. The 120-ton barge *Mary Edwards*, with all her gear, was sold in Plymouth for £5 at about that time; I doubt whether she could have been sound, but her ground tackle alone was worth more. When Mr Arthur Bennett bought *June* of Rochester, in 1933, a perfectly sound barge, with all her gear, and the advantage, for conversion purposes, of having a steel keelson, she cost him only £50. Her story he has told in his enchanting book "*June* of Rochester—Topsail Barge", which is referred to later. I am delighted to learn that a second edition has recently been published.

Running expenses were very small; barge owners were not expected to pay so highly for their requirements as were yachtsmen. The domestic staff required to run the barge-yacht might consist of a barge skipper as master and his wife as mate-stewardess. It need cost little more than what was required for a small house, and would be more than paid for by the saving of rent and rates. The principal cost, in fact, in making one's home in a barge, was the actual cost of the conversion. This, however, would entirely depend on where the work was done. By placing it in the hands of a small yard, where overhead expenses were light, the work would be done for a very reasonable sum, especially if the owner were an amateur enthusiast able to do a good part of it himself.

Mr Ionides did this. Having bought his barge and loaded her in London with the wood and other materials required, he sailed her round to a quiet Essex port to convert her; and there, employing two working carpenters to assist him, did the greater part of the conversion. The result was that, having paid originally £140 for the barge, the cost of conversion amounted to £235 19s., inclusive of petty cash expenditure, making the total cost of the floating home £375 19s., which, it will be agreed at once, is very little for a vessel having the accommodation provided by the *Ark Royal*. This accommodation was arranged in the following way, which may be better understood by referring to the plan (Fig. 32).

Right forward was a storeroom for lamps, lamp oil, paint, etc. On the starboard side of the old fo'c'sle was a maid's cabin; on the port, the larder and scullery, with the kitchen just abaft it on the same side. Abaft the maid's cabin was the owner's cabin, 12 feet by 6 feet 10 inches, and the bathroom was on the opposite side of the passage. Large water-tanks were arranged next, on either side of the ship, and a boiler for providing hot sea-water baths, or fresh-water baths when plenty of water was available. The dining cabin was next, aft on the port side; and on the starboard side another cabin opening out of the saloon. This saloon was a fine large cabin, extending the full internal width of the ship (14 feet 10 inches) and 16 feet in length. There was another small cabin opening out of it on the after side to starboard, and to port the entrance lobby or hall, with the companion ladder leading up to the deck. Right in the stern was a two-berth cabin, which was the original crew's quarters in the barge's trading days.

The ship throughout had over 7 feet full head-room under the hatches. The hatch-covers were raised to form a deck or roof, supported on stout pillars rising from the coamings, and the intervening space was filled with opening glass windows, making everywhere very light and airy below. As a barge under way lists, or heels over, very little, ordinary house furniture can be used aboard; and barge-yacht

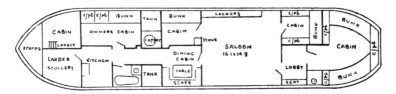

FIG. 32 Cabin Plan of the *Ark Royal*

owners have told me that, unless in expectation of bad weather, it is not even necessary to stow china and glass ornaments when going to sea.

The *Ark Royal* was a small barge, and although this made her easy to handle, it entailed several disadvantages. Her total length was only 74 feet, and she was 17 feet beam at the level of the deck and 15 feet on the bottom. She had carried no more than about 90 tons of cargo, and in so small a barge the head-room under the decks (as apart from under the hatches) was naturally very little, varying from 4 feet 3 inches to 5 feet 8 inches. A further disadvantage—and perhaps the most serious objection—in the small barge conversion was that the keelson appeared everywhere above the floor. In a sailing barge, this great baulk of timber, measuring about 12 to 14 inches square, runs down the middle of the ship, giving her longitudinal strength, but dividing the floor space into two equal compartments. If the cabin floors are raised high enough to cover this, the head-room is insufficient; and if it is merely cased in, it is in the way. The only remedies are either to have a barge large enough and deep-sided enough to enable the cabin floors to be laid over the keelson (as in the *Cawana*, described later), or to make use of the keelson by arranging the accommodation in such a way that it will serve as a seat, a step, a support for a table, the bottom shelf of a book-case and so on. In some places it will, however, be a nuisance. A few barges, like Arthur Bennett's *June*, have keelsons of T-angle iron or steel, and in these, as the keelson is not raised so high above the floor timbers, the cabin floors can be laid above it and an unbroken surface obtained. In the *Ark Royal* this could not be done, and the slight disadvantage of this projecting timber had to be put up with. Nevertheless, when one compares the total cost of considerably less than £400, with the ample and comfortable accommodation it provided, one cannot help being impressed with the economical aspect of such a delightful home afloat. Unfortunately, the figures given by Mr Ionides represent the cost of a conversion made a few years before the First World War and bear no relation to the astronomical figures which must be expected in 1951. Even as late as 1933, *June* of Rochester was converted by W. D. Inglis, of the Canal Basin, Gravesend, for a contract price of £150 (it actually cost £300), which included the cost of shifting the barge from Northfleet, where she was lying when purchased, with all charges incurred lying at Gravesend, and shifting in and out of the Basin. Add to this the £50 price of the barge, and it will be seen that sixteen years ago such a floating home, fully rigged and equipped and fit to go anywhere that a barge might sail, could be obtained for no more than £200. Although prices have fallen in the last few months, I would hardly dare to guess at the cost to-day; but £2,000 to £3,000 would be nearer the figure.

The *Ark Royal*, as far as I am aware, never had an engine installed, even after Mr Ionides sold her. But other barges, converted on somewhat similar lines, have generally had auxiliary engines put into them. The convenience of having power for manoeuvring easily in docks and narrow waters enables the amateur to handle his own vessel without an expert bargeman as crew, so long as he has some reasonable experience in the management of craft.

Cyril B. Ionides was not the first to convert a barge into a yacht, however; and a much earlier example was the *Four Brothers*, owned by the late W. L. Wyllie, the marine artist, and H. O. Arnold Foster, M.P. She was built as the *New Zealand* by A. Keep at Greenhithe in 1879, and her dimensions were: length, 81·9 feet; beam 18·5 feet; and depth 6·6 feet. It was in her, during the nineties and at the turn of the century, that Wyllie was painting his incomparable pictures on the Thames and Medway, and an account of some of her adventures

PLATE 61 *Veronica* with staysail set outside crosstrees as spinnaker

[*Photograph by courtesy of Eng.-Cdr H. Oliver Hill, R.N.*]

is contained in Mr and Mrs Wyllie's book "London to the Nore". She worked out at 115 tons Thames measurement, and disappears from the Yacht Registers after 1904. Commander Harry Vandervell knew her well and once spent a couple of weeks' holiday aboard her in about 1900 with Mr Harry Keep, the son of her builder, who had chartered her from the Wyllies.

A barge somewhat similar to the *Ark Royal*, which was converted into a yacht, was the old *Volunteer*, 57 tons, originally built by Cann of Harwich in 1879 for Richard Horlock of Mistley. She loaded about 120 tons, and is said to have gone from the Nore to Harwich in 3¾ hours, as a trading barge. She was very comfortably arranged and fitted, and was rather larger than *Ark Royal*. She was converted by Mr C. A. Badcock in 1914. The *Volunteer* was an auxiliary barge and she was driven by twin screws, with a pair of engines in a commodious and well-appointed engine-room aft. These were not fitted until after the 1914–18 war, however. One engine was a 35 h.p. Thornycroft, the other a 30 h.p. Atlantic. She had a Gardner electric lighting plant, which gave much satisfaction. Hot and cold fresh- or sea-water baths could be obtained in the well-equipped bathroom. Her saloon was large and comfortable. When I visited her, lying in the Thames off the Cadogan Pier in about 1930, I learnt from the owner of the long and regular cruises she had made. During the summer she was cruising constantly, rarely stopping in one port for any length of time, and ranging the European coast from Ushant to the Elbe. She carried an efficient crew of three or four uniformed hands, and although a capable ship, was economical in upkeep in those days.

The arrangement of twin screws in the *Volunteer* is worthy of comment. It might well be considered the most suitable arrangement for auxiliary power in a barge, whether for trading or pleasure purposes. The central installation of a single large propeller, with a slow-speed engine, which is found most satisfactory in the majority of heavy craft, is quite unsuitable in a barge that is often—and a barge-yacht invariably—sailing light, and drawing very little water. A large propeller therefore is not practicable, and a small one on a shaft piercing the stern-post works in dead water and can only churn, with great slip and loss of power. Two small propellers driving under the quarters, however, are always submerged and working in an unobstructed stream of water. Very little power is lost.

*Volunteer*'s owner very sensibly kept her general external appearance in accordance with standard practice in smart working barges. In this he was, in my opinion, much to be commended. It is a mistake to try to make a converted barge resplendent with enamel, bright

18

varnished deck-houses and shining brass. Kept as a barge, she can be a smart, clean and able vessel and a pleasure to the eye of the sailor, for she does not lose her character.

Arthur Bennett in converting *June* also very wisely kept her character as a barge. Externally, she was a clean, smart, efficient ship, easy to run and economical to maintain; a thing of beauty, and a joy to the eye of the sailorman, for she remained perfectly fitted for her work. Her owner became a thoroughly competent amateur barge skipper, able to take her anywhere without professional help, and often with his charming wife as his only crew. Below decks they had a comfortable, roomy and certainly delightful home. I will not write more of *June* of Rochester, for those who have read Mr Bennett's

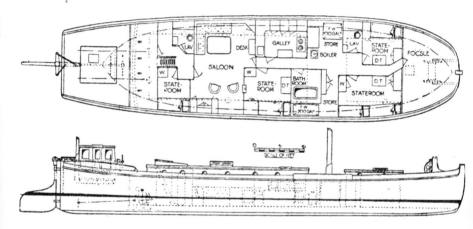

FIG. 33  Cabin Plans of the *Haughty Belle*
[*By courtesy of the Editor of the "Yachting World"*

book will know her already; and those who do not will find her story in the new edition. There must be many who have envied him his carefree life afloat during the years that she was his home; and even the city train must have been less repulsive when one could leave for one's office from a different port each week, and return each evening to one's own fireside in a mobile floating home.

The ever-increasing number of barges converted between the wars included the lovely *Haughty Belle* (Fig. 33 and Plates 62 and 63), converted by Cooper's of Conyer for Captain A. C. Radford in 1934, as described in the "Yachting World" for 25th May of that year. Having an iron keelson, her cabin floors could be kept low, allowing 7 feet of head-room under the hatches. Her full sailing gear as a spreety was retained, but she was fitted with two Kelvin Ricardo F2 15 h.p. paraffin engines, driving twin screws. On deck, a small sunk wheelhouse was built aft, but it was very unobtrusive in appearance and did not interfere with the mizzen. The plans reproduced herewith (Fig. 33), by kind permission of the Editor of the "Yachting World", give an excellent idea of her accommodation.

Later she was owned by Mr Pemberton Billing, M.P. Unhappily, she became a war casualty, and is now lying awash in Chiswick Dock, where she has been ever since her stern was blown off by a V.1 which exploded near her at four o'clock one morning. Two ladies living aboard her at the time fortunately escaped uninjured.

Another conversion was *Plinlimmon*, which dead-heated with *Harold Margetts* in the Medway Barge Race in 1927. Her owner arranged to have a "garage" in part of the hold, so that he could carry an Austin "Seven", of the early miniature type, which he could sling ashore with his sprit; thus adding the pleasures of Continental motoring to the joys of cruising in European waters. In September 1935, when bound from Newhaven to Dover, she carried away her steering gear when off the Cuckmere Valley. The anchor started to drag and she was driving ashore, when she was picked up by the steamer *Pulborough* and towed into Newhaven. Sir Alan Herbert, a keen amateur "sailorman", and his two daughters were aboard at the time.

Other pre-1939 conversions were the *George*, for Lieut.-Colonel R. C. Bingham, D.S.O.; the *Herbert Gordon*, for the Hon. Jestyn Phillipps, now Viscount St Davids; and the *Silver Wedding* for Mr Antony Hippisley Cox, who with his sister Tacina, wrote "Galley Wise", a guide to "Boat Cooking", with a rich assortment of dishes prepared and tested in *Silver Wedding's* galley.

*Silver Wedding* unhappily came to grief when she was tacking up the London River on a flood tide on Sunday, 10th May 1936. At 0.55 a.m., while on the starboard tack, they sighted the starboard light of a steam-vessel rounding Jenningtree Point. As, or soon after, her port light came into view, they thought she blew three blasts. There were two other vessels coming up astern of the *Silver Wedding*, so she stood on. The steam-vessel then blew two short blasts; and *Silver Wedding* still stood on. When she was about a barge's length away, the steamship let go her anchor, but her bows crashed into the barge just forward of the main horse. As she was on the starboard tack, the chine took the first impact, and was broken. The thrust of water on the rudder made the wheel whirl round—the barge having chain steering gear—and the professional skipper was hurled overboard and picked up some distance upstream by the tug *Vincia*. They managed to get the barge beached alongside the South Metropolitan Gas Works Wharf, with the water an inch or so above her keelson.

Poor *Silver Wedding* was so badly damaged that her sailing days were over; but her owner, Mr Antony Hippisley Cox, to whom I am indebted for the foregoing account, next bought *Dipper*, which he sold soon after the beginning of the war.

The number of barge conversions since the Second World War has exceeded all previous figures. One yard alone, the Whitewall Boat, Barge and Yacht Co., Ltd., of Hoo, on the Medway, which has made a speciality of this work, has converted no less than twenty-three barges between the end of the war and the time of writing. These were *Good Templar, Tricolor, New Acorn, Louise, Sidwell, Leslie, British Lion, Magnet, Primrose, Harold Margetts, Shield, Winifred, Cereal* (re-named *Lyford Anna*), *Beryl, Swift, Gonda, Iota, Gladys, Venta, Henry, Alice May* and *Wolsey*. Costs, however, have naturally been much in excess of pre-war figures, starting with the price of the barge. Owing to the big demand, prices are high for a sound barge suitable for conversion, such as the *Cereal*, for which I am informed the sum of £1,000 was paid.

Barges converted to yachts in these post-war days have certainly not been content to lie idly at anchor and many of them have made extended cruises. *Gladys*, for example, has been twice to the Clyde. In August of 1947 she was in trouble off the Pembroke coast, when bound home for Chatham; having sails blown away and a spar broken. This did not prevent her repeating her cruise in the following year, and on her return voyage to the Medway she called at Boulogne on her way. *Good Templar*'s cruise in 1948 was to the Channel Islands, and she made a very good passage to Guernsey, in spite of bad weather. *Iota* was at Burnham Week in 1948 and later made a trip up the Thames as far as Sunbury—a very creditable performance, with no professional assistance for taking her through bridges.

One of the most active post-war converted barges has been the *Black Swan*, belonging to Mr A. H. Hoare, and, as a member of the Royal Yacht Squadron, sailing under the White Ensign. She was originally the *Shamrock*, of Rochester, of 45 tons, built at Sitting-bourne in 1893, and was in the Thames Estuary ballast trade before the war. *Black Swan* is a fully powered auxiliary, with twin screws. Her mizzen has been removed and she has no bowsprit. She is always kept in fine condition, and her passage making is not limited to the summer months. In November 1947 she dragged her anchors lying in Bridlington Bay and drove ashore a little north of the town; but, grounding on a sandy beach, was in no danger, and refloated easily

PLATE 62 *Haughty Belle* as a Barge Yacht
[*By courtesy of the Editor of the "Yachting World"*

PLATE 63 The Saloon of the *Haughty Belle*
[*By courtesy of the Editor of the "Yachting World"*

PLATE 64 *Sarà* in the Thames Race of 1935

when the weather had moderated. Early in March 1948 she was reported in Great Yarmouth; and in February 1949 was lying alongside H.M.S. *President* by the Embankment—a privilege accorded to her because she was flying the White Ensign.

Other barges which have been converted to yachts include *Challenger, Pride of Ipswich, Mermaid, Swale* and *Dipper* (converted before the war); with *Five Sisters* converted since. *Beryl*, a big barge, loading 180 tons, was having her gear taken out and a motor installed at the time that she was bought for conversion; and it is pleasant to report that this process was then reversed, and that, on being turned into a yacht, she became once again a fully rigged sailing barge. Some barges have been converted into mere houseboats, and these include *Hibernia, Northumberland, Berwick, Frederick William* and *V.C. Spurgeon* is awaiting conversion.

A number of converted barges have permanent winter quarters, to which they return when their summer cruise is over. *Waveney* and *Mermaid*, for example, have berths at the head of the dock at Conyer Creek, with their own private gardens on the shore alongside. In summer they have berths outside, and lie afloat in the Swale. *Henry and Jabez* is another "regular inhabitant" of Conyer. *John and Mary* and *Harold* winter at the Marina Club at Hoo. *Harold Margetts* favours Beccles, by the Broads; and *British Lion* spent the winter of 1949 at Chichester. The converted barges have certainly increased and multiplied since the pioneer days of W. L. Wyllie and Cyril B. Ionides.

A curious reversal of the usual process of conversion occurred with the *Vigilant*, the barge made famous in E. G. Martin's book "Sailorman", who served in her as mate under "Chubb" Horlock. In 1932 she was sold by R. R. Horlock to Mr Clifford for conversion to a yacht, and a remarkably fine barge-yacht she made. Now, the process has been reversed, and she is trading again, as a fully powered motor barge, under Captain Norton.

Thus far I have been considering only vessels which have begun as trading barges and have afterwards been converted into yachts. But there have also been a number of yachts built on barge lines, and in these, of course, more sumptuous cabin accommodation is generally possible; for it is not necessary to make the best use of an existing cargo hold, into which cabins have to be fitted by dint of much careful thinking out and contriving.

Of barges originally built as yachts, one of the best known is undoubtedly the *Cawana*. She was the barge-yacht built by Gill of Rochester in 1904 for Mr R. Hill Dawe, who sold her after the First

World War to Major Younger, by whom she was presented to the Portsmouth Sea Scouts, and run by W. L. Wyllie and his son Harold Wyllie, as a sea-going training ship for two years. The model from which she was built is now in the Science Museum at South Kensington. As far as the shape and build of her hull are concerned, *Cawana* was a typical trading barge, except that, as in the *Haughty Belle* when first launched, she had a short elliptical counter-stern, since removed. She is built of oak, with Kauri pine decks, and is 96 feet in overall length, 85 feet between perpendiculars, 22·6 feet in beam and 6·4 feet deep. Aft she draws about 4 feet of water. She is 162 tons, Thames measurement. Under the cabin floors, which are laid across the keelson so that a level deck is obtained, she carries 47 tons of iron ballast. A full 7 feet of head-room is obtained under a large, wide, raised cabin-top occupying the greater part of the upper deck, and opening portlights in the sides of this make the ship both light and airy below.

The *Cawana* is, of course, a much larger vessel than Mr Ionides' *Ark Royal*, and much more accommodation is possible. From aft are steps down from a comfortable companion-deckhouse into a lobby, which is part of a very commodious engine-room, and from this one enters a passage with two large double cabins on the starboard side, one of them with tapestry panelled walls, and a single cabin, w.c., and bathroom with w.c., opposite to port. The forward end of the passage opens into the saloon, which is a most spacious and beautifully fitted cabin. It extends to the full width of the ship, and is panelled throughout in oak. The fireplace, on the starboard side, is like that of a country house on a small scale, and has a glowing slow-combustion stove which is equipped with a boiler supplying the central heating installation which warms the whole ship. This is a great comfort in cold weather, and enables all the principal cabins to have airing cupboards. Forward of the saloon, on the port side, is a marble-floored pantry, the galley or kitchen and the steward's cabin. To starboard is a small cabin, and beyond it a larger one, sacred as the owner's "den". Forward is the fo'c'sle with quarters for a crew of four if needed. Hot or cold fresh- or sea-water baths are easily obtained, and hot and cold water is laid on to lavatory basins fitted in every sleeping cabin.

It will naturally be imagined that such a large and luxuriously appointed ship needs a large and expensive crew to run her. Nothing could be further from the truth. Actually, *Cawana* (or *Mamgu*, as she is now called) is regularly handled by her present owner and his wife, with or without any friends who may happen to be aboard. She is well kept below, and makes a fine and roomy floating home.

The ease with which she is handled, however, is largely due to the fact that in her engine-room aft a powerful and efficient motor is installed, and her working sails were cut down to foresail, main try-sail and mizzen. She no longer carries topmast, bowsprit, spreet or gaff. In fact, for some years now she has carried no sails, and I con-fess I am sorry to see the change. Her first engine was installed after the 1914–18 war, and was a 26–30 h.p. twin-cylinder Kelvin paraffin engine; but this was later replaced by a 50 h.p. Thornycroft four-cylinder petrol motor, running at 1,500 rev. and geared down. Driving a single propeller through the quarter, it gives a speed under power of 6 knots. An auxiliary "Delco" 32-volt lighting plant is fitted in the engine-room.

Among other barges specially built as yachts, perhaps the most palatial is *Thoma II*, built by Howard at Maldon in 1909. In shape of hull she is not unlike the *Record Reign*, with clipper bow and counter-stern, and being 100 feet in overall length with a depth of 7·9 feet, she has a clear 7 feet of head-room under a flush deck. Of 91 tons gross and 67 net, she draws 4·8 feet on a waterline length of 80·1 feet; and her Thames tonnage works out at 134 tons. Before the Second World War she was fully spreety-rigged, setting some 4,500 square feet of canvas. At the time of writing she is lying at the Marina Club at Hoo, on the Medway, where she arrived late in 1948. Much of her gear was lost during the last war, but her present owner, Mr Geoffrey Burge, has re-fitted and re-rigged her completely.

She is certainly a very lovely vessel, built to the order of Mr R. Callingham, under whose ownership from 1909 to 1914 Captain J. Stone, of Mistley, was her skipper; and during the time he had her she made voyages down-Channel, across to the Continent, over to Ireland and to the West Coast of Scotland. Once on a passage from Maldon to Guernsey in 1912, with the wind nor'easterly off Portland Bill, the barge suddenly flew up into the wind, her rudder-post broken. There were still about 2½ hours of east-going tide to run; so Captain Stone stood off until high water, and then jogged into the land, and took her into Weymouth, not using the rudder but by skilful use of the main brails, jib and mizzen sheets.

After the 1914–18 war she was owned by Mr Christopher Turnor, and in his time she crossed the Bay of Biscay four times; on the first occasion, to and from the French and Spanish coasts, and the second time, in 1926, for a six months' cruise in the Mediterranean. While there, she was surveyed at Leghorn, and so appears in the Merchant Navy List for some years after. Her sail out from Cowes to Gibraltar, where she arrived on the morning of the eighth day out, must surely be an all-time record for a barge; and I do not know of any barge that has been further afield, excepting only the *Goldfinch* and her contemporaries, which were sailed out to South America. Theirs, however, were one-way passages. *Thoma II* was just cruising!

In 1928, when she was owned by Sir Matthew W. Thompson, Bart., she had two Kelvin petrol-paraffin engines installed, of 30 h.p. each, with twin screws driving through the quarters; but she remained fully rigged. She used to be a fine sight in summer, lying in her usual berth off Brightlingsea Creek. Under her new owner, she is now sailing again, and she took part in the 1950 Medway Barge Match.

Another very beautiful barge-yacht is the *Daisy*, built by Gill at Rochester in 1907 and often to be seen during the yachting season lying at Burnham-on-Crouch in Essex, and afterwards at Poole in Dorset, during the early 1930's. She had originally been built to go through the French canals to the Mediterranean, and her beam was therefore about 2 feet less than normal, enabling her to pass through the locks, but reducing her stiffness and rather spoiling her for sailing. The voyage through France never took place, so that she might have been built on normal lines. Commander Harry Vandervell, who bought her later, found that she was a little tender at times.

The foregoing ships have all been comparatively large vessels, and I have considered the converted barge rather more from the "floating home" than from the "yacht" standpoint; but a number of the smallest sailing barges have also been converted for use as ordinary cruising yachts for week-end and summer holiday sailing. Such craft, however, are very limited in their possible cruising range. The very small barge is intended only for river work, and is not suitable for sea-going purposes. There are perhaps exceptions to this; one is the little *Sea Gull II*, built by Gill for the War Department in 1901, to load 40 to 50 tons of cargo, and later converted into a yacht. She was lying off Harty Ferry in the East Swale in 1948, looking very smart. Another very pretty little barge-yacht is the *Dinah*, built as a yacht by Gill at Rochester in 1890; still going strong, she was completing her refit at the Whitewall Yard in 1948. Her lines have been taken off, and a new yacht-barge of very similar type, which is probably a prototype for a new series, was being laid down in November 1948.

In a different category are the small barge-yachts, built originally as yachts, whose only link with the barge type, properly speaking, lies in their flat-bottomed and chine-built hulls, with lee-boards. Of these there have been quite a number built, and they are the English equivalent of the small Dutch yachts of the *boeier*, *botter* and *hoogarts* types.

The pioneer of the small English barge-yacht was the late Mr E. B. Tredwen, and one of the first yachts of this type was the *Susti*, built by J. W. Shuttlewood, a barge builder, at Paglesham, to the design of Messrs Tredwen and J. E. W. Robinson. She later had her name changed to *Doreen*, and a model of her, made by Mr R. H. Draper, who owned her for a time, is now in the Science Museum. She was built with a perfectly flat bottom, and was 25·3 feet between perpendiculars, 8·3 feet beam and 3·8 feet deep. She was designed to obtain a maximum of cruising accommodation for her size, with shoal draught for "ditch-crawling" among the estuaries, and reasonable speed and seaworthiness when a longer passage had to be made. Her flat bottom enabled her to sit upright on the mud flats when lying in a place where she had to dry out at low water. To prevent her making leeway she had a pair of iron lee-boards, each weighing 2 cwt.; they were raised and lowered with small tackles, and a narrow iron bar passing outside them at the level of the yacht's chine prevented the weather lee-board trailing out from the side of the ship like a broken wing and throwing strain on the fastenings. In some barge-yachts this difficulty has been met by fitting the lee-boards working inside the ship in cases like centre-board cases, and dropping down through the bottom at the sides. Of this type was the barge-yacht *Swan* owned by Mr Maurice Griffiths at one time. It not only has the disadvantage of much reducing the width of the internal accommodation, but it has the effect of duplicating all the disadvantages of the ordinary centre-board. Head-room in the *Susti* was reasonably good thanks to a raised cabin-top, and a self-draining cockpit for steering from was intended to make her tolerably safe at sea. Her yacht measurement tonnage was about 6 tons. Sloop-rigged, she had a gaff mainsail, roller foresail and jackyard tops'l.

Mr Tredwen subsequently built many more barge-yachts, of which his last was the *Pearl*. In her he voyaged right down the Channel to Cornish waters. She was a larger ship, of about 13 tons, and well known in yachting circles. Mr Tredwen was a wonderful old yachts-man, and sailed winter and summer alike. At the age of seventy-one he sailed from Burnham-on-Crouch to Heybridge Basin entirely single-handed in the depths of winter. Leaving Burnham at 10.15 a.m. on Saturday, 29th December 1923, with frost-covered decks and frozen rigging, he arrived at Heybridge Basin at 2.30 p.m. on the following day. Writing to the "Yachting Monthly" at the time, he concluded: "So ends 1923 season. The 1924 season commences on Friday, 4th January, when I rejoin the ship at Heybridge, and I'm seventy-two in April, but it is yachting keeps me young."

One of the best of small modern barge-yachts is the *Growler*, a Bermudian yawl belonging to Sir Alker Tripp, who, writing as "Leigh Hoe", describes her in his fascinating and popular book "The Solent and the Southern Waters". I saw her some twenty years ago turning into Queenborough, and she is certainly a handy and workmanlike little ship; she has, moreover, proved herself in quite long cruises.

But in spite of the advantages of shallow draught, flat bottom, big accommodation, cheapness of construction and ease of handling, I am convinced that the small barge-yacht is not a good proposition for anything but the most restricted ditch-crawling. Although I am a great admirer of the ordinary full-size sailing barge, when a very small craft of the same type of construction is built she is too shallow and too much of a box to be safe at sea. The big barge is heavy enough to stand up to a press of sail and to carry enough way to smash her bluff bows through the short Channel and estuary seas in which she works. The small barge is too light to carry sail and she will not go to wind'ard in a breeze, as any sea knocks all the way off her immediately. Although initially stiff, she will capsize very easily when once the danger-point is reached, and this is reached far sooner than in a big and heavy working barge. To get comfortable head-room, since draught is limited, she has to be built high-sided and with a high and heavy cabin-top. All this increases windage, and makes her sluggish and unhandy. In fact, the small barge-yacht is generally a straight, ugly, crank and slow vessel.

Trouble always arises when it is attempted to adapt a type of craft that has been evolved for a certain purpose to other uses. The large yacht-barge is a fine, seaworthy and comfortable ship. The small barge-yacht is a mistake for anything but estuary sailing.

Arthur Bennett asks me how *Nancy Grey*, who beat all the barges in the 1950 Medway Match, fits in with my views?

I'm afraid she doesn't!

# CHAPTER XVIII

## Recent Years

GREAT changes have taken place in the Thames Sailing Barge fleets since the first edition of this book appeared in 1931. Changes were already taking place when, in 1939, the storm of war burst upon us and swept so much away. The competition of modern shoal-draught motor coasters was already having its effect on the sailing craft; and bargemen remember well the lean years of the nineteen-thirties, when a barge might be for weeks at Woolwich buoys—"starvation buoys" as they were called—hoping against hope for a freight to offer. Since barge crews were paid by the share, it would sometimes happen that, even when a freight had been obtained, skipper and mate would still be in debt to their owners after the cargo had been carried, delivered and discharged, owing to the long time they had been living on "subs", advanced to keep them going while waiting for work.

In those hard times many bargemen were forced to give up the sea and take whatever other employment they could get ashore. Not only had bargemen to take up other work, but many of the smaller barges, which would no longer pay, were laid up or sold for very small sums for conversion to yachts, as already recorded. A few of the larger barges were converted to auxiliary power, though this movement did not gain impetus until after the war. In spite of all difficulties, however, the more enterprising barge owners and bargemen were able to get a living, even in the worst times; and the money spent by small men as well as big, in fitting out the barges for the annual barge sailing matches, was evidence enough of this. Some restrictions on the freedom of foreigners to exploit our own coastwise trade with modern motor vessels might have helped to keep all our barge fleet busy; but there were reasons of high international policy which prevented this apparently simple remedy from being adopted at that time.

Since the war, until recently, there has been no lack of work for the barges which are left; it is the bargemen themselves who are lacking. The life is too hard, the hours of work, governed by wind and tide, too unattractive for the young men of the weary post-war world. A comfortable, safe job ashore, with a lot of money, short hours, little work and no risk is too often the ideal. In the new welfare state, where the free will of the individual counts for less and less, there is no longer the same encouragement for the rugged individual endeavour which we inherited from our Elizabethan ancestors. The sailing bargeman, believing in the unfashionable traditions of co-partnership in private enterprise and in the spirit of the gentlemen adventurers, on which his sturdy independence has been founded, is inevitably in danger of extinction. We may regret it or not; we may think something better has taken its place—that is a matter on which politicians may argue, but with which this book is not concerned. The simple fact must, however, be recorded, and every bargeman knows it: the young men of to-day will not go bargeing. The skippers are mostly older men, and the young, keen, enterprising mates who should follow on in time to take their places simply do not exist.

The barge fleet of to-day is but a small fraction of its pre-war strength; and the reasons for this are various. In the first place, of course, there is the inevitable wastage of age and decay, which would have continued in any event, war or no war, but which was greatly accelerated by six years of comparative neglect. It is now some eighteen years since the last sailing barge was built (with one small exception, for a special purpose); and barges, like everything else, wear out or decay in the end. Pathetic examples of barges which have reached their last berth may be seen at West Hoo Creek, on the Medway; where *Bessie Hart*, winner of the 1865 barge race, is now helping to prop up the sea wall of the creek, together with Brice's *Partridge*, *Metropolis* and *Henry Wood*, and Mercer's *Violet*. Most of the barges which were on war service, particularly those employed on mine-watching or balloon barrage work, were returned to their owners in a deplorable state, many of them too far gone to be worth repairing.

One of the most potent factors in the reduction of the sailing barge fleet has been the disproportionately great increase in the cost of all sailing gear. Whereas before the war a barge's mainsail would cost from about £37 to £47, according to the size, in 1947 a new mainsail seemed reasonable at £130 to £140; and to-day the cost would be even higher. Tarred hemp for head-ropes and bolt-ropes was almost unobtainable after the war; and a sailmaker told me, in 1946, that he was having to pay 6s. 6d. a pound for it, wholesale, on the black market. Big spars for masts and sprits are hardly procurable and the cost is fantastic. When wear and tear are added to the initial cost, it is undoubtedly cheaper to equip and run a fully powered motor barge than a sailorman.

The great increase in commercial road transport has also adversely

PLATE 65  Passing the Royal Naval College, Greenwich, with the Queen's House beyond

PLATE 66 *P.A.M.* approaching a Low Bridge on the Medway

*[By courtesy of Captain George Blake*

PLATE 67 "Stone-walling": Kentish rag is shot aboard

*[By courtesy of Captain George Blake*

affected the barge. For the comparatively short distances that the average small barge carried her cargo, the motor lorry is a serious competitor; for it can deliver its load right to the customer's door. In the old days a barge would make her way to some little farm creek; but, as likely as not, she would be loaded or unloaded by farm wagons, in which the goods were carried for the beginning or end of their journey. The motor lorry can go almost anywhere, and local transport and trans-shipment costs are avoided. The lorry carries its load right through, in one operation, from door to door. It is also independent of delays caused by weather—an important consideration in these days, when life moves so much more rapidly.

Greater regularity in delivery can undoubtedly be obtained by fitting auxiliary engines, and many barges now have motors. These, however, are not by any means a certain answer to the problem of making barges pay. In the first place, the barge must carry more cargoes and earn more in freights to cover the cost of the motor plus interest on the additional capital involved. But the space given over to engine-room, and the weight of the engine itself reduce to some extent the carrying capacity of the barge; so that, although she may carry more cargoes, each cargo is smaller and earns a smaller freight. The running cost of the engine is a small item when compared with the cost of upkeep of the sailing gear; and if the engine is powerful enough to give the barge a reasonable turn of speed, there is a tendency to use this power more and more and the sails less and less. When the sails wear out, there is a strong economic argument in favour of landing the gear and continuing as a purely motor vessel. That has happened with a considerable number of craft.

Barges generally may be divided roughly into two classes. The older, smaller barges have naturally suffered more from age and decay. Their upkeep is proportionately more costly. They require the same crew as a bigger barge, but earn smaller freights. Their hatches are small and often cannot accommodate modern machinery for discharging cargo. If an auxiliary engine is fitted in a small barge, the proportionate loss of space and carrying capacity is greater. Thus it is that the small old barge is ceasing to be a profitable proposition. That is why so many of these craft, which are still sound enough to be serviceable, have been sold for conversion to yachts.

It still pays to convert the larger barge to auxiliary and many are so trading. But, as already pointed out, there is a tendency to go one stage further and turn them into fully powered motor vessels.

Where purely motor craft are concerned, the modern small motor cargo vessel, properly designed for the job and built of steel, is obviously a more satisfactory and economical ship to run; and that is why, in my opinion, both the purely sailing barge and the auxiliary are doomed to ultimate extinction, though I hope that for many years to come the survivors will carry on and keep alive not only the undeniable beauty and romance of sail, but also the fine standards of tradition and seamanship which are found so highly developed in the bargemen.

In this chapter, therefore, I will try to give a general picture of what is happening to the barges at the present time; of their adventures and misadventures; of the cargoes they carry; and of those that have been or are being converted to auxiliary power.

When the war ended, the spritsail barge fleet had been reduced to no more than a small proportion of its former numbers; but by January 1949 it had been slightly increased, since a number of coasters had been refitted. The total number of those using sail alone then stood at about 140; the names of many of them are given in Appendix II. There were, in addition, perhaps 40 auxiliaries.

Not only is the fleet much smaller, but the pattern of post-war trading has considerably changed. Voyages to the Continent have almost ceased and the sailing barges no longer work so far down-Channel. Nevertheless, they are still, at the time of writing, trading as far north as the Humber and as far west as Weymouth. Most of the traffic, however, is between London and East Anglia, with a considerable trade to the Medway and some to the North Kentish ports. Cargoes of every sort are carried—timber, coal, sugar, explosives, cattle-cake; anything that offers, in fact. In spite of the motor lorry, barges still reach country wharves far inland up rivers and creeks.

Let us consider for a moment some of the cargoes carried, beginning with timber. The increase of timber imports to London after the war brought much trade to the smaller London River barges in the summer of 1946, when it was again fairly common to see spreeties with high deck loads sailing down the river. Goldsmith's, in particular, had a number of their barges in this work, including *Thetis*, a 65-ton barge built of steel at Sittingbourne in 1897. Early in April 1947 she broke adrift in the Thames Estuary in a heavy gale, and drove, stern-first and crewless, out to sea. The Southend lifeboat *Greater London* chased her for some miles and managed, after a struggle, to tow her back with her large deck cargo of timber intact.

Other barges owned by Goldsmith's and employed in this work were the three 64-ton steel barges *Lorna*, *Carina* and *Calluna*, all built at Southampton in 1898; and the 67-ton *Siesta*, also built at Southampton, but in the following year. Their big *Viper*, 81 tons, built at Sittingbourne in 1898, was likewise in the timber trade in the summer of 1948, carrying timber to Ipswich, as were *Carina* and *Calluna*. Shrubsall's *Gladys*, of Dover, took timber to Maldon after her annual refit, late in the same year. The *Siesta*, by the way, was in trouble in the winter of 1948–49, when she drove ashore at Leigh; she was light at the time, and fetched up within a few yards of the main railway line, but was refloated without damage four or five days later. It is sad to have to record that in April of 1949 Messrs Goldsmith's sold all but the two favourite barges of their fleet, *Briton* and *Scot*, to the London and Rochester Trading Company and even these have now been sold.

In January 1949, the *Kitty*, one of the finest barges in the large fleet owned by Francis & Gilders of Colchester, was repairing at Maldon with stem damage, following a collision when laden with timber which started a real chapter of accidents. Just before the collision, the *Kitty* of Harwich, a bowsprit barge of 65 tons, built at Harwich in 1895 and once owned by Horatio F. Horlock of Mistley, was loading timber in the Surrey Commercial Dock. She took a big deck cargo to clear her steamer, and when moving in the dock took a sudden list and lost it overboard. Crews of several other barges loaded the timber into the *General Jackson*, belonging to the same firm; but she also was run down by a motor vessel, the *Grampian Coast*, in Erith Reach soon after leaving the Dock. Damage proved to be more serious than was at first reported, and the *General Jackson's* bow was deeply cut into by the stem of the motor coaster. She was beached at R. Norton & Co.'s Barge Yard at Charlton to save sinking, and the *Leslie West* picked up her cargo of timber. The *General Jackson* is a 49-ton barge, built at Ipswich in 1896, and after being repaired, she was sold for conversion to a yacht, and now lies at the Marina Club. The photographs of parts of her gear, which appear in this book, were taken while she was lying at Norton's Yard awaiting a decision.

Coal is a less frequent cargo than in pre-war years; but coal for the gas-works at Margate has given employment to at least two of Everard's big coasters. The *Will Everard* took coal from Goole to Margate in the summer of 1948, resuming a trade she and her sisters carried on before the war. In July, in the same year, she visited Colchester with coal from Keadby. The same owner's *Greenhithe* was also carrying coal to Margate in 1947; and one passage at least in this trade is noteworthy, for she sailed from Hull to Yarmouth Roads, some 105 miles, in 15 hours, laden with 172 tons of coal.

In this connection, a typical summer month's trading by the *Greenhithe* in pre-war days, as shown by her log, is of interest. At the beginning of the month she sailed from Purfleet to Hull with a cargo of empty barrels. Thence she went to Keadby, light, where she loaded coal, with which she sailed to Margate and discharged. From Margate she proceeded to Grays, Essex, where she loaded cement for Weymouth. She had reached her destination and started to discharge when the month ended. To do all this between 1st July and 31st July is pretty good going, under sail alone.

A comparable post-war example is afforded by the performance of the big wooden auxiliary *Cabby*, belonging to the London and Rochester Trading Co. Launched in 1928, she was the last barge built at Gill's lower yard on the Medway; and is one of seven auxiliaries owned, at the time of writing, by the same company; the others being *Marie May*, *Pudge*, *Thyra*, *Alan*, *Scone* and *Vera*. *Cabby* began life as a sailing barge, and raced in the Coasting Class in pre-war days, but was later fitted with an auxiliary engine. In June 1947 she loaded four freights of coal from Boston for the South—which is good work for one barge in a single month, even with an auxiliary. She is also one of the few barges to trade to Wells since the war.

The sand and ballast trade also employs a number of barges, including Piper's *Adriatic*, a steel spreety of 61 tons built on the Humber in 1900. She was in this work in 1947, and was in distress in the Thames Estuary in April of that year. She varied this trade by taking an occasional cargo of wheat. In the summer of 1948 she was on the blocks at East Greenwich for a much-needed refit. The famous little racing barge *Fortis* of Rochester and the 85-ton *M. Piper*, "the Big Iron Pot", built at Greenwich in 1914, were both in the ballast work in 1948, though the *M. Piper* also took a cargo of wheat to Ipswich in the summer of that year.

The adventures of the *British Oak* of Rochester deserve a special mention. This 68-ton barge was built at Maidstone in 1903 for a local owner, and later passed to Samuel West Ltd., of London. In September 1948 she had come off St Osyth Beach, where she had been loading ballast, when she was caught in a hard Sunday-evening blow. She started to leak, and sank off the N. Buxey Buoy about midnight. Her crew tried to row ashore, but were unable to make it; so they lay in the boat astern of the wreck until Monday midday, when they were rescued by the Clacton lifeboat. On the same day the *Greenhithe* was bound from the north with coal for the gas-works at Colchester. When off Southwold she had to run back, and was not able to bring up until she was off Happisburgh, on the Norfolk coast.

It was the end of the *British Oak*, however; and her wreck was reported as having been blown up by Trinity House in January 1949.

This was not the first time that she had been in trouble; for in 1935, when bound from Goole for Hayling Island with coal, she was caught in a severe gale off the North Foreland, and, trying to make Ramsgate harbour, missed the entrance, struck the stone pier and drove up on Ramsgate sands with a smashed bowsprit.

Before the First World War she took part in a number of Thames Races, coming in second in the Coasting Class in 1905. The barge which narrowly beat her on that occasion was the *Violet Sybil*, still trading, but laid up and for sale early in 1951.

Wheat is to-day one of the most important cargoes carried by sailing barge—particularly in the Ipswich trade. A big freighter at Cliff Quay, Ipswich, still attracts a fleet of barges; as many as twenty have been seen there together, even as late as 1948. It is a cargo that needs a sound and tight barge; but the longevity of these craft is such that there are some still in the work that have been trading for over half a century. The 50-ton *Millie* of Colchester, for example (Plate 54), owned by Horlock's, and built at Brightlingsea in 1892, was surveyed at Mistley in the summer of 1948 and found sound enough, despite her fifty-six years, to continue in the grain trade. Two of Goldsmith's barges, the *Thetis*, built at Sittingbourne in 1897 (see page 286); and the *Kismet* of London, 73 tons, built at Deptford in 1899, were carrying wheat in the summer of 1947 and 1948 respectively. In addition to Ipswich, Colchester in Essex and Whitstable in Kent get barges carrying grain; as do a number of other ports.

Sailing barges are still being used in the powder trade, carrying explosives; they are particularly suitable for this, having no engines, which inevitably involve a risk of fire. Two of Wood's barges in this work are the *Gipping*, 59 tons, and the *Orwell*, 51 tons, both of Ipswich and built there in 1899. They were reconditioned, after long idleness, late in 1948, by Wood's at Gravesend, and, like the same firm's *Edith and Hilda* of Rochester, 56 tons, built at Milton-next-Sittingbourne in 1892 and also in this work, are easily distinguished by their green rails above a red wale.

Reference has already been made to the revival, since the war, of stack work, carrying deck cargoes of Essex straw to the paper mills near Queenborough, in Kent. Much of this goes from Colchester to Ridham Dock, on the West Swale, and barges which have been in this trade include Everard's *Lady Mary* and Daniels Brothers' *Violet*, a very sweet-lined little Maldon barge, both trading in the summer of 1948. Sully's big auxiliary *Arcades*, ex-*Olive Mary*, of 100 tons, built by Wills & Packham at Sittingbourne in 1921, was burned to the water's edge by a fire starting by the mast-case when she was

19

carrying a stack of baled straw from the Colne to Ridham Dock in June 1947. Her burnt-out hulk now lies at Sittingbourne; her engine was installed in the same firm's *Oxygen* in the autumn of 1947. The motor was unreliable, and on her first trip as an auxiliary, from London to Ipswich, it broke down and *Oxygen* had to make her passage under sail. The old *Olive Mary* was a fine barge, and that well-known bargeman, Captain J. Keeble, had her for many years.

A particularly interesting trade, and one involving considerable risks for the barges engaged in it, is that with Kentish ragstone from the Medway quarries near Maidstone, over to the Essex shores, where it is used for repairing the sea walls of the low-lying islands on the northern side of the Estuary. My friend Mr Arthur Bennett has sent me some notes on this work.

There is still a real demand for Kentish ragstone by the Essex County Council and the Essex Catchment Board. When the Essex County Council recently rebuilt Mersea Strood, Wakeley's *Lancashire* did the bulk of the work, berthing right up at the Strood. Being a light-draught little barge—bought during the war from Eastwoods, the brickmakers—and comparatively shallow-sided, she was popular with discharging gangs, as it was not such a big "throw". Her skipper was that famous bargeman "Tubby" Blake, who seemed equally happy with or without a mate, and who, for a long period recently, was sailing the *Lancashire* single-handed. One can but record one's admiration for the man who tackled so lightheartedly the task of sailing a working barge about the Estuary entirely on his own. That he did so successfully is sufficient evidence of his supreme skill as a master mariner.

Other barges regularly in this work are the auxiliary *P.A.M.* and the motor barge *Windward*, both belonging to Wakeley Bros. The Kent Catchment Board also run the *Llandudno*. They load at Tovil, just above Maidstone, and also at Allington, where the stone is trundled aboard in barrows and tipped into the hold. *P.A.M.* has steel plates on the ceiling to protect the wood. The discharging berths are pretty crude sometimes, and the barge has to berth to suit the job. Concrete blocks are being used in Essex, but do not do the job as well as rag, which is not always forthcoming. Wakeley Bros. always did the bulk of the work, though "Black Jack" Rayfield had a number of barges on the job, including *Afternoon*, which Arthur Bennett remembers as a regular trader to the Blackwater, working right up behind Osea Island. The towage up and down the Medway is a heavy item for a sailing barge, amounting to about

£10; and the barge also suffers from being knocked about a bit by reason of the nature of the cargo and of the discharging berths. The trade pays quite well, however. The Essex County Council pays 8s. per cubic yard, with four days' "purposes". The barges mostly load back with sand for Leigh, Pitsea and London River; usually from Alresford Creek, just above the swing bridge that carries the railway to Brightlingsea.

I am also indebted to Captain George Blake, master of Wakeley's *P.A.M.*, for a first-hand account of this work, in which he has been engaged for some fourteen years, first as mate with his father, "Tubby" Blake, then master of the old *Southwark*, of whom Arthur Bennett has written so delightfully in "*June* of Rochester", and later in a barge of his own. I cannot do better than quote it in full, and I would like here to express to him my thanks for this admirable picture of one form of bargeing.

"Seawalling isn't the best of jobs," he writes, "especially during the winter months. I've spent just on fourteen years working rag-stone from the Medway quarries to the Essex sea walls. Mishaps have come my way, and are expected with a job of this sort. Four occasions have found me and the barge washed up the walls, fortunately little damage being done, apart from torn chines and smashed boats. I think myself very lucky.

"Sometime in 1934 I went mate with my father in the old *Southwark*, and started my first experience with the stone-walling. Having done several jobs below, there came an order for Deal Hall on the front of the Crouch. It was while we were berthed on here that my first real knowledge of the job came home to me. We discharged on the day tide, but not early enough to save our water off. During the night the wind shifted to the south-east and blew a gale.

"Unfortunately for us, the holding qualities of the mud off there are not too good, and the anchor came home; with the result that the old barge washed up and down the sea wall like a balloon. My father and I spent two of the most uncomfortable hours of our lives crawling around the decks on hands and knees, trying to ease the position. After the tide had left and daylight came, we surveyed things and found little damage, and we got away on the day tide with the help of moorings which the unloaders had put down for us.

"I had two or three little mishaps with my father, but they never really amounted to anything. It is all right when there is someone at your side to do the worrying. I suppose it is a different story when you take a barge of your own and decisions have to come from your own head.

"In 1943 I took over the little *Estelle* and started working her to Foulness Island with ragstone. Many people with nautical knowledge will realise that the island isn't one of the easiest places to stick a barge alongside, particularly in the Crouch area. Plenty of people would think twice before doing so. It is a different tale when the skipper is given an order for delivery of stone to replace a bad section of wall.

"I berthed *Estelle* late one afternoon, on the high water. The weather was tame enough and had every appearance of staying so. The following morning found a fresh sou'-west wind off the shore; in fact, we put out extra kedges over the wall to keep us in our berth. Rain put the unloaders out by noon, and they pushed off home, leaving the barge with just under thirty tons of stone in, most of it on the port side.

"At three o'clock next morning, I was disturbed by roaring of wind and poked my head out. The wind had flown into the north-west and was blowing a full gale. This put us on a lee-shore, and the problem of holding her on was now far from my mind. The question of getting her off was my only worry. Luckily, I had berthed my anchor off in the stream fifty odd fathoms, so with the mate I went forward. Letting go all shore ropes, we manned the windlass. I think I did more work in an hour then than I have in my life before, with the result that we got her clear with only the loss of the barge's boat. When daylight came, the wind moderated; and the first sight that met my eyes was the four sailing barges that had been anchored over on the north shore off Coney Hall, but now on the south side just below the Shell Banks on the Foulness Sand, their sails in ribbons. I suppose I realised that it was one of the worst gales we had had.

"The following day I sailed to Burnham and 'phoned my guv'nor. He was quite relieved to hear my story and to know that the only damage was the loss of a boat. I owe the saving of the *Estelle* only to allowance for freak weather—something that is always to be reckoned with on these jobs. The anchor off with a good lead of cable is the mainstay. If that fails, well—it's all up. I know the *Estelle* would never have worked another freight if she had gone up on the sea wall that night.

"In the Medway above Allington Lock sometimes we find the land water a bit difficult. One or two good downpours of rain, and down comes the water, twisting its way to Allington around the narrow bends. To navigate craft safely, the water must be still; at times we only just find height under the low bridges with the mast lowered flat on deck. A quick rise in the land water holds us up there for a week or more. The latest addition in sluice-gates were erected at Allington some years ago, and these have eased the position. They are quite automatic, with gauges in the Lock Master's office, giving an accurate reading of depths every minute of the day. This enables the water to be maintained at one level all the year round, but it has not solved the problem of land water. It only helps matters.

"With all these little troubles we usually get by, and carry on the ragstone trade, which is necessary to the farmers of Essex to prevent their land going to sea. Taking things by and large, it is just another job, and something to keep the old barge going."

As we are now reaching the last stage in the barges' history, it is perhaps worth while to run briefly over some of the ports where barges are still trading, taking them in geographical order, and including those ports where to-day barges are still being repaired and refitted.

Reference has already been made to the Humber ports of Goole, Keadby and Hull; and to two of the barges trading there to-day —Everard's *Will Everard* and *Greenhithe*. Samuel West's *Olive May*, once mulie-rigged but a pure motor craft to-day, is another of the very few barges—even including auxiliaries—now seen in Yorkshire ports. Some London and Rochester Trading Company's barges are working to the Humber; and their *Scone* actually ended up, after a bad blow, in Bridlington Harbour, in December 1950. The Lincolnshire port of Boston, in 1947, saw the same Company's auxiliary *Pudge* in addition to *Cabby*, already mentioned.

Farther south, the smaller East Anglian ports of Wells and even Blakeney had barges trading up to 1939. Most of the Everard barges, including the boomy *Martinet*, worked to Wells before the war. Deep-draught coasters could only enter Wells at spring tides; and at least once *Alf Everard*, with a cargo of 285 tons of oil cake, just missed her tide and had to anchor for over a week off Wells bar before she could cross and reach the quay. Since the war this trade of Everard's has not so far been renewed; and Wells and Blakeney now have very little trade, although the quays are well kept. One of the few barges to visit Wells was the *Cabby*, in 1947.

An involuntary visitor to Blakeney in June 1948 was the 49-ton *H. Brouncker*, built at Frindsbury in 1882 and now a pure motor barge, owned by Whiting Bros. She arrived unexpectedly, after she had grounded a mile or so from the harbour, when bound from Gravesend for Grimsby, and had to enter for repairs. Farther south, Walberswick in Suffolk, which forms Southwold Harbour, has, so far as I know, had only one sailing barge in port since 1939. This was the small spreety *Gold Belt*, of Faversham, 43 tons, a skipper-owned

trading barge which arrived in June 1946 on a private "yachting"
cruise, without cargo, at a time when freights were scarce and her
owner wanted a holiday! Built by Gill of Rochester in 1892, she was
originally named *Orion*, and built to the order of Payne & Co., the
Faversham millers. She was, in fact, says Hervey Benham, in "Last
Stronghold of Sail", the last of the 100-ton coasters to be built before
the millers required larger barges for their bigger silos, and the closing
of many of the smaller barge ports made the smaller barge not such a
good economic proposition.

On London River she was known as "the little yacht barge", and
was engaged in stack work, from Essex to the Kent paper mills, after
the war. Her original name, *Orion*, was bought by the Orient Line for
their new liner just after a change in the regulations had made it
impossible to register a new ship in a name that was already on the
register. The Orient Line particularly wanted to use the name
*Orion*; but could only do so if the little barge had her name changed.
Naturally, her owner was in a position for driving a hard bargain; that
he did so I learnt from a director of the company, who felt that they
had had to "pay through the nose" for the name they wanted. The
little *Orion* was then refitted and re-named, most appropriately, *Gold
Belt*. She was bought in 1939 by an actor turned bargeman, who
preferred to spend his life as skipper of a barge rather than in a
theatre. She later had a 26 h.p. auxiliary fitted; but I understand she
has now been sold, and her owner is back on the stage.

Hervey Benham, who in the winter 1948 number of "Spritsail"
tells the story of her "yachting trip" visit to Southwold, writes of
the "civic reception" which they received on arrival. "Our cup of
joy was finally full," he writes, "when we heard an unmistakable
colonel identify us as a Norwegian type of craft. He was annoyed
when we refused to confirm this diagnosis, and learning that we were
a sailing barge observed testily, 'I thought you fellows always stuck to
the Broads'." *Sic transit gloria mundi!*

Skipper-owned barges are rare these days; it is not easy to get
enough freights to make a living. One other barge in this class, however, is the *Defender*, a very sweet-lined little Maldon barge of 63
tons, built there is 1900. She is an ex-stackie, and was loading sugar
in East Anglia in the latter part of 1948; but has been laid up at
Pin Mill since 1941.

Great Yarmouth still gets a few barges; *Trilby* and *Convoy*, both
fully powered motor barges since the war, were there in December
1947, the latter being one of the few Rye-built spreeties. E. J. & W.
Goldsmith's *Thetis* was there in the summer of 1948; Everard's *Lady*

*Mary* visited the port in September and October, and *Beatrice Maud* and *Will Everard* in December of the same year. *Centaur* and *Veravia* went there under sail alone in 1949. *Cambria* and *Greenhithe* have visited Lowestoft, the latter being fixed with sugar from East Anglia in the winter of 1948.

Of all barge ports, however, Ipswich is to-day the most important. A brisk trade between London's Dockland and Ipswich in grain, sugar, timber and flour employs some fifty craft, many being owned by Cranfield Bros. and R. & W. Paul Ltd. Twenty-four big coasting barges, for example, cleared from London for Ipswich, Felixstowe and Yarmouth in the first ten days of October 1946. Among them were the *Colonia*, *Repertor* and *Remercie*. Cranfield's fleet includes *Gladys* of Harwich, a fine Cann-built barge of 68 tons, which has recently completed a major refit at the St Clement's Shipyard; *Petrel* (since sold for a yacht); and *Spinaway C*. The last two barges were both built by Orvis & Fuller at Ipswich, on the typical Ipswich model, hollow bow lines combined with a fine sheer, finishing in a shallow transom: "sweeter lines one could not wish to see," as a writer in "Spritsail" described them. Paul's *Alice May*, *Ena* (of Dunkirk fame) and *Thalatta*, with Sully's *Raybel*, are regular traders there; as were the latter's *Valdora* and *Scotsman* until they were sold and converted to yachts. *Scotsman*, of 44 tons, built at Sittingbourne in 1899, was a very smart craft. Her skipper was a Horlock, and she always looked as if she had just come off the yard. *Thalatta*, once a boomy, used to trade regularly to the Bristol Channel in days gone by.

*George Smeed*, another barge trading to Ipswich, a real old-timer, built at Murston in 1882, is a bluff-bowed craft, beamy and with a narrow stern; a great contrast to the sweet-lined East Coast built barges. She originally belonged to the Smeed Dean fleet, was rebuilt in 1922, and, after surviving the depressed years of the 1930's, was bought by the Associated Portland Cement Manufacturers. When their well-known "Blue Circle" sailing barges were disposed of she was acquired by Francis & Gilders, who still own her. Under her skipper, Captain G. Mann, she took potash to Ipswich late in 1948. Other Ipswich traders are the auxiliary *Gravelines I*, ex-*Hilda*; *Dannebrog*, one of the largest coasters sailing between London and the River Orwell and a sister ship of *Alice May*; *Greenhithe*, *Veravia*, *Beatrice Maud*, Goldsmith's *Calluna*, *Viper*, *Briton*, *Yarana* and *Kismet*, with *Fortis* and *M. Piper* belonging to T. Scholey, the last two, however, being usually in the sand and ballast work.

Felixstowe Dock has a considerable trade, in which many barges

trading to Ipswich are engaged; *Ernest Piper* was among those seen
there in the spring of 1948. Mistley too has barges actively trading
there. *G.C.B.* of Rochester was bound there with maize from the
Victoria Dock when she dragged her anchor off Southend Pier in one
of the gales at the end of 1948 or beginning of 1949. Her skipper,
Captain W. J. Giggins and his young mate were taken off, suffering
from exposure, by the Southend lifeboat, but were put aboard again
when the weather moderated and the barge had been towed inshore.
She reached her destination safely a week later.

Colchester is famous for Francis & Gilders' large fleet, of which
*Kitty* and *Centaur* are two of the finest. Marriages have one sailing
barge left, the *Leofleda*, which trades to their East Mills right up the
Colne, above the road bridge. She was in trouble in March 1947, when
she broke adrift in the Colne in a gale and was in collision with
another barge lying near her. *East Anglia* of Rochester, 46 tons, built
there in 1900 and owned by the London and Rochester Trading Company, was bound from London to Colchester with wheat in December
1948 when she capsized and sank in the Thames Estuary off the Isle
of Grain, after being in collision with the power barge *Glenway*. The
crew were able to get away in the boat before the barge sank, and she
was successfully raised a few days later by the P.L.A. Salvage Department, but was never fitted out again. Francis & Gilders' barges
trading regularly to Colchester, in addition to those already mentioned, are *British Empire*, *George Smeed*, *Clara*, *Dawn*, *Falconet*,
*Ethel Ada*, *Lady Helen*, *Leslie West*, *Mirosa* (ex- *Ready*), with *Alaric*
and *Varuna*—the last two being auxiliaries. Their beautiful little
*Saltcote Belle* was also a Colchester trader until recently, when she
was sold to become a yacht. All but *Alaric*, *Ethel Ada*, *Lady Helen*
and *Leslie West* are at least fifty years old. The 73-ton *Alaric* was
originally named *Shamrock* and was built at Sandwich in 1901. In
March 1943 she was machine-gunned by six German fighters;
her skipper, Captain Harry Eves, died of his wounds within a few
minutes, but his son Alan escaped practically uninjured. The barge
was badly damaged, but was afterwards extensively rebuilt, and
doubled.

To Major W. D. Gosling, of Gay Bowers, Danbury, I am indebted
for full information on the barge trade to Maldon, on the Blackwater,
once such a famous port for building barges; together with a detailed
analysis of the barges trading there from the beginning of January
1948 to the end of February 1949. He was assisted by Mr J. G. Sadd
of Messrs John Sadd & Sons Ltd., Mr Taylor, a director of Messrs
Francis & Gilders, through whose agency the barge trade to Maldon

is now handled, and Mr A. Wright, the River Bailiff. To all these my thanks are due.

It is sad to record that to-day only one barge is owned in Maldon, the *Ethel Maud*, belonging to Green Bros. The *May Flower*, their other barge, was sold in the summer of 1950 to become a yacht. There is, nevertheless, a busy trade with visiting barges, and this was particularly so during the war. The year 1943 saw 293 barges unload at Hythe Quay, Maldon, with rubble from London for use on the local airfields. Many brought only half a load, but were paid for a full freight. Since the war the trade has generally been with grain from London, and sometimes from Ipswich; as well as with cargoes of timber. The barges either return light or carry flour or grit. Regular traders in 1948 and 1949 were the sailing barges *Falconet, Ethel Ada, Saltcote Belle, George Smeed, Dawn, Mirosa, Leslie West* (now being converted to motor), *Centaur, Kitty* and *Lady Helen*, all belonging to Francis & Gilders; with Goldsmith's *Briton*, Samuel West's *British Oak* (until she was lost), Shrubsall's *Verona* and Prior's (of Burnham) *Mayland*; together with Francis & Gilders' auxiliary *Alaric*. Barges making five or six trips during the period were *Leofleda, Gladys, Ardwina, Oxygen* ("Chubb" Horlock's barge), *P.A.M.* and *Lorna*. In addition to these, twenty-seven other barges made one or more occasional trips.

I have recorded this information fully, to give a good idea of the extent of the post-war barge trade, and I hope it may be of some historical interest.

The barge trade on the River Crouch seems to have fallen to rather small proportions since the war, though a few barges still trade to Hullbridge and one—*Beatrice Maud*—to Battlesbridge. *Saltcote Belle* discharged her grain cargo at Hullbridge instead of Ipswich, after being in trouble in July 1948. Two barges owned by A. M. & H. Rankin Ltd., trade regularly to their owners' mills at Stambridge on the River Roach, below Rochford. These are the *Lord Roberts* of Maldon, built in 1900, and the *Joy*, built at Teynham, Kent, in 1914.

An active trade is still carried on with Southend. In 1948 timber, ballast and coal were the inward cargoes, with breeze from the local gas-works as outward freight. A large number of barges are in this work, including most of Piper's fleet. The last barge to be owned in Southend is the *Ashingdon*, and she keeps up an average of one trip per week. Goldsmith's *Viper* was also a regular trader there, but has now become a yacht.

By way of contrast, Leigh had less than a dozen arrivals in the first ten months of 1948. Wakeley's *Violet Sybil* took a few cargoes to

Leigh that summer, and in November some timber was discharged at Bell Wharf; the latest arrivals being *Maria* and *Squawk*. On the other hand, a fleet of barges is still owned in Leigh by Messrs W. H. Theobald & Co., a firm of contractors and builders, trading under the name of Leigh Building Supply Company. Their barges fly a plain blue "bob" bearing the letters "L.B.S." in white. The barges of this firm were employed carrying timber, and ballast for new roads, between London and Southend and Leigh, where the firm has a wharf in Leigh Creek. One of their barges was the *Spurgeon*, which was sold for conversion as a yacht and was the Club Barge of the Thames Barge Sailing Club during the summer of 1948. In 1946 Messrs Theobald were converting their barges to full motor power, and none are now left as sailing craft nor even as auxiliaries. First to be fitted with Diesels were *Maid of Munster* (formerly *Bexhill*) and *Maid of Connaught* (ex-*The Monarch*). These were followed by *Persevere*, *Ada Mary* and *Mary Ann*. *Paglesham* is laid up out of service, as a result of damage following a collision between two steamers in the Thames in 1947; she was sunk in the Surrey Docks, and, though raised afterwards, was condemned; *Russell* and *Primrose* (of Ipswich) have, like *Spurgeon*, been sold for conversion to yachts.

Coming now to the River Medway and the Kentish ports, it may be fairly stated that, on the whole, Kent barges have succumbed to the inroads of motor craft to a greater extent than the Essex fleet. Many were already being converted to motor power by the summer of 1946. Mention has already been made of the sea-walling trade in Kentish ragstone from the quarries near Maidstone; but of course many other cargoes are carried, including, rather unexpectedly, coir. *Flower of Essex* was bound from London to Maidstone with coir when she sank in the Jenkin Swatch on 29th October 1948. She was raised a day or so later, to berth at Queenborough. She never resumed trading, but lay at Crown Quay, Sittingbourne, until sold for conversion to a yacht. Not long after, the *Albert*, converted to full power and likewise carrying coir for Maidstone, struck a submerged wreck in the Jenkin Swatch, not far from the spot where the *Flower of Essex* sank. *Albert* also sank, but was less fortunate, for she later broke up and became a total loss.

The barge trade to Rochester and the Medway barge ports like Gillingham has sadly fallen off in recent years. At one time Messrs Eastwoods, the brickmakers, had a fleet of forty-five sailing barges carrying bricks; by the end of the war they had only part work for three—motor lorries had replaced the rest. The Associated Portland Cement Company's trade is carried by fully powered craft or by lighters towed by tugs. Plenty of barge repair work is done on the Medway, but not many barges find work there, although a few trade fairly frequently with grain or flour. Until she was sold recently, Paul's *Alice May* was sometimes seen there, for example. Plenty of cement is also carried away from the Medway by barge—largely to the Docks for export. The revival of the stackie trade to Ridham Dock on the Swale is described earlier in this chapter; and Faversham has a few barges still trading, such as the staysail barge *Pretoria* and the *Esther*. Both are also registered at Faversham. The yards at Sittingbourne are still finding plenty of work rebuilding and refitting barges and installing engines in many of them.

Next to Rochester, Whitstable is perhaps the most important barge centre to-day on the southern side of the Estuary. The Whitstable barges *Azima*, *Savoy* and *Trilby* still seem to find plenty of work from the London Docks to the North Kentish ports, as did *Nellie* and *Lord Churchill* until sold to become yachts; while the auxiliary *Kathleen* trades to Ramsgate and Dover, with *Vicunia*, now a fully powered motor barge. Shrubsall's big coaster *Veravia*, ex-*Alaric*, after refitting at Grays, took 750 quarters of Canadian wheat to Whitstable as her first freight, which she discharged there in September 1948. From there she proceeded to Ipswich, in company with the *George Smeed*. Sully's *Hydrogen* was there after Kentish wheat late in 1948. This powerful barge, of 98 tons, was originally, like *Oxygen*, a tank barge, boomy-rigged, and was built at Rochester in 1906. She was originally owned by Burt, Boulton & Haywood, and once made a trip to the Firth of Forth. Later, when owned by Smeed Dean, she was working to the Humber, before the Second World War. Mr H. Butcher, of Sittingbourne, sailed in her for eleven years eight months, only missing one trip, before he "swallowed the anchor" in 1932. In 1921 she made a remarkably fast passage from the Humber to Kent: Spurn Head to Milton Creek, Sittingbourne, in twenty-four hours. It must have been a wonderful sail! "Chubb" Horlock describes her as a very fine barge, and she is always very well kept up. She is now owned by Sully, and the late Captain A. Coward, one of the most famous of racing bargemen, was her master until recently.

*Centaur* was also in Whitstable, late in 1948, loading Kentish wheat. Captain Hewson had her then, having recently come from Everards. At one time he had the *Teetotaller*, working to the Queenborough Gas Works. Coming out of Sheerness with a cargo of barrels in the hatchway, he was once hailed by a yachtsman, who shouted at him, "You're a fine sort of chap—calling yourself *Teetotaller* and carrying a cargo of beer!"

The *Lord Churchill* referred to above is the last of the English & Continental Shipping Company's once numerous fleet of "Lord" barges. Originally ketch-rigged, they sailed to the Rhine and to the West Country. *Lord Churchill*, like her sisters, was once a boomy, and was built by Harvey of Littlehampton in 1888. Her hull was an unusual shape for a barge, deep-sided and very fine forward, with hardly a straight plank anywhere, and the exceptionally heavy draught, light, of 3 feet 9 inches. She had a new ceiling fitted at Whitstable late in 1948. As well as Whitstable, she also traded to Ramsgate. *Savoy* is another Ramsgate trader in these days.

The barge trade to Ramsgate was picking up a little towards the end of 1948, when the port was getting one or two barges a week. *Kathleen*, owned by Daniels Bros. of Whitstable, after being refitted and converted to an auxiliary, was trading there regularly from London, with *Lord Churchill*, *Savoy* and *Vicunia*. The latter, with *Kathleen* and Shrubsall's *Veravia*, were working to Dover.

Barges are seldom seen down-Channel these days, but Sully's *Trilby*, as a fully powered motor barge, went to Southampton in November 1948. The *Glenwood*, also fully powered, has traded to Newport, Isle of Wight. She was bound there from Rochester in February in the same year, when her engine failed in heavy weather, and she had to be towed into Ramsgate by the Ramsgate lifeboat, fortunately without much other damage. Weymouth is about the western limit of trading for post-war barges, though a voyage there has now become a very rare event.

The time has come, however, to end a long chapter and an even longer story. One could fill many volumes with tales of the barges and bargemen, but I have had room to include only a selection from the great mass of material which I have been collecting for over a quarter of a century. That selection I have tried to make as representative as possible. As with the clipper ships, so with the barges—interest seems to increase as the craft themselves diminish, and no doubt others will take up the tale where I must leave it. There is much still to tell in the volumes yet unwritten. Hervey Benham's new book "Down Tops'l" is itself a mine of information, for example.

Already there is, however, one important and, until recently, growing addition to the literature of the sailing barge. A new quarterly publication, "Spritsail", devoted exclusively to sailing barges, is now being published by the Thames Barge Sailing Club, founded in 1948 at an inaugural meeting at the National Maritime Museum, Greenwich. Unhappily recent difficulties have caused the temporary suspension of this journal after seven issues; but it is to be hoped that these may soon be overcome so that publication may be resumed. The objects of the Club are to keep alive the traditions of the barge and to bring together all who are interested in sailing barges, whether they be professional bargemen, amateur seamen, model-makers, artists, photographers or maritime historians. Through the generosity of the London and Rochester Trading Company, the famous old *Arrow* has been lent to the Club at a nominal rent, as a Club ship. She was roughly converted to accommodate a crew of twelve during the winter of 1948-49, so that during the sailing season she can sail every week-end in the Thames Estuary, with a professional barge skipper in charge, and be crewed by members of the Club and their friends. During midweek she can be chartered by members for a small sum; and whether in this way or at week-ends, sailing members can obtain first-class sailing at extremely low cost. They can also learn much of seamanship and acquire something of the bargemen's fine traditions. Full "Sailing Members" pay a guinea entrance fee and a two-guinea annual subscription. Members of recognised yacht clubs may join as "Maritime Members" for a guinea a year, without entrance fee, but pay a higher subscription for their week-end sailing.

In addition, a class of "Endowment Members" provides the working capital in the form of interest-free debentures; and "Associate Members", who also receive "Spritsail" and partake in all the activities of the Club, but who may not wish to indulge in practical barge sailing, pay no entrance fee, but contribute a half-guinea annual subscription. Professional Members pay the same half-guinea rate.

A further possible development, of great importance to the survival of sailing barges, is a scheme under consideration for professional sail training in a fleet of these craft. The cost and difficulty of running a blue-water sail training ship for British Merchant Navy Officers would be so great that many hold such a proposal to be impractical in present-day conditions, however desirable it may be. Might it not be possible, however, to run a fleet of sail-training barges, as a venture almost economically self-supporting, in which, under ordinary trading conditions, large numbers of apprentices could receive a short period of training in sail, counting for sea-time, in which they would receive a very valuable grounding in real seamanship of a kind which they could never gain in steam? This is not the place to argue the value of sail training; but I do venture to suggest that some of its benefits might well be obtained cheaply, but very effectively, in sailing barges.

So I reach the end of my story. He is a rash man who ventures on a prophecy, and I am not going to discuss at length the future of the sailing barge. None has been built since the early 1930's. Unless for sail training, it is hardly likely that any will be built now. The passage of years and the ever-present hazards of the sea must take their toll. As I finish this book in the Spring of 1950, changes in the barge fleets are occurring all the time; and so rapidly that much of what I have written will be out of date before it can be printed.

The sailing barge is, however, a very tough customer; her longevity and toughness are almost phenomenal. As for the bargeman, in an age of mechanical power he is one of the few real sailors left in the world to-day. Let us end therefore with the hope that both ships and men may live for many years to come, for sad indeed will be the day when there are no more sailing barges.

# APPENDIX I

## BARGE OWNERS' "BOBS", 1949

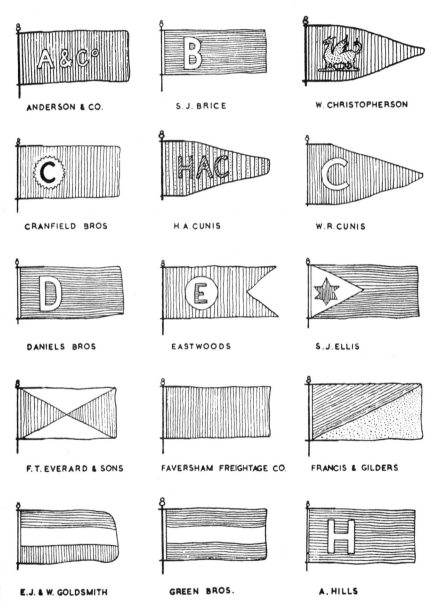

ANDERSON & CO.

S. J. BRICE

W. CHRISTOPHERSON

CRANFIELD BROS

H. A. CUNIS

W. R. CUNIS

DANIELS BROS

EASTWOODS

S. J. ELLIS

F. T. EVERARD & SONS

FAVERSHAM FREIGHTAGE CO.

FRANCIS & GILDERS

E. J. & W. GOLDSMITH

GREEN BROS.

A. HILLS

**M.F. HORLOCK**

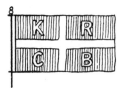

**KENT RIVERS
CATCHMENT BOARD**

**LONDON & ROCHESTER
TRADING CO.**

**E. MARRIAGE & SON**

**METCALF MOTOR COASTERS**

**R. & W PAUL**

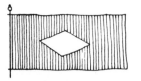

**S.J. PETERS**

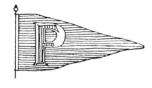

**J.R. PIPER**

**R.J PRIOR**

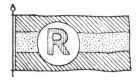

**A M. & H. RANKIN**

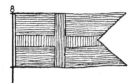

**H.P. SHRUBSALL**

**G.F SULLY**

**WAKELEY BROS.**

**SAMUEL WEST**

**WHITING BROS.**

**T.F. WOOD**

**KEY**

| | | |
|---|---|---|
| BLUE  | RED  | GREEN  |
| ORANGE  | GOLD YELLOW }  | PURPLE MAROON MAUVE }  |

# BARGE OWNERS' "BOBS" 1930

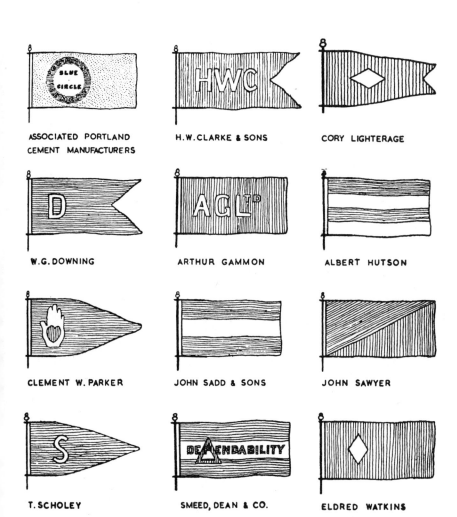

ASSOCIATED PORTLAND
CEMENT MANUFACTURERS

H.W.CLARKE & SONS

CORY LIGHTERAGE

W.G. DOWNING

ARTHUR GAMMON

ALBERT HUTSON

CLEMENT W. PARKER

JOHN SADD & SONS

JOHN SAWYER

T. SCHOLEY

SMEED, DEAN & CO.

ELDRED WATKINS

# APPENDIX II

## PART I. BARGES TRADING UNDER SAIL IN JUNE 1949

Arranged under owners, alphabetically, with house-flags or "bobs".

Information is given in the following order: name, port of registry, place and date of building, net tonnage, official number, and signal letters where carried.

Steel-built barges marked with an asterisk (*).

Barges laid up or under major repair marked with a dagger (†).

Auxiliary barges shown as "(Aux.)". Barges not so indicated are trading under sail alone.

Fully powered barges, whether steadying sails are carried or not, are NOT INCLUDED.

The list is as complete as widespread researches could make it, with the gratefully acknowledged help of the owners concerned. The barge fleets have been somewhat reduced since the list was compiled, but where changes have taken place, these are shown in the form of footnotes, bringing the information up to the end of March 1951. I am indebted to Mr. L. Vandersyde, and to Mr. F. S Cooper, for kindly undertaking this final revise to ensure that the list gives a completely reliable picture of the trading barges as they exist at the beginning of the second half of the twentieth century. "Now" in the footnotes means early 1951.

ANDERSON & CO.
44, Oxford Street, Whitstable.
White "A & Co." on a red flag.
Major of Harwich (Aux.) . . . b. Harwich 1897 67 tons 105424 MQZB

SOLOMON J. BRICE.
Point Barge Yard, Rochester.
White "B" on blue flag. Dark blue, white and dark blue bands on sprit.
G.C.B. of Rochester . . . b. Rochester 1907 63 tons 118299
Nelson of London . . . b. Sittingbourne 1905 63 tons 120590
Plover of London . . . b. Swanscombe 1898 62 tons 110026 MGXN

| | | | | | |
|---|---|---|---|---|---|
| *R. S. Jackson* of Rochester[1] | . | b. Upnor | . | 1895 | 48 tons | 104324 | MJDF |
| *Rowland* of London | . | b. Ipswich | . | 1895 | 65 tons | 105752 | |
| *Violet* of London | . | b. Ipswich | . | 1896 | 64 tons | 105853 | |

[1] Laid up.

### WILFRID CHRISTOPHERSON.
6, Dial Lane, Ipswich.
Gold Griffin with the legs of a Suffolk punch on red pennant.

| | | | | | |
|---|---|---|---|---|---|
| *Memory* of Ipswich | . | . | b. Harwich | 1904 | 65 tons | 113758 | MJKQ |

### CRANFIELD BROS., LTD.
College Street, Ipswich.
Black "C" in serrated white disc on red flag. White ball in topsail.

| | | | | | |
|---|---|---|---|---|---|
| *Beric* of Harwich | . | . | b. Harwich | 1896 | 63 tons | 105421 | |
| *Dannebrog* of Harwich (Aux.) | . | b. Harwich | 1901 | 71 tons | 109881 | MFFZ |
| *Ethel* of Harwich | . | . | b. Harwich | 1894 | 68 tons | 99453 | |
| *Felix* of Ipswich | . | . | b. Harwich | 1893 | 68 tons | 97686 | MGTP |
| *Gladys* of Harwich (Aux.) | . | b. Harwich | 1901 | 68 tons | 109882 | |
| *Kimberley* of Ipswich | . | . | b. Harwich | 1900 | 65 tons | 109209 | |
| *May* of Ipswich | . | . | b. Ipswich | 1891 | 57 tons | 97680 | |
| *Orinoco* of London (Aux.) | . | b. East Greenwich | 1895 | 70 tons | 104862 | |
| *Spinaway C.* of Ipswich | . | b. Ipswich | 1899 | 57 tons | 109207 | |
| *Venture* of London | . | . | b. Ipswich | 1900 | 58 tons | 112769 | |

### CHARLES CREMER.
50, Newton Road, Faversham.
*See* FAVERSHAM FREIGHTAGE CO.

**FREDERICK CREMER.**

Churston, St Anne's Road, Tankerton, Kent.

*See* FAVERSHAM FREIGHTAGE CO.

**HORACE A. CUNIS, LTD.**

Albion Wharf, Holland Street, Southwark Street, London, S.E.1.

"H.A.C." in purple on orange pennant with square end.

| | | | | | |
|---|---|---|---|---|---|
| Glencoe of Rochester [1] | b. Rochester | 1905 | 64 tons | 118221 | |
| H.A.C. of London (ex-*Invicta*)†[2] | b. Sittingbourne | 1896 | 55 tons | 105551 | HQWC |
| Mafeking of London*†[3] | b. Beverley | 1900 | 60 tons | 112777 | |

[1] Laid up, for sale at Sparks Yard, Limehouse, since late 1949.   [2] Sold, lying Ramsgate, connected with dredging operations in harbour.   [3] Sold for breaking up.

**W. R. CUNIS, LTD.**

Royal Woolwich Wharf, Woolwich Church Street, Woolwich, S.E.18.

White "C" in red flag.

| | | | | | |
|---|---|---|---|---|---|
| Glenmore of Rochester (Aux.) | b. Rochester | 1902 | 53 tons | 113710 | MGJS |

**DANIELS BROS (WHITSTABLE), LTD.**

78, Harbour Street, Whitstable.

White "D" on blue flag.

| | | | | | |
|---|---|---|---|---|---|
| Azima of Faversham (Aux.) | b. Whitstable | 1898 | 50 tons | 104941 | |
| Kathleen of Rochester (Aux.) | b. Gravesend | 1901 | 53 tons | 113708 | MNBQ |
| Lord Churchill of Faversham [1] | b. Littlehampton | 1888 | 60 tons | 94389 | |
| Nellie of Faversham [2] | b. Faversham | 1901 | 43 tons | 114452 | |
| Savoy of Dover | b. Rochester | 1898 | 69 tons | 105555 | MCBB |
| Trilby of Dover | b. Sandwich | 1896 | 53 tons | 91829 | |
| Violet of Maldon [3] | b. Maldon | 1889 | 45 tons | 96482 | |

[1] Sold 1950 for conversion to yacht; lying Nine Elms.   [2] Sold 1950 for conversion to yacht; lying 'Hoo.   [3] Laid up 1951.

## EASTWOODS, LTD.

47, Belvedere Road, London, S.E.1.

Blue "E" in white circle on red swallow-tailed flag. "EASTWOODS, BRICKMAKERS" in large white letters on sails.

| | | | | |
|---|---|---|---|---|
| Westmoreland of London . . . | b. Conyer Quay | 1900 | 43 tons | 112733 |

## SIDNEY J. ELLIS.

153, Bell Road, Sittingbourne, Kent.

Red star on white triangle at hoist in blue flag.

| | | | | |
|---|---|---|---|---|
| Maria of Rochester [1] . . . | b. Sittingbourne | 1898 | 58 tons | 109923 |
| Pimlico of Rochester (Aux.) [2] . | b. Borstal, Kent | 1914 | 59 tons | 107263 | MJDK |
| Victoria of London [3] . | b. Sittingbourne | 1897 | 54 tons | 108233 |

[1] Sold to L.R.T.C. Now aux.   [2] Laid up Sittingbourne since sinking of Erith, Oct. 1950.   [3] Sold for conversion to yacht early 1950; now at Southampton.

## F. T. EVERARD & SONS, LTD.

The Wharf, Greenhithe, Kent.

Flag quartered diagonally: red at hoist and fly, white above and below.

| | | | | |
|---|---|---|---|---|
| Cambria of London . . . | b. Greenhithe | 1906 | 79 tons | 110199 | MCSJ |
| Greenhithe of London *[1] . | b. Great Yarmouth | 1923 | 89 tons | 147562 |
| Lady Marjorie of London [2] . | b. Chiswick | 1893 | 66 tons | 102783 | MJQK |
| Lady Mary of London [3] . | b. Greenhithe | 1900 | 49 tons | 112692 |
| Lady Maud of London . | b. Greenhithe | 1903 | 59 tons | 118305 | MJLK |
| Marguerite of London [4] . | b. Bergqvara, Sweden | 1901 | 63 tons | 114808 | MJKT |
| Princess of Harwich [5] . | b. East Greenwich | 1902 | 58 tons | 116171 |
| Sara of London . . | b. Conyer Quay | 1902 | 50 tons | 115858 |
| Veronica of London [6] . | b. East Greenwich | 1906 | 54 tons | 120691 | MJDQ |
| Will Everard of London *[7] . | b. Great Yarmouth | 1925 | 150 tons | 148677 | MBSF |

[1] Laid up early 1951 pending B.O.T. survey.   [2] Sold for conversion to yacht, Queenborough, Sept. 1950.   [3], [4], and [5] Laid up; Greenhithe.   [6] Laid up, damaged, Greenhithe, late 1949.   [7] Now aux.

## FAVERSHAM FREIGHTAGE CO. (Formerly JAMES CREMER.)
Faversham, Kent.
Plain red flag.

| | | | | | |
|---|---|---|---|---|---|
| Edith of Rochester | b. Sittingbourne | 1904 | 48 tons | 118208 | MJDY |
| Esther of Faversham | b. Faversham | 1900 | 43 tons | 104945 | |
| James and Ann of Faversham | b. Teynham, Kent | 1903 | 42 tons | 114455 | |
| Pretoria of Faversham [1] | b. Faversham | 1902 | 44 tons | 114454 | |

[1] Laid up.

## FRANCIS & GILDERS, LTD. (Merged with L.R.T.C., March 1951.)
28, Hythe Quay, Colchester.
Flag divided diagonally, purple above at hoist, orange below at fly.

| | | | | | |
|---|---|---|---|---|---|
| Alaric of London (ex-Shamrock) (Aux.) | b. Sandwich | 1901 | 73 tons | 105560 | MGYP |
| British Empire of Colchester | b. Brightlingsea | 1899 | 50 tons | 109616 | |
| Centaur of Harwich | b. Harwich | 1895 | 60 tons | 99460 | MQRV |
| Clara of London [1] | b. Sittingbourne | 1896 | 60 tons | 105829 | MGWR |
| Colonia of Harwich [2] | b. Sandwich | 1897 | 62 tons | 105422 | |
| Dawn of Maldon | b. Maldon | 1897 | 54 tons | 105902 | |
| Ethel Ada of Ipswich [3] | b. Ipswich | 1897 | 48 tons | 109202 | |
| Falconet of Rochester [4] | b. Strood | 1899 | 49 tons | 110951 | |
| George Smeed of Rochester | { b. Murston 1882 / rebuilt Murston 1922 } | | 64 tons | 84430 | MGWB |
| Kitty of Harwich | b. Harwich | 1895 | 65 tons | 105418 | MFXT |
| Lady Helen of London | b. Rochester | 1902 | 56.tons | 114844 | MFJP |
| Leslie West of London (Aux.) | b. Gravesend | 1900 | 57 tons | 112762 | |
| Mirosa of Maldon (ex-Ready) | b. Maldon | 1892 | 49 tons | 96485 | |
| Saltcote Belle of Maldon [5] | b. Maldon | 1895 | 49 tons | 96490 | |
| Varuna of London (Aux.) | b. East Greenwich | 1907 | 59 tons | 125614 | |

[1] Laid up.   [2] Sold to Daniels Bros Aug. 1950.   [3] and [4] Laid up.   [5] Sold for conversion to yacht mid 1951; now at Pin Mill.

# E. J. & W. GOLDSMITH, LTD.

110, Fenchurch Street, London, E.C.3.

Round-shouldered flag, divided into blue, white and red horizontally.

| | | | | | |
|---|---|---|---|---|---|
| *Briton* of London*[1] | . . . | b. Southampton | 1898 | 80 tons | 109988 MJFP |
| *Esterel* of London*†[2] | . . . | b. Southampton | 1899 | 67 tons | 110200 MJND |
| *Scot* of London*[3] | . . . | b. Southampton | 1898 | 80 tons | 110008 MJCW |
| *Trojan* of London*†[4] | . . . | b. Southampton | 1898 | 79 tons | 109987 MLXT |

[1] Sold to Sadd of Maldon 1950; now a lighter.  [2] Sold to T. Walker, Northfleet, as a wrecking lighter.  [3] Sold to owner at Queenborough for conversion to yacht mid 1950.  [4] Sold to Sheerness Motor Barge Co. early 1950 and now fully powered.

# GREEN BROS (MALDON), LTD. (Now Baker, Ltd., Maldon.)

Maldon, Essex.

Flag divided into dark blue, white and dark blue horizontally. White "G.B." in topsail.

| | | | | | |
|---|---|---|---|---|---|
| *Ethel Maud* of Maldon | . . . | b. Maldon | 1899 | 45 tons | 96483 |
| *May Flower* of Rochester [1] | . . . | b. Frindesbury | 1888 | 48 tons | 94558 |

[1] Sold for conversion to yacht mid 1950; now at Leigh-on-Sea.

# AUGUSTUS HILLS.

Annandale House, Greenwich, Kent.

White "H" on blue flag. White "H" in topsail.

| | | | | | |
|---|---|---|---|---|---|
| *Surge* of London [1] | . . . | b. East Greenwich | 1904 | 54 tons | 118448 |

[1] Sold for conversion to yacht.

# M. F. HORLOCK & CO., LTD.

High Street, Mistley, Essex.

White Maltese cross on blue pennant.

| | | | | | |
|---|---|---|---|---|---|
| *Adieu* of Harwich*[1] | . . . | b. Mistley, Essex | 1929 | 79 tons | 161035 MQMQ |
| *Millie* of Colchester | . . . | b. Brightlingsea | 1892 | 50 tons | 98325 |
| *Portlight* of Harwich* | . . . | b. Mistley, Essex | 1925 | 68 tons | 145405 MQMS |
| *Redoubtable* of Harwich (Aux.) | . . . | b. Harwich | 1915 | 99 tons | 131904 MGRQ |
| *Reliance* of Harwich [2] | . . . | b. Ipswich | 1900 | 62 tons | 109879 |

**M. F. HORLOCK & CO. LTD.—Continued.**

| | | | | | |
|---|---|---|---|---|---|
| Remercie of Harwich (Aux.) . . . | b. Harwich | 1908 | 67 tons | 123936 | MQMT |
| Repertor of Harwich* . . . | b. Mistley, Essex | 1924 | 69 tons | 145404 | MQMV |
| Xylonite of Harwich* . . . | b. Mistley, Essex | 1926 | 68 tons | 145408 | |

1 Fully powered motor barge late 1950.  2 Laid up; Mistley.

**KENT RIVERS CATCHMENT BOARD.**

Brunswick House, Maidstone, Kent.

White St George's cross on red flag, with white letters "K.R.C.B." in the red quarters.

| | | | | | |
|---|---|---|---|---|---|
| Llandudno of Rochester . . . | b. Sittingbourne | 1892 | 43 tons | 99911 | |

**LONDON & ROCHESTER TRADING CO., LTD.**

Canal Road, Rochester.

Red flag with white crescent in the hoist.

| | | | | | |
|---|---|---|---|---|---|
| Alan of London (Aux.) . . . | b. Battersea | 1900 | 61 tons | 112679 | MDKD |
| Arrow of Rochester 1 . . . | b. Rochester | 1897 | 54 tons | 108516 | |
| Asphodel of London* . . . | b. Deptford | 1898 | 70 tons | 109978 | MJKW |
| Astrild of London* . . . | b. Southampton | 1899 | 69 tons | 110162 | MJKG |
| Brownie (The) of Colchester . . . | b. Gravesend | 1901 | 60 tons | 113696 | |
| Cabby of Rochester (Aux.) . . . | b. Frindesbury | 1928 | 73 tons | 160687 | |
| Calluna of London* . . . | b. Southampton | 1898 | 64 tons | 110043 | |
| Cambria of London* . . . | b. Southampton | 1899 | 66 tons | 110199 | MJKV |
| Carina of London* . . . | b. Southampton | 1898 | 64 tons | 110044 | MJNB |
| Federation of Colchester . . . | b. Brightlingsea | 1900 | 54 tons | 111381 | |
| Geisha of London* . . . | b. Deptford | 1898 | 70 tons | 169999 | MJLS |
| George and Eliza of Rochester . . . | b. Rochester | 1906 | 50 tons | 118226 | MGKR |
| Kismet of London* . . . | b. Deptford | 1899 | 73 tons | 110077 | |
| Lorna of London* . . . | b. Southamptom | 1898 | 64 tons | 110042 | MPSP |

| | | | | | |
|---|---|---|---|---|---|
| Marie May of Rochester (Aux.) | . | . | b. Maidstone | . | 1920 | 72 tons | 127270 | MKFN |

| | | | | | | | |
|---|---|---|---|---|---|---|---|
| Marie May of Rochester (Aux.) . . b. Maidstone . | 1920 | 72 tons | 127270 | MKFN |
| Pudge of Rochester (Aux.) . . b. Rochester . | 1922 | 68 tons | 127274 | MJNV |
| Scone of Rochester (Aux.) . . b. Rochester . | 1919 | 65 tons | 127269 | MJFW |
| Senta of London* . . b. Southampton . | 1899 | 69 tons | 110161 | |
| Sirdar of London . . b. Ipswich . | 1898 | 53 tons | 110033 | |
| Speranza of London* . . b. Southampton . | 1899 | 67 tons | 110054 | MJFS |
| Thyra of Rochester (Aux.) . . b. Maidstone . | 1913 | 62 tons | 127262 | MGBJ |
| Vera of London (Aux.) . . b. Limehouse . | 1898 | 44 tons | 108369 | |
| Yarana of London* . . b. Southampton . | 1899 | 69 tons | 110126 | MQDQ |

1 Club barge, Thames Barge Sailing Club.

## E. MARRIAGE & SON, LTD.
East Mills, Colchester.
Yellow fleur-de-lis in blue flag.

| | | | | | |
|---|---|---|---|---|---|
| Leoflæda of Colchester . . b. Harwich . | 1914 | 48 tons | 132906 | |

## METCALF MOTOR COASTERS, LTD.
4. New London Street, London, E.C.3.
White "M" on green swallow-tailed flag with narrow white border.

| | | | | | |
|---|---|---|---|---|---|
| Ardwina of London 1 . . b. Ipswich . | 1909 | 66 tons | 129016 | MFKS |
| Ernest Piper of London 2 . . b. Greenwich . | 1898 | 65 tons | 110000 | MJFR |

1 Sold to Daniels Bros early 1951. 2 Sold for conversion to yacht early 1950; now at Portsmouth.

## R. & W. PAUL, LTD.
Ipswich.
Small broad white diagonal cross in red flag. White diagonal cross in topsail.

| | | | | | |
|---|---|---|---|---|---|
| Alice May of Ipswich 1 . . b. Harwich . | 1899 | 70 tons | 109205 | MCCB |
| Anglia of London . . b. Ipswich . | 1898 | 54 tons | 110029 | |

## R. & W. PAUL, LTD.—Continued.

| Name | Built | Year | Tonnage | Number | Signal |
|---|---|---|---|---|---|
| Ena of Ipswich (Aux.) | b. Harwich | 1906 | 73 tons | 122974 | MGVR |
| Gravelines I of Ipswich (ex-Hilda) (Aux.) | b. Ipswich | 1905 | 77 tons | 120785 | MGLW |
| Jock of Ipswich (Aux.) | b. Ipswich | 1908 | 86 tons | 122975 | MGXS |
| Lady Daphne of Rochester (Aux.) | b. Rochester | 1923 | 85 tons | 127276 | |
| Lady Jean of Rochester (Aux.) | b. Rochester | 1926 | 86 tons | 148366 | |
| Marjorie of Ipswich | b. Ipswich | 1902 | 56 tons | 113753 | MGST |
| Serb of London [2] | b. East Greenwich | 1916 | 75 tons | 149324 | MGWY |
| Thalatta of Harwich (Aux.) | b. Harwich | 1906 | 67 tons | 116179 | MGXL |
| Tollesbury of Ipswich [3] | b. Sandwich | 1901 | 70 tons | 110315 | MGSB |
| Wolsey of Ipswich (ex-Robert Powell) [4] | b. Ipswich | 1908 | 65 tons | 118205 | MJFV |

[1] Sold for conversion to yacht late 1949; now at Hoo.   [2] Sold for conversion to yacht early 1950; now at Hammersmith.   [3] Aux. 1950.   [4] Sold to Prior, Burnham, early 1950. Now converted to a yacht at Hoo, bound for Portsmouth.

## SAMUEL J. PETERS.

Hermine Yard, 66, Eastern Esplanade, Southend-on-Sea, Essex.
White diamond on red flag.

| Name | Built | Year | Tonnage | Number |
|---|---|---|---|---|
| Ashingdon of London | b. Conyer Quay | 1913 | 59 tons | 135916 |

## JAMES R. PIPER (including T. SCHOLEY).

Piper's Wharf, East Greenwich, Kent.
White "P" with red "F" superimposed, on blue pennant. Device repeated on blue ball in topsail.

| Name | Built | Year | Tonnage | Number |
|---|---|---|---|---|
| Adriatic of London* | b. Beverley | 1900 | 61 tons | 112756 |
| Brian Boru of London [1] | b. East Greenwich | 1906 | 59 tons | 123705 |
| Fortis of Rochester* | b. Great Yarmouth | 1898 | 53 tons | 109922 |
| M. Piper of London* [2] | b. Greenwich | 1914 | 85 tons | 136819 |
| Thelma of Rochester [3] | b. Rochester | 1901 | 50 tons | 113701 |

[1] Laid up since sinking in Feb. 1950; Southend.   [2] Sunk March 1951, Grain Spit. Since raised but not refitted.   [3] Laid up since late 1949; but on film work in 1950. Now used as mooring hulk.

## REGINALD J. PRIOR.
38, Mildmay Road, Burnham-on-Crouch.
Flag divided into red, white, red horizontally.

*Mayland* of Maldon[1] . . . b. Maldon — 1888 — 45 tons — 82399

[1] Laid up and for sale.

## A. M. & H. RANKIN, LTD.
Stambridge Mills, Rochford, Essex.
Red "R" in white ball on flag divided horizontally into green, yellow and green.

*Joy* of London[1] . . . b. Teynham, Kent — 1914 — 56 tons — 136718

*Lord Roberts* of Maldon[2] . . b. Maldon — 1900 — 63 tons — 105909

[1] Now for sale.   [2] To be aux.

## SHAWS OF KENT, LTD.
Bloor's Wharf, Rainham, Kent.
1950 "bob" is swallow-tailed flag, horizontally divided, blue above and red below, bearing a vertical diamond with white "S" on red top half and white star on blue bottom half.

*Virocca* of London*[1] . . . b. Southampton — 1899 — 69 tons — 110123 — MJFQ

[1] Aux.

## HORACE P. SHRUBSALL.
34, Dartmouth Court, Blackheath, London, S.E.10.
Red cross in blue swallow-tailed flag.

*Gladys* of Dover[1] . . . b. Sandwich — 1900 — 64 tons — 105558 — MGJY

*Veravia* of London (ex-*Alarm*) . . { b. Sittingbourne — 1898 / rebuilt East Greenwich — 1925 } — 72 tons — 110031

*Veroma* of London . . . b. East Greenwich — 1905 — 56 tons — 120497

[1] Sold mid 1950; now converting to motor barge at Hoo.

## G. F. SULLY.
110, Fenchurch Street, E.C.3.
Red "S" in white ball on green pennant.

| | | | | | |
|---|---|---|---|---|---|
| Beatrice Maud of London (Aux.) . . | b. Sittingbourne | 1910 | 76 tons | 129122 | MFJL |
| Edith May of Harwich . . . | b. Harwich | 1906 | 64 tons | 116180 | MGLV |
| Hydrogen of London (Aux.) . . | b. Rochester | 1906 | 98 tons | 123640 | MDLF |
| Oxygen of Rochester (Aux.) . . | b. Rochester | 1895 | 69 tons | 104329 | MGKC |
| Raybel of London (Aux.) . . | b. Sittingbourne | 1920 | 79 tons | 145058 | |
| Scotsman of London [1] . . | b. Sittingbourne rebuilt | 1899 } 1933 | 63 tons | 110106 | |
| Valdora of London [2] . . | b. East Greenwich | 1904 | 56 tons | 118442 | |

[1] Now converting to aux. at Sittingbourne.　[2] Sold to Queenborough for conversion to yacht late 1950.

## WAKELEY BROS & CO., LTD.
74, Bankside, London, S.E.1.
White cross on blue flag.

| | | | | | |
|---|---|---|---|---|---|
| Lancashire of London . . | b. Teynham, Kent | 1900 | 43 tons | 112734 | |
| P.A.M. of London (Aux.) . . | b. Rochester rebuilt London | 1901 } 1945 | 43 tons | 114801 | MFFY |
| Violet Sybil of London [1] . . | b. Ipswich | 1898 | 59 tons | 109992 | |
| Water Lily of London (Aux.) . . | b. Rochester | 1902 | 58 tons | 114334 | |

[1] Sold early 1951 to Appledore, N. Devon, for conversion to yacht.

## SAMUEL WEST, LTD.
53/55, Central Buildings, Southwark Street, London, S.E.1.
Flag divided into dark blue, orange-red and dark blue horizontally.

| | | | | | |
|---|---|---|---|---|---|
| Glenway of Rochester (Aux.) . . | b. Rochester | 1913 | 73 tons | 127260 | MFWZ |
| Gwynronald of London (ex-Charles Allison) (Aux.) . . | b. East Greenwich | 1910 | 90 tons | 125703 | MFJN |

| | | | | |
|---|---|---|---|---|
| Lady Gwynfred of London (Aux.) . | { b. Gravesend<br>{ reconstructed Gravesend | 1904 ⎫<br>1935 ⎭ | 66 tons | 118441 | MFKB |
| Leonard Piper of London (Aux.) . | . b. East Greenwich | 1910 | 90 tons | 129071 | MGFW |
| Saxon of London (Aux.) . | . b. Gravesend | 1902 | 82 tons | 115904 | MFJR |

### F. A. WHITING BROS.
39, Baker Street, Chatham, Kent.
Dark blue "W" on large white diamond touching edges of dark blue flag.

| | | | | | |
|---|---|---|---|---|---|
| Nellie Parker of London (Aux.) . | . b. Ipswich | 1899 | 53 tons | 112619 | MFFV |

### SUCCESSORS TO T. F. WOOD (GRAVESEND), LTD.
Denton Wharf, Gravesend.
White "W" on a red flag.

| | | | | | |
|---|---|---|---|---|---|
| Ardeer of London . | b. Rochester | 1895 | 46 tons | 105731 | |
| Asphodel of Portsmouth . | b. Rochester | 1900 | 52 tons | 113689 | |
| Dreadnought of London . | b. Sittingbourne | 1907 | 70 tons | 123849 | MFJW |
| Edith and Hilda of Rochester . | b. Milton-next-Sittingbourne | 1892 | 56 tons | 98816 | MFKC |
| Ethel Ada of London . | b. Paglesham, Essex | 1903 | 49 tons | 118352 | MFJY |
| Gipping of Ipswich . | b. Ipswich | 1889 | 59 tons | 97676 | |
| Orwell of Ipswich [1] . | b. Ipswich | 1889 | 51 tons | 95310 | |
| Revival of Harwich (ex-Eldred Watkins) . | b. Ipswich | 1901 | 54 tons | 109210 | |

[1] Laid up for repairs since sinking in collision late 1950.

PART II. OWNERS AND "BOBS" OF 1930

Owners in 1930 who no longer have sailing barges

ASSOCIATED PORTLAND CEMENT MANUFACTURERS, LTD.
Tothill Street, London, S.W.1.
"PORTLAND CEMENT" in white letters on a blue circle in a yellow flag, "BLUE CIRCLE" in blue letters on white interior of circle. Similar device in topsail.

HERBERT W. CLARKE & SONS, LTD.
Bqnk Chambers, Erith, Kent.
"H.W.C." in white letters on red swallow-tailed flag.

CORY LIGHTERAGE, LTD.
Cory Buildings, Fenchurch Street, London, E.C.3.
Small white diamond on red swallow-tailed pennant.

WILLIAM G. DOWNING.
30, Plough Road, Rotherhithe, S.E.16.
White "D" in blue swallow-tailed flag.

ARTHUR GAMMON, LTD.
Holborn Wharf, Medway Street, Chatham.
"A.G.Ltd." in white letters on red flag.

ALBERT HUTSON.
Earl Street, Maidstone.
Flag divided into light blue, white, light blue and white horizontally.

CLEMENT W. PARKER.
Bradwell-on-Sea, Essex.
Red heart in white hand on blue pennant. (An Oddfellows' emblem flown on his barges for over forty years.)

JOHN SADD & SONS.
Maldon, Essex.
Flag divided into dark blue, white and dark blue horizontally.

JOHN SAWYER.
Brightlingsea, Essex.
Flag divided diagonally, mauve above at hoist, red below at fly.

T. SCHOLEY.
Dawson's Wharf, East Greenwich. (*Now* JAMES R. PIPER, *see above.*)
White "S" on blue pennant.

SMEED, DEAN & CO., LTD.
Sittingbourne.
Red triangle in a blue flag with "DEPENDABILITY" in blue letters on horizontal white band across the flag. Red triangle in white border in topsail, with "DEPENDABILITY" in white letters on red base of triangle.

ELDRED WATKINS.
Griffin Wharf, Robinson Street, Stoke, Ipswich.
Small vertical white diamond on a red flag.

## Additional Devices in Sails, 1930

In addition to the devices in sails mentioned above, the following barges also had designs painted on their topsails in 1930; and might often be seen in the London River at that time:—

1. *Daisy Little*, a cement barge belonging to Gillingham, had a bulldog in her sail. She once carried this device in the barge race.

2. Meux's beer barges carried a horseshoe in the topsail.

3. Sankey's paint barges had a white spinning-top in the topsail, with "SANKEY'S TOP BRAND PAINTS, TRADE MARK" in black letters.

4. Tunnel Portland Cement barges had a white circle in the topsail, and "TUNNEL PORTLAND CEMENT" in black letters, and a black tunnelmouth therein.

5. *Orion*, owned by Green of Brantham, Essex, had a large white "G" in her topsail.

6. Broads, Ltd., of Blackfriars (Alpha Cement) had the device :—

$$\text{B}\genfrac{}{}{0pt}{}{\text{ROADS}}{\genfrac{}{}{0pt}{}{\text{LACKFRIARS}}{\text{RAND}}}$$

WAKELEYS
HOP      on a green sack in the topsail.
MANURE

7. *Southwark*, owned by Wakeley's of Bankside had

## Additional Devices in Sails, early 1900's

1. Lees, Ltd., of Halling, had a white ramping horse over the word "INVICTA" in white letters on their *black* mainsails.

2. The West Kent Portland Cement Co. had a white five-pointed star in the mainsail.

3. *Sepoy*, *Savoy*, *Envoy* and *Convoy*, belonging to Crundall of Dover, carried a blue "C" on a white ball in their topsails.

## APPENDIX III

### BUILDERS' SPECIFICATION FOR BARGE *Phoenician*

AGREEMENT made the 7th day of April One thousand nine hundred and twenty two BETWEEN Edmund Alfred Horlock and Alfred Sully 32 shares each of 64 shares, A. Sully to be Managing Owner (hereinafter called "the Purchasers") of the one part and Wills and Packham, Limited, of Crown Quay, Sittingbourne, Kent (hereinafter referred to as "the Builders") of the other part.

WHEREBY IT IS AGREED AS FOLLOWS:—

1. The builders contract and agree to build for the Purchasers in accordance with the Specification attached hereto and signed on behalf of the Builders and the Purchasers, One sea-going Coasting Vessel of the following dimensions:—

Length overall not exceeding . . 84 ft.
Breadth to outside planking . . 20 ft. 6 in.
Depth of side amidship . . . 6 ft. 9 in. under deck
Capacity . . . . . 140 tons (approx.)

2. The vessel shall be built under the inspection of the Purchasers (or their Representative) who shall at all times during working hours have free access to the Yard and Shops where the vessel is being built. All materials used in the construction to be of the best quality obtainable for this type of vessel.

3. The Builders to proceed with the work as expeditiously as possible, but it is agreed that the Builders shall not be bound to a definite date, although they shall use the best means in their power to complete the vessel with all possible speed.

4. The Purchasers shall pay to the Builders the sum of £2,500 (two thousand five hundred pounds) for the vessel complete delivered afloat at the Builders' Works this price to include Board of Trade Fees.

The payment of the Contract Price to be made in the following manner:—

£600 with order;
£600 when vessel is framed out;
£600 when vessel is planked up and decked;
£700 on completion and delivery afloat at the Builders' Yard.

In the event of the Purchasers requiring by an order in writing that certain alterations shall be made or extra work performed in the vessel or in any part thereof otherwise than as set out in the Specification, the Builders shall execute work or alterations for which they shall receive extra payment, the amount of which shall be mutually agreed upon, and payment for such work shall be made with the final instalment.

5. The Vessel and all material connected therewith shall be held by the

21

Builders at their own risk until the Vessel has been completed and delivered to the Purchasers. The Builders shall at their own cost keep the said Vessel and material connected therewith insured for the full Contract Price against loss or damage by fire and all other risks during construction and until delivered to the Purchasers.

6. The Builders undertake to make no departure from the Specification attached to this Contract without definite authority in writing from the Purchasers.

7. If any dispute or difference shall arise between the Purchasers and the Builders relating to or concerning these presents or specification signed by both Parties as aforesaid or any clause thereof, the matter of difference shall be referred to two Arbitrators, one to be appointed in writing by each Party in difference, and also an Umpire to be appointed by the Arbitrators prior to entering upon the reference, and this Agreement shall be deemed to be a submission within the meaning of the Arbitration Act 1889 or Statutory modification or re-enactment thereof for the time being in force the provisions whereof shall apply as far as possible.

8. Every effort will be made by the Builders to carry out this Contract but the due performance of it is subject to variation or cancellation owing to an Act of God, War, Strikes, Revolutions, Lockouts, Fire, or any other cause beyond the Builders' control, or owing to inability to procure materials or articles.

Signature of Purchasers.
ALFRED SULLY.
E. A. HORLOCK.

Witness to Signature of Purchasers.
A. G. GREEN, 31 Homfrith Road, Stratford, E.15.

Signature of Builders.
G. H. WILLS. ⎫ Directors          Seal of
ERNEST PACKHAM. ⎭          Wills & Packham Limited.

Witness to Signature of Builders.
ERNEST E. STOKES, Secretary.


# SPECIFICATION
### for
Sea-going Sailing Barge to carry approximately 140 tons

————

DIMENSIONS.

| | | | |
|---|---|---|---|
| Length overall not exceeding | . | . | 84 ft. 0 in. |
| Breadth of deck | . . . | . | 20 ft. 6 in. |
| Depth of side amidships | . | . | 6 ft. 9 in. under deck |

GENERAL. The vessel to be built with straight stem and transom stern. To be generally built of English Oak and Elm with Oregon Pine bottom. The material to be of best quality and workmanship, of the highest class for this type of craft. Timber to be as far as possible free from sap shakes or defects. All spikes and fastenings to be galvanised and iron fittings on deck galvanised in the usual manner. The vessel to be rigged with a sprit mainsail and mizzen, and having a running bowsprit. A 14-ft. Dinghy to be provided and the outfit supplied to be in accordance with the present B.O.T. requirements for this type of craft, working in home limits. All seams to be made watertight. Every effort will be made to ensure a first-class job in every respect.

SCANTLINGS. KEEL. English Elm sided 12 in. moulded 4 in. and well scarphed together with hook scarphs properly bolted. The moulding to be increased at the ends in order to form efficient connection with stem and sternpost.

STEM. English Oak, sided 10 in. and moulded 11 in. and bearded on fore edge to 3 in. below wales, and fitted with outer iron stemband 4 in. × ¾ in. well bolted.

FORE DEADWOOD. English Oak, well fastened to stem and keel.

STERNPOST. To be of English Oak sided 9½ in. and well secured to keel and transom.

TRANSOM. To be of English Oak, sided 5 in. and moulded as required.

BOTTOM. To be of Oregon Pine 3 in. thick in as long lengths as possible and well fitted with tar and hair seams to be tie bolted as necessary. Bottom to be fastened to the floors with 1⅛-in. Oak treenails driven upwards and sheathed inside with 1-in. tongued and grooved yellow fir and galvanised fastenings.

UNDERCHIMES. To be English Elm 4 in. thick well fastened.

FLOORS. English Oak 7-in. sided, and moulded 6 in., spaced 20-in. centre to centre, and fastened with 1⅛-in. Treenails to bottom.

TIMBERS. To be of English Oak, and sided in hold 7 in. and moulded 6 in. at heel and 5 in. at head, well connected to floors by halved dovetailed and bolted with galvanised bolts. Knees of galvanised iron 3 in. × ½ in. to be well fastened to timbers and floor with galvanised bolts and nuts. Knees placed on every second frame.

BEVELLED FRAMES FORE & AFT. Frames before and abaft the fore and after bulkheads respectively to be doubled with timbers each sided not less than 5 in. moulded as required and fastened with two bolts each side of butt. The frames to be well bolted and butts shifted to give sufficient strength where the butt on the keel and short floor to be worked across keel and well bolted to keel and frames.

APRON. Of English Oak, sided 6 in. moulded as required.

WALES. To be of English Oak, sided 3 in. 20 in. wide in two widths of 10 in. Butts to be properly shifted and bolted. Wales to be through fastened to inwales with clenched bolts and galvanised spikes and dumps.

SHEATHING ON WALE. To be of Oak 1 in. thick.

SIDE PLANKING. To be of two thicknesses. Inner planking to be of P. Pine 1¼ in. thick full well fitted with tar and hair joints. Outer skin to be of 1⅜-in. P. Pine well fastened with galvanised spikes and treenails. Tar and hair to be worked hot between both skins and seams. Oak chafing to be put round bows for anchor, in lieu of iron. To be made thoroughly water-tight.

CHIMES SIDE. To be of English Elm rabetted 4 in. thick about 18 in. wide and well fastened to under chimes with 7-in. galvanised spikes and dumps about 6 in. apart. To be bolted with through galv. clenched bolts to chime keelsons, one in each frame.

RUNS. To be of English Elm worked in two thickness 1½ in. and well fastened with galv. spikes and oak treenails with tar & hair between. Elm to light water mark, above that English Oak to chimes.

CHIME KEELSONS. To be of P. Pine in one length extending well fore and aft and bolted to floors and timbers with ⅞-in. and ¾-in. clenched bolts.

MAIN KEELSON. To be of Oregon Pine about 14 in. square fastened through each floor and keel with 1 No. 1-in. screw bolt.

STRINGERS. An English Oak stringer to be worked on top of each end chime keelson to extend as far forward and aft as possible. To be 3 in. thick and well through fastened with $\frac{11}{16}$-in. clenched bolts, and galv. spikes and dumps.

INWALES. English Oak or P. Pine 3 in. × 14 in. worked fore and after under the beams and through fastened with $\frac{11}{16}$-in. clenched bolts to be worked from stem to stern.

LINING. To be of P. Pine 2 in. thick and fastened with 5-in. galv. spikes and to extend well forward and aft as far as possible.

CEILING. To be of P. Pine 2½ in. thick and fastened with 5½-in. galv. spikes. Limber strakes to be worked in portable lengths about the 2nd strake from side keelson. Slice pieces to be fitted under the 1st strake on each floor to raise ceiling.

BULKHEADS. To be well fitted tongued and doubled with tar and hair in between. Bulkheads to be built watertight with a steel plate and angles at an extra cost.

FILLINGS. Filling between beams and carlings to be fitted of English Oak and well fastened.

BREASTHOOK. Of English Oak 7 in. and well fastened with $\frac{13}{16}$-in. clenched bolts in arms and 1-in. nut and screw bolts through throat.

BEAMS. To be of mild steel T bulb round up about 13 in. in whole length. Hold beams to be 6 in. deep × ⅜ in. fitted with bracket plates at ends and well secured to side with angles. 4 beams under mast case.

MAIN BEAMS SHIFTING. To be of steel plate and angle fitted with bulb on lower edge. The middle piece to be made portable and the end pieces to be well fastened to the side with bracket plates and angles. An iron standard to carry fore and afters to be fitted to main beam and made portable.

CARLINGS. Deck carlings to be of mild steel, 3 in. × 2½ in. × $\frac{5}{16}$ in. turned down and well connected to side with nut and screw bolts.

QUARTER KNEES. Of English Oak, sided 5½ in. and well fastened to transom and sides with ¾-in. bolts clenched.

DECKS. To be of selected Oregon Pine, 3 in. thick and worked 5/6 in. wide. To be well fitted to beams and fastened with ½-in. galvanised nut and screw bolts. Under side to be planed and beaded. To be well caulked with 3 threads of best Navy Oakum, and payed up with Marine glue. Ends of deck to be square butted into covering board. Heads of fastenings to be covered with turned wood dowells.

COVERING BOARD. To be of Oak 3 in. thick and 11 to 12 in. wide to be well fastened to wale, with 6½-in. galv. spikes, spaced about 6 in. apart. Inner edge fastened to beam and fillings with galv. dumps and spikes.

GUNWALE BANDS. To be of segmental iron 3 in. × ¾ in. well fastened, one on top of wale and one on bottom of wale.

PAWL BITT. To be of English Oak, 9 in. square and well fastened to beams and at heel.

WINDLASS BITT. To be of English Oak sided 5 in. and moulded 12 to 14 in. above deck tapering to 9 in. at heel. To be well secured to bitt beams and at heel with ¾-in. bolt.

WINDLASS BITT KNEES. To be of English Oak sided 5 in. well grown to form and bolted to beam partners and bitts with $\frac{11}{16}$-in. bolts. Scuppers to be cut out in bottom of knees to free water.

KNEES IN HOLD. 5 galv. iron knees each side to be worked in hold at angle of chime and properly through bolted with ¾-in. dia. bolts.

COAMINGS. To be of Oregon Pine 4½ in. thick to stand about 20 in. above top of deck and top of inner edge rabetted to receive hatches. Well fastened to beams and carlings with ¾-in. screw bolts and joints well fitted with paint and white lead between. A bracket knee to be worked each side at main beam of steel plate and angles and well secured. Also board for stack in hatchway to be supplied. Coaming to be fitted with batten hooks and rings for lashing as required. Segmental iron bands to be worked on coamings and headledges to prevent chafing.

HEADLEDGES. To be of Oak, sided 3½ in. and well fitted to deck with tar and hair between. To be fastened with nut and screw bolts to beams and dovetailed to coamings at end. Fitted with batten hooks and cleats to carry fore and after for hatches, and angle irons at corners.

HATCHES. To be properly constructed with Oak Carlings and Fir Boards.

FORE & AFTERS. To be of Pine or Fir, 2½ in. × 12 in. portable fitted to cleats fastened on headledges and arranged to carry hatches.

MAST CASE. To be galv. steel plate and angles properly made and fitted. To be well secured to beams and partners with ¾-in. nut and screw bolts.

PILLARS. To be fitted under mast and efficiently secured at head and heels.

WASHRAILS. Of Oak 3 in. thick to be worked fore and aft round the vessel and well fitted and fastened with ¾-in. bolts and to stand about 5 in.

in board from edge of gunwale. Height of midship rail to be about 12 in. above top of deck. Scuppers to be cut as required. The rails to be well fitted at joints and a hollow moulding 1½ in. wide to be worked about 4 in. above top of covering board and parallel to it. The length of half round segmental iron band fitted at top to midship rail to stand a rack iron in, one each side. Height of rail at stem 1 ft. 6 in. tapering to 14 in. at fore horse.

QUARTER BOARD. To be worked on top of washrail at after end of vessel from transom to main coaming after headledge. To be 2 in. thick and about 12 in. wide forward and tapering to about 8 in. at end. (See Captain before working these for measurements.)

A neat oak capping to be worked on top 2 in. thick and 4 in. wide with rounded edges to form nosing.

HAWSE BOX. English Oak, hawse pipe chock to be fitted to stem and bow rail to properly house hawse pipes.

HAWSE PIPES. A case iron hawse pipe to be fitted on each bow and properly secured large enough to take shackles of cable.

COMPANION. A sliding companion to be fitted forward for access to forecastle properly framed and fitted.

WINDLASS. A 36-in. windlass fitted with ruffles and pawls to be supplied and properly hung with gunmetal bearings or centre pawl windlass at Purchasers' option.

CABLE PIPE. A cable pipe to be fitted on fore deck to take cable to chain locker.

FORECASTLE. To be arranged to accommodate two men and to be fitted with 2 cot frames, cooking stove, rope racks and all lamp cupboards as required.

STEERING GEAR. A screw steering gear (Seager's Make) large size to be supplied and fitted with teak steering wheel brass bound with name of vessel engraved round ring, and hull builders name on hub.

LEEBOARDS. Leeboards to be of English Oak, sided 3½ in. at head tapering to 2¼ in. at tail, to be strongly bound and braced with segmental iron bands 3 in. × ¾ in. properly riveted. Head plates to be well secured and arranged to take mushroom-head toggle shackled to leeboard clamp bar strongly secured to deck beam. Leeboard to be about 18 ft. long and 7 ft. wide at widest part. Pennants and falls to be chain galvanised.

LEEBOARD CRABS. Leeboard crabs fitted with independent drum on end to be fitted one each side abaft main horse to raise and lower leeboard.

MAIN BRAIL WINCH. To be supplied and fitted as required.

PUMPS. Cast iron pumps 4 No. complete with boxes and gear to be supplied and fitted as required with lay pipes etc.

CAST IRON BOLLARDS. 4 No. to be fitted as arranged one on each quarter and one on each bow.

FORE & MAIN HORSES. Of English Oak to round up as deck and to be strongly secured at ends to Oak chocks well fastened to rails and deck.

An iron traveller to be fitted to each horse. Iron segmental band to be fitted under main horse to take chain. Fore horse to be arranged to unship. Chocks for main horse, see Captain before making.

CABIN. To be arranged aft for Captain and Mate. To be fitted with lockers and cupboards and to have stove and fittings as usual for a vessel of this description.

RUDDER. Rudder post to be of English Oak 12 in. × 12 in. at head. Tail of rudder to be solid of Fir and English Elm and well bolted. To be hung with 3 No. forged rudder irons well bolted to rudder. Dia. of rudder bolt 2 in.

BOAT. A Dinghy of Elm 14 ft. long with all necessary gear to be supplied with davits, blocks and falls complete.

MAST. To be of Pitch Pine with usual standing and running rigging 13 in. clear square.

MAIN BRAIL WINCH. A Main brail winch to be supplied and fitted as required.

SPRIT. An Oregon sprit to be supplied about 58 ft. long fitted with 3 eyed hoop muzzle, yard tackle band etc. complete.

TOPMAST. Properly fitted to caps with rigging complete to be supplied. Dia. at cap 9 in. to 10 in. Captain's option.

BOWSPRIT. A running bowsprit to be fitted about 24 ft. long outside stem, and to heel in suitable bitts. Chain shrouds with lignum vitae dead eyes iron bound.

MIZZEN SPARS. To be properly made and fitted as required.

STANDING RIGGING. To be of galvanised steel wire well fitted and spliced and served up a reasonable distance not less than 10 in.

FORE STAY. To be 4 in. circ. wormed and fitted with cringles complete.

SHROUDS. To be 3 in No. each side for mainmast. Main shrouds to be 3 in. circ. fitted at lower end with lignum vitae deadeyes and wire rope lanyards.

STANDLIFT. To be 3 in. circ. fitted with a loop to go over masthead and lower end fitted with a tightening screw to engage with 3 eyed hoop on lower end of sprit.

TOPMAST STAY. To be of 2-in. F.S.W. Rope fitted with double and single blocks and tackle at lower end. Part galv. chains, length of bowsprit.

STANDING & RUNNING BACKSTAY. To be of 2½-in. F.S.W. Rope fitted at lower ends as topmast stay. Two pieces of small chain about 10 ft. long with hook and eye to be fitted to line of backstay.

RUNNING RIGGING. To be of good quality tarred hemp or manilla sufficient in quantity and size for the purpose required and to be in accordance with rigging plan.

RIGGING CHOCK. To be 10 in. wide at bottom tapering to 8 in. at top and shaped to take leeboard head worked each side abreast of mast and well secured to take chain plates. Iron chafing bands to be worked to prevent leeboard chafing.

TAFFRAIL AFT. Of English Oak sided 5 in. and well fastened. Two galvanised fair-lead snatches to be fitted, to be of good quality iron or mild steel, and well galvanised.

SAILS. To be well made and fitted and in accordance with sail and rigging plan. Sails to be made of Haywards extra G. and of the following numbers:—

Mainsail No. 1.
Topsail No. 2.
Foresail No. 2.
Mizzen No. 3.

All sails to be made to fit as per Captain (A. E. Horlock) instructions.
Jibs to be of Navy duck sails to be dressed or left white as required.
Sails to be dressed and ropes tarred.

TARPAULINS. 2 Sets to be well dressed Merchant Navy canvas and well fitted.

SIDE CLOTHS. To be of green rot proofed canvas and well made.

BLOCKS. Stem blocks to be 10-in. dia. sheaves, lower block with 4 sheaves upper block with 3 sheaves to be galvanised iron except as hereunder specified. Size of blocks to be wood fitted with patent sheaves. Main sheet block as shewn on rigging plan.

Fore Vangs
Vang Block
Main sheet block
Topsail Halyards
Sheet Block          } These blocks to be wood fitted with
Fore Halyard blocks    patent sheaves.
Mizzen sheet
Davit blocks
Jib purchase

ANCHORS & CHAINS. The following anchors and chains to be supplied and fitted:—

Anchors.　1 No. 4 cwt. Bower Anchor.
　　　　　1 No. 3½ ,,　2nd Bower Anchor.
　　　　　1 No. kedge about 1¼ cwt.

Cables.　60 fathoms 1⅜-in. tested cable chain shackled at every 15 fathoms.
　　　　　45 fathoms ¾-in. galv. short link cable chain.
　　　　　50 fathoms 2½-in. F.S.W. Rope with shackles complete.

MOORING ROPES, ETC.

1 60-fathom 8-in. Tow warp (bass)
1 40 　,,　 6-in. 　,,　　,,　　,,
1 40 　,,　 5-in. Manilla warp
2 60 　,,　 3-in. (Tarred Manilla) Horseline
1 80 　,,　 Track Line (1½-in. Manilla)

SIDE LAMPS. 2 Sets port and starboard best galv. plain lenses navigation
    side lamps (Davey's patent) to be supplied and fitted with all necessary
    lamp stanchions and to pass B.O.T.

ANCHOR LAMPS & STERN LAMPS. 2 No. Galvanised lamps with stanchions
    aft.

CABIN LAMPS. 1 Cabin Lamp in gimbals to be supplied and fitted.

OUTFIT. To be as follows:—

    1 Spinnaker Boom
    2 Side Lamp screens
    1 sea anchor
    8 lifebelts
    3 lifebuoys
    2 galvanised water tanks one forward and one aft
    1 water breaker
    1 snatch block
    1 lead line and lead
    2 hold shovels
    2 hand spikes
    2 crowbars
    1 cold chisel
    2 pails
    2 brooms
    2 deck scrubs
    2 mops
    1 axe
    1 saw
    1 hammer
    1 fog horn
    1 bell
    1 binacle and compass
    2 oil cans
    1 oil feeder
    6 fenders
  100 batten wedges
    4 boat oars
    4 setting booms
    1 ensign
    2 boat hooks
    1 marline spike (iron)
    1 spindle and bob.

NAME. Name to be neatly cut in on bows and stern with Port of Registry
    and gilded.

PAINTING & BLACKING. Vessel to receive two coats of tar and well black-
    leaded below wale.

    Topsides and rails to be painted an approved colour and varnished
    and grained.

A streak about 1½ in. wide to be cut in on lower edge of washrail, and neatly painted.

Spars to be varnished.

SKYLIGHT. A neatly made skylight with galv. iron fittings to be properly secured on after deck and to be in accordance with best practice for this class of vessel.

The vessel to be measured by B.O.T. Surveyor and load line and plimsoll mark cut in one each side as instructed. No departure or additions to be made to this specification unless by written instructions from the Purchasers, who will pay any additional cost, if any, by the alterations.

Signature of Purchasers      Witness to both signatures

ALFRED SULLY.            A. GREEN.

E. A. HORLOCK.

BLOCKS

*Vang falls Blocks*

     2 10-in. Double I.I.B. Patent Sheaves with Lugs & Screw Pins also beckets.

     2 Double ditto without becket.

     2 single 10-in. with oval eye (for Fairleads).

*Main Sheet*

     2 11-in. I.I.B. P.S. with oval eye in line of sheave and shackle.

     1 11-in. double, outside bound P.S.'s with stout hook and pin through sheaves to belay main sheet pin (1½).

*Runners Falls*

     2 5-in. double iron with lugs and screw pins.

     2 5-in. single with lugs and screw pins & beckets.

     Runners: 2 6-in. iron blocks with oval eye.

*Running Tackle Falls Backstays*

     2 5-in. double iron blocks with hooks.

     2 5-in. single iron with hooks & beckets.

*Rolling Vang Falls*

     2 9-in. I.I.B. P.S. double wood blocks with hooks.

     2 9-in. ditto with hooks & beckets.

*Main Tacks*

     2 6-in. iron with hooks.

     1 double 4-in. iron with hook.

     1 single ditto with hook & becket.

*Brails—Peak Blocks*

     4 4-in. iron *single* with round eyes *single*.

     2 4-in. iron double with round eyes.

*Main Brails*

     2 6-in. iron, for wire.

*Lower Brails Blocks*
    4 5-in. single iron with eyes for shackles.

*Yard Tackle Blocks*
    1 5-in. iron with hooks & beckets.
    1 5-in. with *eye for screw pin.*

*Topsail Sheet Blocks*
    1 5-in. iron with lug and screw pin and swivel.
    1 7-in. wood P.S. I.I.B. with lug and screw pin.
    1 6-in. iron P.S. with *lug and screw pin* to fit $3\frac{1}{4}$-in. wire.

*Topsail Tack*
    1 4-in. double iron with eye for shackle.
    1 4-in. single with eye for shackle and becket.

*Topsail Downhaul.*
    2 single 5-in. iron with P.S. with large *round eye.*

*Topsail Halyards*
    1 single 5-in. iron with lug and screw pin and swivel, halyards 2 single 5-in. blocks P.S.

*Crosstree Lifts*
    2 3-in. single iron with *oval eye.*

*Fore Halyards*
    1 6-in. iron with swivel and oval eye.

*Fore Tack*
    1 double 4-in. iron with hook.
    1 single ditto with hook & becket.

*Downhaul*
    1 5-in. wood I.B. with oval eye.

*Topmast Heelrope*
    1 6-in. iron block with oval eye.
    1 5-in. *sheave* jin with lug, screw pin & swivel.

*Leeboard Falls*
    2 6-in. iron with lugs and screw pins.

*Jib Halyards*
    1 5-in. iron block with hook in line of sheave.

*Jib Stay*
    1 6-in. iron block with hook in line of sheave.

*Jib Downhaul*
    2 4-in. wood block (plain).

*Jib Sheets*
    2 3-in. Cat eyes Lig: to take $2\frac{1}{2}$-in. rope.
    3 $2\frac{1}{2}$-in. Bull-eyes.

*Jib Stay Purchase*
    2 double iron blocks, 5-in. P.S. one with becket.

*Staysail Halyards*
    1 4-in. iron block with eye.

*Topmast Stay Fall*
>    1 4-in. double iron.
>    1 4-in. single ditto with becket.

*Bobstay*
>    1 6-in. iron with lug and screw pin.

*Uphaul*
>    2 2-in. iron blocks.

*Bowsprit Shrouds*
>    2 double 5-in. iron lug and screw pin.
>    2 single 5-in. iron with beckets and oval eyes.

*Topping Lift*
>    5-in. iron block.

*Purchase*
>    1 5-in. wood I.B. P.S. *single* with lug and screw pin and becket.
>    1 5-in. ditto with lug and screw pin.

*Peak Halyard*
>    1 5-in. iron with hook.

*Throat Halyard*
>    1 5-in. iron with hook.

*Trice Line*
>    1 4-in. iron with large eye.

*Reef Tackle*
>    1 4-in. I.B. wood P.S. double block with long hook.
>    1 4-in. I.B. wood single P.S. with hook & *becket*.

*Mizzen Sheet*
>    1 7-in. wood I.B. P.S. double becket & lug & screw pin in line of sheave.
>    1 7-in. ditto without becket but pin across the sheave.

*Davit Falls*
2 6-in. double I.B. P.S. with becket and lugs and screw pins.
>    2 6-in. double I.B. P.S. with stout swivel hooks.
>    2 9-in. wood clump double blocks for stropping.
>    2 9-in. single ditto.
>    10 11-in. Wood hoops.
>    9 12-in. ditto.
>    8 13-in. ditto.
>    24 Spring hanks to fit 2-in. wire.
>    24 2-in. cringles.

## APPENDIX IV

### The *Record Reign* and Transatlantic Barges

#### 1. *Motor Ketch "Record Reign"*.

*Built by* HOWARD & SON, MALDON, 1890

| | | |
|---|---|---|
| Keel and chine planks . | . | . English elm |
| Sheathing and lining | . | . Pitch pine |
| Timbers | . . . | . English oak |
| Keelson | . . . | . Pitch pine, boxed with steel top and two sides |
| Gross tonnage | . . . | . 200·32 tons |
| Nett registered tonnage | . | . 138·92 tons |
| Dead-weight capacity . | . | . 275 tons |

*N.B.* She has carried as much as 282 tons of stone.

| | | |
|---|---|---|
| Length B.P. | . . . | . 112·2 feet |
| Breadth | . . . . | . 24·15 feet |
| Draught laden | . . . | . 10 feet |
| Draught unladen . | . . | . 7 feet |
| Depth | . . . . | . 12 feet |
| Hold . | . . . . | . 58 feet |
| Hatches: | | |
|   Main hatch . | . . | . 31 × 13 feet |
|   Fore hatch . | . . | . 9 × 9 feet |

Engines. Two 40 H.P. S.C. Bolinder. Oil storage tanks, 1,600 gallons.
Speed (under power only), 6 knots.

Consumption: No tests made recently. Last test, 810 sea miles on 660 gallons.

Cargo machinery. One Bolinder derrick winch.

This vessel was used as a Q-ship during the First World War. See pages 245 to 248.

#### 2. *Schooner Barge "Goldfinch"*.

*Built by* J. M. GOLDFINCH, FAVERSHAM, 1894

Built of wood; oak frames; put together by tar and hair set work. No caulked seams anywhere except two under top plank.

| | | |
|---|---|---|
| Gross tonnage | . . . | . 144 tons |
| Nett registered tonnage | . | . 117 tons |
| Dead-weight capacity . | . | . 250 tons |
| Length B.P. | . . . | . 98·5 feet |
| Breadth | . . . . | . 22·75 feet |
| Depth in hold | . . . | . 9·0 feet |
| Draught laden | . . . | . 7·8 feet forward |
| | | 9·25 feet aft |

Three hatches

Sailed out to Demerara from Plymouth in 1930 in 45 days. See page 100.

3. *Ketch Barge "Clymping".*

Built *by* J. & W. B. HARVEY, LITTLEHAMPTON, 1909

Built of wood to Lloyd's; oak frames, pitch-pine and oak planking.

| | |
|---|---|
| Gross tonnage . . . . | 121 tons |
| Nett registered tonnage . . | 99 tons |
| Dead-weight capacity . . . | about 220 tons |
| Length B.P. . . . . | 93·0 feet |
| Breadth . . . . . | 23·3 feet |
| Depth in hold . . . . | 8·25 feet |
| Draught laden . . . . | 7·5 feet forward |
| | 8·5 feet aft |

Sailed out to Demerara from Plymouth in 1929 in 38 days. See page 100.

4. *Ketch Barge "Kindly Light".*

Built *by* J. & W. B. HARVEY, LITTLEHAMPTON, 1904

Built of wood with galvanised iron fastening, to B.O.T. Certificate.

| | |
|---|---|
| Gross tonnage . . . . | 111 tons |
| Nett registered tonnage . . | 90 tons |
| Dead-weight capacity . . . | 200 tons |
| Length B.P. . . . . | 91·3 feet |
| Breadth . . . . . | 22·25 feet |
| Depth in hold . . . . | 7·8 feet |
| Draught laden . . . . | 8·0 feet |

Sailed out to Demerara from Plymouth in 1926 in 40 days. See page 100.

# INDEX

Names of vessels are printed in italics

Named Barges—see List at end of Index

# BARGES NAMED